Tales from America's Golden Age

Books by Malcolm Bell

The Turkey Shoot: Tracking the Attica Cover-up
Grove Press, 1985

reissued as

The Attica Turkey Shoot:
Carnage, Cover-up and the Pursuit of Justice
Skyhorse Publishing, 2017, paperback, 2022

Roses in the Night
Mayan Sisters Confront CIA-Backed Terror
Fresh Look Press, 2023

Overdue Heresies
And the Search for Truth
Fresh Look Press, 2024

Tales from America's Golden Age
A Life on the Privilege Spectrum

Malcolm Bell

Fresh Look Press
Randolph Center, Vermont

Tales from America's Golden Age
A Life on the Privilege Spectrum

Malcolm Bell

Fresh Look Press
Randolph Center, Vermont USA
freshlookpress.com

Cover photo by Alan Golin Gass, a classmate of Brown Moore Meggs, left, and the author, right. Background: Dunster House, their Harvard College dormitory. The car is Meggs's second-hand 1939 Cadillac. Barely visible to the right of its grille is the Charles River. Time: the spring of 1951. Earlier that day, the sign, which says "PRESIDENT'S HOUSE 17 Quincy Street," adorned the lawn of the President of Harvard University, Dr. James Bryant Conant. See "Virtuosity" at page 38.

A previous version of "Ramallah Friends" appeared in the February 2012 issue of *Friends Journal* under the title "An Afternoon at Ramallah Friends School."

Book design: Kitty Werner, RSBPress, Waitsfield, Vermont

ISBN 979-8-9889080-6-7 tradepaper
ISBN 979-8-9889080-7-4 ebook

Library of Congress Control Number: 2025917188

For Erin and Brian

Life flames. The words that tell
how it was remain as embers.

Contents

Introduction

This book is an impressionist memoir. Its many short and very short stories stand alone like many-colored daubs of pigment on an impressionist's canvas. But if you step back and view them as a whole, they become a portrait of a white guy who has lived along the privilege spectrum during a shining stretch of America's sprawling saga.

"You were a privileged little kid," my cousin Josephine told me around the time she turned ninety and I was in my seventies. I had always enjoyed Josie's candor, but maybe not this time. Thinking it over, though, I saw she was right. Obviously. How had I missed it? There are, however, degrees of privilege.

I grew up mostly on Brooklyn Heights, a part of town that's fancier now than it was then, and rode the BMT subway to a private high school called Poly Prep far across the city. When I started at Harvard, many of my classmates who had attended one of New England's real prep schools—St. Mark's, St. Paul's, Choate, Groton, and so on— would ignore my "Hi!" and pass me by on the walkways of The Yard as though I did not exist. That hurt, until I stopped saying "Hi!" to them. My class was about half preppies, and we understood that they held the grading curves down for us high schoolers who'd gotten in on our brains. Not that it took that many brains to get into Harvard in 1949. The fact that my father and all three uncles had gone there probably didn't hurt.

My brothers David and Richard and I were all listed in the Social Register of Cincinnati, Ohio (a.k.a. the *Blue Book*, not to be confused with the *Blue Book* of car values), where our father had some notable forebears. Those listings enabled David and Richard (a.k.a. Tigger) to be listed in the New York Social Register and invited to a number of debutante parties. I never got around to being listed or invited to those parties. Nor did the Cincinnati forebears' money follow their genes. Some of my distant cousins were wealthy and maybe still are, but my immediate family lived comfortably thanks to my father's intelligence, work ethic, good luck, and white skin.

The first half of my life and all but the stories in "Beyond the Law" and the Epilogue occurred during what I think of as America's Golden Age, to the extent that it had one, from our entry into World War II until President Ronald Reagan decided to make the rich richer and the labor unions weaker. Between 1981, when Reagan took office, and 2021, when Trump's first term ended, spendthrift tax cuts and various deregulations moved about $50 trillion from the bottom 90% of Americans to the top 1%.[1] At the time, I didn't see those years as being either golden or an age; and for a great many people, they weren't; they were the same old struggle. Nonetheless, it was an era when vast numbers of working class and middle-class families led relatively comfortable, worry-free lives (unless they worried about being nuked) before the 1% began ripping off the rest of us more effectively than usual. Then the nation slid down the slope from Golden Age to another Gilded Age. But the slide didn't affect me. Privilege again perhaps.

Not until I considered these stories as a whole, did I realize that besides being discrete (sometimes indiscreet) daubs on the canvas of my life, they portray fair chunks of the life and culture of the United States during the rise and plateau of its Golden Age. Would that we could recover the best of that era: a great many families living comfortably, very few filthy rich, while the progress that many, though far from all, of us have enjoyed since then continues in medicine, tolerance, and the sciences. And this time, no homelessness. All it would take for a new golden age in this richest nation on Earth is for enough good people to tackle the prevailing corruptions.

The two stories in "Prosecutor" get a separate section of the book because they began a major change in how I thought and lived. The title of "Beyond the Law" signifies my life after leaving the practice and also the civil disobedience that my wife, Nancy, and I committed then. In several stories in the latter section, I relate my small roles in the endeavors of four exceptional women; those stories are part of this memoir because my participation meant much to me. Nancy, too, supported the women's endeavors and helped them where she could.

The longest story in the book, "Inner Journey," relates what I believed and how I lived the beliefs (or didn't) from my earliest memories until now. It's a spiritual memoir within the memoir. Many of its events, secular on their surface, contributed to shaping my spirituality. For me at least, there is no bright line between the secular and the spiritual, maybe no line at all.

Rereading the book reminds me that I did many stupid things especially while young, and they cost me little. Partly, I suppose, a perk of privilege.

"Tell us a story, Daddy," my children used to say, and I did—all of them make-believe and most lost in the sunshine of those years. It took my first divorce to start me writing down the present stories. All the stories except "Flights of Fancy"— in which I'm not tethered to reality—are as true as memory permits, apart from an occasionally changed name. Though I composed these, too, for my children, they are not children's stories. Erin and Brian stayed with me regularly after their mother and I split, and I believe they knew me as well as a child may know a parent. All the same, I wrote down many of the events I'd enjoyed or endured—embers of the life I led and the times in which I led it—for them to read when they grew older. As they aged, they were fun to keep on writing. I hope they will be fun to read. Perhaps they will prompt a memory or two of your own.

Malcolm Bell
Randolph Center, Vermont

Boyhood

Hourglass

What is time? When I was around nine years old, I took a pencil and a sheet of yellow paper from the white wooden cabinet that held my toys and boxes of games, intending to write the answer, an answer that was straining inside my head though I had not yet found the words to express it. Holding the pencil, I regarded the page. Empty, it looked infinite. I could write anything I wanted. Infinite, too, was my sense of time, gathering like a sneeze about to burst forth from the front of my brain where thoughts become words. Yet the sheet remained empty.

What I did next is lost in the dust that hung in shafts of sunlight on that winter afternoon in Brooklyn, the year before the United States entered World War II. Gone too are my toys and games, and my granddaughters have long since outgrown theirs. What is time? If I address the question in my old age, the sheet of yellow paper will still remain empty.

Security

Reading *Mary Poppins* and *Wind in the Willows* aloud and, above all, the wonderful foursome by A.A. Milne, my parents affirmed my sense of security during the desperate doldrums of the 1930s. World War I, which my father had been lucky to survive, lay in the remote past. Roosevelt, not Hitler, was the bogeyman. A few evenings, my father's cousin Herbert called at our front door, his truck parked in the street outside, as he sold apples across the city to sustain his family and their orchard on the slopes above the Hudson River. But in those comfortable books as in our blessed home, all was stable and no one went hungry. Then my mother read me *The Snow Goose* by Paul Gallico, about a brave, misshapen man who used his little boat to rescue British soldiers from the bloody sands of Dunkirk until a German pilot machine-gunned him, and I began to realize that the world was not as I had known it.

Discovery

If you climbed one of the long-needle pine trees on the hillside and rocked it, you could grab the next treetop and step across onto one of its branches, and so on from tree to tree. My brothers and I discovered this lofty pathway one autumn afternoon and swung forever around the grove, shouting now and then to our parents whom we could hear surprisingly well at our cottage across the valley. Dark green needles pricked through my sweater, and one stuck my eye, making it feel sleepy until I forgot about it. Dusk came on and chilled the air. We climbed down the branches like the rungs of a ladder, our hands gummy black and smelling of pitch. The next summer we walked back to the grove and climbed a tree or two, but it wasn't the same.

Fishing

Jimmy Farmer and I fished from a large gray rock that the sun had warmed above the current lapping at our toes. Or clutching our poles and a can of freshly dug worms, we climbed along a half-submerged tree that had fallen into the pond in an ice storm, each footstep on the branches sending ripples across the water. Or we clambered down a gorge of white boulders to a clear basin upon which a waterfall splashed a slender tattoo in the summer's drought.

One afternoon we waded into a strange pond on boards that we pushed under with our feet so that we would not sink into the dead leaves and muck that covered the bottom to a depth we did not know. Standing in my rolled-up overalls, I noticed through the brown water that wriggling leaches were fastening painlessly onto my bare legs. Others were feeding on Jimmy's. We had to dig into their slimy, snaky bodies with our fingernails to rip off the dark mouths that trailed our blood as they came loose. We splashed towards shore as fast as we could on the boards, ripping away more leaches and grasping the boards that angled free as we stepped off them.

Usually, though, we fished quietly and spoke as boys will about our deeds and problems and what we were going to do when we grew up. My heart would quicken when the rod dipped in my hand and silvery life flashed on the line. Then the wide-eyed fish lay on the grass with a twig through their gills and did not move.

Later, when I had children of my own and did not see Jimmy for years at a time, I decided that the fishing had meant more than the fish, and wondered that I had ever felt otherwise.

Woods

In the summer the grabby green leaves and sweaty feeling—not to mention several snakes I nearly stepped on—discouraged me from exploring the woods around our valley. Then came crisp October, and off I'd go, sometimes with one or both of my brothers, often alone. I climbed short cliffs of old gray rock that could come loose in your hand. Or pushed over small dead trees along the way, watching out not to crown myself with a rotten top that might break off and plummet straight down if I pushed the bottom too sharply. Sometimes I'd stop on an island of moss that shone rich green above the brown, stick-strewn forest floor and listen to the hush of red and yellow leaves raining through the sunlight.

The war was on, and I planned where I'd hide out with my .22 rifle if a German invasion reached Easton. When I first got the rifle—a birthday present from my parents—I shot a few birds for sport, but killing the little creatures wasn't sport and soon repulsed me. I quit doing it. My brothers and I stayed close to home in November when hunters from the cities cannonaded through the hills. One spring I found the skeleton of a deer that had outrun the person who'd shot her. I kept the long lower jaw on a shelf, where it rocked when I poked its small, neat front teeth.

On a gray winter day, I came upon a stream that had frozen and thawed on top and frozen again, and went crashing up the middle past bushes bent with snow, my galoshes breaking through the first layer of ice but not the second, so my legs stayed dry. All the while I roamed the woods, I felt that I was searching for something. Part of it I found by searching. Part I recognized only decades later, not by trudging up another ice-covered stream, but by stopping to listen to the silence of the snow across the floor of the forest.

Yet peace has limits. In the forest that I perceived as silent, the fox and lynx and hawk and owl must kill God's weaker creatures or find carrion or die.

Tears

A stream sluicing down a mountain takes eons to carve a groove through the granite beneath it, yet tears flowing across a person's cheek may carve their way into one's memory in a moment. During the late '30s and World War II, my mother employed one young woman and then another to do light housework in exchange for room and board and maybe eight dollars a week. Eighty years on, I remember little about these women except their tears.

Janet was about twenty and had an open face and dark hair. Her family had come from Poland. During breakfast time one bright summer morning—it must have been in September of 1939—a voice from the kitchen radio reported that the German army was rolling into Poland, and Janet burst into tears.

Next was Agnes, whose family were Czechs. My bedroom in the city adjoined the bathroom that she and I shared, and one night when she was in it getting ready for bed, I pretended to be sleepwalking in order to walk in on her. I didn't know whether sleepwalkers can turn a doorknob, but I turned it and in I went. She shrieked. The problem was that I knew that sleepwalkers can't open their eyes, so I couldn't see whether any of her interesting parts were showing. She became involved with a sailor, and boyish logic told me they went all the way, as copulation was sometimes called then. He led her to believe he'd marry her before he sailed out of her life. She would sob, and Mom would try to comfort her.

Then Amelia, elderly, heavy, black, and from Trinidad. Each evening at nine she would turn on her radio and listen to the newscaster Gabriel Heatter, who said whenever he could, "There's good news tonight...." She wept softly after her family sent word that a torpedo from a German U-boat had exploded against the dock where her brother was working and killed him. I didn't know that the Germans blew up docks on Caribbean islands and supposed that maybe the torpedo had missed the ship it was aimed at. Amelia had so little, and now she was more alone.

Stamps

I must have begun collecting postage stamps by the fifth grade because that's when I went to work for A.E. Anderson in his Stamps for Collectors shop on the second floor of the old Arbuckle Building, a large square structure that had high ceilings, big windows rounded at the top, and two fire escapes across its face. Either from design or decades of soot, the building, now long gone, was black. It fronted on Fulton Street and the plaza that lay before Brooklyn's stately Borough Hall. Across the plaza, rose the tall office buildings of Court Street that separate the government buildings from mostly residential Brooklyn Heights.

Mr. Anderson had a slight frame, wore glasses, and often chewed on an unlit cigar. He seemed like an old man. An L-shaped counter transected the room in which he earned his living. Between it and the two big windows that faced the view, he kept his desk, safe, stocks of stamps, and occasional young helper. Customers would come in from the hall and make their selection by sitting down at the other side of the counter and going through books on each page of which he had affixed with small, transparent hinges a variety of stamps. They'd pull the stamps they wanted to collect off the pages under his watchful eyes.

My main job was to take these books from time to time and, using the *Scott Catalogue* number* written behind each stamp, replace the stamps that had been bought with duplicates from his stock. Very carefully. It would not do to put a stamp worth a dollar into a book of penny stamps. I had no set hours. After school when I wanted to, I'd take a short detour from my usual walk home and work for an hour or two. On a few Saturdays, I worked much longer. Often I spent all my earnings on his stamps for my collection.

This was my first paying job, twenty-five cents an hour, bumped up to thirty cents during sixth grade. My father gave my brothers and me a smaller allowance than most of our friends received, and in hindsight I'm glad he did, because he wanted us "to learn the value of

---

* The *Scott Catalogue*, which was revised annually, assigned a number and value to every stamp in the world and was ubiquitous among dealers and collectors. It invariably assigned a higher value than Mr. Anderson charged. In those days, it was all in one volume; today it's in fourteen.

a dollar." Mr. Anderson taught me the value of a quarter and of thirty cents.

His most valuable lesson, to the extent that I could absorb it, was to see what lay before my eyes. "Be observant, Malcolm. Be observant!" Small differences in the color or design of two apparent duplicates might show that they were actually different stamps, one more rare and valuable than the other. Another lesson came when he asked me for an eraser and instead of walking it over to him, I tossed it. As we crawled around on the floor looking for it, he scolded me about the time that attempted shortcuts often wastes. Do boys and girls pay as much attention as they used to to old men's words? His lessons have stayed with me, at least sporadically.

Collecting stamps marked my first and, fortunately, my last compulsively acquisitive phase (except for one summer of saving bottle caps). I mounted most of them in a large, blue-covered album, using those ubiquitous hinges; sometimes I looked up the value of one stamp or another in my *Scott Catalogue*; and more often than was useful, I counted them, reaching more than ten thousand different stamps before I lost interest shortly into puberty. My father couldn't stand FDR, but I found it almost redeeming that he, too, was a philatelist, as my father had been in his youth.

I'm not sure how I came to work for Mr. Anderson, though I think it was through a friend named Nick Spence, who was already working for him. Nick's parents had sent him here from England to escape the German bombs and threatened invasion. While he was still in grade school, he undertook to write a paper about the Prussian Junkers, a venerable clan of so-called nobility that had owned vast amounts of land and included Otto von Bismarck, the "Iron Chancellor" of Germany in the Nineteenth Century, and many other militarists. I knew the word *Junkers*—the *J* is pronounced *Y*—only as a producer of bombers that were smashing London and killing Brits, and it impressed me that Nick had the brains and drive to undertake this project. It still does. When it became safe, he returned to England. I'm sorry I lost track of him.

After sixth grade, I changed schools and no longer had the time or interest to work for a stamp dealer. It had been a good experience, and I was glad that my parent accepted it. Only when I became less self-centered, did I realize that I had learned almost nothing about A. E. Anderson except that the A was for Alfred. Why had he chosen to sell stamps for collectors? Was he doing well or barely making it? Did he have a wife—I sensed that he didn't—or any children? The one question I wondered about at the time was whether I was worth my twenty-five cents an hour, if, say, it took me that long to replace twenty-five one cent stamps in a sales book. The follow-up conclusion, which I did not draw at the time, was that he was probably a lonely old man who felt comfortable having Nick and me around. Perhaps we were the grandsons he never had.

My stamp collection, along with Dad's, has passed to my granddaughter Noa.

Handiwork

Besides collecting stamps, I had another hobby, this one my own invention. Starting when I was maybe seven or eight and continuing into my teens, I took paper and adhesive tape, soon supplanted by the sheets of cardboard by which the laundry stiffened my father's shirts and the rolls of sticky brown paper that he bought me; and I cut them up and stuck them together to make boats, airplanes, all manner of guns, a slide trombone, and boxes that only opened when you tilted them to let the marbles I'd secreted inside roll a certain way. You could blow into the back of my bolt-action rifles and shoot spitballs out of the rolled-up paper barrels—my brothers were not amused. Or a sword whose tinfoil-covered blade collapsed into the hilt, giving the impression that you'd plunged it into your gut. All manner of things.

During grade school and beyond, I was often home in bed with a cold or the flu or whatever, which gave me lots of time to construct this stuff. (Seldom made anything while I was well.) I was often at it while the radio played "soap operas," so called because soap makers sponsored many of them: *Stella Dallas*, a story of mother love and sacrifice. *Mary Noble, Backstage Wife. Lorenzo Jones*, whose inventions made him a character to the town but not to his wife, Belle, who loves him. *Our Gal Sunday*, can a girl from a mining town in the West find happiness as the wife of a wealthy and titled Englishman? (Not mentioned: can he find happiness with her?) *The Romance of Helen Trent,* which asks whether a woman can find romance at thirty-five and even beyond. The dramas came in fifteen-minute episodes (less commercials and theme music), and I sometimes stayed sick a day longer than necessary in order to find out what happened next.

My pleasure in making these cardboard objects would serve me well decades later when I started my own law practice and couldn't afford to hire someone to assemble the briefs and other booklets that I typed out and filed in New York's state and federal courts.

The War Touches Home

During Sunday dinners in the early 1940s, usually a chicken with mashed potatoes and gravy, Dad often turned on the radio, and we would listen to Edward R. Murrow reporting the news of the German bomber blitz, his calm, firm voice intoning, *"This...is London."* To make his reports, he was risking his life under the bombs and shards of exploded antiaircraft shells, and his words went deep. Even today, recordings of the rising, falling wail of the Banshee—the air raid sirens that foretold the bombers droning towards the embattled city—move me to tears.*

On Sundays after the mid-day dinner, Dad would sometimes take my brothers and me for a walk across Brooklyn Heights and the storied Brooklyn Bridge, sometimes as far as his office in a nearly darkened building in a canyon of lower Manhattan. On the cold, clear Sunday afternoon of December 7, 1941, he took us ice skating in the below-street-level rink at Rockefeller Center. When we got home, Mom, who was very pregnant and had been listening to the radio, told us that the Japanese had bombed Pearl Harbor. Britain's war became ours too.

A few weeks later my little sister, Mary Elizabeth, was born, but she lived for only five days because of an Rh factor incompatibility that was nearly always fatal back then. I believe her death was the greatest loss my mother ever suffered. It was the only time I saw Dad weep. When Kay's and my daughter Erin was born, we chose Elizabeth for

---

* In Irish lore, a banshee was a female spirit whose wail portended a death in the family. During those air raids, German bombs killed nearly 30,000 civilians in London.

her middle name, for Kay's sister Betsy, for my cousin-and-almost-sister Betty, and for tiny Mary Elizabeth.

On some mornings later on, my mother would put on her gray Red Cross uniform and leave the house before dawn to serve coffee and doughnuts on the Brooklyn docks to soldiers who were boarding ships for Europe. My parents must have known that many of these young men would not return, though they didn't mention it, at least not around us kids; and it didn't occur to me that those steaming cups from those gray-clad women were the last kindly act these lads ever received in their homeland. Only much later did it occur to me that Mom was doing God's work in a war that God had not prevented. At the time, I simply knew I admired her for doing it.

My father had served in France during World War I—that pointless slaughter that rearranged the Western World and paved the path to World War II—but had not been sent to the front before the Armistice came, unlike his cousin (and mine) Tommy Haughton, who grew up in Cullybackey, Ireland, and whom two German machine gun bullets killed on July 1, 1916, the first day of the Somme, the bloodiest day in the history of the British army, in which Tommy would not have been fighting if the Brits had stayed the hell out of Ireland centuries earlier. I learned from family letters that crossed the Atlantic back then, that Tommy's parents had clung to the belief that his death accomplished something, and they never got over losing him. Dad barely survived the flu epidemic that followed the War to End All Wars, as many called it and some believed, until Hitler invaded Poland and Janet wept a bare twenty-one years later.

Dad was too old to serve in this war but signed up as an air raid warden for our neighborhood. We kept buckets of sand in the attic and an "Indian pump" that enabled you to squirt a stream of water from a tank strapped to your back, in case a German incendiary bomb plunged through our roof. The sand was for the fiercely blazing thermite bomb itself, and the water was for the fire it would start, probably on our old wooden attic floor. We hung blackout curtains snugly around our windows, not so much against the bombers that never came—though there were air raid drills with sirens wailing in the Brooklyn night—as to do our part in keeping the glow of the City from silhouetting American ships in the periscopes of the U-boats that lurked offshore. There was still too much glow in the sky; many ships and men and much materiel fell prey to German torpedoes in nearby waters.

As the war continued, Dad sometimes took my brothers and me to Coney Island on Sunday afternoons to walk on the empty beach, climb across the rocks of the breakwaters, and ride the one merry-go-round that stayed open during winter. For much of the trip to and from the beach, the subway became an elevated train, and we would count the stars in the small red and white banners that hung in many upper story windows of the houses we rumbled past. Each blue star stood for a person in the household who was serving in the armed forces. A gold star meant the person had been killed.

After the war, a memorial for the mariners whose lives the Germans had taken in our coastal waters went up in Battery Park across the bay from the Statue of Liberty, huge white blocks like oversized dominoes with four thousand six hundred names marching neatly across them, each the name of a man who had been blown up, burned to death, or drowned in American coastal waters. While I was young and still worked downtown, I'd sometimes walk among the white blocks during lunchtime and wonder at all those men who died so close to New York. Were the salt tears that their loved ones shed, along with the tears of Amelia and Tommy's parents and the millions of loved ones of the other dead of World Wars I and II, enough to carve a groove through that granite? If they were, they were not enough to prevent the wars that followed.

On Brooklyn Heights

I grew up on Grace Court, a dead-end block that pointed to the southernmost waters of the East River, the Staten Island ferry slips at the south end of Manhattan Island, and in the distance, New Jersey. We had such a good view because the block ended at the edge of the plateau called Brooklyn Heights, letting us see over the roofs of the piers and warehouses that lined the waterfront below. Opening onto long and busy Hicks Street at its other end, our block had little traffic, making it ideal for roller skating and playing stoop ball, stickball, touch football, and hopscotch, also known as potsy and sometimes as a girls' game, as well as shooting marbles in the gutter and enjoying the thrill of winning puries. My family and I would remark on a large merchant ship flying a white flag with a red circle on it, the Rising Sun of Japan, that sometimes dominated the view at the end of the street. After Pearl Harbor, the ship no longer docked there.

At the dead-end end of Grace Court, an oval of widened pavement and narrowed sidewalk gave cars room to turn around. An iron fence with a streetlight standing at its midpoint separated the sidewalk from a brief, flat lawn that ended in a short drop-off to a hillside of tufted grass sloping down to a flat concrete shelf a few yards wide that ran along the top of a cliff that stood maybe two stories up from Furman Street below.

One day I had a fight with a kid named Cue Ball Benson on the hillside and concrete shelf. Everybody called him Cue Ball because he had a very round skull, its roundness accentuated by his perpetual crew cut. I think the fight happened because he wanted it to. I was bigger and stronger, so not in much danger, or so I thought. At one point we were holding each other's hands or wrists on the concrete shelf and swinging round like partners in a square dance when I realized that if I let go of Cue Ball, he would fall backwards off the shelf and down to the pavement. So I did not let go.

After the war, the City destroyed the hillside and cliff as a part of building the two-tiered Brooklyn-Queens Expressway along the whole west edge of Brooklyn Heights. We kids played on the construction now and then as it progressed. After it was finished, we'd see the top portions of large trucks sailing past the end of Grace Court. A block to the north, at the foot of Remsen Street and cantilevered over the Expressway, began the stately Promenade, which ran more than a third of a mile along the edge of the Heights and provided walkers with magnificent views of the spiky Manhattan skyline, the Brooklyn and Manhattan Bridges, the Staten Island ferry terminal, the Statue of Liberty, and the waters of New York Harbor. If you faced the other way, you saw into the backyards and rear windows of a long row of venerable, red brick mansions that had once been very private along the street called Columbia Heights. Now everyone could enjoy the same panorama as the rich folks who lived there. Some years after the

Promenade was finished, I would wheel my tiny daughter Erin in her baby carriage along it and sit and read while she slept.

Alternative

I stared through the windshield of our pre-war Plymouth station wagon at one green Ohio town after another as my father slowed the car under the tunnel of trees that shaded the frame houses where the highway served a short stint as the town's Main Street. They must roll up the sidewalks at nine p.m., I thought dismissively as I had thought on other drives across Ohio, and the annual church picnic must be *it* for the year. The war had ended and so had gas rationing, and my family was making its annual visit to Cincinnati, from whence my father had come a quarter of a century earlier to seek his fortune in the canyons of Manhattan.

Books on social history, which my mostly staid high school teachers had not assigned but I had read anyway, had persuaded me that my father was serving as a private to the captains of industry—a vest with every suit, evenings at an office that never yielded wealth, usher at our church, encounters with men whose stature in the world of business Dad somehow implied.

"How would you boys like to be growing up in a town like this?" he asked my brothers and me as he slowed down for another green town, breaking my reverie. "I once gave a lot of thought to living my life in a town like this."

I turned to the man who was holding the wheel between his hands and looking down the road. Suddenly I saw Dad anew, a stranger yet a human being more like me than I had supposed.

Dodgers

Because there was nothing else to do, I supposed, my brothers and I sprawled in the cool of our parents' bedroom on sunny summer after-noons and listened to Red Barber and Connie Desmond broadcast the Brooklyn Dodgers' baseball games. Though there was no TV then, I'd watched enough games in Ebbets Field to imagine what the pitches and plays looked like in that small, tall, dark green stadium as the voices from the radio described them. Who will win? Can the Dodgers hold their lead or come from behind? Who will take the pennant? And the nearly perennial Brooklyn battle cry, Wait till next year! Between innings one of us sometimes roused himself to pull an ice tray from the refrigerator and fetch glasses of cold Pepsi Cola.

Dixie Walker "patrolled the pastures," as Red Barber put it, under the short right field fence in front of Bedford Avenue, and fought it out with Stan the Man Musial of the St. Louis Cardinals for the National League batting crown. So we named our tortoise-shell kitten Dixie. One winter after she had grown to cathood, a trap set for foxes in the woods near the farm that delivered our milk caught her in the snow. By the time the farmers found her, they had to amputate her left foreleg. Undaunted as animals often are, she developed a powerful right leg with which she sometimes pinned down large rats long enough to bite them dead. Once after she'd swallowed one, I watched her walk across the grass with the tip of its tail protruding from her mouth. Nothing squeamish about Dixie! She hobbled back and forth to rub against the legs of the people she cared about, and she bore litter after litter. One August we left her for a few days at the farm and returned to find a large dark spot on the white guest room bedspread. She had found her way home to bear her kittens.

In those days that cat led a more interesting life than we did. "Never a dull day with the Dodgers," Red Barber used to say. But we were the ones dodging, and however pleasant, those were the dullest afternoons of my life. It's fine with me for other people to enjoy hanging out, but it makes me restless. So does lying on a beach in the sun, and after trying it a few times, I stopped doing it. So it may be paradoxical that years later I would look forward to the hour of sitting still in the silence of a Quaker Meeting.

Curiosity

During several years of our youth, my brothers and I sometimes played with a friend named Freddy Dobbs, who was younger than I and older than my next brother David. One afternoon shortly after Freddy and his family had moved into a brownstone on Remsen Street a few blocks from our house in Brooklyn, the four of us decided to find out what lay beyond the wall at the far end of the Dobbses' new backyard. We climbed onto the wall and, to our disappointment, beheld another little yard that had almost nothing in it except for a slab of weathered wood, maybe the size of a wide door, that was lying at the foot of the wall and apparently flat on the ground.

I didn't consider the slab or why it might be lying there as I lowered myself from the top of the wall and jumped backwards the last few feet towards its far side. My mind was on exploring the yard, not that there looked like much to explore. My feet did not land on the slab. Instead, they crashed through it, and I found myself standing on a narrow ledge a bit below ground level as the rest of the rotten wood I had just shattered fell onto the concrete floor maybe ten or twelve feet below my precarious perch. The slab had actually served as a lid over the opening into an underground cellar. The yard was its roof.

It looked dark down there except for the pale brown fragments of newly shattered wood that lay scattered across the floor where I would be lying and picking myself up, or not, if that ledge had not been there and my feet had not landed squarely on it.

This was the first of four events in my young life where I realized that improbably good luck, or maybe a Divine hand, saved me from serious injury or worse. Before the second event, Freddy Dobbs would disappoint me and I would disappoint him.

Tipping Point

A big kid in my class seemed to get his jollies out of hurting me when he saw an opportunity. Once when I ducked under an arch that he and another kid made for me with their arms, he banged their clasped hands down on my head. Once when he was holding a big metal door for me to go through into the school chapel, he banged the door into me as I passed. I don't think he planned these attentions, which struck me as sadistic, but I don't think he missed an opportunity. Why me?

One bright spring Saturday morning, he started to inflict some new pain, I forget what, as he and I and several other boys were standing at the end of my block beside Grace Church and the traffic rolling past on Hicks Street. I'd reached my limit. I raised my knee into his nuts. He cried out and doubled up onto the sidewalk. I didn't plan it, just took the opportunity. After that he didn't bother me.

Ghost

Below the arch of the concrete bridge, the Saugatuck River broadened and deepened into a swimming hole called Devil's Den. On one side, mossy rock rose from the water with setbacks slanting upwards. The brow of an enormous gray stone whale overhung the other side. Dark green spruces rose from the cliffs, shadowing the water in gloom most of the day. Looking down from the bridge, you could see the trees and between them a jagged stretch of sky reflected in the water like a photo's negative. White pebbles turned darker and darker brown, the deeper they lay off a submerged beach where the river grew shallow downstream. The water was always too cold to stay in it very long before we would have to climb the trail above the cliffs and dry off on the sunny blacktop road above.

Mostly we dove off the setbacks rather than the gray overhang because it was easier to climb back up, even though the higher you got, the harder you had to shove outwards in order to miss the rocks below. We dove from a ledge about five feet high the first time and worked our way up, taking more time and mustering more courage at each level, to a ledge maybe twenty feet over the water. That's a lot farther to plunge from than to look up at, and seemed plenty high to us. It took me nearly half an hour the first time I dared to dive off it.

Watching the big kids go off the bridge always scared us. It was more than twice as high as our highest cliff, and they were really moving by the time they hit the water. That was exciting, and we always watched. Besides being scary, it was truly dangerous. The water was still quite shallow under the bridge, and now and then one of them would laugh about crashing into the rocky bottom when he went in too straight. It was deeper on the side with the overhang, so they tried to come close to that big stone slab without landing on it. Sometimes a big kid jumped feet first, but we knew that his buddies looked down on this, and they usually dove. Some of them wore tee shirts to lessen the sting when they smacked the water.

One day when we weren't there, a big kid we didn't know misjudged his dive and broke his neck.

The town sent men to cut down all the spruces on both sides. It was as though they were trying to make up for having paid too little attention to the danger and not foreseen the fatal accident. Now the bushy treetops slanted into each other in the water with their trunks resting on the rocks above. When my brothers and I looked off the bridge, it was all sunny and naked-looking down there, and the branches lay so thick you could hardly see any water at all, much less swim in it. A year or so later the trees were gone, but we thought about the big kid who had died, and none of us cared to swim there again.

Precaution

My brother Tigger and I were walking home on Rock House Road near dusk on a cloudy autumn day after trudging through a part of the woods we'd never explored before. Up ahead Dad stood on a wooden ladder over the stone wall in front of the barn, sawing a large dead limb off the lofty elm that would later succumb to the ravenous Dutch elm disease.

"A piece of wood that big can really jump around," I told Tig. Coming up to Dad, we insisted that he tie himself and the top of the ladder to the tree with a rope that we fetched from the barn. Laughing, the weekend tree surgeon complied. Fifteen more minutes of sawing, and the limb cracked free, sprang back, and snapped the ladder in two as it crashed down onto the grass and stone wall. Dad dangled safely above the rocks.

In an unexpected way, perhaps, two children were father of the man.

Years later I reflected on that afternoon of my misty youth as I stood high on an aluminum ladder sawing a dead limb off the big oak in front of Kay's and my house in exurban Norwalk, Connecticut. Since I had placed the ladder well around the tree from the limb, I did not sense any danger as the limb began to crack. Rather, it was a sense of my obligation to the memory of saving my father that prompted me to climb down, find a rope in the carport, and lash myself and the ladder to the tree trunk. A few more strokes with the saw, and to my surprise, the falling limb sprang back and smashed the ladder off its footing. Safe but stranded, I called to a neighbor to put the ladder right, so I could untie myself and climb down.

Prank

The prank, when it occurred to me, seemed like an interesting challenge, though if I'd thought beyond my desire to pull it off, I'd have seen it was also dumb.

The classroom of Mr. Virgil Dechert, the chemistry teacher, was directly over the entrance hall of my high school; the chem lab that adjoined the classroom was directly over the office of Dr. Joseph Dana Allen, the venerable headmaster who was known around the school as the Bunny because he looked like one. A white glass bowl formed an ample lampshade around the light bulb that hung from his office ceiling. In the lab were several rows of wooden counters at which we fifth formers (eleventh graders) stood while performing our experiments. Each workstation had a sink sunk into the counter, a stack of drawers down to the floor beneath the sink, and a faucet rising beside it like a shepherd's crook.

On day I took some short pieces of rubber hose and connected them with pieces of glass tubing to make a fairly long hose. When I thought no one was watching, I wedged one end of the hose onto my faucet, put the other end into one of the drawers beneath the counter, and closed the drawer gently so as not to pinch the hose. As the lab period ended, I turned on the water, the room emptied, and we all went to our next classes. Later that day, word filtered through the school that Dr. Allen's chandelier had filled with water, and water was falling onto his desk. This was more success than I'd anticipated and a bit sobering.

A year later Dr. Allen recommended me to his friend, the dean of admissions at Harvard College, and for better or worse, I became a Harvard man. If the cascade onto his desk had been traced to me— if Mr. Dechert had remembered which student had been standing where—would this have happened? Dr. Allen was a wise man who took the long view. I wondered later whether he had learned the truth and decided not to let an ill-considered prank impair my future.

This was not the last time that the idea of a prank would blind me to the possible consequences.

Truth

I have never wholly understood why I blackballed my longtime friend Freddy Dobbs from Sigma Psi, my high school fraternity. The reason I gave the brothers—and myself at the time—was simple: He had lied to my mother.

Freddy was brash, lively, and engaging, qualities that aroused mixed feelings in me even as we played in each other's houses during countless afternoons after school. One summer evening when he was visiting us in the country, as we called the family cottage in Easton, he and my brothers and I decided it would be fun to pull an empty box on a rope across a lonely stretch of the Blackrock Turnpike. The headlights of oncoming cars would catch it, and drivers would come to screeching halts. We had not considered what would happen next, which is why we got caught. A driver got sore enough to slam out of his truck and grab us in the bushes before we had the sense to retreat through the darkness, except that Tigger wasn't caught right away because he had climbed into a tree. The driver took us to my mother to let justice be done. She admonished us, quite rightly, that we had done a dangerous thing. After the driver left, Freddy assured her with persuasive sincerity that we had not done it.

Truth mattered to me. "No legacy so rich as honesty" was the quote that the classmates who worked on the Poly Prep yearbook would place under my graduation picture the next year. Freddie's lie shocked me, yet it crystallized who he was, not a bad person but quick to sacrifice the truth for convenience. He made a terrific impression on the brothers at pledge time and seemed set to be voted in, until my simple report about his lying to my mother persuaded half of them to join me in blackballing him.

Fraternity proceedings were supposed to be secret, but that same evening the brother who was his biggest supporter told him. I expect it crushed him, until he adjusted to what he must have seen as my betrayal. He soon pledged to another fraternity, and we were back to saying "Hi" by the end of the year.

I suppose that my mother was sorry to see him hurt, glad that his vain effort to deceive her had angered me, and probably surprised that I'd taken it as far as I had. I don't recall discussing it with her. I suppose, too, that things were awkward for a while between her and Freddy's mother. Mrs. Dobbs had been baptized in our church only a few years before and had chosen Mom to be her godmother.

It occurred to me later that I also spoke against Freddy because he was too much of a wise guy to fit in with the brothers and I wanted to spare us his noise. Maybe, too, I feared that he would upstage me, he the witty showman and I usually quiet even in a group I knew well. And maybe I was finally clarifying my mixed feelings about him. I am sure, though, that I would have held my peace and we would have voted him in if I had not felt strongly about his lying to my mother.

Up till then, I had had little experience with the hard choices that conflicting values may present. Now here it was: friendship versus truth. I hoped that the incident became a growth experience for Freddy. I know it did for me.

Teacher

Making fun of a high school teacher is as likely to signify affection as disrespect. We derided Doctor Miles Merwin Kastendieck for his pointed nose and sometimes pointed tongue, for still parting his hair in the middle, 1920's-style in the 1940's, for... What does it matter? In a school that boasted many fine teachers, he stood out.

Doc K roamed around his vast subject, English. "Lady Macbeth said, 'What's done is done,'" he told us, "but the point is that what's done is not done." He talked about a prediction that houses with glass walls would grow common, a theory that whether the gunman shoots one person and spares another may depend on how they have lived their lives up to that moment. He coached track; walking with him in the halls, I found it hard to keep up. After many a day of classes and coaching, he would take the subway to Manhattan to review a concert for one City newspaper or another, living as fully as he taught.

I believe I surprised and maybe pleased him thirty years later by quoting his vanished words. "First impressions are often right." Quite so. "Never force an issue." I disagreed but forced fewer issues after he said it. He predicted during tenth grade—rather safely, I realized later—that within the next year most of us would love and lose. "I hope you do," he added with a grim smile. I did—her name was Carolyn—

and realized through my pain that he was right: a person who has not lost painfully cannot be complete.

He taught us to outline and underline, to seize upon what matters. (I still underline nearly all the non-fiction I read, a habit I use to justify buying books instead of borrowing them from the library.) "Discriminate!" he commanded, but discriminate first about how one discriminates, not against people different from one's self, but against shoddy books, movies, attitudes, and what would later be called lifestyles, against whatever diminishes life. The works he expounded— Shakespeare, Ibsen, O'Neill, Dickens, Conrad, Hardy—taught us the profound lesson that most people are much like ourselves.

He dramatized. "I-*knew*... an-*actress*... once...." We mimicked him, but he held us. He had values and urged us to have values. Be fearless of mind. Do not compromise your integrity. Take a stand for what matters. He disparaged our custom of re-electing our bland class president year after year; and I wondered, but didn't think to ask him, what he expected a high school class president to stand for.

In those days the school still had fraternities, and they accepted fewer than half the students. Most of the class who were "in" got in; most who weren't didn't. If Doc K realized that this perverted the discrimination he preached, I did not hear him say so. He was the faculty advisor of Sigma Psi, where I became the *archon*—Greek for president—and he was more like a father to us than many fathers doubtless were to their sons.

Unforgettably, he arranged for us brothers to see the magnificent musical *South Pacific* shortly after it opened on Broadway. After the final curtain, he led us on a short walk to 43rd Street and into the Blue Ribbon restaurant, with its interior rich in dark polished wood, for a bite to eat and a round or two of Rhine wine. I took one of the long-necked green bottles with me as a souvenir, and it was well that I did since, through no fault of Doc K's, my evening could have ended badly without it.

The subway from Times Square to Brooklyn was fine, but as I walked along dark, empty Remsen Street two blocks from home, a large man stepped out of the brownstone doorway at the top of a flight of steps. I brandished the bottle, ready to smash its base on the curb and defend myself with the jagged rest of it. The man stepped back into the shadows. Glancing constantly up at the doorway, I passed unmolested.

Many an evening when my parents assumed I was at my homework, I was playing solitaire, slapping card on card and stacks of thirteen on my desk, while soft music murmured from the radio. Much of high school contributed little to my education. But I knew a teacher once....

Crushes

When I was thirteen, my mother decided that I had best learn to dance, specifically by attending Miss Hepburn's Dancing School in the parish house of Grace Church, which was only a few doors up the block from our house. Miss Hepburn's was an institution in Brooklyn Heights, and most of the kids I knew attended it. Since my body was maturing more slowly than my classmates'—somewhat embarrassing then, but pleasant now I'm in my 90s—Miss Heppie and Mom decided that I should attend a younger class. I resisted going to the school and wearing the white gloves that even the boys had to wear, but I succumbed.

My class had, as I recall, eight boys and eight girls. I nearly always chose one or another of four girls as a partner and paid no attention to the other four, for reasons I can't recall. Nancy was a nice girl, about my height, and easy to talk with, and so was Jean, who was shorter. I have no memory of my third partner. The fourth was Barbara, with whom I was soon smitten and found myself tongue-tied. I thought about her constantly; she was the reason I looked forward to the classes. Since she lived on my block, I'd see her sometimes on the sidewalk, though I never tried to talk with her there either. She was beautiful; years later I would compare her to the tennis star Martina Hingis. Once I spent days working up the nerve to ask Barbara to the movies—it would be my first date—but when I phoned, her mother told me she was out, and I never mustered the nerve to phone again.

My crush on, infatuation with, and zillion daydreams about Barbara continued for maybe two years, though not having talked with her, I barely knew what she was like. I never told anyone how Barbara filled my fantasies and wondered whether my mother suspected. At age fifteen I had my first date, not with Barbara but with a gentle, intelligent, thoroughly nice girl named Joan. She lived in Flatbush, which surprised me with its grass, trees, and detached wooden houses when I climbed the stairs from the subway and walked several blocks to pick her up. We went to a movie. It turned out that Miss Hepburn had taught her father, too. I really liked her and enjoyed talking with her, but I wasn't smitten.

The next blinding crush after Barbara came in my junior year with Carolyn, again a gentle, intelligent, and thoroughly nice person, plus she lived in an apartment house only a short walk from home. As it happened, my fraternity brother and close friend, Jim Keller, was also smitten with her. As you know from "Handiwork," I had made models of ships and guns and other things out of cardboard and sticky brown paper; this time I made a copy of my Sigma Psi fraternity pin using gold tin foil, black paper, and a safety pin and presented it to Carolyn. Not to be outdone, Jim offered her his real Sigma Psi pin, and she accepted it. I was desolate, lonely at the parties I attended, a lost soul for weeks. I recalled Doc K's hope that each of us students would soon love and lose—as a growth experience, I supposed. Score another one for Doc K! My growth, if any, hurt. Carolyn told me later that just because she was pinned to Jim, she never expected me to stop dating her.

A year or so after my crush on Barbara had subsided, I had a happy encounter with her. My brother David was having a party in the family living room with a few kids his age, including her. I walked in and, as the others paired off, I asked her to dance with me. The phonograph came on, the lights went out, and we danced the Y, so-called because the partners' feet were apart, their torsos were as one, and they rocked slowly from side to side, suggesting an inverted Y—not a step that Miss Hepburn taught. I hugged Barbara and she hugged me, tightly and warmly. We slowly rocked as one body for a long time, still never saying a word to each other, and I was very happy.

Barbara grew even more beautiful but considerably taller, and though I now had whatever it took to talk with her, I did not have the social courage that Al Pacino would have with Diane Keaton in the *Godfather* movies—or that a fine guy named George Hanson had with my Cousin Josie, whom he married—to be seen with a taller woman. Barbara went her way, I went mine.

I did not choose to be attracted to her, Joan, or Carolyn, or to Linda, Bonnie, or beautiful black-haired Sue. Instead, I simply found it happening—as is typical, I understand, for most teenagers. Why, I have often wondered, do many people forget, ignore, or defy the way that their own sexual urges emerged, and insist that some boys and girls consciously choose to join the abused minority that prefer members of their own sex? It's not gay boys and girls who defy Nature. It's the folks who fault them for being who they are.

Instinct

The second time that anger moved me past my tipping point and a darker instinct took over came on a warm spring day in my senior year. Several of us started having rock fights during the school's lunch hour. Truly dumb, but I can't go back and change it. The air was warm, the world freshly green, the tension of trying to get into college slackened while the admissions offices made up their minds, and nobody thought how David's fight with Goliath ended.

Tom's team and mine circled on opposite sides of the pond, down the long driveway from the school, but it is hard to find stones in the mud, and you had no chance of hitting anybody at that distance because he could see a stone coming in plenty of time to dodge it. Both teams charged up to the driveway and moved towards each other, using the trunks of the trees that lined it for cover.

Tom stepped from behind a trunk and hurled a chunk of concrete at me. I was caught in the open on the driveway about twenty or so yards away. Seeing the object coming low, I jumped up. It hit the driveway and slowed down. As I landed, it bounced into my shinbone.

Pain shot through me bringing fury. Almost without thinking, I scooped up the concrete and a small stone, threw the stone at Tom to drive him behind the tree, and after pausing for second, fired the concrete where I expected his head to reappear. The jagged chunk went surprisingly true. Bark split from the tree beside his startled face. That ended the rock fights, as we finally realized how stupid they were. It also made me more circumspect, seeing, as I had not seen when I raised my knee into the bully's nuts a few years earlier, that I had it in me to turn vengefully violent.

Wonderful

Between high school and college, I took a summer job assisting an aging tree surgeon and landscape gardener named Fred Colter. One afternoon we finished trimming the shrubbery on one of the estates he tended and drove off towards Bridgeport. I don't remember what the hurry was when a downpour hit, but we were barreling along faster than I realized on a slick road in the family's pre-war, partly wooden station wagon. I learned later that the speedometer read fifty when it meant sixty-five, and I should have known that the rear tires were as smooth as a baby's butt. For that matter, so should my father.

I pulled out to pass a slowpoke. Alongside him I saw a car coming at us through the rain. I tromped harder on the gas to sneak on by. That did it. The station wagon spun half around and started skidding broadside towards the oncoming car. My foot hit the brake and froze. Time slowed as an onrushing tree trunk beside the road grew huge before my eyes. As we left the blacktop, the front fender took over a mailbox, spinning the car farther around and pointing the back end at the tree. The rear wheels plowed into a bank of soft soil that, thank God, was somehow there, stopping the tailgate a foot from the tree. Had the soil been ordinary, the station wagon would have rolled over it and collapsed like a strawberry box against the tree trunk. Rain on the station wagon roof made the only sound. The wipers slanted motionless. I had braked the engine dead.

"Wonderful! Wonderful!" Fred said. "Wonderful! Wonderful! Let's go before someone comes about the mailbox."

Fred had enough vitality left in him to wed his longtime girlfriend the next winter and enjoy married life in Florida for four more years. I have been through college, served my country, raised my children, and done decades more living since we back-ended into the unaccountably soft soil along that country road.

Who lives and who doesn't? I was the same age that rainy afternoon as hosts of young men had been six or eight years earlier as they waded towards shore to wrest the islands of Tarawa and Iwo Jima and Okinawa from their Japanese defenders. How many of them had miraculous escapes, we'll never know. By the time the station wagon slammed into the soft soil, the rains and rot and tides of the blue Pacific had long since cleansed the sand of last traces of many thousands of lads, American and Japanese, whom nothing had saved and whose children, had they been born, would have been a few years older than mine.

Imagination

One moonlight night after I got my driver's license, Bonnie and I parked on a dirt road and climbed into the woods. We pushed our way upwards through thick undergrowth reaching easier trees and came out onto a pasture close to the top of a hill. The katydids sang in good voice. Meadows and woods and an occasional house lay blue below us.

As we started into the meadow, several cows walked towards us. Calves stood behind them. I had milked a cow secured in her stanchion once or twice and had thought them gentle beasts. Now, though, Bonnie and I asked each other whether they ever attack. We felt very alone. As they kept coming, their heads low, we retreated back among the trees, and they stopped at the edge. We lay down and necked and looked out at the pale blue countryside as the August night resounded around us. After a while, we found an easier path back to the car.

Bonnie and I had dated for some time and liked each other, and the possibility of going farther than necking had not seriously occurred to me. This was back in the day when a great many youths in high school and even in college didn't do it—a folkway that was somewhat easier than it might have been, I imagine, because I didn't know what I was missing. All the same, I often found it hard.

My parents told me that when I stayed out late, they worried that I would have an accident with a drunk driver, and I was sure they worried that I would have sex. I doubt, though, that they ever imagined I might be gored by a cow.

The Harvard Years

Trees

Timmy plunged out of the tree, one of his shoes fell off, and a sock fluttered down. The back of his head smacked a root, and he lay still on the ground. I stayed with him while Sherman Briscoe, my partner in our summer day camp, went to phone the doctor. The other boys ambled around, sober and scared, no horseplay. After a while, Timmy began to moan. Thank God! He kept crawling onto his feet and trying to walk before he could stand. His eyes were only half open, and he was crowing nonsense. On my knees, I held my hands around his little chest so he wouldn't fall over, and each time he stumbled laid him down as gently as I could.

After a long while, Dr. Grevatt, Redding's all-purpose physician, drove up, put Timmy in his car, and drove him to the Danbury Hospital. No 911 in those days. Timmy turned out to be all right, but his mother pulled him out of our camp, for which Sherm and I did not blame her. It was so unusual for people to sue people back then that it never crossed our minds that she might—nor had the idea of insuring the day camp. We kept the boys out of the trees for the rest of the summer.

They say that most accidents can be prevented, but I'm not so sure. When we climbed a tree, we tried to obey the Rule of Three—always hold on with one hand and both feet or both hands and one foot—but most boys take chances, and sometimes some lose. All my life, it seems, a boy has come plunging out of a tree.

Chivalry

The first autumn of my college education, I discovered a Chilean version of Rhine wine sitting humbly in a squat green bottle that could become a modest candlestick after it was emptied. Cheap, tasty, effective. That first Christmas vacation, I brought a bottle to Bonnie, whom I'd been dating that summer. She finished it before dinner except for the few swallows I took, and she made up for those with her father's scotch. Since I was invited for the night, there'd be no problem of driving after drinking, right?

Her uncanny capacity to act sober in front of her parents got us through the meal in their cozy, brightly lighted dining room. How little, I thought, these hearty grown-ups suspect. We had a few more drinks and drove her father's car, me at the wheel, down to Compo Beach to park. I do not recall the trip too clearly except that we ended up as the only car beside the historic pair of cannons that the Town of Westport had placed near the rocky breakwater—no one but us to watch the lights on the far shore dancing across icy Long Island Sound.

The dark expanse of sand and patches of snow made a literally polar contrast to the day I had driven Bonnie to that beach, and nearly to a fatal accident, on a warm summer day a few months earlier. We swam out to one of the floats and lay in the sun and talked and talked—we always had a lot to talk about. When it came time to leave, I asked her to sit on the edge of the float so I could dive over her. I ran a few steps, cleared her head, and plunged towards the water at an angle that would have been okay if the tide had not been going out while we were gabbing. Most of my body was still in the air when my outstretched hands hit the sandy bottom, jolting me terribly. I didn't think my head had struck the sand until I discovered that my hair was matted with its dark gray grains. I hope I thanked God that my neck hadn't broken. I managed to drive back to her house then to mine, but the next morning, my back was so stiff I could barely get out of bed.

Now in bleak midwinter, my body had long since healed, and my head was nearly clear. Hers wasn't. Drunkenness came roaring out like a bear that won't hibernate. Between bouts of necking, she kept staggering over the sand and snow towards the water.

"Come on! I'm going swimming."

I kept hauling her back, which was quite a struggle—she was about my size and very strong—and the struggle may have excited her.

"Malcolm, I love you. You can do anything you want to me. You can do anything."

I didn't think it would be gentlemanly to do that when she was soused, which made her, among other things, not particularly attractive. And I didn't want to take advantage. After a while she vomited beside the car, and I drove us home. With few inhibitions and no seat belt to restrain her, she kept trying to kiss my mouth, which made it hard to steer, and even to see out the windshield, but it may have kept me awake.

A year later, she told me that the morning after a fraternity party at Cornell, her lovely blond roommate had wept, her virginity gone, and no idea how or who. Having no recollection of our evening at the snowy beach, Bonnie, too, had no idea—and I never told her—that she had nearly beaten her roomy to the same awakening.

Old Sport

John Hermann and I were fraternity brothers in high school and roommates during our freshman year of college. Our rooms were in Grays Hall at the south end of Harvard Yard, fortunately it turned out, on the ground floor. We often talked into the night, deciding for instance that most romances are pseudo love, and the strongest emotion a man and woman can feel for each other is real pseudo love. We both discovered *The Great Gatsby* that year and ever afterwards called each other "Old Sport," Jay Gatsby's affectation becoming ours.

A subject I'm quite sure we did not discuss was religion. John was a Jew by heritage though I didn't know the extent, if any, to which he was observant, and I suppose he knew as little about my Christianity. Like many Jews, he did not, in the term of the day, "look Jewish"; so that at least twice back at Poly Prep, someone in a group we were in passed an antisemitic remark. He didn't seem to notice, and neither did we who knew he'd been insulted and probably hurt. I don't know whether he experienced the same in college, but wouldn't be surprised if he did, given the bigotry that existed then and survives today.

John joined a social circle that I did not and learned to dance the Charleston, as I did not. A university curfew that forbade us from having women in our rooms after seven p.m. led to a night I remember well. After I had gone to bed, John, another guy, and two women burst in. They turned on the lights, put a record on the phonograph, and began to Charleston, their arms and legs flying. Suddenly came a pounding on the hall door. John and his friend hustled the girls across the foot of my bed and out the window seconds before a campus cop entered the room.

Though John and I joined separate groups in separate dorms the next year, we remained friends and co-adventurers. Who were the two guys in tuxedos rowing a canoe around the indoor swimming pool after a dance at Mount Holyoke College? How was the local newspaper able to run a photo of the canoe beached on the campus lawn the next morning? Driving late at night, John and I would enjoy the country music that radio station WWVA, Wheeling, West Virginia, cranked out across New England after many closer stations had gone off the air.

The caper that nearly got us arrested happened as we were driving back to Cambridge in his car to begin our sophomore year. As good Harvard men, we wanted to do something about the two Yale Bowl signs that flanked eastbound side of the Merritt Parkway where it approached New Haven, one in the grassy median, the other just off the right shoulder. Each sign was about four feet wide, two feet high, and bolted onto a post. Each said "YALE BOWL" in black letters inside a big white arrow that pointed towards the exit for drivers coming to watch the football games in that huge arena.

It was a warm, sunny day. Traffic was light. John pulled onto the shoulder near one of the signs and raised the hood as though to fix something in the engine. I crossed the pavement to the sign in the median. During several intervals when few cars were coming, we unscrewed the signs from their posts and laid them in the back seat across the stuff we'd packed for college. He eased the car onto the parkway, and off we went. A few minutes later, a state police car roared past.

John hung his sign in his rooms in Adams House so that it pointed down at the toilet bowl. Mine hung in the garage for decades, with much of its paint flaking off, before I gave it to my stepdaughter Katrina. John became an accomplished New York City ophthalmologist with an office on Park Avenue. He and his wife sometimes had dinner with Kay and me until we moved to exurbia; but he continued to care for my gradually increasing nearsightedness. It was always good to talk things over with him during the brief time that my annual appointments allowed. "Old Sport! How's it going?"

He knew how to live, I thought, closing his office and playing golf on many Fridays. A cerebral aneurysm took him at the age of forty-nine.

Outstanding

In my sophomore year, my parents drove up from Connecticut to visit me for the Harvard–Yale football game, which was always the last game of the season.

"You're not doing one thing that's outstanding," my father snarled afterwards as the three of us walked among crackling brown leaves towards the red sun after Yale won.

Most people don't, I fumed in silence.

Dad's anger that afternoon and mine in response, I realized later, sprang from a deep difference between us. Growing up in Cincinnati, he had had to be sufficiently outstanding in high school to get into Harvard, where his grades were sufficiently outstanding to win his election to Phi Beta Kappa, which is said to be the most prestigious honor society in the country, and admission to Harvard Law School where his grades earned him a place among the editors of the prestigious *Harvard Law Review*. His legal work in Manhattan earned him the money to send my brothers and me to well-regarded Poly Prep, and me to this college and this weekend.

While I was in high school, he asked me to read two or three books by Horatio Alger that he had read during his youth. In them, a young man rose from humble origins to conventional success through hard work and bits of luck. That was more or less Dad's story, though as the son of a physician with locally prominent forebears, his origins weren't exactly humble. But from the privileged position he had earned for me, I didn't care all that much about conventional success.

While I tried to perform my various tasks thoroughly and well and didn't like to disappoint Dad, I did not particularly care about pursuing excellence either. Sons often disappoint successful fathers, it seemed to me, not because they are necessarily lazy or less intelligent, but because their values differ. Though I was probably hurting my grades by reading books that were not assigned—Hemingway, Fitzgerald, Steinbeck, Shaw, G. K. Chesterton, and so on—at the expense of some books that were, I would graduate from Harvard with honors, get myself into the same law school, climb from the bottom third to about the middle of my class, and land a job with the same Manhattan law firm that Dad had started out in—all of which neither of us knew on that autumn afternoon when I was actually planning to become a professor of college English.

For better or worse, I felt that there is more to life than being outstanding. Would Dad agree today that ours was a generational difference, not a cause for anger? As Hemingway wrote in another context, isn't it pretty to think so?[2]

Runaway

The fall of my sophomore year saw considerable friction between my father and me. One weekend prior to the Harvard–Yale game, I went home to Connecticut but arranged with my then girlfriend, Scottie, to spend one of the nights at her house. For some reason that Dad never explained, this infuriated him. That evening he drove the seven or so miles from our house to Scottie's, and in front of her and her family in their warm living room, he ordered me to come home with him. Rather than expand the painful scene, I obeyed. I had never felt so humiliated.

Until right after Dad and I reached our own warm living room. The house guest that weekend was white-haired, dignified Dr. Joseph Dana Allen, who had recently retired after thirty-two years as headmaster of my high school and whose good opinion of me had been instrumental in getting me into Harvard. In front of Dr. Allen and Mom—I don't recall where my brothers were—Dad made it clear that what I had done was shameful.

Again, I did not expand the scene by saying a word in self-defense. But I did not, and to this day do not, see anything shameful about what I had done. The previous Christmas vacation, I had spent two or three nights at the home of my friend Bonnie and her family, as you read in "Chivalry," without arousing Dad's ire. There was no way that Scottie and I would have made love in her small family home; and if we had, I would have considered it indiscreet, not shameful. I have often wondered what Dr. Allen thought of my father's tense little tirade. So, at either end of that seven-mile car ride, my father inflicted the two most humiliating moments I have ever experienced.

Thanksgiving weekend completed a trilogy of father-son dust-ups during the waning of that year. Again, I was home in Connecticut. I forget what Dad lit into me for that Saturday evening, but it totally pissed me off. I phoned Bonnie, who was home from Cornell for Thanksgiving too, then went to my room, closed the door, opened the window beside the bed, and crawled out into the night. Maybe half an hour later, Bonnie met me at a nearby crossroads and drove me to the Bridgeport railroad station. I took a train to New Haven—don't recall why I only went that far—walked to the nearby Yale campus, and had the good luck to find the rooms of guys I knew from high school who had left their door open and lights on.

After a short sleep on their couch, I finished the trip back to college, and later in the day talked to my mother on the phone. She had thought I was sleeping late that morning and was horrified to find the room empty and the window open. I never learned whether His Nibs felt any contrition for what he had done to her and me—he wasn't one to talk about feelings—and I suppose he managed to blame me and not himself. On the other hand, he was not a fool and must have been a bit shaken by the empty room, open window, and Mom's distress. Did the episode do him any good? I have no idea.

All was not lost with Dad. Some months later, he visited me for a weekend, slept on the couch in Brown Meggs's and my rooms, and joined me at one or two of my Saturday lectures, all in all a good visit. That same year—I don't recall whether it was before or after Dad's visit—I had a terrifying nightmare. The faceless man was pounding on the door, trying to break into the rooms. I never identified the man to myself, but of course I knew who he was. The summer after my junior year, Mom, Dad, my brothers and I packed up the family's yellow Ford convertible and had a warm, wonderful adventure exploring as far west as Montana's Glacier National Park, as I relate in "Walk."

Only a Game

I was trailing five games to two in a friendly set against Johnny Balch, whom I had barely managed to beat the Sunday before in the finals of the annual Redding tennis tournament. Mom and Dad were swimming in the nearby pool as afternoon shadows lengthened across the water and towards the court. Now, one game from a friendly defeat, I noticed Dad standing up to his knees on the ladder at the deep end of the pool watching with the stern look I knew so well.

I had aroused his anger by staying out until two o'clock the night before, and had avoided the inevitable confrontation all day. I knew, too, that if I lost this fun set, my late date would serve as the handle for a verbal lashing by that tiger of the hearth. So, I won the next five games, taking the set, glancing from time to time at Dad still frozen on the ladder. Shaking hands with me over the net, Johnny said, "I don't know what happened to me."

Afterwards Dad and I did not discuss my victory, which was not unusual, or my staying out late, which was. I have never forgotten the figure on the ladder, and several years passed before I thought of it without feeling anger rise within me.

The sources of Dad's temper puzzled me. Undue righteousness contributed, or was it only an excuse? Same question for the time I pissed him off by striking out at a baseball game. Everybody strikes out. Even he. I wondered whether his temper had to do with his own father, my Grandpa Bell, who had died before I had a chance to know him. Yet Dad's younger brothers were not like him. Uncle Proc and Uncle Winslow were gentle, companionable men whom I did not see enough of.

Whatever caused Dad's anger—besides my brothers' and my transgressions of course—what made him think that expressing it, even in the restrained way he did, was acceptable or constructive? It struck me as self-indulgent. He had many fine qualities, was a nice guy most of the time, and did many thoughtful and generous deeds; but he would unleash his semi-contained rage at me—clenched teeth, curled lip, barely raised snarl, or else furious silence—into his old age, as the feelings he aroused in me turned from anger into dismay.

In other ways he was less expressive. When I was happily married and in my sixties, years after he had died, a therapist asked me to tell her something he had praised me for. I searched my memory in silence and found myself sobbing. Anger and criticism, never offset by words of love or approval, had apparently mark me more deeply than I had realized.

My relationship with my mother, in contrast, was pleasantly simple. I loved her, respected her, and considered her a dear friend. From my teenage years until the end of her life, we would talk things over. Nor did I fault her for not trying to protect my brothers and me from Dad's fear-inducing anger. I saw that it marked her as it marked them and me. In the main, though, I was exceptionally fortunate to grow up in the family that Mom and Dad created.

Education

I used to think that, given the physical intimacy, the emotions that may arise unbidden, and the child that may be conceived if precautions fail, there is no such thing as casual sex. Even the whores I would see later in German bars would have a drink with soldiers and get to know them a bit before leading them to their rooms. Then came the so-called sexual revolution and all it brought. Now that hook-ups and one-night stands are said to be common in colleges, my concern about a student I'll call Clara, belatedly as it came, may seem quaint. But I remain glad I felt it.

I took my turn at being as heedlessly horny as the next guy, I suppose, and maybe more so when I met her. She had big breasts, a pudding face, and a brilliant mind; and I asked her out because I heard you could fuck her on the first date—a deed not so common back then as it would become. I had asked Brown, my roommate, to absent himself. Alone in the rooms with Clara, I fed her a couple of sea breezes—grapefruit juice and gin—and talked with her as long as seemed necessary to show her I wasn't simply interested in her body. Then I made my move, and sure enough. Not being very experienced, I was baffled that the anticipation outdid the deed.

The first time I'd done it was with a high school senior named Ellen whom I'd felt I loved, in the back seat of a Ford parked off a country road on a dark autumn night several months earlier. At the moment of truth came an immense feeling of purity. So this is what it's all about, I thought, so much more powerful than I'd been led to believe. I think it was Ellen's first time too. We broke up a couple of months later while Patti Page was turning "The Tennessee Waltz" from a catchy country song into a poignant American classic. When I asked Ellen the next summer whether she had any regrets, she said no. I didn't either.

In its wisdom, the college let us upperclassmen entertain women in our rooms only on Wednesday and Saturday evenings. I wasn't about to blow a Saturday on Clara, so my friends called her my Wednesday night pig. Later I heard that a guy I considered a friend was saying that I'd stick it into anything. That hurt, and hurt long after Clara was gone. She was very interesting to talk with and particularly enjoyed my record of *Petruchka*, while I preferred *The Rite of Spring*. At least we both appreciated Stravinsky. In fact, I felt at the time that I was not being fair to her fascinating fund of conversation while I drove her back to her dorm or ate with her in the House dining room or the other times we couldn't spend in bed.

One weekend I met a girl I could really like, so I called Clara and broke our Wednesday date and never heard of her again. Long afterwards it occurred to me that from my vantage atop her flattened breasts, I never appreciated the person underneath, and I asked myself, who was then the pig?

Tricks

Once when I was a carefree undergraduate, opposed to dirty government and dirty business and everything else that paid my way, a friend named Charlie Herbst came to Brown and me with a desperate tale. The week before, it seemed, he had hidden under a bed in the room where his roommate was trying to score. (Score in those days meant copulate, not buy drugs.) Now he had a date with a sure thing, and he feared that his disgruntled roomy would find an embarrassing way to retaliate.

We said what any red-blooded American boys would say: Of course he could borrow our room, so long as he didn't dicker with Brown's new hi-fi.

On the fateful day, we safety-pinned a microphone into the folds of one of the drapes in the bedroom and ran the cord out the window to the room next door. Unfortunately, Charlie did play the hi-fi, which sat on a dresser between the couch and the drapes; and by the time the first LP ended, he was too preoccupied to turn it over or off. When we listened to the tape afterwards, the click-click of the needle in the last grooves overrode the better part of the moans and entreaties that we heard, or thought we heard, and the squeaking of the couch springs.

That was not the only anticlimax. The sure thing turned out to be a tease, and though Charles may have come close to scoring, in the end he struck out. A miss is as good as a mile, and this miss wasn't playing ball. Having his failure taped was probably what would have bothered him the most, had he known about it.

Brown and I had promised the other guys on our corridor that we'd play them the tape. Since it left much to be desired, we improved it by dubbing in more moaning and rhythmic squeaking. The guys huddled around the machine. We all listened in silence, straining to make sense of the ambiguous eruptions on the tape. Apparently I had sounded too much like myself during the dubbing because one of guys turned to me and said, "Did you say something?" We did the decent thing, of course, and did not tell them that the strikeout victim was Charlie. He later confessed to me that he had played Brown's hi-fi, but he was sure Brown did not know because he had put everything back the way it was.

The Korean War was on by then, and the army drafted Brown the next summer. Somehow the story of bugging our buddy's failed tryst came up during his placement interview. It impressed the sergeant who was asking the questions so much that Brown found himself in the Counter Intelligence Corps and spent two years in Japan gathering information and playing electronic tricks on the Soviets.

Protest

Whoever laid out Memorial Drive along the Charles River banked the curve outside Dunster and next-door Leverett Houses the wrong way. Come the warm spring evenings, you could pretty well count on sooner or later hearing a noise like metal garbage cans falling off a roof, and you'd know that a car had smashed into one of the trees that lined the curve.

This was years before Ralph Nader, and the rare person who mentioned the obvious merits of seatbelts was thus considered a commie, sissie, or both. In one crash, an old man flopped out onto the back of his head and died. Another night we ran out and found that a tree trunk was standing between a car's front wheels where the axle should have been, the driver was unconscious though moaning. Twenty minutes later, someone realized that another person was crumpled under the dashboard beside the engine. He survived. It was too much to expect the city to regrade the curve, but an orange blinker light might have saved a life now and then.

Brown and I had had enough. We borrowed a headstone from nearby Mount Auburn Cemetery, filled a couple of cardboard cartons with earth, and set up a fresh grave on the Dunster House courtyard lawn beside a blinker light that I'd fashioned out of cardboard and colored paper. The message was graphic and quite brash for 1951. We hoped people would get it.

The Establishment, however, had chosen the dorm super well. He recognized his duty. Early the next morning before almost anybody saw our mute, mordant message, he dismantled it. Nothing left but the mound of earth that looked like a giant brown molehill on the grass.

But all was not lost. A few days later, the Harvard *Crimson* ran an item about a mysterious gravestone that nobody knew what to do with. We had found channels to get our story to the editors, along with instructions on where to replace the stone in the maze of the cemetery. The *Crimson* followed up. Brown and I did not claim credit for the blinker light that the City of Cambridge finally erected on the curve.

Not that Harvard could be trusted to take a joke or forgive a prankster who got caught. My favorite story has it that in the late 1920s, when the university's president, A. Lawrence Lowell, a Boston aristocrat, opposed the building of a subway kiosk in Harvard Square, the following headline appeared in the *Crimson*: "PRESIDENT LOWELL FIGHTS ERECTION IN HARVARD SQUARE." Lowell, then in his seventies, might have welcomed this testament to his virility, but instead, he expelled the editor of the *Crimson*. Today he has lain many years in his grave while the erection he fought still stands.

Virtuosity

To us virtuosity meant taking a chance that you didn't have to. A mild example: At several parties where I ushered my date along the receiving line, I would introduce myself and her as Nick Caraway and Jordan Baker, two of the well-known characters in *The Great Gatsby*. The bored-looking strangers whose hands we shook never caught on.

Less mild virtuosity: Walking back from class one warm spring afternoon in 1951, I saw, as though for the first time, on a trim, white post beside a white gravel driveway, a trim, white sign that said "PRESIDENT'S HOUSE, 17 QUINCY STREET." It signified the residence of the President of Harvard University, who was then James Bryant Conant, a chemistry prof who had worked on developing poison gasses and the atomic bomb. (Another Harvard chemistry prof, Louis Fieser, led the team that developed napalm.) This struck me as a good time and place to test a theory that I (among others, I suppose) had conceived, that if you do an outrageous act calmly enough, no one is likely to say anything.

A man was cutting the freshly green lawn with a power mower beside Conant's redbrick, white-trimmed, Georgian mansion. I watched as he walked towards me behind his sputtering machine. When he turned and followed it the other way, I followed his back up the driveway, lifted the sign out of its hole in the grass, and carried it upside down, the post under my arm, the five blocks through Cambridge to Dunster House. I avoided eye contact with the people walking towards me. None of them said anything.

The second virtuosity came that evening. The signpost was a neatly painted pipe filled with concrete. Welded to its top were two crossbars to which the sign had been screwed. It looked like a lot of trouble to replace, and it seemed a shame to steal more than we needed. I put the screws into a small paper bag and attached it to the post with a rubber band. After dinner Brown and I drove back to the President's house in his secondhand Cadillac; I walked up the driveway, and dropped the post back in its hole, which I found easily in the freshly cut grass. The few people passing on the sidewalk paid no heed. We may as well have been the only conscious souls in the city.

I felt a bit like Robin Hood. In fact, the whole caper felt so good that we did it again the next month after the university replaced the sign, so that Brown could have one too.

I took my sign home and hung it on a wall of my room. My father knew immediately which President it signified. He didn't say much at the time, but many years later he told me that after he saw it, he increased his annual donation to Harvard. I guess he had his own theory of virtuosity.

Whim

On a whim more or less, Brown had purchased his Cadillac for $500 fairly early in our sophomore year. It was a 1939, meaning of prewar quality. One rainy night when our friend Frank Finch was driving it and I was dozing in the back seat, a taxi stopped suddenly ahead of us on terrifying Route 9 to make a left-hand turn. Frank hit the brake. We skidded into the taxi, smashing in its whole rear end. The Caddy was not scathed.

Frank had a girlfriend named Margee at Vassar in distant Poughkeepsie above the Hudson River, but no transportation. What to do? Frank and Margee fixed Brown up with a blind date named Nancy Meachen, who soon became the love of his life. Brown and Frank made the long drive to Vassar quite a few times that year, and I once—the time the Cadillac smooshed the cab—to visit a girl named Bitsy Thompson, whom I knew from Brooklyn.

Brown would go on to lead a full life, becoming the chief operating officer of Capitol Records and signing up the Beatles to distribute their deluge of music in America. He told me that he took precautions lest those young men involve his son Brook in marijuana. He wrote four well-received novels and sent me copies—I liked *The Matter of Paradise* best—while I sent him *The Turkey Shoot*, which he kindly called "a magnificent achievement." He went on to become the President of Angel Records, which specialized in classical music, the only music he truly cared about, and he found it hard to quit the job because it was hard to find a successor who understood both business and classical music, that is, who had his breadth. For all his success and the life it offered, Nancy brought him his greatest happiness and her death from pancreatic cancer in 1990 at the age of fifty-nine, his greatest sorrow. Had he not happened to buy that Cadillac, she'd not have entered his life.

Brown was one of the best friends I ever had and Nancy, one of the rare people for whom I ever felt unalloyed admiration. After she died, he moved from Pasadena to San Francisco, where my wife (also a Nancy) and I saw him several times when we visited our sons who lived there. Back in college he and I used to debate faith in God. I always had it; he was a lapsed Catholic. When his Nancy was so cruelly taken from him, he said, as best I recall, "Fifty-nine days from diagnosis to funeral! Where is your fucking God now!" The primal scream of a civilized man. There was nothing I could answer that would lessen his grief, which, I believe, is ultimately what led to the stroke that took him at the age of sixty-six.

Plans

"MYSTERY TREE BLOCKS PIKE," the front page of the Boston newspaper blared. "Huge Oak Felled Across Main Artery to City," explained the subhead. I bought the paper in the middle of the afternoon, too groggy from a short morning's sleep to be more than a little elated, still not sure we had escaped, and stupidly grateful that no one had been hurt, except for the nick in my knee where Charlie had let go of his end of the saw.

Charlie and his roommate Bedwell had thought it would be fun to make Bedwell's girlfriend Noodle late to work. She had dropped out of college and drove to work in Boston every morning on the then four-lane Concord Turnpike, a.k.a. Massachusetts Route 2. Charlie and Bedwell masterminded the project as carefully as they could to assure that no one would be hurt. They stole the necessary red lanterns and sawhorses that said "Detour" from a local construction site and recruited the rest of us, calling on me mainly because they knew I had felled a few trees and thought I could drop one where they wanted it. That was not strictly true, though I did well on the night of the caper.

We arrived at three a.m. at the ideal site they had chosen along the Turnpike. What with scrambling around in the dark and diving out of the headlights and into the bushes every time a truck roared past, we took nearly two hours to make the opposing cuts in the trunk, while Jason waited a quarter of a mile down the hill with a sawhorse, two red lanterns, and a flashlight to wave cars onto a side road that began a perfect detour, and Rick waited with a flashlight at the top of the hill about eighty yards above us, ready to try to flag down any cars coming up the other side. Bedwell, Charlie, Warren Sides, and I took turns on the saw. Sides was also supposed to set out red lanterns at the last minute above and below the spot where the tree was supposed to fall, as another warning for oncoming drivers, but though he had gotten all A's in his freshman year at Harvard, he managed to misplace the lanterns directly under the place the tree was to fall. Their shattered remains must have puzzled any cop who wondered how they had reached that pavement before the tree.

Light tinged the sky as the tree began to tick towards the highway. Charlie and I got an All Clear from Jason below and Rick above. Nothing happened. I suddenly remembered how long it takes big wood to fall. As I waited in dread for some oncoming car, the tree arced interminably downwards across the dim sky. We heard two cars racing more and more loudly from the far side of the hill, the shafts of their headlights scissoring overhead as the tree swung downwards a bit faster. One driver was trying to pass another, who was trying not to let him, Rick told us later. He tried to wave them down with his flashlight, until he had to jump out of their way.

Bedwell, Charlie, Sides, and I were running through the woods away from the tree and towards the car we'd parked on the detour road behind the Turnpike. A bush came between Charlie and me. We hesitated, and he dropped his end of the saw. I did not feel its teeth bite into my knee, though I still bear the scar. Hearing a desperate squeal of brakes behind us, I turned to see a tangle of headlights and branches before I plunged on.

As we drove off not knowing what had happened at the tree, Bedwell exclaimed in terror, "My God! I left my coat. It has my name in it."

He and Sides hid with the saw behind some bushes while Charlie and I drove onto the Turnpike and joined the gathering jam-up of cars. As we topped the hill, we saw the tree lying across three of the four lanes and the center island. No wrecked cars or injured people! Thank God! If the tree had taken five seconds longer to fall....

While no car could pass on the Boston-bound side, the cars on our side were able to evade the tips of the branches by driving with two wheels up on the grass shoulder. Charlie and I passed Rick as though he were a stranger. It was light enough now so we could see Jason at the foot of the hill faithfully waving cars onto the detour road as we had arranged.

One or two drivers had stopped at the tree to explore the scene. We joined them, examining the neatly cut stump and agreeing with them what a terrible thing this was. When we left the car, Charlie was wearing a coat and I was not. When we returned, we both wore coats. While we were gone, Bedwell had vomited on the ground behind the bush.

A highway inspector was the first official to reach the scene. He did nothing except compliment Jason for being on the job, and drove off. Next came two cops who treated the whole scene as a big joke and jokingly asked Rick if he had done it. Rick jokingly said no. By the time the traffic had backed up for a quarter of a mile in each direction, Jason and Rick decided they were no longer needed and hitchhiked back to Cambridge. Noodle was indeed late for work. She told Bedwell that as soon as she saw the tree, she knew who was responsible.

I do not subscribe to the theory that what you learn from a bad experience generally makes it worth the while. Too often the tuition comes too high. Not to learn from experience, though, is unpardonable and often unpardoned. I learned from the slowly ticking tree that the world has little tolerance for the best-laid plans and humbles the most careful planners. We had played with fire. Only by the grace of God was no one burned. I probably owed it to the drivers racing each other over that dimly lit hill that I come to those conclusions.

Fans

Several evenings during the spring of sophomore year, Brown and I drove into Boston and rolled slowly between the silent redbrick houses looking for a space without a fire hydrant to park his car near Symphony Hall. The best seats cost the least, fifty cents. We made the front of the ticket line, then raced the other cognoscenti up the stairs to sit as close as possible to one tip or the other of the lofty horseshoe called the second balcony. From there we looked down on Arthur Fiedler, the white-haired lion of the Boston Pops, conducting his mighty orchestra in marches and show tunes and overtures, punctuated by the pop of champagne corks, often in time with the music, at the expensive tables on the floor below us.

We watched Fiedler wait between taking his bows, hidden from the applauding floor by a huge fan of flowers that stood behind the podium. We saw before the rest of the audience the placard that a man at the back would hold up to announce an encore—there were several encores per concert. We could watch each move that each musician made. Once we heard the piano soloist commit several dozen errors among the swarms of notes that comprise the Khachaturian *Piano Concerto*—if not mistakes, then William Kapell, whom the *Washington Post* called "America's first great pianist," had gone way wrong on the LP that Brown's Nancy had given him and we often listened to in our rooms—but it sounded great, and the applause rolled on.

One evening during graduation week two years later, my classmates, our dates, and I boarded a line of busses at Harvard and roared off towards Symphony Hall with motorcycle cops leading the way and other motorcycle cops racing ahead to block off the side streets as the convoy thundered past, an annual reminder of who mattered around there and the most practical way to get the hundreds of us to the Pops on time. A bunch of friends—not Brown, who had left the college—took a couple of tables down on the floor and drank champagne with our girls and the local aficionados. We saw little of what was going on, though in a sense we were part of it, and the acoustics were not as good as they were in the second balcony, which I looked up to from time to time.

Rule

I had a good lead off second base and ran at the crack of the bat. A hard grounder bounded straight to the third baseman, who swept it up in his mitt and stood waiting in my path, about ten feet in front of the bag, with the ball raised in his fist to tag me out. I threw an arm across my face and crashed into him, pushing him backwards and inadvertently keeping his hand with the ball in it over our heads. As we reached the base, I slid between the surprised guy's legs before he could bring the ball down to tag me.

"Safe!" The umpire's hands whipped wide, palms down, smoothing the air above the grass.

Skipper Toth, the visiting coach, reached the umpire first. Our coach, grizzled Jesse Sanford, ran up shouting, "Don't get your Hunky blood in an uproar, Skipper!" The rhubarb that followed lasted half an hour as voices and gesticulating hands rose and fell. No one had a rulebook, though I felt that whatever it might say, I couldn't be called out on a play like that.

I sat in the sun on the square white base enjoying the spectacle and chatting with the third baseman, who sat on the ground beside me, both of us spectators to what we'd started. Fortunately for my sense of justice, the umpire held fast. For umpires, holding fast is the rule.

Good Call

When the regular first baseman did not show up for the game against Newtown, old Jesse moved me in from center field on the theory that all you have to do at first is catch the balls that come your way, which is what you do in the outfield anyway. He moved the regular right fielder over to center and put a kid in right who was too small to be a regular but might draw a walk at the plate.

Everything went fine until the fifth inning when I had to lunge to my left to knock down the third baseman's wide throw. I picked it up by the foul line and tagged at the batter as he charged past me. The only umpire, who usually stood behind the pitcher's mound, had come over to cover the play, but could not see what happened when the batter ran between him and me. I was sure it looked as though I had tagged the guy out.

"Safe!"

I did not protest. Between innings, I asked the umpire about the call.

"I could see by your face that you missed him."

Approval

Considering the suspense in the way we played baseball, the crowd that came to our games was not large. Once someone threw the ball, you never knew if it would go where he aimed it or be caught if it got there. Actually, we were not bad for a town team, and our following wasn't that bad either, considering how sparsely their homes lay scattered across the hills of Redding, Connecticut, which was a country town and zoned to stay that way.

The spectators sat with the team under the maples along the stone wall that more or less served as our bench, or they sat in maybe a dozen cars parked around the big chain-link backstop way behind home plate. Sometimes three or four of them honked their horns when they liked a play. We seldom gave them much to honk about at the plate or on the base paths, but out in the field we tried for everything and sometimes looked good. We strove to make up in hustle what we lacked in ability.

One hot Sunday afternoon we were losing to a Class D team, which definitely wasn't Class A but, for our league, played darn good ball. Lenny Bergquist, our pitcher, was doing quite well in spite of being a run behind, and the other team had yet to hit the ball out of the infield if you don't count two bounders that went through our shortstop's legs.

They say outfielders spend so much time watching a game that they ought to pay admission; and I was fretting idly under the sun inside my scratchy wool uniform out in center field. Partly to keep my mind on the game, I yelled the usual encouragements to Lenny. "Work easy, babe!" "He can't hit!" "No sticker in there!" "Put a little blood on the ball!"

In the top of the fourth, Hiker Wells, their cleanup hitter, strode to the plate with one out and runners on first and second. Lenny tried and failed to smoke one past him down the middle. Hiker lined a deep drive into the hole between center and left. There was no one there, just a lot of parched grass.

I raced to my right, leaped in the air as the ball began to sink, and, smack, right in my glove. All the horns cut loose. They were still honking after I fired the ball into the infield to drive the lead runner back to second. The great Joe D couldn't have felt better. I can't remember who won, though it's not hard to guess. Those horns I've never forgotten.

Reality

One snowy night as I was hitchhiking out to Wellesley College to see a girl, the jerk from the Harvard Business School who picked me up made a stupid left-hand turn in front of a car that was coming slowly down the white-coated bridge ahead. In the streetlights, I could see the other driver hit the brakes, not because his car came any slower but it started sliding on a diagonal, straight for my door. It must have slowed a bit because I saw it was going to hit behind me and relaxed about the time the jerk first noticed the danger.

"He's going to hit us!" he said. No shit.

A mild jolt spun us in a three-quarters circle on the snow like a careful billiard shot, hurting no one. The jerk and the other driver copied their information while the snow fell on them through the streetlights, and I pulled the jerk's right rear fender out from where the other car had mashed it in against the tire. He did not notice the problem or my solution, and I did not mention them. When they got their cars moving in the right direction and we were warm inside with no more snow melting on our faces, the jerk explained how it was all the other driver's fault. Jerk though he was, he showed a sound instinct for shifting the blame.

The System made it quite likely that a few years later the jerk would be earning three or four times more than me, but I don't think it ever occurred to him how lucky we had been that another car had not slid down the slope into both cars while he and the other driver were blocking the slick white road.

Luck?

Hitchhiking was much safer and easier during the decade after the war than it is today, and having little money and no car in college, I did a lot of it and met a lot of interesting people. Between visiting home and girls at Wellesley, and the frequent need to hitch more than one ride to get somewhere, I estimated that my total was around two or three hundred rides. This story is about the most perilous ride I ever took with anyone anywhere.

It was growing dark and snowing lightly at the diner where we stopped for coffee a few miles after the sailor picked me up on an afternoon I was hitchhiking home from college. He had been driving fast and seemed unaware that the snow was making the road slick. The diner, which stood beside Route 20, the old three-lane highway that ran from Worcester, Massachusetts, to the Connecticut border (long since superseded by I-84), provided my last fair chance to hitch another ride or stay put until the snow ended and the road improved.

In those days the first vehicle into Route 20's center lane got to use it for passing, and Heaven help everyone if an oncoming driver did not realize that he was not there first. From the state line to Hartford the road was two-lane with wide shoulders that a decent truck driver would pull onto if you wanted to pass his rig going up a hill, because there was almost always someone coming the other way. South of Hartford it was all four-lane to New York City.

What the hell, I figured, it's bad weather for finding another ride. I didn't really consider waiting in the diner for the snow to stop and the road to be cleared, out in the proverbial middle of nowhere. A few miles later we picked up another hitchhiker, and I climbed out to let him sit in the middle of the cramped front seat.

The sailor's driving went from bad to much worse. The other guy and I tried to talk him into slowing down, tactfully because we both sensed that if we angered him, he'd speed up and surely kill us. Fearlessly he took the center lane to pass other cars even though he had his car under control only now and then and none of us could see much through the steamy windshield except the snowflakes swirling endlessly out of the gloom and into the headlights. As it happened, no oncoming truck occupied the center lane while we did, where we could not possibly have moved to the right in time. A recurring vision would haunt me afterwards: our car is in the center lane pointed diagonally towards an enormous tractor-trailer that is coming at us in its own lane but we don't hit it because we are in a skid and the car is sliding straight down the center of the road instead of moving where it is pointed, into the oncoming lane. The sailor actually did this several times.

We finally talked him out of using the center lane—less, I think, because reason prevailed than because there were now very few cars on the road for him to pass. But he still seemed hell-bent to kill us, like when he started tailgating a truck that had a load of pipes sticking out the back at about the level of our windshield—just right to impale us if the truck stopped and we couldn't—and we obviously could not stop as quickly as the truck.

"Our heads would look pretty silly sticking out the back window on those poles," I said.

"You shouldn't talk like that," the sailor replied, but he dropped back a few yards.

He decided to pass someone again and moved us out into the center lane and could not get back to the right. I strained to see death in the gloom. Suddenly we came upon a car stalled squarely across the road, completely blocking the lane we should have been in. Had we been there, we never could have stopped in time; but we sailed past the car as though it were a photograph and eventually were able to ease back to the right.

I do not know how we made it as far as the state line. I have never been so terrified for so long in my life. When a nightmare strikes, at least you wake up.

The car was able to climb the desolate hills north of Hartford as long as we kept up some speed, but we had to slow down on one of them and lost traction and could not get going again. The car moved slower and slower, and it looked as though we were going to be stuck right there midway up the hill. When we had almost stopped moving, the other guy and I climbed out into the slush and started pushing the car. He kept the front door open and I kept the back door open to get good grips, and our pushing was doing the job.

Suddenly headlights flashed behind us. We turned to see a great bulk coming over us, and barely leaped back into the car when huge tires splashed through our footprints and an eighteen-wheeler shaved past on the shoulder of the road, its engine snarling in my ear. I guess the truck driver hadn't wanted to lose traction either.

Both of us left the sailor in Hartford. He sounded disappointed. A train got me to New York by midnight with seventy cents in my pocket, the only train I ever took home from college. If I were a rational person, I would have been warm and dry and safe back in the diner in Massachusetts. If this were a rational world, the sailor, the other guy, and I would have lain mangled in the snow.

Routine

A decade before hippies invented themselves, Jason seldom shaved or bathed or went to class or bed. Brilliant and easily bored, he would schmooze all night with Cambridge cops in a diner near Harvard Square, then wander back to Dunster House by the river and sleep serenely on the increasingly rancid couch in his sitting room while people like his roommate Harry listened to esteemed professors and studied in the library. Virtually unused, Jason's bed stayed fresh for months.

Harry would have preferred to study in their rooms, but Jason's recumbent presence on the couch bothered him. Not having undressed, Jason was dressed when he awoke, so he seldom donned clean clothes. Once when he had worn the same necktie for several months, Harry found it on the floor, poured lighter fluid on it, and made a little pyre on the hearth. Jason's next tie became as filthy as the first, but he guarded it by keeping it loosely knotted around his collar.

One sunny noontime when Jason happened to be out and I had returned from my classes, Harry and I were sitting opposite Jason's couch trying to figure why his lifestyle bothered Harry. Jason never did anything to him and did not smell except up close. I suggested that whatever the reason, we should cut the knot.

It seemed logical. There was no discussion. We picked up the couch, eased it out the door and the double doors of the House—fortunately the rooms were on the ground floor—across Memorial Drive during a break in the traffic, and out to the middle of the graceful, white and redbrick Weeks Footbridge that crossed the Charles. The couch poised momentarily on the parapet and fell with a soft splash. It didn't sink but drifted slowly downstream, nearly submerged, a hazard to college crew shells and other navigation.

"Where's my couch?"

"It's in the river."

His routine broken, Jason's life changed. He tried flopping onto his bed with his clothes on, but it wasn't the same. He slept fitfully and muttered in his sleep. He took to staying up all night less often and to sleeping between clean, white sheets. He attended more classes. They interested him. He crammed less madly for exams, and his marks improved. Later the army aged him, and academe captured him. He became a professor of advanced physics at a major university.

Wall

Recognizing one summer that my parents' cottage needed a cookout, I asked them if they would like me to build them one. This was before the age of gas-fired, hooded grills that you wheel out of the garage when you want to rough it. You still made a fire of wood or charcoal under a grate. That was less convenient, but the hamburgers tasted better. Mom and Dad agreed, though it meant that during the weeks that the job took, I'd not be earning any money towards my senior year in college.

Working six hours a day, I dug a trench twenty by three by two feet deep in the rocky Connecticut soil, dismantled a stone wall along a road near the back of the property, and brought in the rocks, only a few hundred pounds at a time so as not to break the springs in the old family station wagon as I drove slowly on the meadow from the road to the trench. With them, I built a massive rectangular block that showed three and a half feet above ground with two fireplaces squared out of its front. It was dry wall all the way up except for the top layer of flat stones that I cemented together to make a firm counter for the meats and salads and bottles of dressing, ketchup, mustard, and booze. In effect, I tore down part of a long, low, rambling stonewall to build a short, thick, higher one. I had no right to take those stones, but the woods they came from belonged to the Bridgeport Hydraulic Company, and I doubt that they cared or even noticed. Crucially, my lawyer father had no problem with it. Realizing that this horizontal monolith was the most tangible thing I had ever done, I asked a friend to make large photos of it.

During the work, I conjured up an image of manual labor transfusing life from a person into a product through a tube of time. Does capitalism, I wondered, mean that when a man builds a wall, the wall becomes more valuable than he is?

Walk

The same summer that I built the stone cookout, we five Bells loaded up the yellow Ford convertible and drove across the nation to northwestern Montana's Glacier Park (which still had significant glaciers), taking in the Badlands of South Dakota, Devil's Tower in Wyoming, and other magnificent sights along the way, the greatest of our family's trips and one of the few that wasn't to visit relatives.

A morning or so after we reached our cabin, which faced St. Mary Lake and the jagged mountains that march along the far side of the water, my parents and brothers dropped me off by the roadside where the Gunsight Pass Trail begins. I walked for several miles along the valley floor among tall trees, scattered bushes, and green ferns, passing a lake with whitened branches sticking up from the black water around the edge. At the end of the valley, the trail doubled back and began to rise across the side of a mountain. It had never occurred to any of us that I might meet a grizzly, and I didn't.

If you are in any kind of shape, you can climb all day at a thousand feet an hour, and this trail was graded for that kind of walking. The trees grew shorter and disappeared, leaving grass and dark green moss and rock in the morning sun. The trail doubled back again, and I continued up. The wind soughed, and now and then a marmot cried out like the scream of a woman in distress, but most of the time I heard only my sneakers on the gravel and the silence under the peaks and the sky.

A slanted field of dirty snow blocked the trail, with melt water gurgling through cracks beneath it. Some time ago, someone had squared off a trail in the steep snowpack, but the sun had melted it soft and rounded. If I started across, I might slide down the snowfield onto the rocky slope below, but climbing up or down to go around it would have meant rough scrambling for several hundred yards either way. Since my sneakers, which had done me well so far, were too soft to kick toeholds into the mush, I unsheathed my knife, drove it into the corn snow above the trail and, facing uphill, planted my feet carefully onto it. I plunged the knife into the snow again a yard to the right and moved my feet the same way. It may have been silly to risk sliding down the snowfield onto a rough stop on the rocks below, but I made it across.

A mountain goat loped on the trail a few yards ahead of me and sometimes loped incomprehensibly up the rock and moss that rose sharply from the trail, turned and stared down at me with his hairy white face like a vacant old man who might know more than I suspected. Being up on roofs and bridges usually frightened me, but this trail, no wider than I am tall, left me calm even when the valley fell two thousand feet off to my right.

An hour or so higher, the trail broadened into a field of rock that formed a saddle between two peaks—Gunsight Pass. I sat on a boulder facing the way I had come, barely able to distinguish the place where I'd left the family, and ate my sandwiches. I had climbed two or three times the height of the Empire State Building, which had been a pinnacle of my youth in the City, and decided that it might not be so tall after all.

In the afternoon, the trail zigzagged down to an oval lake on a shelf of the mountain and up over another pass, rock all the way. Ice and wind had carved the ridge of the next mountain so thin that a patch of blue showed through the rock wall below the jagged crest. As the sun declined, I came to a log lodge standing low among the boulders and dined long and well with six hearty people who had hiked up the shorter trail, which the supply mules used, on the other side. Alone again, I finished reading a paperback of John Dos Passos's *Manhattan Transfer*, the essential inessential that I carried in my bag, by a kerosene lamp beside the bed.

However simply, I had chosen to commit to the adventure of a long walk over the mountains. Tired and happy, I turned out the flame with a sense that today's solitary walk had brought me closer to humankind's adventure on Earth.

Fire

Thomas Wolfe wrote that he once set out to read the one million books then in Harvard's Widener Library, a project, I thought, that showed more energy than taste. Some days I cut class to read from half a dozen books that lay around the room, going from one to another as I wished, finishing this one or that one the same day or a week later or never, buying new paperbacks, or taking hardcovers from the

House library. Professors spoke of books in their lectures. Friends and reviews spoke of books. Books suggested books. I finally had to write down a list of the ones I burned to read. Ever afterwards, the more I read, the longer grew the list.

Often in later years I wanted to read half a dozen books all lying open around the room, but incomprehensibly, there has not been time. College doesn't offer an education. In four years? It offers merely the fuel, shelter, and fellowship to begin one, and to start a fire that will not die until the heart stops pumping to the brain.

US Army

Praise

The US Army took me on August 17, 1953, a few weeks after the shooting stopped in Korea. A basic part of its basic training was learning to hit your target with your M-1 rifle. The M-1 was said to be slightly less accurate than the Springfield that soldiers had used during World War I—think of Gary Cooper in the film *Sergeant York* "touching off" German soldiers with his Springfield—but the M-1 was still highly accurate, and unlike the Springfield, it could fire off a clip of eight bullets as fast as you could pull the trigger. To aim it you look through a tiny hole in a metal disk atop the rear of the weapon and position your target to sit on a small blade atop the muzzle. The disk could be adjusted to allow for your distance from the target and the wind, if there was one. Line up the hole, the blade, and the target. Squeeze the trigger. The rifle bangs back against your shoulder. (Only fools and movie heroes shoot from the hip.) An instant later, the bullet tears through the target, be it a sheet of paper or a human being.

After a period of drilling, lectures, too little sleep, and ridiculous orders designed to break our willfulness and teach us to obey orders, the lads of my company were finally going to fire our M-1s. On a warm September morning, several buses drove us from our drafty, wooden, World War II barracks to a desolate, flat, sandy patch of Fort Dix, New Jersey, called the KD Range. KD means known distance because, unlike in battle, you do not have to guess how far you are from the targets. A bullseye counted five points. The next rings outwards diminished from four points to one. The targets hung on wooden frames that men in a long pit below them would pull down to count the bullet holes and attach fresh targets. After each shooting exercise, they would raise a marker on a pole to show how many shots had punctured each ring. For a shot that missed completely, they raised a rag called Maggie's drawers.

The .22 caliber rifles I was used to growing up had little or no recoil or "kick," but the M-1 propelled a much heavier bullet with vastly more power. The kick from my first shot banged the butt of the metal receiver into my cheekbone. Ouch! I moved my face back along the rifle's wooden stock. No more bruising.

After we'd shot for a while, my company's first exercise to determine our rating—how good we'd become or inept we'd remained—had us shoot, as best I recall, from a standing position a hundred yards from the targets. Next, we sat on the ground at two hundred yards with our ankles crossed and our elbows in the pockets of our knees. Then prone at three hundred yards. We may have fired from a kneeling position too, but I don't recall it. I was hitting the target pretty well, not a surprise given all the shooting I'd done with those .22s.

The greatest challenges were the two "sustained fire" exercises. In a short time, you had to fire a full clip of eight shots plus one more cartridge that you loaded by hand. For the first one, you sat at two hundred yards. My rifle jammed twice, and I had to slide the bolt back and forth with my hand to seat the next cartridge. Still, I managed to get off all my shots in the allotted time.

Up came the markers. I had seven bullseyes and two shots in the four ring, for a score of forty-three out of a possible forty-five. That was the highest score in that exercise by any of the thousands of soldiers who had trained at the KD Range in recent weeks. Several commissioned offices from my company, other companies, and maybe the range commander—they didn't tell me their jobs—came over and complimented me. I had been raised on the theory that praise spoils the child, and this was by far the most praise I had ever received for anything in my life. And my shooting so far put me within easy reach of "expert," the highest rating a rifleman can earn.

Then came the other sustained fire exercise, prone at three hundred yards. This time the rifle did not jam. A friend who was watching said I fired so fast my rifle looked like a machine gun. Up came the markers, two shots hit the outer rings and all the rest were Maggie's drawers.

How awful! What had I done wrong? Had I jerked the trigger instead of squeezing it? Had I adjusted the rear sight incorrectly? Or was it the praise? At least, my total score earned me the rating of "marksman."

Stationed at Fort McClellan in the mountains of northern Alabama the next summer, I qualified for my company's rifle team. We were all good shots—a laconic Native American sergeant was the best—and any praise was cursory. "Good shooting, Sarge." Our team won second-place medals in the fort's competition.

Humanities

Tolstoy and Dostoevsky had loomed before me in high school like giants in the mist, but fortunately no one expected us to take them on yet. Freshman year in college, several friends took a course called Humanities 2, which assigned those authors and more. The endless pages they had to read each week intimidated me, slow reader that I am, though their enthusiasm for the prof's deep and moving analyses sounded great.

And so the mist lifted, showing the giants more terrifying and seductive than ever. Their insights must be awesome, but what a price I'd pay under a late-night lamp if I took Hum 2 while books for other courses lay uncracked. I devoured a speed-reading course, but promptly fell back to my plodding pace and never saw how I could afford the time to take Hum 2. I was sorry to miss the prof, the widely praised John Finley, and kicked myself later for not sitting in on some of his lectures.

It was the army that gave me ample time for reading, which I occasionally enlarged by bugging out from my duties—such as endlessly servicing a jeep that seldom moved—to a quiet chair in the post library where no one ever thought to look for me. I devoured *Crime and Punishment, Anna Karenina, The Brothers Karamazov*, and more. *War and Peace* might come later. It still might.

The giants shrank to life size, but what life! Though their insights were usually less than profound, they saw humanity as most of us may see it but few have the patience and precision to give it the words it deserves. I came to see those books, not as larger than life, but as broad as life; and I often recognized myself and the people I knew within that life. The giants grew into everyperson.

After a year in the States, I got myself transferred to the army of occupation in Germany—really an army of weak and temporary defense against the Red Army should it attack—and ended up stationed in a former SS barracks a few minutes west of Soviet bombers. On some days Soviet tanks thundered down on the border between their zone and ours, and our unenvied fellow GIs who faced them never knew whether these iron monsters, which had outfought Germany's best panzers a decade ago, would halt in time. How bizarre, I thought, that we stand poised on the brink of war against a people who produced and still read such literature, who open our eyes—if not the eyes of their leaders or ours—and let us see the humanity of all peoples. And equally bizarre that the nation that both armies had conquered and now occupied had produced such giants as Bach, Beethoven, Brahms, Kant, Goethe, and Thomas Mann.

Dawn

I had never appreciated dawn until basic training at Fort Dix. The first red light, more clear than sunset, opened the world to eternity, as though all time lay on the red horizon and I could as well be wearing skins or armor as my green field jacket, until the whitening sky slipped the day into its little slot in the summer of 1953. Marching to the drill field after breakfast, I sometimes saw the shadow of my helmet and rifle crossing the yellow barracks wall like a ghost of countless slain or countless others who waited out the years for wars that did not come.

Never had I been so cold as the winter I finished basic at Fort Mc-Clellan among the rounded mountains of northern Alabama. So much for the sunny South! Smokey coal stoves in the barracks and the mess hall gave off such heat as there was, not much when a recruit assigned to tend the fire through the night fell asleep on the job. As I recall, it was seldom more than ten degrees that December when we fell out on the Company street for the first formation after breakfast.

The first job when you drew KP was to start the coffee and the GI soap, which looked like the Fels-Naptha that my brothers and I used to wash with after brushing against poison ivy. You cut up bars of the yellow soap with a knife and set them simmering in a vat of water on the black iron stove, so you'd have something mop down the floor with after the hundred and twenty GI's had trooped through for breakfast. You made the bitter GI coffee in a vat beside it. Both vats bubbled a little and looked pretty much alike. In the years since serving my country, I have missed the explosive force of GI coffee for jolting me into the day.

I was never much at five a.m., which was a long way from December's dawn. One morning on KP, I accidentally filled the coffee pitchers from the GI soap vat and set them steaming on the tables to wait the troops. One hundred and twenty bodies filed sleepily through the chow line. One hundred and twenty sat down to eat and sip. You know how a single voice sometimes stands out in a crowd. Part way through the meal I heard one voice among the many, "This coffee tastes like GI soap." Others agreed. I changed the pitchers. I don't think my error damaged anyone. In fact, GI soap can do wonders to liberate a sluggish intestine.

Topping a rise in a snarling three-quarter ton truck on those cold dawns, I saw the eternal army camp below. Long lines of coal smoke hung in the air like charcoal sketched across the red and whitening sky.

Eden

The weathered regular-army corporal was explaining life in the service to another draftee and me as he drove us in a World War II-style jeep over a flat dirt road back to the base at the end of a hot Alabama summer afternoon. We saw ahead the back of a figure in green fatigues walking by the verdure on the left. The corporal slowed the jeep as if to pick him up, and the man turned towards us expectantly. The corporal leaned out of the jeep and said softly in the man's face as the jeep crept on past, "Suffer, motherfucker, like you made me suffer."

He gunned the jeep in first gear, leaving the man in a swirling tan cloud. "That smartass left me out here in the boondocks last week," he explained. "Said there was no room for me in his vehicle. Brought it on his self."

Through the plastic rear window, I saw the unforgiven person toiling in the dust under the sun.

Gallantry

Six guys were pushing the jeep off the lieutenant when I reached him. I had seen him around the Company but never so close. Lying in the weeds at the edge of the trees, he looked young and lean and had a complexion of tiny red volcanoes. He was widely considered a gung-ho prick, constantly yelling at soldiers who didn't play Eagle Scout, which meant nearly everybody; but I was sorry to see him lying there hurt.

He had had his recon driver bombing too fast down the dirt road when they rounded a bend hard onto the end of our convoy. The driver hit the brakes skidding back and forth like a snake across the road, barely missing several of our jeeps and finally tipping his into the ditch. The dust from their skid hung briefly in the warm air.

I was the only first-aid man in the Company, which meant I'd had six mornings of lectures and accidentally broke two needles in another trainee's arm when we simulated injecting an antidote for nerve gas, which is supposed to kill you instantly anyway. I told the lieutenant to lie where he was. That's what you say when the spine may be hurt, which can obviously happen to a person who is thrown from a vehicle onto his back. But I didn't even have the stripe of a private first class on my sleeve, and gasoline was spilling into the weeds beside him, so he mumbled something about fire and moved himself about twenty feet along the ditch.

The jeep's driver had a sprained wrist or maybe it was a little bit broken. He became hysterical and sat in an empty jeep where I told him to, but the lieutenant insisted on walking around and flexing himself. Said he wanted to work the stiffness out of his back. That sounded like his way of saying that the accident hadn't happened. I tried again to get him to lie down, then decided the hell with it. Each time he mentioned his back, he stretched himself like a lady greeting the dawn.

When the ambulance came, the lieutenant tried to make his driver with the hurt wrist lie on the stretcher that served as a bed while he would sit up front. We ignored his protests and eased him onto the stretcher. I think he was actually glad. His spine was broken. The doctors staked him out in bed so he couldn't move for six weeks, but it did no good. The next time I saw him walking around, he was the same prick, yelling at a soldier for not having shiny boots on a dusty road.

The Right Thing

The M-3 smoke generator was a clever green machine in which a staccato of tiny gasoline explosions turned cheap oil into compressed white steam that burst out of three nozzles at one end of it. The machine was about three feet long and a lot lighter to carry and safer to operate than the World War II machines we had been using that constantly threatened to blow their lids fifty or so feet in the air. Not that the M-3 was wholly safe. The gas tank built into the top sometimes grew ominously warm from all those explosions beneath it, and sometimes the whole machine caught fire, igniting the grass or bushes or whatever else was nearby. While the US happened not to be fighting a brushfire war that year, it seemed as though I spent a good bit of my summer in Alabama fighting real brushfires.

A few dozen M-3s placed properly to the wind could screen a friendly advance, disorient an unsuspecting enemy, or hide a bridge or gun emplacement from unfriendly eyes and bombs. My platoon's job was to train junior officers to operate the M-3 and show them how it could help in combat. The fog oil did not hurt your eyes and did not feel unpleasant to breathe. One of our sergeants had worked with it for eleven years and still seemed healthy, though I would not have insured his life. The only time I knew it to threaten anyone during my time at Fort McClellan was the warm day that the wind blew a white cloud of it down the hill from our training area and into the open doors of the post hospital, making it impossible for anyone to see where he or she was walking or pushing a gurney in the corridors.

Of course there were the auto accidents. During maneuvers in Germany, many civilians drove as though the smoke from our little machines was not blinding them—the way oblivious Americans drive in a heavy fog today. Then our government had to pay for the German drivers who were dumb enough to kill themselves or someone else. The closest that my outfit came to tragedy was when a three-wheeled truck piled high with cabbages tipped over off a road in a smokescreen, sending the vegetables rolling everywhere. Our soldiers righted the truck and helped the driver to re-pile his load. By the time I reached Germany, the toll had become too expensive, or our government had grown more cooperative with the Germans, and the army had stopped making actual smoke. It merely simulated it on maneuvers. That meant we unloaded the generators from the trailers behind our jeeps and set them up beside heavy, 55-gallon oil drums, and everybody pretended they couldn't see what they were looking at.

One day while still in Alabama, I was driving our platoon's lieutenant down a dirt road that suddenly ran close to an M-3 that was belching out its dense white cloud. We could not see beyond the jeep's hood. The lieutenant, a likable guy, said he would lead me. I urged him to stay inside the jeep until I lost sight of him up ahead. He called me to follow him, and I did the best I could by looking straight down at the edge of the road, though the fog often hid even that. Out in the sunlight we found that I had driven past him and would have driven into him if I had followed better. As tactfully as a private can, I told him not to be such a hero, though he probably thought at the time that he was doing the right thing.

A few weeks later a bunch of us were standing on another dirt road near an M-3 that caught fire with the petcock at the bottom of the gas tank half open. Since no one could get close enough to turn it off, a thin stream of gasoline kept squirting onto the fire, squirting harder as the flames licked the gas tank and built up the pressure inside. The other soldiers moved back, but it seemed ridiculous to me to let a good machine burn up like that. I went up and flung handfuls of dust onto the fire until I got it out. We checked the gas tank. Its sides were bulging ready to blow. I had nearly incinerated myself in a couple of gallons of gasoline to save a silly machine, though it seemed at the time like the right thing to do.

The M-3 could pump out great beauty. Several times when the weather cooperated, I saw columns of white smoke rise fifty or so feet above each machine in the calm red dusk and merge into a single cloud that abided through the night and still hung over us in the red dawn.

Where and When

We set up our .50 caliber machine gun at the edge of a woods. It was late summer and nice among the trees. If this had been combat, we could have stitched anything that moved on the cobblestone road below with the large bullets that had terrified German soldiers during World War II because they would rip up their bodies up or tear off their arms. Imagine the damage from a pointed Civil War Minié ball that was zipping along at high velocity. The weapon was originally designed near the end of World War I and is still in service in this year of our Lord 2025.

The next morning someone took a deuce-and-a-half—a truck with a two-and-a-half ton off-road carrying capacity—with four of us standing tightly together in the open bed with our arms on the roof of the cab as the truck bounced through one bumpy green orchard after another, and we grabbed dark red apples and sometimes ducked a limb as the truck sailed into the shadows under a tree. Apples never tasted better.

We filled the pockets of our field jackets for our buddies who were not lucky enough to be there. The Germans pretty much accepted our maneuvers. I guess they figured we were better than the war and the Russians, not to mention that we had beaten them ten years earlier. At least, the Americans who were there before us beat them and, for all I know, died in these same green orchards. Life and death in the army is all in where you are and when.

Less than a century earlier, the where had come for my great grand-father George Stoddard in a Confederate hellhole called Libby Prison in Richmond, Virginia. I'm not sure about the when, though it was probably late in the war. He grew up in Massachusetts, joined the Union army, and died in that prison—I can only imagine the circum-stances—without ever seeing the little girl that his wife, Henrietta, bore them. The young widow survived in part by becoming a paid wet nurse, suckling her own little Georgietta and another woman's child at the same time, the two baby girls being affectionately called milk-sisters. Georgietta grew up to become my Grandma Locke. The man she married, Frank Locke, was the son of a Union soldier who survived the war.

The main reason the Civil War took the lives of George Stoddard and more than 600,000 other American men is that a bunch of South-ern gentlemen and ladies—the "1%" of their place and day—persisted in enjoying the life of privilege that they got by stealing the freedom, labor, and lives of millions of kidnapped Africans and their American progeny. Nations like Great Britain, France, Russia, and Brazil ended the abomination of slavery without a bloodbath. The United States did not. Wax eloquent if you will that States' rights or some other issue as the cause of the fratricide—many have done so—but for me, this is the truth of it.

Train

I flew for the first time one winter afternoon in early 1955, hitching a ride, as soldiers could, in an old military DC-3 from Frankfurt in the American Zone to Berlin deep in the Soviet Zone. As the plane chugged into the sky, I wondered what kept it up. Above the overcast, I searched the sky for Soviet MiGs, which had been buzzing our planes lately, but saw only the sun setting above red and purple clouds.

Dusk fell on Tempelhof Airport about the same time that we did. As the plane touched down, it tipped crazily and started to cartwheel off the runway. Dark green grass rushed towards my face. The pilot gunned the ancient engines and we managed to rise and circle for another try. The wheels touched the runway again, again the green, again the pilot's skill and engines' power lifted us to temporary safety. A slim sergeant walked quickly past me to work on the malfunctioning rudder inside the tapered tail, while we rode above the lights of the city.

He must have succeeded because we landed on the next try. A concrete monument in front of the airport memorializes the fifty-five American, British, and French airmen who died during the Berlin Airlift of 1948–1949. At the end of my visit, I decided to forget about hitching a ride on another military flight and instead to brave a train back through the Soviet Zone.

The homes around the station reminded me of Flatbush in Brooklyn; and before the train pulled out, they played the music they used to play on commercial flights in America to soothe the passengers before takeoff. It all felt very homey. The gruff Russian soldiers who boarded the train soon after we left and yanked open the door to my compartment to check my papers and luggage did not disturb me at all.

Butt

The Hole in the Wall Gasthaus in downtown Wiesbaden was about the size of a large kitchen and always filled with people and cigarette smoke. When you went to the can, you took another soldier with you to hold the door so the whores wouldn't walk in while you were pee-ing down the hole in the floor between your feet. You usually had a buddy along anyway in case of a fight, and if he weren't holding the door, any whore who wanted to take a leak would push her way in. Not very romantic. The fights you might have were with soldiers from other outfits. The Germans were very peaceful if you didn't count the prostitutes rushing in to pee.

The Hole in the Wall was a drop for black market cigarettes. When you went to the can, you left a carton, which cost you two dollars at the PX, in a bag on one of the little tables. When you returned, the bag was gone and you picked up the twenty-mark note that was lying there, worth five dollars. The MPs seldom came in. Crowded as the place was, nobody took what he or she wasn't supposed to. Here, at least, the black market worked on the honor system.

One evening I was standing in the crowd having a beer with George Unger, the Company usurer, who was amassing a young fortune by lending my friends five dollars now for ten on payday, which was often only a week or so away. I never used him and vice versa, so I was one of his few friends. The soldiers did not repay him out of fear—he was meek and inheriting the Earth, a big help if I got in a fight—but because they knew they'd need him again. He did not lend to soldiers who were coming due to rotate home.

I had just lit up a Chesterfield and neatly rebuttoned the pack into the left pocket of my brown wool Ike jacket, when a sergeant I had never seen before asked me for a cigarette, as GIs often did and irritated me every time. The line, which was seldom actually used, went, "Have you got a cigarette? Have you got a match? All I've got is the habit."

To my surprise, I took the Chesterfield out of my mouth, shoved it between the sergeant's lips, and snarled, "Screw!" He turned and disappeared among the heads in the smoke.

"What did you do that for?" stammered Unger.

I did not know. I'd never done anything like it, it felt good, and it worked. I had the sense never to do anything like it again.

Incidentally, it would be my daughter Erin who persuaded me to stop smoking when she was about nine and I was forty. Well that she did. I was recently diagnosed with early emphysema.

Power

Drinking a cup of coffee with the other officers in the Company lounge, Second Lieutenant Larry Bunsen looked pleasant and conventional, he laughed, not a bad guy. I saw how we might have been friends if we had known each other before or after the army—but not during. He had elected to stay in the Reserve Officers' Training Corps whereas I had decided after one year of ROTC, that I was wasting a good part of my years at Harvard. Learning to draw azimuths on contour maps was not my idea of a liberal arts education. I'd take my chances as an enlisted man, start out as a private, and maybe learn stuff that was outside the course my life seemed to be taking.

This turned out to be a more significant decision than I realized when I made it. As my cousin Josephine would later put it, I'd been a privileged kid; and the rest of my life figured at that point to pass among privileged people. But in the army's entry-level enlisted ranks, no one is privileged. Spending nearly two years there broadened my outlook and showed me that I could make it among the less privileged—at least the ones who didn't resent my Harvard education.

Lieutenant Bunsen turned out to be another prick. He never lost a chance to hassle me, and it bugged him when he thought he'd caught me at something and I had an answer that he couldn't refute. One day he came to the heart of it and accused me of shirking my responsibility by not wearing gold bars on my shoulders like his on his, and thus not being personally liable for the awesome amount of pricey equipment that the army had made him sign for. I guess he took their intimidation to heart, and the responsibility of being an entry-level officer scared him. Whatever the reason, he couldn't stand to see me having fun, which I'd have had more of if it weren't for him. They say private first class, which I was by then, is the best rank in the army. Sometimes it is.

One gray January morning because I was late returning from breakfast in the mess hall, another second lieutenant ordered me to hit the prone and do push-ups on the ice-covered earth with no gloves and the wind whipping like needles through my summer fatigues; but this guy did not begin to piss me off like the constant jabs from Bunsen.

Lord Acton's nugget has it that power corrupts and absolute power corrupts absolutely. Often I saw the alchemy of gold bars on the shoulders turn nice people into pricks, not all, but many. (I would encounter similar abuse while I waited table for fellow students in my law school eating club, and I'd say a silent no-no by swinging the coffee carafe close to their heads as I served them.) I had been right in college about learning stuff outside my path, but I had not foreseen how lucky I'd be in experiencing the pressure that mounts inside us when the other person abuses his or her power. During my time in the service, I never punched anybody; but my instinct was that if I had run into Bunsen during the first year or so as a civilian, I'd have decked him. In fact, I had a fantasy in law school: I'm walking on a crowded sidewalk. I recognize him. *Bam, biff, bam!* If I felt that strongly after the army, what does an ex-convict feel after enduring years of crap in prison, or a Black person feel in America?

Men

During my time in the army, I saw no combat but many fights.

In basic training, a kid from Maine who bunked below me slept with his bayonet under his pillow, and I hoped he didn't grow defensive during a nightmare and thrust it upwards. Did his caution have anything to do with the fact that the army had welcomed him by pulling most of his teeth? I did not ask. Some evenings he would march up and down the aisle between the bunks with an ugly look on his potato-white face and the blade sticking up from his fist, challenging anyone who looked at him to fight. The guys who noticed laughed, but a woman in the town outside the base took him seriously enough to con him into marrying her. One Sunday night he returned to the barracks radiant. "We drove up and down the road in her convertible. Up and down. Christ, I never been so happy."

An encounter, more dangerous than sad, simmered between a bossy, feline Black man named Ronson and an old-line, canine white man named Raycroft.[3] The night it boiled over, neither man landed a solid punch. Ronson finally pulled Raycroft's fatigue shirt over his head, trapping his arms inside. With his free hand, Ronson grabbed a boot off the floor and raised it to beat on the green bulge that contained Raycroft's head. Despite the imminent danger Raycroft was in, the two of them looked silly. We bystanders laughed. Ronson paused with the upraised boot, inspected the writhing green sack, and laughed too.

A small, self-possessed Mexican named Bert Jones spent odd moments honing a two-inch blade on a little gray whetstone that he carried in his pocket. When another trainee commented on the size of the knife, Jones would tell him the advantages of not killing the person you cut. A smoldering, black-haired Anglo-Saxon from Louisiana named Spiker saw it differently. Now and then he honed his long-bladed fish knife muttering, "If a certain sergeant doesn't stop messing with me, I'm going to leave him along the way."

During my summer in Alabama, my squad sergeant was a dutiful, simple, quiet man. He had been in a dozen years, never been demoted, and never rose above the three stripes of a buck sergeant, a rank that many recruits reached in two years. His idea of reveille was to walk through the barracks and shake the foot of each bunk. That got to me. I brooded about it for a while, then asked him quietly, in a tone I did not recognize or like, to stop it. He didn't shake my bunk again.

During my service, I never awakened to the sound of a bugle playing the traditional reveille, even on a loudspeaker. Typically a corporal would enter the barracks and shout, "Wake up and piss, the world's on fire!" or simply "Drop your cocks and grab your socks!" Not that raunch was only for men. After Fort McClellan became a Women's Army Corps center, several of us were driving past a WAC training area when we heard a drill instructor shout to her trainees, "When I holler 'Attention,' I want to hear forty twats snap!"

A man's eagerness to fight often kept the peace. I was nearly knocked over one morning when a short corporal marched like a tank out of our mess hall. A soldier inside had started talking tough to him. Sometimes men trade insults back and forth, climbing a pyramid until each has reached a point of no return. Not the corporal. He told the other man to step outside and walked out without looking back. His antagonist did not follow.

"The Old Man has no right to talk to me like that," said Master Sergeant Beard, his dignity still smarting after twelve hours and five bottles of the army's 3.2% beer. We were sitting in the Enlisted Men's Club on a bath-warm Alabama Saturday evening. Beard, my platoon's chief non-com, had survived combat in World War II and Korea and made it through half of his twenty-year hitch. His pride equaled his experience. At inspection that morning, Captain Stark, the Company's new CO, had charged our platoon with a host of chickenshit demerits, the third platoon he'd done that to in as many weeks, his way of asserting himself and shaping up the company, as we all knew.

"Come on, Beard," I said. "You're paid to get yelled at by company commanders. That's your job."

"Damn it, Gus"—which is what they called me then—"sometimes you make me so goddamn mad...."

Beard did not finish the sentence or what might have followed. I had stepped into the path of his anger and trod upon his life, but we were friends drinking together.

And Beard was more of a gentleman than Diller, another twenty-year man. When Diller drank, he would say, "I fight pro for dough"—meaning his combat in Korea. Then he would pick a fight with his friends. Pretty soon other soldiers stopped drinking with him, and his social life vanished until his next transfer.

One day a genial southerner named Marshal explained a Black named Henry to me. "You don't understand, Gus. Henry is a *negra*," meaning that Henry was not wholly a human being. Marshal clearly believed this lie, which underlay America's founding sin of slavery, the vast fratricide called the Civil War, and pervasive racist evils that still flourish. Marshal's attachment to the lie, I believe, lessened his humanity, as it lessens the humanity of millions of similarly self-deceived Americans.

My only fight in the army came on a hot, dry Saturday afternoon when Paul Miller and his friend Hank Muthig and I drove over to Birmingham on a weekend pass and rented a room from an elderly woman who, patriotically, took in soldiers for only a dollar a night. Paul and I were good friends, but I had little in common with Hank, who was taller and thinner, except that we both wore glasses. Still in uniform, I laid out my civvies on one of the beds and emptied the pockets of my khakis onto the dresser.

"What's this?" Hank picked up and opened the little brown notebook into which I jotted my thoughts about life, sex, the army, and other private stuff.

"Give it here!"

I reached for it, but Hank turned away holding the book out at the end of a long arm. Unable to reach it, I scythed an arm across his throat and jerked him backwards into a precarious squat with my knee poised against his spine. Paul, who had been smiling at my plight, looked scared, possibly the more so because he knew that when I'd wrestled in high school, I sent two guys to the hospital (with dislocated shoulders). Hank tried to swing on me. I jerked his head in the thick V of my arm, knocking his glasses off one ear.

"My glasses!"

"My book."

He handed it over. I released him and stepped back. Paul relaxed. The three of us repeated the weekend a couple of more times, though Hank and I never became friends.

In the spring of 1954, I served briefly as a propagandist for a real war. Though I was merely a private, possibly a private first class by then, I had been made the company's "troop information and education officer." Every Saturday morning, I stood at a spindly lectern with everyone in the company who couldn't be elsewhere sitting in front of me and lectured them on whatever was in an info packet that I'd received a few days before. Half way around the globe, a French army was being besieged by local fighters at a place called Dien Bien Phu in what was still barely French Indochina, and President Eisenhower was thinking about sending US troops—conceivably including us—to help them keep that remnant of their empire out of Communist hands. So, on a Saturday or two, I explained "the domino theory," how one country after another would surely fall until all of Southeast Asia had gone Red unless we stepped in. Then Ike decided not to, and I went back to explaining how to use a toothbrush and so on.

Atomized troops, in transit to a new unit or nation, in unfamiliar surroundings with few if any friends, often had a low flashpoint, as though fighting were their security blanket. Most of us sensed this, so you'd hear "After you" and "Excuse me" and "Would you please pass the salt" from guys who usually didn't bother with such delicacy. Big Jim Karst, who was neither tall nor fat but a log of muscle, was brushing his teeth in the receiving barracks at Zweibrücken near the French border, after the troops had left their ship at Bremerhaven and spent the night twisting and turning on the wooden benches of third-class coaches rolling south to the American Zone. A guy brushing his teeth at the next sink warned Jim, "Don't crowd me."

"I'm not."

The guy bounced his fist off Jim's jaw. Jim studied him curiously and began to laugh. The guy cried out and fled through the swinging doors without toothbrush, paste, or towel.

When I reached my Company's barracks outside Wiesbaden, everyone was out in the field on maneuvers—meaning in the woods, towns, vegetable gardens, and gasthauses (the rough equivalent of British pubs)—except for a few men who ran the office. The first sergeant had charge of a broken old private whom the MPs had brought back from going AWOL someplace. The sergeant kept the private locked in a room alone except when someone herded him to chow with a loaded carbine or the sergeant went into the room to punch him around. When the Company returned, the AWOL blew over with no charges. The sergeant's punches were the only punishment.

Second Lieutenant Larry Bunsen welcomed me into his platoon by calling me into his little office, closing the door, and warning me how tough Drogovich, my new platoon sergeant, was. "If you get out of line," Bunsen smirked, "you might walk into a door. You know what I mean?" Tough talk for a guy fresh from college.

Drogovich was indeed tough. Years earlier he had boxed heavyweight—the word was that he fought someone who had fought Joe Louis—which gave him an enormous advantage over nearly everyone he encountered. The other person could see his size but not his experience and may have been disarmed by the hearing aid he wore, a souvenir of his years in the artillery. When a guy wanted to mix it up with Drog in a bar on a Saturday night, he would offer to meet the guy sober on Sunday morning. The other guy would never show up. Thus Drog's delay and maybe his reputation kept the peace.

Not that Drog was always a gentleman. One day when he suspected a private of stealing something, he got the man to confess by holding him by the ankles out a barracks window four stories up. Once the man was safely back inside, he recanted. During noon formation on another day, Drog had words with a skinny soldier named Jefferson and invited him behind the barracks. Jefferson went. The rest of us stood in formation hoping that Drog would be satisfied merely to pound Jefferson to a pulp. Pretty soon Jefferson ambled back and took his place among us. Then came Drog, rubbing a bloody mouth. Jefferson had punched him once and run like hell.

Both Lieutenant Bunsen and Sergeant Drogovich disliked me before they met me. Drog never explained why, though I suspect it was because he had one of the highest IQs in the Company, I had been to Harvard, and he hadn't. As I concluded in "Power," Bunsen convinced himself that I, a fellow college grad, had ducked the lieutenant's responsibilities that scared him shitless.

Reilly, who was another skinny guy, understood boxing and also German. He'd learned the former from his neighborhood in south Philly and the latter from a sleeping dictionary, as we called local girlfriends. One evening, two local men were exchanging snide remarks about Americans in front to the Walhalla nightclub downtown. Apparently they didn't suspect Reilly's erudition until he punched them both to the sidewalk. A congenital lover, Reilly had had two women come down to the troop ship to see him off for Germany, one sitting on either side of him on a visitor's bench and both pregnant by him. He carried two bullet holes in his stomach like extra navels, courtesy of an irate husband. Being a lover is not always a bed of roses, and many's the thorn that comes with a prick.

Like several GI towns in Germany, Wiesbaden had a Hillbilly Gasthaus. For the most part, Southerners knew to go there and Black men knew not to. One Saturday night, though, three Black soldiers walked in. A burly sergeant from the barracks next to ours went for the smallest. One punch from the little guy knocked the sergeant back against the wall. Surprised and probably humiliated, the sergeant pulled out a knife and cut the man's throat. A hush covered our first formation on Monday morning. Everyone knew that a sergeant was missing from the formation to our left and was being held for murder.

My Company dwelt in a solidly built, comfortable, former SS barracks in a base called Camp Pieri, from which you could look down on the Rhine and the city of Mainz on the far side. If the Soviets attacked, our job as a smoke generator company was to lay down a smoke screen at either end of the Patch Bridge—a pontoon bridge built across the river by the US Army in March 1945 and named for General Alexander Patch—to hide it before the Soviets could destroy it. The problem was that it would take us about two hours reach it, set up, and start making smoke; and the bridge was fewer than ten minutes from Soviet attack jets.

Thus we were stationed east of the Rhine and likely to stay there, that is, with no natural barrier between the token US forces that we were part of and the Red Army, which had done more than all other Allied armies combined to defeat the Germans, inflicting around eighty percent of the German battle casualties. For our personal weapons, the army issued us .30 caliber carbines that had become obsolete before the end of the war because, we supposed, they didn't want the Reds taking anything of value from our dead hands. Several of us figured that if we survived an initial attack, we'd find an infantry unit and some hard-hitting M-1 rifles, and maybe stand a fighting chance.

A peculiar peace comes to an enlisted man, unlike anything I've experienced before or since, from knowing who the enemy is, the officers, and what we could do about it, nearly nothing. It fascinated me to see, time and again, how power turned people who would have been pleasant enough in college or at a cocktail party into pricks. When the effects of drinking from a mountain stream in Switzerland, which I learned too late had passed through a barnyard above me, put me in the hospital, one of the nurses seemed to be using the lieutenant's bars on her shoulders to vent the stored-up anger of a lifetime against the enlisted men who were under her care. A private who knew that the army does not hold you responsible for what you do under the influence of medication bided his time until she injected him with some drug. As she pulled the needle out of his arm, he decked her.

Jurgen, a tall man from Kentucky, and I had been good friends for several months before he happened to mention that he had joined the army, on the advice of his lawyer, in order to avoid being charged with manslaughter. Would this news have forestalled our friendship if I'd heard it sooner? He explained that the deceased had been a bastard and had been in several fights the day he died, so Jurgen was only finishing work already begun when he knocked him down and kicked his head outside a bar in Knoxville. Fine, I thought, but the man is dead. Anyway, I spent many enjoyable evenings with Jurgen and his wife in their off-post apartment drinking German brandy and Coca-Cola, a favorite drink among GIs then, a blending of cultures, I suppose.

Jurgen had fought in Korea. I remember his astonishment when he spotted a red-haired kid named Dubois checking into our Company. Each had last seen the other in a firefight that looked hopeless. What surprised them more than their unlikely meeting was the fact that they were both still alive.

Jurgen was usually pleasant and friendly when sober, but a few drinks could make him scrappy. At a platoon party one night, he picked a fight—I don't recall whether there was a reason—with Nick Gentile, who was shorter but more solid, whose smile looked like the ace of spades, and who had been a Golden Gloves heavyweight in Chicago. He was the only man in the Company whom Sergeant Drogovich feared. This evening's collision reminded me of Hemingway describing a bull charging a horse. Though Gentile did no more than he had to, Jurgen wheezed around the camp the next day with several cracked ribs.

Minor differences between men may prove more provocative than major ones, and American soldiers from different outfits somehow made natural enemies. One day when everyone was supposed to be out on maneuvers, Jurgen and I stopped in a country gasthaus for a beer. Three guys from an antiaircraft outfit were sitting at a table across the room. I don't recall what they said that offended Jurgen, though I know it wasn't much. Jurgen went for an ax that was resting against the end of the bar, and the other three went for the door. I put down some money for our beers and reached the street in time to see Jurgen waving the ax over his head as the four of them wheeled around the corner of the cobblestone street. He told me later that he'd begun to feel foolish with the ax and had let them outrun him.

Trouble brewed between other soldiers in a half-empty beer hall one night until florid Joe Fogarty strode in the door and up the center of the room like a one-man platoon, his open topcoat creating an illusion of bulk, demanding in his whiskey-hoarse voice to know what was wrong. Later I saw Fogarty, who considered himself a fighter, in the ring in a camp boxing match, his trunks too big and his arms too small. His opponent clobbered him, his bloody nose deepening his red complexion.

Fogarty's puny arms prompted me to reflect that apart from lacking a tail to balance on, humans are built a bit like kangaroos: the huge hind legs, the erect posture except when grazing, the forelegs inadequate for walking but suitable for boxing. Kangaroos, though, are said to release virtually no methane.

An aspect of the human condition that has only resulted in needless wars so far but may yet end us all: It's the highly aggressive men and women who tend to become the leaders of the tribe or nation, and they are also the people most likely to pick fights with similarly endowed leaders of other tribes and nations.

Late one Saturday night six of us ended up in yet another country gasthaus, across a big room from six guys from the anti-aircraft unit. The place was getting ready to close. No one else was there except the German owner and his large, friendly daughter. I watched them both grow apprehensive as the tension mounted—they didn't need to understand the nasty remarks passing back and forth in English—even though the owner simply sent the army the bill each time soldiers broke up his place. I began to worry how a fight could be stopped, miles from the nearest military police, with nothing short of someone's personal tragedy likely to end it. I think that everyone worrying about the same thing is what saved us. Pretty soon one of our guys who knew one of their guys went over and started talking with him. One by one the rest of us joined in. It turned out we had nothing to fight about.

There was a gasthaus several hundred yards up the hill from our Company's motor pool, where one or another of us walked guard through every night in two-hour shifts. A pious little virgin named Joey Womble from North Carolina was walking his post one evening when a German emerged drunk from the gasthaus and started to fire a pistol at the motor pool—to resume the war, I guess. Many in the Company would have returned fire, knowing he was in little danger from a pistol at that range, if only to see what he could do with a carbine in the dark. Joey, though, sat down behind a truck until the German finished his fun.

A month before, a guard at a motor pool for US tanks across the river in Mainz had shot and killed two Germans from some political faction who were trying to sabotage something. The guard did what he had to, I suppose, but I'd not have wanted to do it. Generally, I sensed a mutual respect, almost a kinship, between the Americans and these Germans, an affinity between victors and vanquished. We understood, though, that Germans in the north would just as soon resume the war. What mix of temperament, culture, and US Air Force bombing in the north made the difference, I do not know. Part of the price of letting a Hitler take over your country.

Every morning the five of us in my squad room pitched in to sweep and buff the waxed linoleum floor. The task was required and worked fine until Philly Powell rotated home and a powerfully built lad named Rufus Ferris moved in. He thought himself above cooperating and lay on his cot while everyone else worked. Naturally, the guy who was guiding the electric buffer around the floor would start banging it into the legs of his cot. He hated the jolts and threatened whoever was doing it. When he threatened Ben Struthers, Ben dropped the handle of the buffer and stood over him with his fist cocked.

"Get up, you son of a bitch! Come on fight! There's no chain on your ass. Nothing's holding you back but fear!"

When my turn came, I did the same—it was Ben who taught me to talk like that. I figured I'd have one good shot at Rufus's mouth as he started to stand up. If that didn't slow him down, I hoped Ben and my other buddies would help me before I got mauled too badly. Rufus never rose to the challenge.

After a week or so, we began to take these confrontations less seriously. We were all very tough of course, but you can't be that tough in your common bedroom day after day. One morning Rufus picked up a broom and started to do his share. He could laugh. He turned out to be a nice guy.

While we were putting on our dress uniforms for Saturday inspection soon afterward, Rufus wanted to show Ben how he used to fight back home in Tacoma. In all innocence, he held the corner of a razor blade between his thumb and forefinger, taking care to keep the point from protruding, and crisscrossed Ben's chest with his hand. Very interesting, we thought, and were rather impressed until someone noticed that the front of Ben's shirt was hanging in loose khaki tatters. The blade had stuck out farther than Rufus intended, and Ben had to break out a fresh shirt.

In our squad room, Rufus and the squad leader were Black while Ben, a guy named Davis, and I were white. I had not had much contact with Black people except for my parents' church and my mother's Trinidadian helper Amelia (mentioned in "Tears"); but in the army, the races were wholly mixed, except that a high proportion of the noncoms we took orders from were Black—several of them told me that their lives were better in the army than in civilian America—and for most of us, the mix didn't seem to matter. Perhaps the best thing that President Harry Truman did to unify the nation was to integrate the armed forces, but the end of the draft in favor of an all-volunteer military in 1973 caused fewer people from fewer strata of the public to receive this benefit.

If all young men and women today were drafted into military or civilian service, they should enjoy the benefits of working in community as I did in the army, do jobs that help the public, and reduce race prejudice. Putting the lives of privileged sons and daughters again at risk should do wonders to cut the number and length of US wars. But I digress.

Downtown on a Saturday night Ben rarely missed a chance to defend his honor, and his face often showed a new lump or two on Sunday morning. "I'm easy to get along with," he liked to say, and he was, if he fought someone often enough to relieve his pugnacity. His needed to fight the way most people need to pee. One evening in the Gasthaus Walhalla, he tried to hook me up with Wiesbaden's most beautiful and popular prostitute, but she was sitting at another table with other soldiers and didn't seem inclined to move. He drew laughter, though, from the whole room when she stood up too long and he shouted, "Sit down, you big-titted whore!"

Camp Kilmer steamed under humid June. The troop ship USNS Upshur had dumped roughly eight hundred of us short-timers off the cool Atlantic onto Staten Island the day before, and a hot bus had driven us past greenery and junk into the interior of New Jersey. Not surprisingly, tempers grew short as our hours in the service dwindled. Two big guys who had needled each other all across the ocean drew bunks on the ground floor of the same barracks, and the fact that neither of them really wanted to fight had prevented it so far, which made it all the more likely to happen now, like water deepening behind a weak dam. Now their angry voices rose above the sounds of "I Love Paris" on a radio I was listening to in the sun outside. I entered the barracks as their fists lashed out, their feet pounding the wooden floor as they circled each other.

"WHAT THE FUCK!" I bellowed.

They understood and separated before they turned and saw that I had no authority beyond my disgust. The stride of their fight broken, they mumbled sulkily at each other and busied themselves at opposite ends of the long room.

As a boy, I hadn't liked to fight because it seemed like a pointless way to risk getting hurt. Not that I never fought. Later, I didn't want to hurt the other person no matter how much he'd angered me. Yet as I have listened to men in genteel settings abuse each other with words after I left the army, I have considered how much more civil they might be if a rude remark might draw a punch in the mouth.

The soldiers I've mentioned were, of course, only a handful of the millions of men whom Uncle Sam had trained to kill and die in the perceived national interest *du jour*. Did they keep the peace among themselves, or fail to, much as nations do? Would the world be more peaceful if women led more nations? Consider Angela Merkel, but also Margaret Thatcher. If Hillary Clinton, not Mikhail Gorbachev, had led the Soviet Union when it broke up, would war have ensued?

Four decades after leaving the army, I visited the Korean War Memorial on a lonely corner of the Washington Mall. It consists of a band of larger-than-life steel figures wearing the fatigues and ponchos that my fellow soldiers and I used to wear and carrying the weapons that we used to carry. The poor bastards, I thought, sweating and freezing, killing and dying, in a cause that they, and the nation's leaders who sent them, little understood. Gazing at them I wept.

Wall Street

Words

Home in bed with the flu back in my teens, I was fooling around with some coat hangers and a pair of pliers when, lo, I invented a novel device for cooking hamburgers over a fire. My father looked it over and offered to help me try to patent it. In May of 1947, the lawyer he hired filed the application; and soon the Patent Office asked me, isn't the device the same as Shenton's, isn't it the same as McHarg's? Around doing my homework in the evening, I drafted little essays for the lawyer explaining why my device differed from these two and several others—an easy job once I brought myself to focus on it, also tedious and fun. Those other devices were so different from mine that I wondered how the Patent Office could even ask. It finally granted my patent—Number 2,538,440, Culinary Implement—in January 1951; but before I could figure out how to market the device, technology superseded it. So I netted nothing except, unbeknownst to me though surely not to my father, a taste of a career.

Doing the research for my college honors thesis on the controversial House Un-American Activities Committee several years later led to the second taste. Apart from a well-balanced book by a Catholic priest, almost everything written about the bumptious, anti-communist Committee struck me as being unduly polemical on one side or the other. Fortunately, though, some people whom the Committee had charged with contempt of Congress had fought back in court. Reading the opinions of judges I had never heard of—Prettyman, Holtzoff, Edgerton, and others—I marveled at the clarity and power of their words.

If my lawyer father wanted me to choose the law, he never said so, so it never occurred to me to resist him.

Between two and four o'clock one night while I was walking guard in Germany and looking down on the lights of Mainz reflecting off the Rhine, the idea of The Law descended on me like the "brooding omnipresence in the sky" that the venerated Supreme Court Justice Oliver Wendell Holmes had said he did not believe in. It filled me up, ending the plan I had enjoyed since high school to teach English literature. Indeed, I needed only one more reference to complete my application to enter a University of Michigan Ph.D. program. But now students would not go forth from my lectures and do whatever. Instead, I would make decisions, take actions, win and lose cases, and, I hoped, relieve my client's troubles.

Even though I had decided on my career, I applied to only one law school, Harvard. Dumb, but I was probably still a bit half-hearted about the law. And there was another problem. In order to take the law aptitude test, which was given down in Heidelberg, I had to get around Sergeant Drogovich, who was then tearing up my weekend pass applications. I pleaded my case to the Company commander, Captain Craig—who was known as Tankhead because his skull was so large that he had to take the webbing out of his helmet liner before it would fit him—when I managed to drive his jeep one day. I told him I felt strongly enough to go AWOL, if necessary, to take the exam. The pass came through; and I spent a glorious weekend in the old city on the banks of the Neckar, except for the long Saturday morning itself, during which I was dismayed to find that serving my country had rusted my brain. The law school accepted me.

Thus I entered the world of urbane minds and contentious mouths. After several years at my Wall Street firm, the law, and to some extent the rest of civilization, fell into perspective when Erin, who was then four or five, asked me, "What do you do at the office, Daddy?"

"I read some papers, and write some papers and talk to some people."

Reference

About the reference that I still needed for my application to the University of Michigan: It was to be from Archibald MacLeish, who had survived combat in World War I to become an editor of the *Harvard Law Review*, an expat living in Paris along with Fitzgerald, Hemingway, Gertrude Stein, et al., a Pulitzer Prize-winning poet, the Librarian of Congress, and a professor at Harvard. (He would win another Pulitzer for his 1958 play *J.B.*) In my senior year, he admitted me to his seminar on expository writing, a privilege that enriched my mind and required me to turn in a thousand-word essay every week. He once told me that I could "write like an angel" when I felt strongly, which wasn't often because I procrastinated the weekly assignments, once or twice starting round ten p.m. and writing though the night before it was due. Too often for my own good, I turned in what was little, if any, better than a first draft. It pleased him, though, that I actually wrote expository prose. He told me that most of the essays he received were thinly veiled fiction by students who hadn't made it into his fiction course.

I had wanted to be a writer for as long as I can remember; but I didn't suppose I could support myself as one; and I didn't think much of the lives that I saw writers leading. Take Hemingway and Fitzgerald again—two drunks, and the former a prick. No, I would rather have a richer experience in the real world—as I supposed experience and the real world to be—before presuming to offer my writings to readers I'd never met.

It did not occur to me on the night that the spirit of the law banished my plan to teach, that a life at the bar would probably give me more experiences worth writing about than would expounding literature, though for many years my law jobs didn't leave much time to write for pleasure. Not that I wasn't warned. I heard early and often, starting with Dean Erwin Griswold's welcome to my entering class at law school, "The law is a demanding mistress." The Dean didn't mention how often she'd fuck us.

Preparation

The first class of my first year at the Harvard Law School arrived on a warm sunny morning in September 1955. The course was civil procedure—as opposed to criminal procedure, and meaning federal procedure not the procedures that vary dizzyingly from state to state. It was also first class for the law school's new hire named Abram Chayes, who had graduated *summa cum laude* from Harvard College, won a bronze star for heroism and purple heart for being wounded in combat during World War II, and been first in his law school class and president of the august Law Review; he then clerked for legend-

ary Supreme Court Justice Felix Frankfurter and worked two years at
the powerhouse Washington firm of Covington & Burling. I did not
know all this on that sunny morning, only that he looked pleasantly
energetic and must have taken a pay cut when he left that firm in order
to stand at the foot of the theater where a hundred or so of us One L
students awaited in a rising semicircle of seats.

He glanced down at his seating chart, looked up, and called on me.
I had taken only a cursory look at his brief assignment and fumbled
with his questions until he mercifully called on someone else. Dumb
not to have prepared better, I thought, and embarrassing to be exposed. Welcome to my chosen career!

Being a slow reader, I found that by spending most afternoons and
evenings in the huge Langdell Law Library, I was able to read and
usually to outline the cases assigned in my courses, but not to master them sufficiently to feel I could answer a profs' probing questions
intelligently in class. Most students, the smartest group I'd ever been
part of, sat in their assigned seats and carried on the class discussions.
The rest of us sat in the back rows and were not called on.

Professor Calvert Magruder was one of the ornaments of the law
school, mainly because he also served as a judge on the distinguished
Court of Appeals for the First Circuit, which was an ornament of the
federal system. Perhaps his signature decision had come in the landmark case of *Sampson v. Channell*, which dealt with civil procedure.
The day that Professor Chayes assigned the case, I read it with growing dudgeon. It's logic sucked. Why all the fuss over it? It was wrong!

For the next class, I sat in my assigned seat. Professor Chayes, surprised no doubt to see me there, called on me to state the case. That
meant reciting the facts, reasoning, and result, which was what students nearly always did to start the discussion. But this case incensed
me so much that as I stated it, I kept interjecting the points where I
thought Magruder had erred. This was heresy! I sensed that Chayes
was delighted.

"The opinion says that ___ is substantive. Mr. Bell says that it's
patently procedural. What do you say, Mr. ___?" he asked, calling on
one of the half-dozen students whose hands had shot up to defend the
iconic judge and decision.

So it continued, me against the received wisdom and all the other students, for the full hour of the class and, when we met again two days later, for a good part of the next hour. It was terrific fun. No other student took my side. I'm sure Chayes enjoyed it too. During the three years of law school, I never did anything like that again and never saw any other student do it.

The event foreshadowed the future. With the notable exception of Ralph Nader, the great majority of my classmates would serve the Establishment while I would become happiest while opposing it. Both endeavors, of course, are essential.

Abe Chayes turned out to be my favorite prof. He was the only one who invited all his classes—in groups of around thirty—to dinner at the home he shared with his wife Antonia Handler Chayes, who was also an accomplished lawyer. During JFK's presidency, he took time out from teaching to be the Legal Advisor of the State Department and had roles in concluding the Berlin crisis of 1961, the Cuban missile crisis of 1962, and the Partial Nuclear Test Ban Treaty of 1963. The hour and a half of class time that he devoted to orchestrating my assault on *Sampson v. Channell* turned out to be the best preparation that law school gave me for the challenges that lay ahead.

Abe was one of the few profs who regularly showed up at our class reunions. At one, he encouraged me to continue my sometimes rebel ways. His vitality and good humor remained so unflagging that his death from cancer at the age of seventy-seven seemed unfairly premature.

Youth

Sam Gilman, my college roommate who had gone on to the Harvard Business School and to work for the Chubb insurance company near my office on Wall Street, informed me during one of our lunches that we young lawyers at the big law firms were "the last exploited class." I could only point out that B-school grads like him got by on their personalities while we lawyers had to fall back on our brains. But apart from last, he had a point. Take a typical evening:

Four other young lawyers and I walk down the dark canyon called Pine Street, a block north of Wall, and take a corner table in Massoletti's at the bottom of the towering Cities Service Building. The restaurant, which is jammed during the lunch hour (and no longer exists), entertains a pleasantly small crowd for dinner. Most of my group order dry martinis with Tanqueray gin, shrimp cocktails, rich entrees, and Crenshaw melon with our coffee. I skip the martini, prefer the crab claw appetizer, and think the melon insipid.

We joke urbanely about points of law, the foibles of several clients, and the tactics of our opponents in the case that is keeping us from our wives and children for the third evening this week, then go on to compare inside information on the current gossip about the Kennedys, and debate about whether Louis Nizer, whose *My Life in Court* is a recent bestseller, writes better fiction than the Wall Street lawyer and society novelist Louis Auchincloss does. Comfortably satiated, we walk five abreast up the empty sidewalk, two of us smoking cigars, back to the office.

The firm we work for on salaries that pay zero for overtime, picks up the tabs for our meals without question. At the hourly rate it charges its clients for our time, it recovers the price of the drinks, dinners and cigars in the first twenty minutes of our evening's work.

Sluggish Compass

So much depends on the universe that we decide, or are forced, to strive in and the direction we take within that universe! Looking back, I am okay about choosing the universe of the law, but annoyed with myself for paying too little attention to choosing a direction within it during the best years to set my compass. During college I decided to teach English literature in a college. In the army, while walking guard one night above the river Rhine and the lights of Mainz across its dark waters, I switched to the law. During law school, my choice was to work on interesting cases with able and congenial men; cases meant lawsuits, trials, appeals, and all that came with them. But in what field of law; in what city or town; at a firm, corporation, government agency, prosecutor's or public defender's office, or maybe solo practice? With little thought, I mostly passed through the doors that opened before me.

Three brisk and sometimes scary years at Harvard, a.k.a. The Law

School, imparted considerable knowledge, a fair idea of how to think like a lawyer, and the then usual indifference to social and economic justice. The firms and corporations that The Law School served sought fresh blood, after all, to help them thread their ways through the System or find ways around it, but certainly not to make the System more just. The people with power were doing fine with the System as it was. It was the 1950's, President Eisenhower was on his golf cart, and all was right with the world. Except it wasn't.

Large Wall Street law firms ranked high among the places for a law student to seek a job, according to the then current thinking at The Law School, even though Dean Griswold told my class that New York City was an impossible place to work, hard to live in and hard to commute to. Residual nepotism, I suppose, landed me a summer job at the then prominent Wall Street law firm called Dewey, Ballantine, Bushby, Palmer & Wood. The Dewey was Thomas E., a crusading district attorney, three-term governor of New York, and twice a failed Republican candidate for President. My father had toiled at that firm in the 1920's and early '30's, when it was much smaller, was called Root Clark, and was on Nassau Street. I liked to think, though, that it was the work I did during that summer stint, in particular a long research paper that the partner I wrote it for circulated among his peers, that earned me an offer to return after graduation, an offer I could have refused but never thought to.

So began nine heady years in lower Manhattan, the capital of capitalism, back when the smell of roasting coffee still drifted through the canyons. The firm set me to work reviewing corporate trust indentures (contracts), each of which ran a hundred or more printed pages, for the Chase Manhattan Bank. Soon I was wearing a vest and a homburg and finding that nearly all the New York court decisions that my research uncovered favored banks over people. To my surprise, the nuances within those long, mostly boilerplate contracts grew somewhat interesting as I worked on them, but they were not the cases I came for. I asked to be transferred into litigation, a field that was said—erroneously, I decided later—to require fewer brains and more balls than corporate law.

Now I worked days that were too short and many evenings and

weekends with able and mostly congenial men on interesting cases that seemed important at the time. There were worse legal sweatshops than mine, and it puffed me up a bit to mention, quietly and only when necessary of course, the name of the firm I served—for the savvy, simply "Dewey Ballantine," which would later become its official name.*

All that overtime made the firm a handy graveyard for dead marriages and may have killed some live ones, not to mention that it kept fathers from their children during the short precious years that cannot be retrieved.

"I know exactly the night I got pregnant," a partner's slightly sloshed wife complained loudly during one of the firm's annual spring dinner-dances, "because we only did it twice last summer." Her husband worked nearly every evening before making a long commute to their home in New Jersey, and it was said around the firm that, through his brilliance and all that work, he kept his finger on the pulse of the SEC. Such were the myths. He died in his fifties.

Litigators at Dewey Ballantine—and at many firms like it, I understand—did not try many cases. Instead, they spent most of their efforts in a glacial dance of pretrial motions (formal requests to the court) and discovery of pertinent facts until their clients discover the most pertinent fact of all, that is, that their causes were not as invulnerable as they had imagined in the cocoon of their executive suites. So they'd settle, allowing the lawyers on both sides to claim victory while not risking defeat.

Delegating responsibility was not the Dewey firm's forte. When it came to trying a case, or even arguing a motion or taking a deposition, the clients were understood to expect the services of one or another esteemed partner. Vast sums were usually at stake, prestige always was, and the firm was afraid not to comply. Small cases that would have trained the young associates were not considered profitable—which was true only in the short run. While lawyers who try many cases early on tend to find brief-writing and legal research tedious—and maybe to wing it rather than look it up—firms like mine went the opposite

---

* In 1990. In 2007 it merged with another firm to become Dewey & LeBeouf. The combined firm had more than 1,400 lawyers in 27 offices worldwide. It collapsed in 2012.

way with a self-defeating vengeance. It was by watching, not by doing, that the senior partners expected us to learn our skills in court. That works as well for trying a case as for playing a violin.

During a long trial of three major drug companies charged with fixing the prices of their new wonder drugs, for instance, a silver-haired partner enjoyed the honor of carrying the briefcase of a more silvery partner, the firm's senior litigator and last man in the firm's name, John E. F. Wood. That was typical. The jury convicted all three companies; the appeals court reversed the conviction; and an equally divided Supreme Court affirmed the reversal. Also not uncommon: lose on the facts, win on the excellently briefed law.

As one of several lawyers who enlarged the defense team now and then during the trial, I didn't learn enough to evaluate merits of the case; but I saw enough to notice the appalling optics that Dewey Ballantine and the other pricey defense firms showed the jury. At the front table sat a rough-hewn antitrust prosecutor named Harry Sclarsky and two or three assistants. Behind them were tables for each of the three defense teams, each team more impressive-looking than the government's and served by messengers rushing up to hand them papers or whisper messages too urgent to wait until the jury left for a recess. All this, obviously to me but apparently not to my seniors, built sympathy among the jurors for the out-numbered, out-resourced, underdog lawyers who championed the United States of America.

Another silver-haired litigator, whom I'll call Mr. Gillis, seldom if ever went to court. When I was still fairly new at the firm, somebody brought a suit in federal court claiming a vast sum of money against one of our clients and several other corporations. The law was clear that the federal court had jurisdiction over the other corporations but not over ours. The right response could not have been simpler: ask the court to drop our client from the case. But it wasn't simple for Mr. Gillis. He enlisted an older associate I'll call Bert and me to assist him, and he kept calling us into his office for seemingly endless hours to discuss problems that barely existed and to draft the simple papers that making the request required. Not greed, I believe, but fear caused him to run up the chargeable hours.

On the morning that Mr. Gillis is to argue the motion, Bert and I wait in the lofty lobby of the federal courthouse as the time the case will be called draws nearer and nearer. No Mr. Gillis.

At last, he rushes into the lofty hall. "Where's the men's room?"

This silver-haired litigator is literally scared shitless and doesn't know where in the federal courthouse to go. Bert and I point. Seemingly ages later, he emerges and we enter the courtroom. When the case is called, Mr. Gillis stammers through the argument that he'd rehearsed and rehearsed with Bert and me, but at least he doesn't make the mistake of overdoing it. The judge grants the motion. The client objects to the size of the firm's fee but pays it.

More bizarre, if less pathetic, was the morning a taxi discharged yet another silver-haired litigator I'll call Mr. Welch, who almost never went to court, together with three officials of DuPont and me, onto the curb between the state and federal courthouses. We had come to oppose a motion that two troublemakers had made to enjoin (block) a distribution of the General Motors stock that DuPont had bought with the profits it made by selling explosives during World War I and, after years of litigation, the courts had ordered it to divest.

The case was in the federal courthouse to the left of where the cab dropped us. To my horror, Mr. Welch led us up the long steps of the state courthouse to our right. Bringing up the rear, I saw no way to stop him and wondered how his blunder would end. On reaching the revolving doors at the top, he mumbled calmly and inaudibly, did a U-turn, and led the puzzled DuPonters and dazzled me back down the steps, across the street, and into the right courthouse.

But after we worked on briefs and affidavits through the night, and after Mr. Wood argued the case, we beat the injunction. The troublemakers—actually they struck me as decent men with a plausible case, but I knew not to contradict the myth—promptly appealed to the august United States Court of Appeals for the Second Circuit. A scant two days later, after dispatching more papers via messenger to the judges at their country homes on the Fourth of July, we won again. Hours later, DuPont poured a billion dollars worth of GM stock into the mail—back when a billion dollars was real money.

As often as commercial cases settle, a trial is the ultimate weapon. The threat of an unpredictable jury verdict often brings on the proverbial settlements "on the courthouse steps"—if everyone is on the correct steps, that is. Since trying cases remains the only way to grow proficient at trying cases, it is obvious that lawyers who lack this experience settle some cases that should be tried and settle others for too much or too little money—because they recognize, and are terrified by, their own incompetence in court. If I were still that green when I came to face those choices, I wondered whether I, too, would seek sellout settlements.

All the same, working on interesting cases was not a goal that required me to try any cases just yet, and it did not occur to me to look for another job. I was having too much fun to notice the years slipping away, and with them, the freedom to change my direction. I sought out all the chances I could to speak in court; and as I relate in "Prohibition," which follows, my best chances came through Legal Aid (the City's public defender office) in Criminal Court, where the main risk of failure was that people who were innocent but poor would spend time in a slammer.

Having a hundred and twenty odd lawyers, Dewey Ballantine was then one of the largest firms in the world. (In many large cities today, that number would make it a mid-sized firm.) Once a month, it held a dinner—at the Yale Club, across short Vanderbilt Avenue from Grand Central Station—for the lawyers to get to know each other and learn what was happening beyond their niches in the firm. The dinners were called "Wranglers" as in "Are you going to Wranglers tonight?" A cocktail hour. Thick cuts of juicy, red beef. Bottles of Dewar's White Label scotch (a brand of client Schenley) alternating with the salt and pepper shakers along the huge, U-shaped, white-clothed table. Occasionally, the oldest partner stood up and told a dirty joke that we always laughed at. Cigars, usually Coronas, came with coffee, during which three or four lawyers told the rest of us what they were working on. Some of their talks were fascinating. Most extolled the firm's skills and some, its myths. Some made me wonder, as I studied the art of the cigar, why such dull stuff excited such smart men.

A clue that I might be working in the wrong place came at one of the firm's Wranglers. Following the meal, I forget which lawyer stood up, amid the eddies of cigar smoke and clink of ice in the glasses of scotch, and spoke about a victory that the firm had just won. As best I recall, the trees of some fruit farmers stood downwind of a client's new factory that was belching out toxic smoke with a predictable effect on the trees' fruit-bearing. The farmers sued the client with what sounded to me like a very strong case. But it never came to trial. My colleagues used one delaying tactic after another—pretrial motions of dubious merit, excessive depositions, whatever it took—to run up the farmers' legal bills while the smoke that continued to damage their crops, cutting their ability to pay their lawyers or even support their families. Eventually the farmers dropped the suit. Another triumph of Wall Street justice. As I sat at the banquet, I had no idea how many, if any, of my fellow diners found this victory as disgusting as I did.

In those days, half the firm's lawyers had graduated from The Law School, and the firm had only one partner, Lenard Joseph, who was known to be Jewish. Governor Dewey would occasionally ask him how "the Jewish community" felt about various stuff, as though the community existed and this lawyer knew the answers. (My own infrequent contact with "the Governor," as everybody called him, was respectful and friendly.) Rumor had it that after another Wall Street firm selected its first Jewish partner, it felt miffed that it didn't receive proper credit because the man's name didn't sound Jewish. Of course, the rumor itself gave the firm the credit it sought, as well as the larger blame that it was too obtuse to understand.

Much anti-Semitism on Wall Street took the form of exclusion. A lawyer I knew who was growing wealthy at the investment bank of J. & W. Seligman & Co. used to boast—lest anyone be put off by the bank's Jewish-sounding name—that it hadn't hired a Jew in three hundred years. In fact, the bank was roughly a hundred years old.

Some associates at Dewey Ballantine, especially those who lacked the favored background, came to the firm, not to stay, but to pick up its careful, though narrow, training and to dress up their resumés. After a few years, they accepted the farewell luncheon in a private room at the Wall Street Club in the Chase Manhattan Bank Building and moved on. For most of the rest, serving clients was incidental to making partner. That would mean wealth, some power in the firm and prestige beyond it, and, foremost for me, tenure—the reasonably secure freedom to keep working on those interesting cases with those men and finally a few women without having to worry about finding medical insurance, negotiating a lease, hiring and firing people, figuring the taxes, or bringing in new clients—the diversions I'd face in a small firm. True, it bothered me when our cases amounted to big clients screwing little people, but my solution was to avoid being assigned to those cases. It's marvelous how we lawyers can delude ourselves.

In those days, about one out of every dozen new hires made partner after eight or ten years of long hours, proven ability, passing congeniality, and a vital though unmentioned degree of conformity. The firm was fairly adept at placing its rejects with its clients, a perk that helped us associates to accept the long odds against receiving tenure and also helped to keep clients loyal to the firm; the same lawyers often kept on working together, but now the former associates held the whip. The firm's Christmas parties did double duty as alumni reunions. It was all very friendly except for the firing itself. Those of us who thought, or were led to think, that we had a fair chance at making partner tended not to dwell on other goals. "It's not so far away," Mr. Wood told me one day as we passed each other in the short corridor to the men's room.

There was a partners' can one floor up, but Wood preferred to pee with the troops rather than climb the stairs. He tried most of the firm's cases and was widely respected, not to mention wealthy, but though he had reached his sixties, he still spent a depressing number of evenings and weekends in the shop. ("Shop" was the folksy term for the monolith, not consciously short for "sweatshop.") If this guy has success, I'd ask myself, do I really want it? I agreed with William Faulkner that the only thing worth doing eight hours a day is work, but sufficient unto the day.... Evenings and weekends are more than overtime; they are the rest of your life.

A good side to our grind was the four-week summer vacation. The bad sides were trying to snare all four weeks out of our crowded agendas and the near certainty that phone calls from the office, always important, would puncture our alleged freedom. Worst was being called back early to work on some job that couldn't wait and no one else could do.

The phone was serenely silent through the vacation at the end of my seventh year with the firm, just as well since Brian had just been born. "That made me feel insecure," I joked to Len Joseph, the able and congenial but less important partner I'd been working for lately. I joked because this was still a year shy of the usual moment of truth, but he looked uneasy.

A few days later, several of us were told that we had been passed over. "Why?" I asked Len.

"There was no enthusiasm for making you a partner," he said.

While that may have been part of the truth, it begged the question. I felt quietly furious that he was this impersonal and opaque after all the meals we'd shared and evenings we'd work and trips to Los Angeles and Washington we'd taken together. But I saw no point in asking further. I had considered him a friend, but he was also a careful man and a team player. As were all the younger partners. I had gone to the college I wanted to, the army I had to, and the law school and job I'd wanted. Being passed over for partner was the first major disappointment (except at love) in my privileged life.

"How does it feel to have your nuts cut?" another lawyer asked me heartily. You crude prick, I did not reply. He had been my last remaining rival for a partner's slot in the litigation department, and the firm had just chosen him. He worked for Mr. Wood, who had recently encouraged me in the corridor to the can. He even smoked Mr. Wood's Edgeworth brand of pipe tobacco. Fifteen years later, he left the firm and the law to help his wife's music career.

If I had been more reflective, I would probably have seen years sooner that, much as I enjoyed most of my work and colleagues, this firm was not the place for me. One clue came when I had an argument with a young associate named John Harris in the firm's library about the proper price to charge for new (and therefore patent-protected) wonder drugs. These often-outlandish prices were a subject of more than passing interest since the firm's clients included the drug giants Eli Lilly and Chas. Pfizer. John held that companies should charge the highest prices for their drugs that their patent monopolies permitted. I countered that Pfizer and Lilly should charge no more than necessary to allow them to do their research and earn a reasonable profit, so that more people could buy the drugs and save their lives. I was sure that John's view echoed the firm's; but since partners rarely entered the library, I was pretty sure that my heresy had not hurt me—except for failing to make me wonder what I was doing there. I understand that John became a gentleman farmer in New Hampshire

A second warning occurred one summer day in southern Massachusetts. The firm was helping the American Optical Company, which was based there, to defend itself against charges of price-fixing, which was a crime under the antitrust laws. Mr. Wood had brought another associate and me to join the client's general counsel and a couple of lawyers for Bausch & Lomb, which was another major optical company and AO's alleged co-conspirator, to decide which corporate papers a Department of Justice subpoena required the companies to turn over to the prosecutors. As the talking dragged on, I became increasingly bothered that these men were twisting the plain words of the subpoena so as to exclude papers that might be incriminating but were clearly called for. I held my peace.

Before dinner that evening I went to Mr. Wood's room in the venerable Sturbridge Inn and told him my concern. He seemed reflective, not angry, and did not try to talk me out of my opinion. The next morning, he and the other senior lawyers closeted themselves while we associates waited in another office. Once we were all together, Mr. Wood announced that the troublesome documents would be given to the DOJ.

I was glad that my point had prevailed and gave no thought to whether it angered the client or hurt its criminal defense or sank my chances of making partner. I did not see the episode for what it was: a senior partner had decided to cut a corner that I would not have, in order to protect a client which, if dissatisfied, could always switch to another law firm, and I had made the charade untenable. Could the firm afford to keep a lawyer like me? It was only as I wrote this episode down that I saw that it foreshadowed a stand I would take some years later about the crimes that law officers committed at the 1971 Attica prison riot.

A third clue came the day that Mr. Wood called me into his office to discuss a sentence in a long memorandum I had written for use within the office about my work for Legal Aid, which I describe in

"Prohibition." Len Joseph stood there too. The sentence: "Our clients pay for the best legal advice in the world, though they don't always get it." All three of us knew it was true. They asked me to delete it. I agreed. It obviously exceeded the candor the firm's culture could tolerate. Anyone who fit in at the firm would have known not to write it.

A shock absorber that helped to make Dewey Ballantine's up-or-out policy tolerable was that the firm allowed us who had been passed over for partnership as much time as we needed to find a new job, though I noticed that the annual pay raises stopped at once. For me, this took a long time, and now and then a partner would nudge me to crawl up into the womb, as I then supposed it, of some corporate client's legal department—years later I would have several years of satisfying part-time work in such a department—but I was still bent on trying cases, and in those days, house counsel did not try anything but hired outside law firms, believing they were getting experts and knowing they were shifting the blame for whatever went wrong.

Assuredly my job search was long and frustrating because I had little of the basic experience in my chosen field. I'd assisted on several important cases, but the firms I was approaching seldom handled important cases, and apart from my brief volunteer work, I still had not tried a case or argued an appeal. I'd never even taken a deposition, which is where you question a witness in an office, the opposing lawyer hassles you from time to time, you threaten to cab to the courthouse and take the big hassles to a judge but you rarely need to, and a court reporter taps it all out on a little machine. It was routine but often-lively work that trained you to frame questions and stick with them under duress and non-responsive answers, and where, unlike at trial, missteps can usually be corrected. A firm would be crazy not to train its fledgling trial lawyers by letting them take depositions, right?

After two and a half years of headhunters, want ads, phone calls, resumés, and the occasional interview, I found a small, midtown firm, Mermelstein, Burns & Lesser, that wanted me, no depositions and all, for a few thousand dollars a year less than I was making. Ecstasy! Shortly after reporting for work, they told me to take the deposition of a famous musician named Ray Davies who led a famous British rock group called The Kinks. Defending him was an able trial lawyer and former federal prosecutor. What's more, I was told to work Davies over for two full days—how does one make up pertinent questions for two long days?—so that maybe he'd see the wisdom of settling the case. Terror! I went into the room, and two days later I came out with my first real confidence in questioning a witness and two LP records of Kinks' music that Davies had kindly autographed for Erin and Brian.

After that, I handled nearly all of that firm's litigation but was out of sync with the people in charge and so moved to another, smaller midtown firm (after parting with my secretary Laurie, as related in "Adieu"), The Law Firm of Malcolm A. Hoffman, where the senior partner turned out to be loath to delegate the jobs that mattered. In the office, he was "Big Mal" being six feet five and heavy; I was "the other Mal." Thence to a state prosecutor's office, and then my own practice, where I made little money; but once you work for yourself, it's hard to find a more congenial boss.

If I'd thought less about my work at Dewey and more about my career, I'd have left after maybe three years for a job, if I could get one, at one of the Manhattan or Brooklyn prosecutor's offices to get concentrated trial experience, then a job at a more compatible law firm, or maybe I'd have remained career prosecutor, since I cared more about doing justice than winning cases or getting rich—which would be useful priorities when Attica came along.

In all, I worked long hours for nine-and-a-half years at Dewey Ballantine, averaging three evenings in the office every two weeks. With each new year and job since then, the disappointment of being passed over faded farther into the past. Finally, I saw it as a passport to freedom, a prize I had lacked the wit to seize, that opened the door to a richer though less affluent way of life and to my main adventures, the prosecutions that arose out of the 1971 Attica prison riot and later the Sanctuary Movement.[4]

Gideon

Framed on a wall of my office is an 18½ by 14½ inch sheet of paper proclaiming that on March 9, 1964, I was "duly admitted and qualified as an Attorney and Counselor of the Supreme Court of the United States." Once lawyers have been admitted to practice in their state courts for three years, they may obtain one of these certificates simply by filling out a form, getting two friends who already belong to the Court's bar to attest to their good character, and paying a fee, $25 when I did it, $200 today. The main purpose of being admitted to this bar is to qualify lawyers to bring cases before the Court, which is something that very few lawyers ever do. But the certificates framed on a wall in their offices impresses their clients who don't know how easy it is to get one; and when they visit Washington with their family, they get to sit in the courtroom while the Court is in session, while the family may have to wait outside, perhaps in the Court's public cafeteria downstairs.

My one success in the Supreme Court—a derivative success, at that—came before I'd been admitted in New York for the required years, so everything I submitted to the Court was signed by Edward Q. Carr, the attorney-in-chief of the City's Legal Aid Society, who assigned pro bono cases to young lawyers like me who volunteered to take them.

The case of *Garner v. Pennsylvania* was being handled by my fellow Brooklynite and Dewey Ballantine associate, Joseph Califano. But he was leaving for Washington to work in the Defense Department and begin a distinguished government career that would include becoming, as the *New York Times* put it, Lyndon Johnson's "Deputy President for Domestic Affairs." So Joe handed me the *Garner* case, and I was happy to receive it.

It seems that a young man named Eugene Garner, Jr., boarded a train in Manhattan some years ago, and tried to stick up the dining car enroute to Philadelphia. Police met him at the station, and he agreed to plead guilty to the crimes of assault and attempted armed robbery. Off to prison he went. All without a chance to talk to a lawyer and maybe assert a defense or plead to lesser charges.

The Sixth Amendment to the US Constitution says, "In all criminal prosecutions, the accused shall enjoy the right .... to have the assistance of counsel for his defense." The Fifth Amendment says, "No person shall be deprived of life, liberty, or property, without due process of law...." So isn't it clear that under the Sixth, Garner should have had a lawyer, and under the Fifth, he should not have been deprived of his liberty because "due process of law" obviously includes having the lawyer that the Sixth gave him the right to? On the other hand, how could it be "due process" for an impoverished person without any legal training to face an experienced prosecutor who had all the resources of the state at his command? But up to now, states like Pennsylvania needn't provide lawyers to people like Garner before locking them away. Joe and I hoped that Garner's would be the case by which the Supreme Court corrected this injustice.

Having paid his debt to society in Pennsylvania, Garner incurred one in New York. He and some other guys tried to rob the apartment of one Arthur Murray, who was well-known for running a string of dance studios. As the police were breaking in the front door, the story goes, Garner and his accomplices were throwing their guns out the back window, so he was only guilty of criminal trespass, which was a misdemeanor. But because he had the previous felony conviction, New York law turned his misdemeanor into a felony. Off he went again, this time to the Auburn maximum security prison in western New York to serve thirteen to fourteen years.

But this was the age of the Earl Warren Supreme Court, which was ruling at long last that the Constitution meant what it said about the rights of ordinary people. In 1954, it had given us *Brown v. Board of Education*, which began the painful and still incomplete process of ending of inferior schools for Black students. In 1966, it would give us *Miranda v. Arizona*, which required cops to tell suspects that they have a right to remain silent and request a lawyer. Now in the spring of 1961, Joe Califano was excited about the growing likelihood that the Supreme Court would soon rule that the Six and Fifth Amendments required that everyone charged with a serious crime (a felony) must be offered a lawyer. He and I hoped that the Supreme Court would end these very common and one-sided prosecutions and that *Garner* was the case by which it would do it.

Before the Supreme Court would consider whether to hear a case like Garner's, he had to "exhaust his state remedies." That meant the Pennsylvania courts had to be asked to vacate his first conviction. Fat chance! If miraculously his first felony conviction disappeared, then the New York felony should go back to being a misdemeanor, for which Garner had long since served the maximum, and he should walk free.

Joe had already applied to the court in Philadelphia where Garner was convicted. It denied the application. Now it was up to me to appeal the denial to the Superior Court of Pennsylvania, again in Philadelphia. I wrote the necessary papers and asked a law school classmate named Edwin Daly to move my admission to the Pennsylvania bar *pro hac vice* (for this case only). The DA's office that was opposing me claimed among other things that Garner's conviction happened too long ago to be reconsidered, and Ed particularly liked my response, "The mere passage of time cannot impart due process to a proceeding that lacked it." That was the nub of the case: had Garner had due process?

Back in law school I had argued before moot courts, but Garner's was my first real case, one that would determine whether or not a man spent more of his life in prison. The panel of black-robed judges who faced me was the most hostile I would ever encounter. In the middle of my presentation, one of them said, as best I recall, "Well I'm not going to decide for you," and stood up and disappeared out the door behind him. Arguing against me that day was an assistant district attorney named Arlen Specter, who would go on to become an accomplished Republican Senator. His argument sounded illogical, but that didn't matter given the judges' attitude.

Sure enough, they agreed that Garner's conviction had been fine. And I got nowhere appealing their decision to the discretion of the state's highest court. Those failures made the case ripe for me to petition the U.S. Supreme Court for a *writ of certiorari*—that is, to ask the nation's highest court to review Garner's case.

These petitions flood the Court, which grants very few of them. My firm's senior litigating partner and my ultimate boss, John Wood, groused that if Garner were a paying client, he and we would probably decide that his chance of prevailing in the Supreme Court was so slim that it wasn't worth our time and his money to go there. Undeterred, I drafted the petition, which was, in effect, a legal brief that described the case, explained why it mattered, and argued that due process required the right to counsel at long last to be honored for everyone including Garner.

Unbeknownst to me but not a surprise, a number of other petitioners were bringing the same issue to the Court. One of them, a man named Clarence Earl Gideon, had gone to trial in Florida without an attorney—though he told the judge that he had a Constitutional right to have one—and was convicted of petty larceny. He wrote out his cert. petition in longhand with a pencil and mailed it to the Supreme Court, which granted it and assigned the prominent Washington lawyer Abe Fortas of the prominent firm of Arnold, Porter & Fortas to represent him. Fortas was close to LBJ and would later sit on the Supreme Court and then have to resign from it. The Court let Gideon's case go forward and held Garner's case and the others in abeyance.

On March 18, 1963, the Court handed down the landmark decision of *Clarence E. Gideon v. Louis L. Wainwright, Corrections Director.* It held that in all state and federal felony cases, the defendants needed to be offered a lawyer.* A month later, it sent *Garner* and the other cases back to their respective state courts to be reconsidered in light of this decision.† Not being sure of the steps to take now, I sought help from Milton Adler, who ran the Legal Aid office in the City's shabby Criminal Courts Building, doing vital work for paltry pay. We quickly got Garner's New York felony reduced to a misdemeanor and his sentence reduced to time served.

As best I recall, I met Eugene Garner only once. That was on the day that corrections officers brought him into court and a judge set him free. He and I had been corresponding for the two years it took to bring him there, and out of stoicism or a sense of humor, I supposed,

---

* The June 3, 1966 issue of *Time* reported that the thousand plus prisoners granted early release in Florida alone as result of the *Gideon* decision had slightly more than half the recidivism rate of the prisoners who served their full sentences (13.6% v. 25.4 %). Anthony Lewis wrote an excellent book, *Gideon's Trumpet* (1964), about that case and the story behind it. A TV movie, based on the book and starring Henry Fonda as Gideon, José Ferrer as Abe Fortas, and John Houseman as Chief Justice Earl Warren, aired on CBS in 1980.

† *Garner v. Pennsylvania*, 372 U.S. 768 (April 22, 1963). PER CURIAM (for the Court, unsigned). The motion for leave to proceed in *forma pauperis* and the petition for writ of certiorari are granted. The judgment is vacated and the case is remanded for further consideration in light of Gideon v. Wainwright, 372 U.S. 335.

he ended each of his handwritten letters, "I will await your reply." Now his wait was over.

Nearly certain that the tough-on-crime Pennsylvania authorities resented the Supreme Court's decision and would take it out on Garner if they could, I offered him a parting piece of advice. "Stay out of Pennsylvania." He readily agreed. Yet I asked myself later, in how many states is a middle-aged Black man free from the risk of being unfairly incarcerated—or worse?

Prohibition

The best parts of my years at Dewey Ballantine had not been spent at the firm. By 1965, I'd been working there for more than six years, mostly in litigation, but as mentioned above, I had yet to try a case or even take a deposition. In those days, the major firms talked about volunteering their young lawyers for work *pro bono publico* (for the public good), but at least at Dewey it seldom happened. I finally grasped the nettle and more or less shamed the firm into volunteering me to the Legal Aid Society to represent indigent defendants in Manhattan's Criminal Court. Besides considering this a right thing to do, I craved an immersion in a courtroom, however brief.

Once in that office, I worked with able and underpaid lawyers who instructed me patiently through five weeks that were almost as strange and unsettling as my first weeks in the army. Milton Adler, who had helped me in the *Garner* case, still ran the office. I spoke in court every day and during the last eleven days, tried sixteen misdemeanor cases. No investigation, no preparation, no privacy, just talk for a few minutes to my defendant as he stood in a crowded holding cell behind the courtroom, then try and usually—but not always—lose the case. Due process, anyone? For professional intensity and pleasure, these weeks came second only to my time building cases against law officers who had committed violent crimes during New York's Attica prison riot.

Starting in law school, I had often heard that it's better for ten guilty people to go free than for one innocent person to be imprisoned. During my stint at Legal Aid, though, I began to see that the reality is somewhat the reverse. In New York City where the criminal justice system is chronically understaffed and under constant pressure to pump cases through, I'm guessing that maybe as many as ten percent of the people behind bars were innocent of the crimes that put them there. A problem for the people who might address the problem is that they don't know who they are. Some say dismissively, "Well, if he didn't commit this crime, he's probably gotten away with a bunch of others." A truly shabby excuse for gross injustice.

Back at the firm I was asked to speak about my Legal Aid experience at one of the Wranglers dinners. Many questions, some of them incredulous or hostile, arose out of the cigar smoke and clinking glasses of scotch, and I had the best time on my feet since holding forth in Professor Chayes' procedure class described in "Preparation." Governor Dewey happened to be there that evening—he'd been out of office for ten years but remained "Governor"—and found himself transported back to his days as Manhattan's district attorney, whose present assistant DAs had just been opposing me in Criminal Court. Gesturing with his cigar, he extolled in his studied baritone the joys of handling many criminal cases at one time, and urged other associates to follow my footsteps to the Criminal Courts Building. As I recall, though, few if any of my colleagues tried to do that, and none could be spared from the firm's important cases. I'd also heard since law school that lawyers should donate maybe ten percent of their time to unpaid work in the public interest. Apart from the Governor's remarks at Wranglers, I did not hear it at his firm.

Heroin underlay most of my cases during those five weeks—people arrested for possessing it, selling it, or stealing stuff in order to pay for it. It was almost as though a pipeline ran from Harlem, where most of the arrests occurred, to the Art Deco, seventeen-story, grubby Criminal Courts Building a few blocks north of the Brooklyn Bridge. At the close of every day, an assistant DA would ask a judge to dismiss a number of cases because the defendants had died from overdoses.

During those weeks, I decided that all drugs should be decriminalized. It's a conclusion that I've tested ever since, and it remains the same. The War on Alcohol that began with Prohibition in 1920, failed absurdly, and the nation had the good sense to end it in 1933—thus ending the crime and corruption and zillions of years of pointless prison time that went with it; and thus gaining tax money, quality controls that prevented most accidental deaths, and a welcome element of normalcy to law enforcement. Not that alcohol does not cause major problems. The same logic and human nature, of course, hold for the prohibition of banned recreational drugs, yet the decades of futility continue except for recent decriminalizations of marijuana by some states.

Perhaps the current epidemic of middle class people addicted to, and dying from, prescription opioids—no one is throwing them in the slammer—may nudge good sense in the right direction. If anyone belongs in prison, it's not these opioid users but the executives who peddled the lethal lie that these highly profitable drugs are safe. The mostly Black and Puerto Rican people whom I stood up for so long ago in Criminal Court were no less human and equally as deserving of help, not prison, as any white, suburban housewife who finds herself hooked on oxycodone.

Anachronism

Old Sturbridge Village in central Massachusetts bills itself as a living museum that captures life in rural New England during the 1790s through 1830s. I'm not sure whom I went there with one Saturday when it was too foggy and drizzly to drive to a ski mountain, but I remember well the extent to which that living page from the past captured me.

The house of old lamps showed us that people in those days had more ingenuity than now, maybe because of fewer gadgets. To withstand the seductiveness of the tour as it progressed, we reminded ourselves that we were visiting an idealized version of how it was, with no city worth commuting to, many women dying in childbirth, and we could not have driven the hundred miles this morning that it took us to be here. A youngster pointed out that we'd have been here already when we woke up.

The blacksmith fascinated me. He ran a discrete manufacturing operation in one sooty room, needn't consult a committee in order to make the nails before the horseshoes or vice versa, and had no one else to blame. I sometimes felt fully on my own when I skied on an icy trail in the late afternoon. He must have felt that as a way of life. The air heated my face as he pumped his giant bellows, the raging coals turned his iron white, he hammered it into the shape he wanted, and he saw that it was good. Progress banished him long ago, but had I lived back then, I might well have been hammering white-hot iron into shape.

Adieu

Sometimes Laurie schmoozed on the telephone with her girlfriend when she should have been typing, and sometimes I yelled at her very quietly, but as bosses and secretaries go, we had a good relationship. I showed her some of these little stories, and some that aren't in this book, and asked her to type them. She showed me some of her poetry. Each of us would sometimes have a "Dear Abbey" talk with the other about the ways that love was treating us away from the office, which was the Mermelstein firm. Each of us mentioned that the other was "good"—good secretary, good boss. That fall I landed another job in another part of Manhattan, and it was not in the cards for her to go with me.

As S-for-Separation Day approached, I noticed that she was taking extra long lunch hours or schmoozing extra long on the phone, or generally goofing off when she knew I had rush work that needed doing as I pushed to clear up my backlog before leaving. I wondered whether she was taking advantage of her approaching freedom—until I noticed that I was landing on her harder than usual, which obviously had nothing to do with freedom. It finally occurred to me that each of us was using these little spats to move farther apart and ease the break that neither of us wanted.

On my last day at the office, we had to work late to finish up, and I took her to dinner.

"I don't want you to go," she said as we stood up from the table and hugged each other hard.

We agreed to stay in touch, and met for lunch every month or so. One day the next spring, she said across our table at Hamburg Heaven, "You know, my boyfriend doesn't want me having lunch with you any more."

"You know, I wouldn't want my girlfriend having lunch with some guy like me either."

"But we'll keep in touch."
"We'll keep in touch."

Business

While I was at the Hoffman firm, business took me from a warm October in Manhattan to Regina on the flat prairie of Saskatchewan. The man I came to see told me during the small talk at dinner that the Indian name for Regina was Pile of Bones. The railroad had ended there, and for a while they used to dump buffalo bones at the end of the line.

In the morning, the radio said it was eight degrees outside. I was staying on the fourteenth floor of one of those vertical motels, very modern. Flickering feathers of smoke all leaned the same way on the rooftops below, like a field of wheat in the wind. Standing on the warm side of the glass door to the balcony, I saw a string of geese heading south straight for my corner of the building. The leader wavered as he came on, as though he could not make up his mind which side of it to fly on. He would have been at a safe altitude, of course, if no one had erected this obstacle.

It's pretty late for you to be flying south, Buddy, I said to myself, it's already eight degrees out there. My room was warm, and if my business went bad, there was always unemployment and welfare.

The goose decided to lead his flock past my side of the building in good time to keep from flying into it. As he flapped past, our eyes met. Then he went about his business, and I went about mine.

Commuter

I commuted daily for only twelve years, from mid-1962 until late 1974, though it seemed like a longer segment of my life. Here's how it looked to me then:

I cross two rivers to home, the oily Harem that splits the city slum and the blue Mianus that divides the white towns east of Greenwich. A scow wallows in one, a sailboat rides the other. I read. I sleep. I work beyond the time-sucking tentacles of the telephone. (No email, texting, or cell phone then!) Years pass. When the train runs, I seldom see the wayside bits of scenery that zip past; when it stalls, I learn the configuration of the sharp brown stones on the track bed beneath my window. Every year or so I forget my umbrella in the rack, and an urchin breaks a window near me with a stone—it seldom breaks the inner glass—and I miss the morning train. The platform is empty. The train is gone and someplace else.

In the morning, rain may threaten in Connecticut, but absorbed in the *Times* or a book, I forget to notice whether it has started in the City before we vanish under Park Avenue and I am in the tunnel for another day. A face on the platform becomes familiar and disappears, and I do not notice that it is gone unless it returns long after. The man sitting next to me does not exist unless his leg invades my territory, prompting me to cock my shoe across my knee so that the next jolt may rub the sole against his trousers, and he usually retreats. One evening I ask him if he will chew his gum more quietly so I can sleep. If the train stalls long enough, strangers talk to each other and life becomes ad hoc. If the delay comes inbound at the 125th Street station, only some of us take the short walk through Harlem to the downtown subway.

The train is organized so that all its cars move at once like one long bar. It has two seasons, home in daylight and home in darkness. One night as I walk across the parking lot, an inbound train rushes past. The pantographs atop the cars sing against the wire, a string of explosions flashing blue in the night, as the train hurries up the line towards the rivers and the City, leaving the quiet town behind.

Besides the Law

Carriage

As Kay's first pregnancy progressed, she and I started looking at baby carriages. I favored a blue, white, and green plaid one that was attractive, light, and easy to handle. But that was not to be. Not even to be discussed. Kay and her parents settled on a wide, heavy, navy blue job with chrome mudguards; and her parents bought it for us. It fell to me, of course, to collapse the monster and wrestle it in and out of the trunk of our compact Mercury Comet. I realized much later that the differences between the two carriages reflected deeper differences between Kay and me. Her values were more mainstream American, and mine, closer to the simplicity of the Quaker I would eventually become. Tiny Erin, I'm sure, would have been equally at ease in either carriage.

Contentment

Yellow leaves floated past the glass wall that put me virtually out-of-doors in the soft October afternoon. I ate Tilsit cheese on crackers and drank a glass of beer at the glossy-grained, brown dining table with my forearms in the sun. A power saw blasted faintly in the distance. After lunch I would finish painting the deck on the other side of the huge windows. My little girl slept in her nursery. My wife slept too, a fact that contributed to the idyllic scene, I realized afterwards. Not yet conceived was the son who would never know what it was like to have Daddy living at home. This is contentment, I thought. This is happiness. What can possibly go wrong?

Birth

"Have you ever had Novocain?" the gray-haired obstetrician asked Kay as she lay on the table in the delivery room. She turned her head and smiled wryly at me as I was trying to adjust my mask so as to stop fogging my glasses. A thunderstorm outside the quiet room had delayed the anesthesiologist, who rushed in wearing a brightly colored Hawaiian shirt and did not give Kay enough oxygen at first when he clapped a cup over her nose and mouth to administer a proper anesthetic.

Kay went unconscious and the OB's arms worked between her legs. In a few minutes he said, "It's a boy!"

He lifted from her a wet, purple figure with a glistening white umbilical cord, who cried lustily for someone so new and small. He laid the baby on Kay's stomach and went back to work on her. She began to mumble and saw her son and smiled contentedly.

Afterwards I sat in the lounge with the doctor while the nurses finished cleaning my wife and child. My awe and happiness swept aside any fear of sounding naive to a man who had delivered hundreds if not thousands.

"It really is a miracle," I said.

"Yes," the doctor said. "It really is."

Morning

To help Kay, I thought in the beginning, I got up a couple of nights a week for the two o'clock feeding, first with Erin and three years later with Brian. After mixing the formula, I'd put a Bach mass on the phonograph at low volume and hold my little baby in my arms guiding the bottle to the eager mouth, helped by tiny hands, while bubbles rose in the liquid and a chorus praised God in the stillness of the night.

I burped the baby on a towel over my shoulder, wiped its bottom into pink cleanness, and cautiously pinned on a fresh diaper. So I cared for them as I had been cared for and, God willing, they would care for their own. I returned to sleep and went to the office a few hours later more tired than on other mornings but more at peace.

Vacation

Kay and I lay on the sand and swam in the Nantucket surf and made love after showering together before dinner. Before the movie, we window-shopped in the town and she telephoned the babysitter to make sure the children were all right. We stopped for beer at the

Jared Coffin House and made love again and slept the sleep of the sunburned and satisfied. The endless week disappeared like a pebble dropped into the ocean of time, and our world resumed at home and the commuter platform and office as though it had never ceased. Long afterwards, we recalled the uneventful vacation better than anything else that happened that year.

Divorce

Yellow jackets buzzed about the marmalade as we ate croissants on the little iron balcony outside our bedroom by Lake Lugano under blue mountains hazy in the sun a year after we married. I tried to shoo them away because they frightened her, but they kept buzzing around us. At night we gambled cautiously and danced on the roof of the casino under the mountains and the stars. The song *Volare* tugs me back to that summer in Italy and Switzerland and France.

Now she is gone and perhaps never was. I see the old friend she finally became, for a few minutes on the days I visit the children.

Horizon

"They will know we are Christians by our love, by our love. They will know we are Christians by our love," sang the blue-robed choir in the church's white sanctuary. Sun slanted onto the maroon cushion next to Erin, who was about eight then, and me in the white wooden pew beside the clear window.

"That song's not right, Daddy," she whispered up to me.

"Why not?"

"Because Jewish people love, too."

Two decades later she would convert to Judaism and marry an Israeli—as her childhood observation foreshadowed.

Song

Angel among angels, Erin stood with her little friends, blue-robed with her dark hair brushing her wide white collar in the white choir loft behind the minister. Late from dropping Brian at the church's nursery school, I slipped into an empty pew under the side balcony during the first hymn. Erin was singing less than searching the congregation. Our eyes met, and her face relaxed with a smile. The choir sat, and the minister stood between her and me for the opening prayer. I slid over on the long cushion so I could see her past him.

Since she was born, I had pictured her like this, the few times a year the children's choir came into church. God willing, she would sing in the youth choir and perhaps, if her husband lived nearby, with the adult choir. She yawned and I could not tell her to cover her mouth. During the Second Lesson, I saw her reading the program and felt the same boredom myself; I decided to suggest that she hold it down out of sight the next time. Again we smiled at each other.

The children's choir always left during the hymn before the sermon. Passing through the door, she was already talking with one of her little friend. I looked down to see where we were in the hymn. When I looked up, the door behind the minister had closed. Unexpectedly the bare loft stabbed me with the future. I saw her gone with her own, from her mother's home and my many weekends, never again my little girl except in my heart and, God willing, in hers. Yesterday I held her to be baptized. Tomorrow I would give her hand. The words blurred in the hymnal, and I did not trust my voice until the final amen.

It turned out that during Erin and Brian's high school years, it was he whom I took skiing weekend after weekend in Vermont—he is an accomplished skier to this day, most often in Squaw Valley in the Sierras of California—while she stayed back with her friends. When she married our beloved son-in-law Michael Cohen, both her mother and I gave her hand.

A Day With Brian

Little Brian sat straight up beside me as we drove home from a church fair with the top down in my convertible under trees that filtered sun shafts off his yellow hair. We had slid down a big slide on a burlap bag together and been whirled around together, and Brian had gone on the rides for the little people by himself. Then we had stopped on a bridge and watched the cars coming on the Merritt Parkway underneath. Erin was off at a birthday party.

"This is my big day, Daddy."

"Why?"

"Because I have you all to myself."

Story

Brian and Erin did not seem to like it much when I read to them—I suspected that TV had made them too impatient—but they loved to have me tell them a story. On Fridays after work or Saturday mornings, I would pick them up for the night. By the time they were ready for bed in my apartment, one or the other always asked for a story.

I invented adventures about skiing in Vermont, swimming in the surf, about volcanoes, about distant lands, and a tunnel like the one in Alice in Wonderland that ran between my apartment and their home. Sometimes I could not think of a story when they asked, and sometimes I was too tired and asked them to remind me in the morning. We had a rule that the story could be partly true but not all true. Erin reminded me of the rule when she thought I was sticking to the truth too long, and I reminded her of it when she said that something had not happened the way I was telling it.

I could almost never think up a new adventure in advance even though I knew they would ask for one. My difficulty surprised me because at heart I had only one story to tell them, always the same story. A little girl and a little boy and their daddy went someplace and did something together and were happy.

Faith

My Sunday school student looked up, all sweet and clean like the child she still was within her full-grown body. Her long brown hair lay splayed across the hospital pillow, her blue eyes dilated by medication. Some friends had slipped four tabs of acid into her soda as a joke two months before.

"Tonight's the first time I've talked to anyone this long, you know, coherently."

I smiled and held her hand to go.

"Do you think I'm going to be all right?" she asked, trusting that I had the answer.

"I'm sure of it," I said. "Aren't you?"

She smiled, and I left.

Paperweight

The Crest of Canada, painted in red, gold, and indigo enamel on a field of burnished copper, is certainly beautiful, I thought, as I browsed through the store beneath the workshop where a man named Albert Gilles and his family crafted lovely copper artifacts. The Gilles shop stood beside the highway that ran along the north bank of the St. Lawrence River eastwards from Quebec City. Kay and I had happened on the store by chance a dozen years before on our honeymoon as we were driving to visit the basilica of Sainte Anne de Beaupré and the Mont Sainte Anne ski area. This beautifully colored crest, mounted on a block of white marble, would make an intriguing paperweight, I thought, not touristy, and quite likely to provoke a comment now and then in my office.

I had driven up US Route 7 into Canada as a lad with three young friends a few weeks before starting college, and learned that my three years of high school French were virtually unintelligible to the Quebecois. Later I had come to the Laurentians and Quebec City, still a lad with my young bride Kay. We stayed in a cozy room in the majestic Chateau Frontenac looking down on the broad St. Lawrence and drank a Courvoisier apiece in the bar after dinner. The summer of our divorce, I'd driven alone through the evergreen hills of New Brunswick and around Cape Breton by the sea. Now the end of my second marriage found me again in Quebec, to ski alone on Mont Sainte Anne at the beginning of winter.

Even someone in the office saying "I see you've been to Canada" would raise more ghosts than I cared to encounter in an average hectic workday. Instead of the signature seal, I chose a cryptic copper fleur-de-lis, also mounted on a block of white marble, beneath which my ghosts could rest in peace.

Evaluations

"You're the best," she said afterwards.

I thought about that for a while. She had allowed to having had dozens of others. I decided it was a sweet way of saying she liked me.

Defined

"This is good and we're happy and that's all we need to think about, right? We don't know what's going to happen, so we won't worry about it, right?"

"Right."

One morning she told me she loved me. I saw that she meant it, or maybe I was sufficiently bored by then to let myself be trapped. I explained that I loved her and desired her but was not in love with her.

Thus defined, our affair deteriorated. I became too busy to see her during the week. Against the future we had once denied, she became more friendly with men she encountered casually. I sometimes spoke objectively of the morning I had hurt her. We agreed to stop taking Saturday nights for granted. I finally told her I would always love her. That seemed like as good a way as any to end the romance, though we remained friends afterwards.

Final

Walking along a crowded summer East Side sidewalk, she mentioned matter-of-factly that her husband had remarried that afternoon. In bed after diner, we held each other in our underpants and did not make love. I awoke in the middle of the night and saw a line of light under the bathroom door and heard her sobbing for a long time, but there was nothing I could do. Several years later she married a very decent guy. They stayed married, and I hoped they were happy.

Storm

A towering mass of black clouds threatened on a warm June after-noon when I picked up Vicky Sanders and her children for the an-nul church picnic. Thunder punctuated the din of our four youngsters chattering away in the back seat.

Before today's venture, I had noticed Vicky singing in the choir, and we had talked longer than necessary when she turned up on my call list for the every-member canvass the previous November. This afternoon, though, was the first time we'd done anything together—a sort of first date—I didn't even know how she happened to be single. Our daughters, on the other hand, knew each other well from Sunday school.

As the thunder cascaded closer, Vicky and I debated whether to continue to the picnic at the beach or head straight for the parish hall, which was the venue in case of rain. The venue for the picnic was not my main interest that afternoon and may not have been hers. We continued to roll under the towering gloom.

As I turned into the road to the beach, a few sprinkles on the windshield became a downpour. I drove on looking for a driveway to turn around in, but before we reached one, the rain suddenly stopped, and the pavement down the road ahead was dry. I ventured a decision. "Let's at least see if anyone else is there."

We spotted the white turtleneck of Sam Fogal, the junior minister, in a group of about twenty people among the dark green picnic tables up the hill from the parking lot. The warm breeze was such that we had to set the food baskets on the corners of the tablecloths to hold them down. Eating one of Vicky's delicious deviled eggs, I noticed several patches of water out in the Sound where rain was erasing the line between sea and sky. A squall was roughing a dark path straight towards the beach and us.

"Look there," I said. "We're really going to get it."

"It looks that way, doesn't it?" said Sam's wife, Annabel, continuing to ladle potato salad onto the paper plates.

I mentioned the squall to several other people. "Oh, yes," one or another replied, politely interested but not moved to do anything about it. I started to mobilize Vicky and our children, wondering whether she thought me an alarmist, but I was loath to desert the group until rain splattered the parking lot and the first big drops hit us on the hill. The sacrament of baptism took on a new meaning as I watched this water arouse these people as words, eyesight, and common sense had not. We had to run through a deluge to reach our cars. Vicky carried my son Brian.

Back at the church, Alfred Schwarz, the senior minister, and about thirty more of the congregation greeted us with big smiles as we straggled out of our steamy cars and into the parish hall. There was enough food for everyone. Being in wet clothes soon ceased to matter.

Vicky and I went our separate ways after that afternoon, a fond memory for me and, I hope, for her. But, as anyone who has read the

Old Testament probably knows, human nature does not alter. As to-day's thunderclouds—climate change, over-population, nuclear anni-hilation—loom ever darker, the people who have the power to save us keep on ladling out potato salad and enjoying their deviled eggs, and we keep electing them to not disturb us.

Ride

I had not ridden a horse in twenty years and not often back then. My eight-year-old niece, Brin, flew past me in perfect command. We slowed to a trot, then a walk as the trail grew steeper up the mountain. My brother Tigger told me to relax in the style of the country. "Let your ass move with your horse." The black-haired beauty who rode with us pretended not to hear. Through a break in the trees, I glimpsed a distant cross standing on a spur of the mountain against the sky.

Long before we reached it, the trail turned downwards, coming out on a road beside a country club. "Do you feel like a beer?" Tig asked. We hitched our horses to the rail by a whitewashed gatepost and or-dered three beers and a coke on the empty patio. Several families who belonged to the club splashed in the pool a few yards away, chattering in Spanish. It's nearly always like spring or summer in the central highlands of Costa Rica where Tigger and his family had been living since 1967.

Looking into the suds against the bottom of my glass and feeling somewhat sore where I sat, I imagined that this was a cantina and I packed a six-gun and we had hitched the horses to the rail in a dusty and dangerous street, even as I had lived it as a boy in Brooklyn's movie houses on Saturday afternoons, the child who was father of the man.

We paid for our drinks, mounted up, and galloped back through the finca at the foot of the mountain. A little behind the others, I let out my horse for as long as I dared, the wind rushing past and the trail rushing under. Seldom in my life had reality so nearly touched a dream. All things considered, I preferred reality.

Anne

What can one say about a love that bad luck kills aborning? That perhaps it would not have lasted? True, but the memory of it, frozen in time, has lasted as long as I have.

The winter after Kay and I divorced, a friend at my office asked me to her house in Flatbush to meet Peter Hurkos, the Dutch fortune teller who turned out to be a friend of hers. After suffering a head injury during World War II, Hurkos had famously predicted, among other events, that the Nazis would kill a friend of his unless the friend avoided a certain street corner at a certain hour the next day. The friend paid no heed, and the Nazis nabbed him there and then. A warm, vigorous, intuitive man, Hurkos sat on the floor working my shoe with his hands—I'd hoped the slush from the Brooklyn streets had dried when he asked me to take it off—and told me secrets about Kay that our marriage counselor had missed.

"Who is Anne?" suddenly he asked. "Who is Anne?"

I thought that Hurkos had finally gotten it wrong, or maybe I should pay special attention to the next Anne I met. Wondering later whether Hurkos had had a flash of psychic insight or had simply chosen a common name, it dawned on me who Anne was.

One hot spring afternoon fifteen years earlier, I sat in a stuffy yellow cube of a room high in the YMCA of Birmingham, Alabama, writing the most open letter I'd ever ventured, about the way the army was treating me, my thoughts about *Anna Karenina* which I had nearly finished reading, how was college treating her, and much more—it probably rambled—and mailed six pages to her at Smith College in cool Massachusetts.

Anne had been very popular but too young for my crowd in Brooklyn, until we started turning up at the same parties when I went home on leave the previous Christmas. We talked for hours in her mother's kitchen. For some reason I found the kitchen the best place to get to know a girl. She had the indefinable difference, and she brought out the life in me in a way I liked. One evening, I was able to take her to the Philharmonic in Manhattan to hear Stravinsky conduct Stravinsky. After I returned to Fort McClellan and she to Smith, we began to correspond.

When she had not answered that letter four or five weeks after I mailed it, I began to wonder whether I had opened myself up to her too far. A week later my mother wrote to me, among the news from home, that Anne had complained of headaches, and the ophthalmologist took one look at her and sent her to a surgeon. The operation to remove a large tumor from her brain failed. She had been nineteen and filled with life and beauty.

For years when I thought of her, I wondered whether I had been just a lonely soldier pouring his heart onto little sheets of paper during a solitary weekend pass. Then, sometime after my meeting with Hurkos that slushy winter evening, my father wrote to me about a conversation he'd had with Anne's mother at a dinner party. She said that Anne had told her that of all the boys, I was "the only one she could get sentimental about"—so long ago when she was still nineteen and filled with life and beauty. I smiled with the answer to my long-ago letter in my hand. Would Hurkos have found me happily married, I wondered, but for a chance as unlikely as it was cruel?

Joe Smith from Brooklyn

Joseph Yeardley Smith was my age and grew up on a street called Garden Place a few blocks from my family's home on Grace Court. During his youth he went by Yeardley, pronouncing it Yardley. We both had black hair, grew to medium height, and needed glasses in our teens. We would roller skate or hang out together for brief periods separated by long intervals—always friends, seldom close—until our late twenties, then lost touch.

First recollection: We are five years old, and classmates trap Yeardley under a large wooden box on the flat tile roof of the Grace Church parish house, which serves as the playground for our kindergarten. Two sides of the box consist of well-spaced boards, making it easy to see him inside, as though he were in a jail cell with horizontal bars. Though the box is too heavy for him to lift off, he does not call for help but sits stoically inside, his arms around his drawn-up knees, until a teacher comes along and frees him.

Fast forward: The Hotel Bossert occupies a block of Hicks Street between Montague and Remsen Streets, where it housed the offices of the Brooklyn Dodgers, about two blocks from my home and four from his. I used to get haircuts in it for fifty cents each, and later danced once or twice in the nightclub on its Marine Roof fourteen floors up. One day when Yeardley was roller-skating past, a woman went out a high window. When her body smacked the pavement, he told me, it quivered for a moment and burst open. Quivered for as long as a moment? Years later, I wondered whether the shock and horror had slowed his sense of time.

Now we are sophomores in high school. Along one wall of the lofty gym runs a brown wooden storage closet with a roof that joins the closet to the wall. The roof begins maybe nine feet up and slants so that basket balls landing on it will roll off. One afternoon I see Yeardley standing on the slanted shelf and a bunch of our classmates hurling basketballs up at him. He catches some balls and hurls them back; others bounce off the wall behind him. Gravity is on his side, numbers are on theirs, and the lopsided game is not benign. I climb up beside him. Now it's two against the bunch. Other boys join the attackers. No one else joins Yeardley and me. The fracas ends without injuries. It's the first time I remember joining an underdog.

Yeardley finished his secondary education at the Choate prep school in Connecticut and entered Harvard when I did in 1949. He had dropped Yeardley, and his occasional nickname Skipper, in favor of Joe.

In mid-sophomore year, he quit college, joined the Marines, and barely survived combat in Korea. Once when he was taking shelter inside a culvert, he told me after he was back in college, a Chinese mortar shell exploded on the ground above his head. If that earth had not been frozen, my account of him would end right here. (In "Wonderful," soft earth saved me; here hard earth saved Joe.) Finishing college in 1958, the same year I finished law school, he returned to Brooklyn Heights about when my wife and I took an apartment there. He'd pay us visits in the evening and talk with me long after she had gone to bed. Sometimes he'd say, "I've stayed too long and drunk too much." Here are two of the stories he told me during those evenings:

The first: After he was back at Harvard, he found himself in a privileged group at an exclusive luncheon and happened to be sitting next to an eminent professor of humanities. "Isn't it nice," the professor told the group, "that we are all here together, and nobody has to sit next to some Joe Smith from Brooklyn."

The other story: He was dating a Radcliffe student I'll call Joanna when he found himself being aced out by John F. Kennedy. The Senator's black limousine would pull up in front of Moors Hall, which was her dormitory, and whisk her away. (She has reportedly acknowledged that her affair with JFK continued after he became President.) Kennedy's cheating on his wife was not my business, but doing it at my friend's expense gave me a low opinion of him that never rose—except that I remain grateful that he was President, not Reagan or Bush-Cheney or hawkish Hillary Clinton, during the 1962 Cuban Missile Crisis.

Joe told me too, I don't recall when, that if whalers found a male and female together, they would harpoon the female first because the male would stick around and try to help her, making it easy to harpoon him next. But if they harpooned him first, she'd disappear. We both found this survival instinct significant.

After those evenings, Joe and I went in separate directions, and I never saw him again. But I kept track of him from time to time.

He became a foreign correspondent for United Press International, serving in Moscow, London, and Warsaw. Later he joined the staff of the *Washington Post* and became their first official obituary writer. Along the way, he rode horses, hunted foxes, and with the help of Alcoholics Anonymous, pulled himself out of an alcoholic nightmare. "The occasion for obituaries is death, which is sad," he wrote. "But the subject of obituaries is life itself, which is wonderful."

He also wrote, "Denying painful memories is to deny part of the life itself." This truth resonates with me because much of what I write about —the US role in mass torture and murder in Latin American; the deadly race riot by the police at the Attica prison—is painful. It is also essential to seeing our great nation as it is. When people avoid or ignore such events, how complete is their understanding of life?

When lung cancer took Joe at the age of seventy-four, his own obituary said that the obits he had written for the *Post* were "occasionally controversial but always honest." That was the Joe Smith I knew in Brooklyn.

Watkins Glen

For me, the legendary 1969 Woodstock Music Festival on Max Yasgur's farm in rural New York crowned the 1960s' youth breakout that, for better or worse, shed many of the constraints that I had grown up under. I loved the Woodstock music, played the albums often enough, and enjoyed the movie. A good part of me was sorry I hadn't been there in spite of the rain, mud, and chaos.

Lo, in July 1973 came another festival and another chance, this time at Watkins Glen in western New York, with fewer performers but what performers! The Allman Brothers, the Band, and the Grateful Dead! I drove there with Erin, who was eleven then, and James and Megan, who were alums of my senior high Sunday school class and had become a couple. Brian, who was eight, asked me to tell people that he "wished to go but did not." I hope I made it up to him later with rock concerts, stock car races, and ski weekends—all three of which still ranked among his pleasures as he entered his sixties.

Early on the warm, sunny Friday that the festival began, we loaded up my Chevy hatchback and made the long drive west. As we neared the site, the thickening traffic looked misplaced on the farmland; and after increasingly tedious delays on the road, we were directed to park in a grassy field that was rapidly filling with cars. From there it was a fair hike with our food, water, and equipment to the vast meadow where the audience was gathering. If the musicians' stage marked home plate, the plot of grass we stopped at was on the third base line; but so dense was the crowd that our space was nearly a hundred yards from the musicians. A reassuringly long line of dark green porta-potties stood on our right well into foul territory.

James and Megan erected their small tent, and we arranged the cartons of bottled water and other stuff in a semicircle around its front flaps to create a tiny island in the sea of people who were flooding over the grass around us and behind us. Distance made the figures setting up equipment on the stage look small, but sets of speakers mounted on poles across the meadow two hundred, four hundred, and six hundred feet from the stage would bring us the music as loud as it needed to be. The equipment was programmed so that all the folks would hear the music at roughly the same time, no matter how far back they were in the meadow.

"Wall-to-wall people" became a common phrase. Eventually so many sat or lay on the ground that it would take us fifteen minutes of stepping around, over, and sometimes on bodies and possessions to traverse the fifty feet to one of the busy and increasingly disgusting porta-potties, and much longer for Erin and me to reach the rear of the crowd on our way to the hatchback to sleep on its flat rear floor later on. As daylight faded, red and blue lights bathed the stage; and plentiful floodlights washed the path to the car in a pale blue glow. The festival's promoters had learned well from the chaos at Woodstock.

This crowd, we were told, reached 600,000; varying reports had put Woodstock's at 300,000 to 500,000. More people attended this festival than lived then in Atlanta, Denver, Cincinnati, Minneapolis, or Seattle; some historians would call us the largest crowd in US history. The event was called "Summer Jam" for the music on offer, and the name surely fit the crowd, not to mention the traffic coming and leaving. Most of the people I saw were older than Erin and quite a bit younger than I. Many wore the tie-dyed shirts and so-called psychedelic colors that hippies had made popular. Some drank, but marijuana was by far the drug of choice.

After Woodstock, New York State in its wisdom had decreed that a music festival could last no longer than one day. Bummer! But the musicians coped with the absurdity by treating us to a "rehearsal" on Friday that lasted from mid-afternoon until midnight. The next morning grew hotter and hotter, while Erin played cards with some of our neighbors. About noon the music began and continued, with a long break during a drenching, refreshing afternoon thunderstorm, until 3:00 a.m. Sensibly, I thought, Erin and I made the trek to the car around midnight. As we trudged along the back of the huge meadow, we saw several guys pushing over, one after another, a row of ancient wooden outhouses. "Is anyone in there?" I shouted. "We don't know," they shouted back. The music followed us over the trees and fields and tucked us into our sleeping bags.

Being surrounded by an unbroken carpet of people in all directions vaguely oppressed us and even frightened us a bit—probably James the most and Megan the least. On Saturday morning, James had tried to escape it all by sitting inside the tent, until a young man tripped over one of the ropes, pulling a peg out of the ground and collapsing the canvas on top of him. He freaked out, screaming and thrashing.

"Take it easy," Megan said. "There's nothing you can do about it. Why don't we go for a little walk?"

"Where the fuck can we walk," he shouted, "with all these fucking people?"

"Calm down, take it easy, it's going to be all right," the man who had tripped said soothingly.

"Hey, I'll put the peg back every time someone pulls it out," another stranger assured him.

Later on, Megan did some weed, prompting a guy camped next to us to ask her in awe, "You smoke pot in front of your father?"

"He isn't my father," she replied, "he's my Sunday school teacher."

Throughout the weekend, the huge crowd freely shared their food, water, territory, and drugs. Grand as the music was, I came to see it as less the main event than the catalyst for all these people to flow together in a mighty tide and share their lives, openly and briefly, before subsiding back into their separate worlds—a grand affirmation that people are good. (Today I would say mostly good.)

Before we left, I was talking with one of the local cops—"rappin' with the fuzz," as Arlo Guthrie had put it at Woodstock. She told me that these 600,000 marijuana smokers had given her and her fellow officers far less trouble than they usually had with the 100,000 beer drinkers who gathered for the Watkins Glen auto races. The drinkers tended to fight, she said, but this crowd didn't; and most of the weekend's injuries came from accidents like people falling off cars or cutting their bare feet.

During the long drive home, the radio played the Pink Floyd's recent *Dark Side of the Moon* album, a perfect complement to the sounds of the North American rock that had rolled over us during the past two days. We also heard a preacher decry the "drugs and fornication and sex outside of marriage" that he imagined at the festival. He particularly condemned the attendees for "doing their own thing."

Later, my church asked me to describe the adventure in its Laity

Sunday sermon so the congregation could hear about the adventure. While most of the congregation seemed to enjoy my remarks, several people criticized me for going and for taking Erin. A woman of twenty-two made bold to say that I should act my age; and others doubted the wisdom of letting Erin see all those people smoking pot. I thought it was good for her to see how easily I had said no to all the joints and pipes that people generously offered us. Erin was sure to see plenty of marijuana in high school, and I wanted her to know that she had a choice about smoking it and need never feel she had to.

Two months after the festival, I traveled again to western New York, this time as a State prosecutor to visit the Attica prison as part of my introduction to the crimes that rioting inmates and law officers committed there two years earlier. At Watkins Glen, though, I had happily joined the fellowship of that huge, mellow mass of humanity and enjoyed life under the sun and rain and stars.

Surprises

"Why do you refer to yourselves as men but call us women 'girls?'" demanded a formidable feminist named Janis. We were standing in the kitchen of the house where twenty or so women and men, all members of the local Parents without Partners, were taking a break during a discussion that I was moderating. Janis had backed me against the refrigerator.

Though this was in the gold-plated panhandle of Connecticut, PWP people were pleasingly diverse. They held these discussions in members' living rooms several evenings a month. Some typical topics, and the wisdom of us single parents who pondered them: Does communal living really work? Only if each adult has a private bedroom. When your child is home from college, is it okay for her boyfriend to share her bedroom? It's your home; your rules govern. How do you persuade a bank to lend to a single mother? Several women related their difficulties, which we then worked to remove. Is it a good idea to have sex on the third date? It depends.

Though I had been a moderator of these discussions for several months, Janis's question was the first time that a feminist had confronted me. I paused, considered, and saw that she was right. My consciousness raised slightly, I called women 'women' when the discussion resumed.

As Janis and I were talking later, she surprised me by saying that she had invited several women to her home the next morning to take off their clothes and squat over a mirror that would be lying on the floor. "Most women," she informed me, "have no idea what they look like down there." Who knew?

Since I found her attractive, and I guess she didn't find my male chauvinism excessive, we started dating. One afternoon several weeks into the affair, we stopped at a local a bar; and she surprised me again by smiling, chatting, and laughing with the guy who was sitting on the stool on the other side of me, not across our glasses of beer on the counter, but literally behind my back. Did she realize or care that she was putting me down and pissing me off? I would not have done this to her or any other woman I was with. I said nothing.

This was the early '70's, and some feminists were proclaiming that since all men screw around, it's fine for a woman to screw around too, especially since she alone owns her body. But all men do not screw around, and I was one who didn't. When I became even halfway involved with a woman, I remained faithful. That meant passing up desirable opportunities, which was a price I willingly paid. I did not know whether Janis saw the guy in the bar afterwards, but I knew she was not for me.

She wept quietly in her living room a few afternoons later when I told her that I was going to stop seeing her because I was looking for a woman I could marry. This time I surprised myself. I had thought vaguely about remarriage, but by saying it to her, I articulated it to myself and began my quest. It would take nine years and a good number of relationships to find the right woman, but find her I did.

Not seeing Janis did not end my encounters with feminists. This was a period of transition. Some women expected me to open the car door for them; others wanted to do it themselves; so I'd ask each new friend which she preferred. I didn't see why I was expected lower the toilet seat in a unisex john when the next user would as likely be a man as a woman, but I usually lowered it. I didn't blame women for calling God She after millennia of being assured that God was a He, but it irritated me to hear some man stress She as if to say, "I'm enlightened, so you listen up." It finally struck me as being sexist to call God either He or She, so I took to repeating God. But correct speech has limits, and I didn't notice any push to stop calling the Devil he.

On the day that Janis and I broke up, I did not mention her flirtation in the bar, but I expect she figured it out. We remained friends; and when I needed work a few years later, she hired me to be her counselor in a personal matter.

Nightbird

Who among us remembers the pleasingly mellow voice of Alison Steele, who called herself the Nightbird? She purveyed progressive and popular rock music and dared to read poetry on New York City's WNEW-FM during my single-parent and Attica periods in the 1970s. Among the groups she favored were Renaissance, Genesis, Santana, the Grateful Dead, the Moody Blues, and various counterculture artists. She became a leading disc jockey in a field dominated by men, was a member of the Rock and Roll Hall of Fame, and in 1976, became the first woman to receive *Billboard Magazine's* "FM Personality of the Year" award. For a time, she hosted a syndicated show on six hundred radio stations across the country. Jimi Hendrix wrote a song to her that he called "Night Bird Flying." She once said that she would adopt the Pink Floyd's "Us and Them" from their 1973 *Dark Side of the Moon* album as her theme if it weren't so long. I think I remember her saying this because that rich, relaxed music fit so snugly into the mood she often put me in.

Her work in radio and television included producing, writing, and doing voice-overs for commercials. She served on the board of a local epilepsy foundation and raised money for cerebral palsy and muscular dystrophy charities and the Humane Society. She was born in Brooklyn in 1937, had a husband for a time, and bore a daughter. She would chat on the phone with late night callers and at times brought her French poodle into the studio. Stomach cancer took her at the age of fifty-eight.

I did not know what she looked like. She was not my muse; and though sometimes lonely, I never had a crush on her. But she brought me, and a great many other people I'm sure, tranquility at the end of days that often lacked it.

Work in Progress

One of my happiest activities during the single parent years was attending the writers' workshop that a woman name Charlotte Hoffman generously hosted every second Tuesday evening in her cozy apartment in Stamford and later in Ridgefield. Half a dozen or so of us aspiring writers would take turns reading from our work and absorbing the group's critiques. I took careful notes because I tended to reject criticisms at first but realize by the next morning that many of them were on target or at least flagged problems that need my attention.

Suggestions, especially by longtime workshop members Agnes Haviland, Larry Hansen, and Charlotte herself, improved my efforts considerably. Carolyn Meyer, who attended for a time, became a successful author of novels for children and young adult. Edward Packard, once a fellow associate at Dewey Ballantine, tried out his *Choose Your Own Adventure* books at the workshop and went on to publish more than fifty of them. I would read aloud sections of *The Turkey Shoot*, which relates my Attica adventure, and their comments proved very helpful. After I met Nancy and she became my main editor, I still sought the workshop's advice.

Apart from *Turkey Shoot*, did I dare try a novel on the workshop? If not now, when? Back in high school, that's what I had wanted to write, though the esteemed Dr. Kastendieck (See "Teacher.") told me I might do better with non-fiction. His suggestion fit with my doubt that even though I had read many good to great novels and several books on psychology from the Brooklyn Public Library, I didn't understand enough about people's minds to enable me to write insightful novels—and a novel without insights is merely entertainment. My doubts would grow stronger when I'd get home from a party and have to ask my wife what had really happened among the people there that evening. I did take two short story-writing courses in college. John Updike was in one of them. I don't recall anything he wrote for it, but he had a talent for cartooning people with a pencil and sketch pad. At Charlotte's workshop, I put aside my doubts and, with their input, wrote a long novel.

Sexual mores were in flux then in the media and among the people I socialized with; and it seemed to me that many purported experts, in their haste to advise their clients that "open relationships" were okay, were giving sexual jealousy short shrift. So I decided to write a novel that would transpose the legend of the Flying Dutchman to exurban Darien, Connecticut, by telling the story of a man who believed that his wife has cuckolded him, and what happened next.

I had been struck by the mini-story that novelist John O'Hara used as an epigraph in his masterpiece, *Appointment in Samarra.** In it, a servant who thinks he sees Death give him a threatening look in Bagdad flees to Samarra, so she won't find him. Later his master asks Death why she threatened him. "It wasn't a threat," she says, "but a look of surprise at seeing him in Bagdad, for I have an appointment with him tonight in Samarra."

Deciding to use the same device, I found several versions of the legend of the Flying Dutchman. The one in Wagner's opera *Der fliegende Holländer* didn't fit my plot, but I was able to blend the others to foreshadow what happens in the book:

> A captain home from the sea judged his wife unfaithful and smote her in his rage. Now he stands condemned to sail forever, without rudder or helmsman, never to reach snug harbor. When your ships pass close, you may see him on the quarterdeck playing dice with the Devil for his soul.

In O'Hara's epigraph, the servant's fate is sealed, and the only question is where he will meet Death. Mine, though, does not disclose whether the smiting is figurative or literal, or whether the wife survives it; and my Dutchman has a chance, however remote, to win the dice game with the Devil and escape the curse. While working out the plot, I went back and forth on whether he succeeds.

My Dutchman, Bill Hague, is a young lawyer married to attractive, somewhat aloof Senta. He commutes to work in Manhattan, as I did then, and they live in a house that Kay and I had considered buying in upscale Darien before we settled on our home in heterogeneous Nor-

---

* O'Hara borrowed his epigraph from British writer Somerset Maugham, who had adapted it from an ancient tale.

walk next door. Bill is not me, and the two women on whom I modeled Senta are very different from Kay, though I borrowed heavily on Kay's background and mine in creating Senta's and Bill's. A few years of work and workshop evenings produced four hundred and fifteen double-spaced pages. But it was a busy time in my life. I did not try to polish or sell my *Flying Dutchman*, but simply put it away for later.

Later has become now or never. After several decades of not opening the manuscript, I recently read it through. While it needs work, I found it better than I'd expected, particularly the plot twists. The characters seem true. I'll see what I can do with it if time permits.

Mind Games

Erika was one of my most intelligent and playful single-parent friends. Her German and Jewish heritages, I supposed, explained why it amused her that "It's very nice" was the highest praise that my Anglo-Irishness permitted me to bestow. Did a lawyer named Howard Squadron, she wondered, deserve a plural verb? It amused her, too, that I would heat the water for tea in a frying pan; she called it "frying the water." Two more workings of her mind stand out among my very nice memories of her:

One warmish March afternoon, Brian and I were cruising down the slopes of the Killington ski complex and she was reading a book in the base lodge maybe a mile away when a patch of corn snow wrenched one of my skis in an impossible direction. Pain exploded through me like a flashbulb going off as I fell, my right fibula broken. I cooled my butt in the mush until a ski patroller carted me off on a tin sled. At the moment the pain exploded, Erika stopped reading in the warm base lodge and said to herself, "Oh, oh! Malcolm's in trouble." So much for the myth that extrasensory perception never occurs.

So ardent was Erika's feminism that she insisted that if girls were raised exactly as boys are, then as many women as men would be playing major league baseball. I argued to the contrary, while her brother Heinz, who was a New York State judge, withheld his opinion. The fervor of her belief in the untenable surprised me, but recalling it decades later makes it a bit easier for me than perhaps for many others to comprehend the fervor that millions of citizens maintain for, say, an ignorant and vengeful politician. Ideology can trump sense in even the smartest of us.

The Sea

Joseph Conrad prepared me to have great thoughts while staring over the rail of a ship; but when the big day came—when I shipped from Staten Island, NYC, to Bremerhaven, Germany, aboard the *USNS Upshur* in 1954—I turned my back on the few soldiers who were lounging topside, and an endless green meadow called the Atlantic bored me silly and frightened me at how easy it would be to slip over the side into eternity. Maybe that was one of the great thoughts that Conrad had in mind.

Returning me stateside the next year, the same troop ship bore a thousand GIs out of Bremerhaven harbor onto a stormy North Sea. I stood at the rail because I wanted to, downwind from a man who was standing there because he had to. On instinct, I ducked as his breakfast flew over my head and splashed on the deck a few yards beyond. After the sea had sickened about half the men, a loudspeaker boomed for the cleanup squads to report for duty because "an unsanitary condition" existed.

My next time at sea came three years later when Kay and I took a freighter to Europe because for once in our lives we had time to spare. In New York harbor the crew spotted a dead man in the water. He stood upright, the top of his bald purple head bobbing in and out of the water. It troubled me that he did not lift his face for air. We named him Hugo and never learned how or why he died.

One evening after we had steamed for several days, I saw the lights of Cape Race in Newfoundland far across the water, and I thought about that promontory leading its lonely life out there in the North Atlantic. A day later a storm blew the waves higher than the rail and moved me deeply with their dark green majesty.

Kay and I ate in the officers' mess at a table with a priest who drank Four Roses by the pint and talked with me about the state of the Church and his disagreements with the Holy Father long after Kay had retired to the small cabin where we lived happily together. She wrote a note that we corked in an empty champagne bottle from the bon voyage party at the dock and threw over the side. The next winter a letter arrived from a man who found it on a beach in Ireland at Christmastime. He wrote that the sea had not gotten in but the few remaining drops of champagne had blurred part of her message.

When I was five, my parents took me to Ship Bottom on the Jersey shore, and I dug tunnels where the waves at high tide made a step in the sand, and I fretted because I could not remember the time they said they had brought me here at my first birthday. As a boy I dove through the high surf at West Hampton, Long Island, and lay in bed at night frightened by visions of the dark, white-fringed water curling above me, and the next day reveled in it again. When I grew bigger, I loved to let the surf break on the back of my neck.

Now I sit alone on the beach and watch my children play in the surf, which sounds like it sounded when I was like them.

Wind

When I was eleven, I lay on my back on the lawn beside the family cottage in Connecticut, and the summer wind swishing through the maples overhead made me think I was going out of my mind. What is it saying? Why won't it cease? When I was thirty, I skied into the wind at eighteen below zero and loved it, but my face grew stiff. The month I turned forty, I sat one evening on a white porch in Edgartown on the island of Martha's Vineyard and listened to people passing on the other side of the hedge and the summer wind soughing through the elms above. A bell across town chimed the hour. Who knows the hour?

Bob Dylan assured us that the answers to several large questions were blowin' in the wind. I guess he meant that the answers vanished before we learned what they were.

I pushed my fingers through the hair that covered my skull. The bare masts of sailboats rocked in the lights of the harbor. One night two summers earlier, a young woman had drowned inside a car off nearby Chappaquiddick Island, and the man who said he tried to save her slept on their secret a few houses down the street. Strange men tried to solve something by dispatching bullets into the skulls of his brothers, and much of the nation wept and wondered.

Below the bell that tolled the hour, a slab of metal fastened to a large stone bore the names of men, mostly young I suppose, who had gone to battle across the oceans and not returned. I caught fragments of today from people passing on the brick sidewalk beside the trim old white houses beneath the elms. If they heard the wind, they did not seem to notice the question I felt it sigh: Does God speak, or nothing?

Sunrise, Sunset

"Do you believe in God?" I asked a well-recommended psychiatrist in Stamford in January of 1967. We would not, I felt, understand each other if he did not. He said he did, scotching my last evasion, and I told him the dilemma that brought me to his office: "I cannot live with my wife, I cannot leave my children, and I will not have affairs all my life."

Kay and I had started seeing a marriage counselor well before Erin was born, and we decided to have children only because we felt the counseling had succeeded. The success was a longed-for illusion. Though I had married for life, the possibility of divorce finally entered my mind after Brian was conceived but before he was born. Now Erin was four and he was one. Tension permeated our home, and the kids often saw us clash.

A French couple we knew about had preserved their marriage, more for their church than their children, but loved other people in other bedrooms. We refused to live like that or expose our children to the home and example that such a lifestyle creates. The psychiatrist and I talked once a week for several months, and I reconciled to the answer that seemed least harmful for Erin, Brian, Kay, and me.

We accepted the order of the day that the wife got custody, and our divorce was so "friendly" that we shared the same lawyer, an old friend from law school. He warned us to expect that I would drift away from the children. "Unlikely as it seems now," he said, "it usually happens. "Fathers who move out lose touch. They acquire new interests and maybe new children."

One day in May day shortly after Erin turned five, I sat in my chair at the dining table, put my arm around her slender waist as she stood beside me, and explained as best I could that I was leaving home.

Her quiet response pierced my heart: "I was happier before you told me."

Since lively little Brian was not quite two, there wasn't much I could tell him.

On June 4, 1967, I backed my car down the driveway of the house that was no longer my home, taking the clothes I'd need for a week of commuting to the office, a few personal things, and a finger painting of a big, droll, orange bunny that Erin had made for me. Backing down the driveway that warm, sunny Sunday was the hardest thing I had ever done.

Not that I left my children except geographically. I backed down that driveway hundreds more times during the next nine years, and another driveway starting in 1976 after Kay remarried and moved to nearby Wilton. I saw Erin and Brian every week or so, usually keeping them for a night or two in one apartment or another, or in my new home in Stamford until that brief marriage ended. Plus the wonderful and so inadequate phone calls.

In spite of the lawyer's warning, I never believed I would lose touch with my children, and I didn't. Some years later, he said he was telling his matrimonial clients about Kay and me as a case where the father did not drift away. Business sent me across the Continent fairly often then, and I have flown to Europe and Central America and Israel, but the longest trips I've taken were backing down the driveway after being with my children.

Though most of the times with Erin and Brian have vanished with the faded leaves of those many autumns, some come to mind: Pushing a cart up the aisles at the Stop & Shop with Erin walking beside me and Brian in the cart's basket until he grew too big. Them showing me what they'd made in school. Walking places with them. Climbing through the fresh-smelling frames of half-built houses and taking care not to fall into the basements. Playing along the snow-fringed beach in winter. Meeting their friends. Visiting their schools on Parents' Day. Going around with Erin, then both of them, then Brian on Halloween and stopping for a brief visit and maybe a drink with the old neighbors. Choosing the pizza place for supper. Talking things over. Making up their beds in one apartment or another. Taking them to Sunday school in our good clothes and sitting beside them in church. Studying the evolution of their furniture and the stuff they fastened onto the walls of their rooms. Fights and unintended slights and squabbles and tears. Christmas eves but Kay had them Christmas mornings. On New Year's Days we would sit in some cocktail lounge and discuss our New Year's resolutions. Climbing through the autumn woods as I kept up a tradition, which Kay and I had barely started, of driving them somewhere to the north on Columbus Day weekend. One October several years after the divorce, the four of us drove to Vermont, had dinner at the Jolly Butcher's, and shared a motel room in Brattleboro, a family having fun again for a weekend.

Several trips to Martha's Vineyard and one around Cape Breton Island and the Gaspé Peninsula. Snagging the Frisbee after it landed on the motel roof up the lawn from St. Patrick's Channel. Spending a night in the only room I could afford high in Quebec City's Chateau Frontenac—Kay and I had had a better room in that hotel during two or three days of our honeymoon—and listening to the music of some Beatles imitators in a courtyard far below. Skiing on one mountain or another in frosty sunlight. Walking around Williamsburg and Washington after Brian broke his leg skiing on Vermont's Okemo Mountain. Driving them to St. Louis for the wedding of my former Sunday school student and lifelong friend James Lumsden, and stopping off at Kent State in Ohio to visit another former student, Biff Fenn, who once said he was going to marry Erin. Rock concerts in Manhattan's Central Park. Dropping off to sleep one by one, as we'd sit on the couch my living room watching "Saturday Night Live." The graduations. Drives to and from JFK or Newark Airport. And on and on as they grew and stopped growing and moved away.

I hope I would have spent such times with them if our home had stayed whole, though I've seen many fathers—and you probably have too—who take their kids for granted or are too busy or easily annoyed to try. I did what I could not to be like the dad in Harry Chapin's painful 1974 classic, "Cat's in the Cradle". Wanting to stay close to Erin and Brian in both senses is why I turned down an enticing law job in Washington, DC, and I remained ever thankful that Kay did not move away. This was little enough for her and me to offer them, considering what we had taken from them. I don't know much about quality time but a great deal about precious times.

Some wounds never heal, they just submerge. Not living with Erin and Brian during the years they were growing up remained my deepest sorrow for most of my life. "Kiss me goodnight, Daddy." "Daddy, tuck me in." In 1970, a gentle folk-rock group called the Sandpipers had a hit song called "Come Saturday Morning," The words say that Saturday morning is when I'm going away with my friend. The ending says that we'll remember our time together long after Saturday's gone. I could not hear that song back then without weeping. I still can't. Same with reading these words. There were so many Friday evenings or Saturday mornings when I'd drive to the house I used to live in and go away with my children so very briefly.

Yet I pity the fathers who spare themselves. I would not have missed those visits, close to a thousand over the years, for anything. My times with Brian and Erin were like the afternoons of September, mostly sparkling warm, now and then stormy, or a penetrating drizzle; and all but a few were treasures.

Erin lives in London now and Brian in San Francisco. We phone each other or FaceTime at least weekly and visited at least once or twice a year—until the Covid pandemic. Our times together feel much the same, I think, as if we had remained a family. Which we always were in the ways that matter most. The orange bunny has been there for me on all my many bedroom walls since June 4, 1967. Beside it hangs a large blue, white, and brown painting that Brian made of an afternoon when he was six and I handed him the wheel of a whaler I'd rented on Martha's Vineyard and he drove Erin and me in loops and zigzags around the bay outside Edgartown, the foam flying.

Erin and the ANC

It all began when Erin, who had started college at New York University (NYU), decided to take her junior year at the London School of Economics (LSE), and I drove her to Newark Airport for a tearful farewell on a summer day in 1982. Actually, her choice was fine with me. I would miss her of course—especially since my current consulting job wasn't far from NYU and it sometimes allowed me to have lunch or attend a lecture with her—but it was what she wanted, it would enrich her life and cost no more, including the air fares, than

NYU. And it would be for only one school year. Right?

London enchanted her. She didn't know anybody when she arrived, but that changed. She managed to stay on and graduate from the LSE. Then she went into a clothes-making business with a friend. The quality of their products was high—I still have the navy-blue, wool jacket with a dark purple lining and Bell-Ferguson label that she made me—but the market depended as much on connections as quality, and they didn't sell many clothes. I can still see her schlepping a backload of their wares to Bergdorf's and Bendel's on Fifth Avenue, and goodness knows what efforts she made to sell them in London. So she became a bartender at Fred's Club, known by some as "one of the defining drinkeries of the 80s." I spent a delightful evening there as she poured and I drank shot after shot of differently flavored iced schnapps. In spite of modest British tipping, she made more money than she had before. But it was a job without a future.

Now it's the summer of 1990. The Berlin wall fell last year, and the nations of eastern Europe have been shedding the Communist yoke. Erin is twenty-eight and studying at the highly regarded London Business School (LBS), whose modest motto is "To have a profound impact on the way the world does business." He boyfriend is a very likable young man named Tom Astor, whose father David Astor has been the editor of the influential British newspaper *The Observer.* David has considerable wealth and his own influence and uses them for good purposes, one of which has been to help the African National Congress (ANC) in its struggle against cruel, racist apartheid in South Africa. He has visited South Africa several times and knows a number of the top ANC people. Their longtime leader Nelson Mandela was a frequent guest at his family home in London before the Afrikaner government sent Mandela to prison for twenty-seven years.

This February it released him, and it is clear that the ANC will be taking over the South African government. But it is also clear that the distorted capitalist system that its members have been living and sometimes violently dying under has given them no opportunity to learn the workings of a sound market economy. That's what they want for South Africa, but the only system they know about is the now-failing Communism that the Soviets had had the wit to teach a number of them in Moscow. This concerns many people in the West including David and Erin. What, if anything, can be done?

Erin is taking a course in economics at the LBS with a young assistant professor named Dr. Stefan Szymanski. She has the fateful inspiration to bring him the concern about the ANC. He, Erin, and David get together and discuss the possibilities. And so, twenty-five or thirty top ANC people, including their leader-in-exile Oliver Tambo though not Mandela, come to the LBS for an intensive, week-long course on the basics of how a capitalist market economy actually works.

Afterwards, Erin marries her business school classmate Michael Cohen, an Israeli with whom I feel more affinity than I did with Tom. When the ANC wins the next election and takes over the government, its approach to the economy for the millions of newly liberated Blacks of South Africa, not to mention the white minority, is surely the better for the week of practical learning that Erin sparked, David and Stefan arranged, and the ANC leaders attended.

Flights of Fancy

Where does time go? The Earth circles the Sun, and a year has gone. Where to?

Earth and Moon swing round each other as both swing round the Sun. Ménage à trois at the hoedown of the spheres.

I happened to be drifting across the sky one morning when I beheld an ancient biplane with twin tails and an open cockpit. Goggles, a leather helmet, and a white mustache encased the pilot's head. The plane did not appear to be moving, and I wondered how it managed to stay aloft. Drawing closer, I saw that the propeller was the hands of a large clock.

"What is your destination?" I shouted above the ticking of the engine.

"The future," the pilot replied.

Prosecutor

Attica

Writing in the Rochester *Democrat & Chronicle* on September 13, 2024, the fifty-third anniversary of the bloody 1971 Attica Prison riot, veteran investigative reporter Gary Craig called the tragedy "a seminal experience" in [lawyer Malcolm Bell's] life." It certainly was.

I related the events that comprised the experience at length in my book *The Attica Turkey Shoot*,* and given their effect on me, it seems fitting to include a much-shortened version in this memoir. The focus in the book is on the events, and their effect on me is secondary. In this story, it's vice versa.

At the time, I heard about the massacre on the news—one more tragedy, and on to the next—and didn't think much about it until a few years later when it changed my life. By then, I had grown disenchanted with civil lawsuits, which mostly amounted to ritualized struggles over other people's money. Of all my work till then, the criminal cases had given me the keenest sense of purpose, not to mention the most pleasure, starting with the *Garner* case (see "Gideon"). So I decided to try criminal law. Better fairly well into in my career than never to find out.

Answering a blind ad for prosecutors—a job that could teach me to how become a defense lawyer—I soon became part of the special prosecutor's office that then-Governor Nelson Rockefeller had directed to focus on crimes that arose out of the bloody uprising. Inmates had killed four people and seriously injured several dozen more. Retaking the prison after four days of negotiations, the police killed 39 people, ten of them hostages, and shot 89 others, mostly without justification. The inmates had knives and clubs, but no guns. After they

---

* *The Turkey Shoot: Tracking the Attica Cover-up* (Grove Press, 1985); revised and updated edition retitled *The Attica Turkey Shoot: Carnage, Cover-up, and the Pursuit of Justice* (Skyhorse Publishing, 2017, paperback, 2022). I use the book's wording several times herein. There's more about the book itself in "Reading and Writing."

surrendered, law officers tortured and otherwise abused more than a thousand of them.

Several hours after the shootings, a State official announced, and the media duly reported, that inmate knives had killed all the hostages who had died. Medical examiner Dr. John Edland received their bodies at midnight and, with his associate Dr. George Abbott, autopsied them until dawn. Later that day, he announced to shocked reporters that bullets had killed them all. Since the police had the only guns, the conclusion was obvious. But it was not what many people wanted to hear. Officials tried to discredit Edland—a Rockefeller aid was quoted as saying "We've got to get something on him."—but ended up confirming his findings.

By the time I joined the prosecutor's office two years later, it had led a grand jury to indict (i.e., charge with a crime) sixty-two inmates and no police. Given who had done what to whom, the disparity stank, though I was told and at first believed, that the understaffed office had simply not gotten around to the cases against the police, which itself stank. The following spring, because I had worked hard and wanted equal justice for convicts and cops alike, I had become chief assistant to the special prosecutor and was put in charge of a new grand jury to correct the lopsidedness of the indictments. As I questioned more and more witnesses, mostly State troopers at first, in front of the conscientious and attentive men and women of this jury, I kept saying to myself, I hope *they* will leave me alone until I finish the job. Who *they* were, I did not articulate, but I was sure they existed.

And they did. The closer I came to securing the indictments of a large number of troopers who had shot or shot at people they shouldn't have, the more obstacles my superiors placed in my path. With a hundred and twenty-eight men shot within an area two hundred yards square in less than ten minutes, for example, I was forbidden to ask eyewitnesses whether they saw anyone shoot anyone. I was forbidden to ascertain whether the police had shortened a video they had taken of the assault from a cellblock roof that, amazingly, showed none of the hundreds of shots fired. And so on and on. In dreary December of 1974, I resigned in protest and charged the cover-up in a letter to, then a meeting with, Attorney General Louis Lefkowitz, who was the ultimate boss of the prosecution, a longtime Nelson Rockefeller ally, and the man I suspected of authoring the cover-up. "These are serious charges, Malcolm," the General said when he had heard me out, adding that he'd get back to me with questions. Instead, he sent a letter wishing me well in all my future ventures. That clinched it for me: if it wasn't his cover-up before, it was now. On December 10, the Senate voted to confirm Rockefeller as Vice President of the United States. The cover-up had shielded his candidacy before their vote.

I wasn't paying much attention to national politics then. My main aim was to salvage the prosecution, and my next steps were to warn Judge Carmen Ball, who was in charge of both grand juries, not to dismiss mine prematurely (and irreparably), and to tell New York's newly elected Governor Hugh Carey that the prosecution of guilty cops was being aborted. I discussed the situation with a friend in Darien who had been a federal prosecutor and whose judgment I respected. "I admire your instincts," he said, reassuring words now that I was searching my way alone. He urges me to send Carey a report in writing, "Then they'll have to deal with it."

Working furiously, I typed out 89-pages on the official cover-up by the police and officials, added 71 pages of supporting papers that I'd kept copies of from the prosecutor's office, fastened them into an orange binder, and mailed it off to Governor Carey. The one person I confided in completely that dark winter was Rev. Sam Fogal, a close friend who was the senior minister of my church. He agreed to lock another copy of my report in the church safe and take it to Tom Wicker at the *New York Times* if I suddenly couldn't.

Wicker was a highly regarded *Times* columnist and editor, and had served as one of the negotiators who risked their lives in inmate-held D Yard trying to prevent the bloodbath. He and others warned Rockefeller that a bloodbath was certain if he did not come to the prison and continue negotiating. But Rockefeller chose not to, even though, as he told President Nixon and Nixon secretly recorded, he knew his decision could result in the deaths of all the hostages and two or three hundred inmates. While I never knew Tom well, he had an impact on my life, by taking my cover-up charges seriously and taking them public in the *Times*, as well as by conversations we had in later years.

He cared deeply about issues that mattered and people who supposedly didn't. He summed up my story in the foreword that he wrote for *The Turkey Shoot:*

> Malcolm Bell's lonely struggle against the New York establishment ... tells us much about politics and criminal justice in America.... The tacit alliance of law enforcement and politics, an omnipresent reality in the American criminal justice system, has seldom been seen more clearly than in Malcolm Bell's painstaking account. The police did the politicians' dirty work, and the politicians covered up for them. Truth was outraged, justice denied, and a cynical example provided of what too many Americans already believe: Of those who those who break the law, the powerless get prison and the powerful get protection.

Those months between resigning and going public were the darkest in my life. For sensitive phone calls, I went out to one pay phone or another. At dusk, I hung a blanket over the vertical rows of windows in the French doors that faced the desk in my second-story barn apartment, so as not to be a target, and I frequently checked the rearview mirror to see if anyone was following me. As I drove alone at night, the headlights in the car behind me actually *knew* me—an eerie anthropomorphism I never experienced before or since.

I suppose that some "paranoia" serves a sound purpose, as one becomes unreasonably alert in times of a danger that is palpable yet too elusive to confront. My testimony and papers could embarrass and maybe convict some powerful people and many men who were handy with guns. It would be foolish for them to hurt me, but the Attica story was full of foolishness. I reminded myself that John Dean had testified against Nixon and survived, but happily, I was not aware that Karen Silkwood had recently been killed in an ambiguous auto wreck while she was on her way to tell a *New York Times* reporter about falsified safety records at a Kerr–McGee nuclear plant. My landlady asked if someone was likely to take a shot at me. Was she worried about having a hole in the wall. "If they do," I assured her, "I'll call the police if I can."

At the outset, I told Erin, then twelve, and Brian, nine, that we would have less money. Erin said, "Does that mean we're not in the middle class anymore?" I replied that we still were because class involves more than money. She recalls that I was very open with them about my excitement at getting the prosecutor job, how it went, and being unemployed. Throughout, she remained more curious than worried. She remembers my taking her on a visit to Dr. Michael Baden at his home near the beaches along Long Island Sound. He was one of the pathologists summoned to repudiate the findings of Dr. John Edland that police bullet, not inmate knives, had killed the dead hostages; but instead, he confirmed Edland's work. He was later the pathologist who explained for my office the specifics of how each of the 39 people shot to death had died. Erin recalled that I thought well of him and enjoyed working with him. Brian recalled my taking him to visit Jack Edland and riding bikes with his daughters that evening. I forgot that I'd hung the blanket over my French doors, and several years ago I denied to a friend that I'd hung it, until I phoned Brian and he reminded me that I'd used the blue and tan blanket.

After three futile months of trying "through channels" to salvage the prosecution of the criminal police, I decided to take my story public. My old friend Bill Looney gave me a stellar piece of legal advice. He had been a roommate in law school, a federal prosecutor, and now headed a small law firm in Boston. "When this thing breaks, Malcolm," he said, "a lot of people are going to make assholes out of themselves. Try not to be one of them."

After several attempts, I gained an interview with Tom Wicker in his office at the *Times*. I'd been allotted twenty minutes, but we talked for forty. It was as though we were back at the prison, as I confirmed what he had long suspected. He stressed that he did not want me to "destroy" myself by going public—very thoughtful of him, I thought. The *Times* ran the story of my charges and their fallout daily, often on the front page, for two weeks. I'd kicked the State's anthill. Officials scurried and postured as they fulfilled Bill Looney's prediction.

One of the press and TV reporters who came to my apartment about my revelations badly wanted a copy of my orange-covered report to Governor Carey. I showed it to him but wouldn't give it up. He promised not to reveal me as the source; but giving it to him would have violated the grand jury secrecy laws, plus if asked, I wasn't going to lie about it. Undaunted, he said that if I left it on my desk when I went to the bathroom, he had "been known to be unscrupulous." So when I went to the bathroom, I took the report with me.

The posturing officials finally initiated an "independent inquiry into the charge that the chief Attica prosecutor covered up possible crimes by law enforcement officers," and appointed a former state court judge named Bernard Meyer, who had no criminal experience, to head it. Meyer had twice run for election to the New York Court of Appeals, the State's highest court, and now said about his desire to sit on that court. "I will go to the grave with that ambition if I don't realize it."

He assembled a staff of lawyers who struck me—during my fourteen visits to his office on Long Island and the 1,400 pages of testimony I gave them—as being generally more capable than the lawyers in the special prosecutor's office. He assigned them to separate elements of his inquiry, but kept for himself the task of putting the elements together and deciding whether they established a cover-up. Result: a three-volume, 570-page report that confirmed most of the facts I had charged, but, no, they merely added up to serious errors in judgment, misordered priorities, indifference, omission by the police in collecting evidence, and so on. The first volume of the report, which contained Meyer's conclusions and some factual background, was released in December 1975; the other two, which allegedly supported his conclusions, were not, on the ground that they contained grand jury material. So the conclusions grinned at us like the head of the Cheshire Cat, without a body to support them, or not. While I read a bare summary of the conclusions when Volume One went public, the pressures of a long criminal stock fraud trial had left me no time to read the 130 pages of Volume One until the trial judge let us out early for New Year's Eve.

Reading it alone in my barn apartment that evening, I was devastated by Meyer's unwarranted assumptions, huge omissions, non-sequiturs, refusals to see or say the obvious, and coddling of officials—the higher their job, the more he coddled them. It was my most emotional moment in the whole Attica adventure. I phoned Tom Goldstein, the

Times reporter who had been covering the aftermath of last spring's dust-up over the cover-up.

"It's bullshit!" I said. "I can't believe it! Do you know what he says?"

"I know," Tom said soothingly.

Once the trial ended and I had a little time, I wrote an op-ed essay for the *Times* that blasted the Meyer Report, genteelly of course. They printed it on February 14, 1976, and gave Meyer a chance to reply to it. He didn't.

One day in 1977, I was one of several people who argued in a Buffalo court to Judge Carmen Ball that it was in the public interest to release Volumes Two and Three in spite of the grand jury info they contained. Meyer submitted papers arguing the same. I wanted the volumes released so I could attack the b.s. that I was sure filled them. I take it as a tribute to his willful myopia that he didn't seem to realize that those volumes would surely demonstrate his pandering incompetence. In 2015, some fragments of Volumes Two and Three were released, and they demonstrated just that. I knew Meyer elsewhere to be an able lawyer.

In 1980 Governor Carey appointed him to fill a vacancy on the Court of Appeals. It is hard to imagine that his dream to sit there would have come true if he had found the obvious, which Tom Wicker summed up so neatly: "The police did the politicians' dirty work, and the politicians covered up for them," and he had pinned the ultimate blame where it belonged, on the recently deceased Nelson Rockefeller.

The turmoil that resulted from my speaking out in April 1975 led Governor Carey to try at the end of 1976 to lay the scandal of the crooked prosecution to rest—to "close the book on Attica," he said—by absolving both inmates and police of liability for the host of murders and other violent crimes they had committed. This was a travesty of the equal justice I had sought, but if I not spoken out, I am quite certain that result would have been that a number of inmates but no cops would have been convicted, with officials continuing to state, falsely but with more people believing them, that most of the officers' shooting was justified and the police detectives had destroyed too much evidence to prosecute the "few bad apples." Those apples were close to half the assault force; the other half showed professional restraint and did not fire their weapons. The truth about the avoidable tragedy and official perfidy would not have been known, and down the road, there would have been even less justice for the hostages and inmates and their families than there turned out to be. Others have told me that I changed the history of the Attica riot.

A highpoint of my post-prosecutor life came a few years after officials cut off my work with the grand jury in the middle. Would the jurors have voted indictments if given the chance? Was the cover-up worth the State's effort or simply a needless precaution? Between the destruction of evidence by the police, my criminal inexperience, and the alleged bias of the jury, would these citizens of Wyoming County actually have indicted law officers if I had been able to finish my presentations?

To find out, I phoned six of them. They told me that most of the jury, more than I needed for voting indictments, had been with me. They appreciated that I was on their side. The officers' crimes horrified them, and they were ready to vote a large number of indictments. They were deeply disappointed when I vanished and my successors merely went through the motions of giving them evidence. Vindication!

But I felt, too, the pain and poignancy of their frustration. We had been in it together, and we had been put out of it together—when it looked likely that we would do the job that the System required but that those who ran the System feared. Some of the former jurors blamed themselves, believing that they had not done enough to set things right, though every time they tried, my former colleagues slapped them down. I felt for these good men and women, even for the few who would not have indicted police, as I had not felt for myself. Their hands were tied much tighter than mine.

"We were a shameful grand jury."

"No. You were conscientious, honest, interested. Your attendance was marvelous. You asked good questions. I was very well impressed." I was very glad I'd made the phone calls that gave me the chance to tell them that. I hoped they felt better about themselves. They deserved to. They were among the people who strove for truth and justice, and to whom I dedicated the new edition of *Turkey Shoot*.

Another happy result of my going public was an unexpected friendship with a lawyer named Donald Jelinek, who was born in The Bronx, started as a lawyer on Wall Street, and spent the bulk of his career in Berkeley, California. I first encountered him in the fall of 1973 as the able "coordinator of the Attica Brothers Legal Defense (ABLD)," meaning the lead counsel for all the indicted Attica defendants, as he argued in Buffalo courtrooms against several lawyers from my office. Two years later, and half a year after I'd gone public, he asked me if we could question each other, with our tape recorders spinning, about our Attica experiences. We did this six hours a day for three days. He slept on my couch and did impressive stretching exercises in the mornings. He asked me about Attica the whole time, after saying that the morning he read my cover-up charges in the *Times*, he literally danced on his bed. He and the ABLD had been charging the cover-up for years, and virtually nobody to the right of the far left had been paying heed.

I ran out of Attica questions for him and learned a whole lot about his three years in the South in the mid 1960s taking part in the struggle for Black people's rights. He eventually wrote a book about it all, *White Lawyer, Black Power: A Memoir of Civil Rights Activism in the Deep South* (Self-published, 2015, University of South Carolina Press, 2020). Here is part of what I said about the book in my Amazon customer's review:

> Sometimes harrowing, sometimes hilarious, always deeply human, and not always politically correct, this book tells a story of courage and resourcefulness, told modestly yet frankly, of one man's contribution to breaching the bastion of oppression that was the "Jim Crow" South. While many talked the talk of civil rights, Don Jelinek spent 1965–1968 walking the walk in Mississippi and Alabama. He nearly got himself killed on several occasions, won some amazing victories, and earned his place among the heroes, black and white, who gave up their time, comfort, and sometimes their lives in the struggle to end this national disgrace.

Don and I remained friends for forty years, until he died in 2016 at age eighty-two. We stayed in touch by phone and email, consulted each other about the books we were writing and much else, and had

two, three, and four-hour lunches, usually in a New York-style deli-
catessen in Oakland, during the annual trips that Nancy and I made
to visit our sons in the Bay Area. He also wrote *Attica Justice: The cruel
30-year legacy of the nation's bloodiest prison rebellion, which transformed
the American Prison System* (Self-published, 2011). It is a fascinating
book, is very kind to me, and tells an essential part of the Attica story.
My two wishes: that a commercial publisher will take it up; and that
he had lived to see the University of South Carolina publish *White
Lawyer, Black Power*. At least his widow, Jane Scherr, had that satisfaction.

In sixteen years and three job changes since law school, I had never
missed a paycheck, and had always been apprehensive about doing
so. That concern was absent during the first months after I resigned.
Maybe I'll find work by March, I thought, though you never know. I
had several promising interviews and understood that I was a finalist
for two or three positions.

Unfortunately, my family and friends did not run the New York
City law firms in which I was seeking a job. After I publicly charged
the corruption in April 1975, the firms stopped responding to my
résumés. An employment agent told me, "A lot of people won't touch
you. They won't say it, but they won't do it." Another agent: "Nobody
who wants to do business with Rockefeller is going to offer you a job."
That covered a lot of business, starting with The Chase Manhattan
Bank, whose chairman and chief executive was Rockefeller's brother
David. Rockefeller's power radiated impact without the need for him
to lift a finger. Plus, plenty of able lawyers wanted jobs; and if I saw a
law firm or one of its clients doing something I considered crooked, I
might report it. Even more basic, where stability matters, who wants
a boat rocker?

I served my time on the lines for the bi-weekly stipend at the Unemployment Office in Stamford and noticed several men from the
Darien commuter platform joining me in this experience of our generation. Some of the people who worked there came to know my story
and liked what I had done. One had me speak about Attica at a neighborhood youth program. Another, who was moving to Boston, said
I could stay with her and her husband any time I went there. It was

heartening that most people I talked with were for me.

A person's status, I'm told, has three traditional sites: job, community, and family. Being without the job took a bit of getting used to. I had not realized that belonging to an organization was a part of me until I did without it, and it disappointed me that I missed the sense of belonging and did not feel as independent as I had fancied myself. One more reminder that I am only human. But it didn't take long to feel that I didn't need to work for someone else in order to be whole. Thus began a freedom I had not realized I had lacked.

"You save it so slowly, it goes out so fast," I told a bank teller named Heidi. She nodded. I scrimped, and Dad's early efforts to teach me the value of a dollar helped. Besides my savings and meager earnings, he was giving my brothers and me $3,000 a year then. I always felt I could go to him for more if need be, but I never did. I ate cheap food like hot dogs and cheese wheels, stopped buying bacon, and started buying oil for the car at the department store. I kept current on the support payments for my children and paid all my second wife's alimony, though sometimes late. She was patient. At noon I ate cheaper, faster, and better at home than I had at Manhattan lunch counters. It mattered to keep getting up at 7:00 a.m. even though I had no train to catch. Having far less to spend changed my life surprisingly little, and I discovered the truth that there are two ways to have money, earn more and spend less.

More often than I would have expected, I kept on seeing my children, kept them overnight, went on local adventures, and even took some trips with them—to Mount Washington, Martha's Vineyard, Williamsburg, and into Canada. We were able to continue skiing together, which could be done quite cheaply in those days. Since they'd be young only once, I was not going to let my conflict with crooked officials deprive the kids or me of the precious experiences we could have only while they were growing up. On the adult level, I met many nice and interesting people, romance was still possible, and usually enjoyable. I contemplated more, relaxed more, and saw more of the beauty of the world.

Though I earned very little money during the next several years, it was exhilarating to have done the right thing; and the experience opened up my perspective on life in these United States. Some said that Attica radicalized me. I believe it simply made me more realistic, allowed me to step outside the bubble. Because my values did not change, my lifestyle had to. I remain very glad.

On the morning of June 29, 1977, I flew to Buffalo and met Gene Tenney, Nelson Cosgrove, and Bill Cunningham, the main lawyers in the hostages' suits against the State for the harm it had done them. My former colleague, prosecutor Dave Flierl, was there for the State. He recited, portentously and a bit self-consciously, the crimes I would be committing under the grand jury and executive secrecy statutes if I went ahead and complied with the subpoena to testify. Sitting at the conference table with these usually pleasant men, I had my most immediate sense of risk over Attica. It was a solemn thing to hear a prosecutor threaten to indict me if I said what I was planning to say, knowing that once said, I couldn't unsay it. In the immortal words of Nixon aide H. R. Haldeman, you can't put the toothpaste back in the tube. The adventurer in me hoped to be indicted, run my own show, question publicly and under oath the officials I believed ran the cover-up, and let it all hang out as far as the courts would let me. On balance, though, the total me wanted very much not to be indicted. But sitting with those men, I said to myself, Fuck it, I'm going ahead.

Dave Flierl sat largely silent as I related, under oath and on the record, much of the Attica story that I had never told before. The unburdening gave me a strange release, finally sharing more of my pent-up knowledge about where the literal and figurative bodies lay. In silent counterpoint while I testified, I planned how I, in Flierl's place, would be building a criminal case against me. During lunch Bill Cunningham said he'd defend me free of charge if I were indicted. He and I smiled. The other two didn't. At the end, Flierl said he was glad I had stayed within bounds.

In 1974, a Brooklynite fresh out of law school named Liz Fink ("Don't call me a liberal! I'm a radical!") had joined the indicted inmates' criminal defense team. The next summer I visited her office several times on Atlantic Avenue in Brooklyn, an easy walk from my parents' apartment, while I was testifying for Meyer and writing *The*

Turkey Shoot, mainly in order to read her transcripts, which I did not have, of what the other Meyer witnesses were saying. We talked, of course, and began to absorb each other's knowledge of how the tragedy went down.

In 1974, too, the inmates began a civil suit in the Buffalo federal court for damages for being wrongfully shot and tortured. By 1982, Liz headed their legal team, which included three male teammates and various help from well-wishers including me. The State owed them big time for what its law officers had done to them, and it fought until year 2000 to keep from paying them anything. Along the way Liz hired Frank "Big Black" Smith as her paralegal. He was the inmate who'd been placed in charge of security during the days of the riot and whom the State Police had forced to lie naked on a table with a football balance between his chest and chin ("If that football falls, I'll blow your fuckin' head off.") while police and corrections officers dropped lighted cigarettes onto him from a catwalk above for a few hours, some burning out on his bare flesh. Then they took him to a small room and beat him senseless.

Liz and her team finally took their first case to trial during the winter of 1991–1992, in the Buffalo federal court, after gross delays by the State's defense and a hostile judge. That jury's verdict effectively established the State's liability to the inmates. Then began the trials to determine the damages due to individual plaintiffs. The first was Black's case, and in 1997 another Buffalo jury awarded him $4 million. Soon a third jury awarded a man who'd suffered far less than Black, $75 thousand.

Liz had used the *Turkey Shoot* and sometimes me in preparing for these trials. "Without you, we couldn't have won," she told me. "Without you, the real story of what happened at Attica would never have gotten told." I had indeed opened the door to the information that she and her team developed, but the main reasons they won were the terrible wrongs inflicted on their clients and their own abilities and perseverance.

In 1999, though, the appeals court reversed the awards to Black and the other man on account of a fatal ambiguity in the jury instructions, and it belatedly suggested that it was time to replace the hostile judge.

Senior Judge Michael Telesca got the case and reportedly told the parties, "Don't tell me you can't afford to settle. You can't afford not to settle." Four months later the case did settle, for $12 million, eight for the inmates and four for the lawyers, who hadn't had a payday during all those years. Liz told me, "The twenty-five years made us settle. We were going to continue to fight and get nothing, or we were going to take chump change, and that's what we did."

So how to divide up the money among the hundreds of inmates and former inmates who were still in the case? During 2000, Judge Telesca held hearings in his courtroom in Rochester and asked all of those men who could get there to produce their medical records and tell him as fully as they could what they had endured; and he accepted written accounts from men and their survivors who could not attend. Many had needed multiple surgeries; nearly all suffered PTSD. The judge found their testimony "for the most part credible" and sometimes "understated." He awarded $125,000 to Black and fourteen other worst-hurt men, $6,500 to the least hurt, and other amounts to men in four categories in between. The majority of the awards, he said, were "of a modest sum," and added that for many of them, "the privilege of recounting their odyssey was of greater value than achieving compensation."

Liz Fink's teammate Joe Heath, who attended the hearings, told me, "What I remember most was the respect [the judge] showed each of the Brothers and that each of them broke down and cried while on the stand."

Judge Telesca and his longtime secretary Joan Countryman were deeply affected by the stories they heard. Afterwards, he wrote and she typed summaries of all 502 of their accounts of what the law officers had inflicted. This is the most complete and accurate record we have or are ever likely to have of law officers' torture of men who had surrendered. The State refused to make a record of it for twenty-nine years. Now anyone can read it in the federal reports online or in a law library, in *Al-Jundi v. Mancusi*, 113 F. Supp. 2d 441 (W.D.N.Y. 2000).

Judge Telesca did not have to create this record. But justice required the great Attica cover-up to be defeated to the extent still possible, he saw a chance to defeat it, and he took it. He told me that he wanted to be open, to let the sunshine in, to let the inmates tell their stories, and let the world know what happened and what the inmates went through.

Nancy and I had several very pleasant visits with the judge in his chambers. He was two years older than I, had been a Marine, and was appointed to the bench by Ronald Reagan in 1982. He was a very likable guy. He said he could talk with me about Attica in ways he couldn't with other people, I suppose because of my outlook. He had not read *The Turkey Shoot* before the year 2000 hearings so as to keep his mind open. Then he read it and assigned his law clerks to read it. For me, he is a hero of the Attica saga and its most exemplary judge.

Before the 1971 riot, the State had maintained the prison as an antiquated and more-dangerous-than-necessary workplace. During the riot, the Governor ordered an assault that was not yet necessary and that he knew could kill all the hostages, in fact killing ten of them. Afterwards, the State swindled the hostages, their survivors, and all their families out of fair compensation for what the State had caused them to endure. During the next nearly three decades, they got along the best they could, some living in poverty, some near it, all of them more or less isolated from each other.

But when they saw the inmates and ex-inmates who had started the riot getting millions of dollars, they were multi pissed. They organized themselves as The Forgotten Victims of Attica (FVOA), which is what they were. A cheerful dynamo named Dee Quinn Miller, who was the eldest daughter of CO Bill Quinn, whom inmates had murdered, became their director. Former hostage Mike Smith, who took four AR-15 bullets through his abdomen (fired by a fellow CO!) and survived by the grace of God and fine surgery, became their chief spokesperson. Public defenders Gary Horton in Batavia and Jonathan Gradess in Albany became their pro bono lawyers. Having no legal remedy this late in the game, they sought to publicize their plight and shame the usually unshamable State into doing right by them. They asked Tom Wicker and me, among others, to help, and we did what we could. Don Jelinek came east from Berkeley to help. Liz Fink offered to help, but because she'd represented inmates, the group declined. On his own, Big Black wrote a powerful letter to then Governor George Pataki on their behalf. During the course of their campaign, Nancy and I became dear friends with Dee and her husband David and Mike and his wife Sharon. In the end, the State paid them, too, $12 million. At their request, Judge Telesca allocated it as fairly as he could among them.

Besides making new friends and sharing new experiences during the FVOA's campaign, Nancy and I and, I believe, many other people who learned about it gained a new appreciation of prison guards. We ask people to do three essential, hazardous jobs for us: firefighters, police, and corrections officers. Nearly everyone thinks well of firefighters. No one thinks better of good cops than I do, but the problem of bad cops is far from solved. And no matter what we think of the prison system, as long as we have it, we need corrections officers. Thanks to various movies and other fictions, and the news when some of them screw up, their image has not been great. But overall, they deserve our full respect and appreciation. Think where we'd be without them.

In September of 2001, Bill Cunningham donated his cartons of Attica papers to Bethune-Cookman College in Daytona Beach, Florida,* and college officials invited him, Big Black, and me to speak on Sunday, the 10th, at a ceremony to receive the donation. Nancy's and my return flight to Boston led to a haunting memory. Landing late that evening, we pulled our carry-ons through the warm, nearly deserted halls of Logan Airport a few hours before a handful of young men with box cutters walked those same halls on their way to change America forever.

We then drove to Attica so I could speak at the Thirtieth Anniversary Memorial Service on the 13th, about a three-hundred-mile drive, no problem. Bill Cunningham was also scheduled to speak, but all civilian flights were grounded following the 9/11 attack. Never easily defeated, Bill drove the nine-hundred-plus miles from Florida, earning the applause of all present at the service.

In 2021, Dee Quinn Miller published her own story, *The Prison Guard's Daughter: My Journey Through the Ashes of Attica*. Gary Craig of the Rochester *D&C* helped her write it, and I was pleased to write the Foreword. Sister Helen Prejean called the book, "A remarkable tale of healing and reconciliation [which] tells us that our better angels

---

* Liz Fink's Attica papers and mine are in the Human Rights Archive of the Rubenstein Library at Duke University.

can prevail." In my favorite passage, Dee describes coming to Vermont with Gary Horton to visit Tom Wicker, at his home north of Nancy's and mine, in 2011 right after Hurricane Irene ravaged the state. I rode with Gary to Tom's house while Nancy drove Dee.

> [T]here were times when the road completely disappeared. Nancy drove the standard transmission SUV as if she were unbothered by the conditions or the occasional lack of road-way. At one point we were literally driving in a creek bed, with water splashing onto the windshield and Nancy calmly flipping on the wipers for visibility.

Liz Fink had a brilliant mind, but she did not start caring for her body until too late, and she died in 2015 at the age of seventy. Nancy and I attended her memorial service at Manhattan's Union Theological Seminary, Mike Smith sent a message to be read, and I was among the people who were asked to speak. I ended by saying that the best people throughout history are the ones who have helped strangers in need, and that's what Liz did.

Every few years there's been a new movie version of the Attica story. The one that has drawn the most attention, nearly two hours long and simply titled *Attica*, is the work of an accomplished documentary filmmaker named Stanley Nelson and his co-director Traci Curry. It premiered on Showtime in 2021 and was nominated for Best Documentary Picture of the Year. Beautifully photographed and produced, it makes a powerful and badly needed case for the humanity of the inmates, which clearly exceeded that of the police at Attica. For that reason, I was glad to see it nominated for the Oscar. But it portrays the inmates as being considerably better and the police as even worse than they were. For example, while the film reports that inmates killed Corrections Officer William Quinn, it fails to mention that they injured thirty-one more prison employees, sending six of them to the hospital. It fails to mention that of the law officers who recaptured the prison, only half joined in the massacre, while the other half showed professional restraint and did not fire their weapons. Incomprehensibly, it portrays a non-existent pause between the two helicopters dropping tear gas on the prison and the officers simultaneously shooting inmates who were holding knives at hostages' throats; if the pause had existed, inmates would probably have finished cutting those throats. So I'm just as glad the film didn't win. A shorter and more accurate film is *Criminal Injustice: Death and Politics at Attica,* which filmmaker Christine Christopher made after doing extraordinarily productive research. Her film was nominated for three Emmy Awards and won one of them in 2013. It was distributed through American Public Television and aired on PBS.

As far as I can tell, the Black Lives Matter movement has paid oddly little attention to the slaughter-with-impunity of Black men at Attica by State Police, many of whom had participated in building up their race hatred during the riot unchecked by the officers in charge, before they began shooting. It's true that all ten hostages and a few of the twenty-nine inmates they shot dead were white, but in the bar of the local Holiday Inn that evening, troopers were heard to brag "Got me a n****r," not "Got me a white man."

Some people called me a hero for resigning in protest and blowing the whistle on the cover-up, but I never felt like one. Many years later, historian Heather Cox Richardson wrote that she came to believe that heroism is neither being perfect, nor

> doing something spectacular. In fact, it's just the opposite: it's regular, flawed human beings, choosing to put others before themselves, even at great cost, even if no one will ever know, even as they realize the walls might be closing in around them.[5]

The flawed part was certainly true for me. The cost wasn't nearly as great as it could have been, and it opened the door to my freedom. Plenty of people knew; spreading the news became the point. And the only walls I noticed were the ones that excluded me. It was my good luck that my whistle-blowing was effective, thanks to Tom Wicker and the *Times.* So many whistle-blowers pay the price, and nothing changes. But they, too, earn the satisfaction of doing right when it matters, and I hope they know it and feel it. All the same, it's okay if some people think I'm a hero—there are plenty who think I'm awful—as long as the thoughts don't affect us day to day.

A true Attica hero was the Rochester medical examiner, Dr. John Edland, who exposed the first great official lie about the massacre, by telling the truth that it was police bullets, not inmate knives, that killed the men who died as a result of Rockefeller's needless order to storm the prison. For his honesty, Jack suffered years of vilification, harassment, and ostracism. His family suffered along with him. For instance, threatening and obscene calls at all hours to their home led him and his wife to tell their girls not to answer the phone.

While Brian, who was eleven, and I were seeing family in Ithaca during the summer of 1976, I drove with him to visit Jack Edland, first in his office—where Brian was fascinated by the skeleton that was hanging there—and as we hit it off and our conversation lengthened to eight hours, with his wife and girls at their home in a residential part of Rochester. The next year as the harassments continued, the Edlands moved away to make a new life for themselves, but the abuse that Jack had suffered for doing his job and telling the truth continued to gnaw at him. He drank too much and suffered from depression, though he continued to do the best he could for his family. In 1991, he died of congestive heart failure at the age of fifty-seven, the forty-fourth fatality of the Attica tragedy.

The abuse inflicted on Jack and his family is but one example of the tenacity with which many people cling to false beliefs that they find comfortable or necessary, and the viciousness with which some of them assail anyone who threatens those beliefs. Truth-teller, beware!

I have long thought it unfair that Jack suffered so much for exposing the first great official Attica lie whereas I suffered comparatively little for exposing the second great lie, that the prosecution was honest. His truth came as a shocking surprise that upset many. Mine merely confirmed what many had long suspected. I told his story as fully as I could, in Chapter 37 of *The Turkey Shoot*, greatly enriching its account, and I remain grateful that he told it to me. Four years before he died, he gave his daughter Gretchen a copy of the book, inside of which he had written, "This is family history. It explains me. I hope it helps you understand why it all happened. Love, Dad."

On My Own

Starting with the new year 1975, right after the Christmas holidays that followed my resignation in protest from the corrupt Attica prosecution, I began looking for work as the litigator, or one of them, in a small or medium-size New York City law firm, sending out résumés and taking the train to the City for several promising interviews. But as noted in the last story, the interviews dried up as soon as I went public about the Attica scandal, implicating as it did the most powerful person in the state, Nelson Rockefeller. Finally, on July 2, Peter Dorsey, the United States Attorney for Connecticut, interviewed me for a job in his office in New Haven. I told him about the pending Meyer investigation of my cover-up charges. "He could come out against me," I said.

"If he does, I'd doubt him," Dorsey answered, to my everlasting admiration.

He offered me a job paying $25,000 a year (about $146,000 in today's dollars); but the longer I thought about it, the more I realized that, somewhat to my surprise, I did not want to be on the prosecution side then. (Dorsey would become the Chief Judge of the US District Court in Connecticut.) If I'd taken the job and held it for a few years, I'd probably then have gone to work for a Connecticut law firm and had a very different life with little or no time for the Sanctuary Movement and what followed, far less time for writing, and a scary chance that I'd have moved to New Haven or Hartford and not met Nancy, the love off my life, at a Darien tennis party. That $25,000 turned out to be roughly five times my adjusted gross income for 1976.

Shortly after I turned down Dorsey's offer, my landlady's son-in-law, Barry Drayer, was charged with stock fraud and asked me to defend him. This led to a strenuous six-weeks trial in the Manhattan federal court the next winter, during which I was lucky to get five hours sleep a night. The jury convicted both of Barry's co-defendants, one of whom was his brother, but they could not decide about him. The judge declared a mistrial; and the prosecutor dropped the case— after telling me while the jury was out that he thought Barry was innocent. I replied that I wished he'd said that to the jury. So began my private law practice.

It's hard to open an office when you have very little money, so I didn't. Instead, I worked out of my home in Norwalk, did all my own typing on an electric typewriter—which averaged about three hours a week with jazz softly playing—did legal research in the law library in the Stamford courthouse and most of the photocopying at the Darien public library. I took the train as needed to Manhattan where nearly all the courts and opposing law firms were, and served my own subpoenas and court papers. I wore a suit and tie when taking a deposition—testimony under oath and transcribed by a court reporter usually in an opposing lawyer's office in the City—or appearing in court. To serve papers or meet with an opposing lawyer though, I wore my usual jeans and flannel shirt, which often led receptionists and secretaries to treat me with minimal courtesy until the opposing lawyer entered the room and greeted me as an equal, and these people realized they needed to do better.

Barry was a plaintiff or defendant in several civil lawsuits that earned me some money over the next few years. One of them gave me a chance to argue, and lose, before the highly-regarded federal Court of Appeals for the Second Circuit.* In another, the Marine Midland Bank claimed that Barry owed it some money, and Barry claimed he didn't. As a sort of tribute to my work, I suppose, the bank's lawyer, Eric Sullivan, resorted to the rare and disgusting tactic of trying to have me disbarred, that is, to deprive me of my livelihood, over this routine commercial case. Even the officials I had accused of corrupting the Attica prosecution hadn't tried to disbar me, though I heard they'd discussed it. Eric's grounds? New York requires its lawyers to have an office within the state. Mindful of this, I maintained a barebones office in my parents' Brooklyn apartment. One day, Eric came there to serve me with some legal papers and rang the doorbell. When I emerged in tee shirt and jeans to sign for them, he realized that his tactic had failed. If he happens to read this, it's not too late to apologize.

A woman I'll call Natalie sought me out after reading about my

---

* The decision is included in the federal law reports as *Drayer v. Krasner*, 572 F. 2d 348-360 (1978). If you go on the internet to this and most later citations, you may learn much more about the cases that I have summarized here.

Attica protest and told me that her former husband, whom I'll call Charles and who was a rising star in a major Manhattan law firm, had custody of their son, and as a nifty way to take custody of their daughter away from her, he had been secretly recording her phone calls to the boy and trying to provoke her into sounding too hysterical to be a fit mother. I didn't particularly want the case, but Natalie said she wanted a "fighter," what she said her husband had done sounded slimy, and the federal statute made it illegal to record other people's phone calls without their consent.

The initial conference with the federal judge had barely started when he called Natalie "greedy," "vindictive," and a couple of other words that led me to conclude he had prejudged the case. I asked him to recuse himself. He declined. I took the rarely used step of petitioning the Court of Appeals for a writ of *mandamus* (an order) removing him from the case. His secretary phoned to say that since I felt that strongly, he'd recuse himself after all. I had later dealings with this judge, came to think well of him, and believe he did of me.

The next judge on Natalie's case contained his emotions but ruled that in a family case like this, the statute didn't mean what it said. When I argued in the Court of Appeals, the judges seemed sympathetic, but that court too carved out an unwritten exception to the plain words that Congress had voted into law. So, it's a crime to punch your ex but not to try to take away her child by an obviously hurtful method that a statute makes illegal. What must those children have thought of their dad? Did the boy look up to him so much that he believed what he did to his mother was okay? Did what he did to the mother cause their girl to distrust men? I don't know, but apparently these possibilities had not deterred Charles and did not deter these courts.

Back in the day, it was fairly common to see banks of self-service luggage lockers standing in airports, railroad and bus stations, and so on. Using them was conveniently quick and impersonal. I often used one. Today they are far less common in the US, and one reason may be the bomb that exploded in a locker in LaGuardia Airport on December 29, 1975, killing eleven people and injuring seventy-four. The bomber and his or her motive were never found, but of course the airport was sued for zillions of dollars. Through mutual acquaintances, I came to represent a young woman whom the blast had injured. I don't recall her name or face or injury. Kreindler & Kreindler, which specialized in suing airlines, represented the most plaintiffs, so became the lead counsel, meaning its lawyers were very much in charge, while lawyers like me could watch if we cared to, which I did, coming to the federal courthouse in lower Manhattan for the pretrial hearings and the days of the trial. The judge was the one who had decided against Natalie and me; and the Kreindler lawyer who tried this case made the cardinal error of pissing him off. When juries deliberate, they often take their cues from hints that the judge, by accident or design, has dropped along the way. As far as I could discern, that's one reason these plaintiffs lost. Another might be that, if I recall the case correctly, it was a stretch to call the airport negligent.

A doctor butchered a myelogram that he tried to perform on a man named Tom Olivieri, who lived in Nassau County on Long Island. A myelogram is a diagnostic procedure in which the doctor first injects a local anesthetic into the patient's spine, then uses a big needle to inject a dye that allows X-rays to locate any abnormalities. This doctor neglected to inject the local anesthetic, then kept trying and failing to push the big needle into the right place despite Tom's screams of pain. This would be my first personal injury case and my first trial in a state court in Long Island, so I drove several times from Norwalk across the Throgs Neck Bridge to the courthouse in Mineola to see how the lawyers did it there.

When the case was called, I did fine with selecting the jury, but the trial did not go well. Tom gave straightforward but undramatic testimony, and the judge thought I should be objecting to more of the doctor's lawyer's questions than I was. My theory, which I'd learned from one of the founders of the Dewey Ballantine firm, was that if the expected answer to an objectionable question looked unlikely to hurt the case, don't give the jury the impression that you're trying to hide it. (In retrospect, I should probably have followed the local custom of objecting to every improper question.) Then I called an extroverted woman friend of Tom's who had watched his agony after the botched procedure. She described it on the witness stand loudly, vividly, and passionately. This excited the judge ("Now we have a *trial!*"), who called a recess and asked us to negotiate. The doctor offered to settle for $25,000 (about $125,000 today), which his lawyer said was all he could afford. The judge was for it, Tom agreed, and I figured the doctor was so inept that he might be telling the truth about what he could afford. So that's what we settled for.

An old friend I'll call Stanley asked me to represent him in his divorce in Stamford. This time too, I didn't particularly want the case, but agreed to take it because he was a friend and he insisted. Another friend kindly got me admitted to practice in Connecticut *pro hac vice*, for this case only. A third friend, who was the court reporter for the wife's deposition, told me afterwards that he was surprised to see me so much more aggressive than my usual self. Another reason I stopped practicing law.

One morning Stanley and I were waiting in the main hallway of the courthouse where the judge assigned to his case was likely to see him, and he was mouthing a big cigar. "Lose the cigar, Stan," is roughly what I told him. "I am who I am, I'm a New York Jew, and I don't care who sees me," he replied. "That's fine, Stan. Now lose the cigar." And he did. He was much less compliant, though, about paying me on our agreed schedule or at all. I kept insisting I that needed the money because my car was dying. He kept promising to pay it when he got it. Then he came into some money and spent it by taking a girlfriend on a jaunt to Switzerland. I was furious. I resigned from the case and never saw him again.

A young man named Arthur Seymore, who had been a quarterback and then one of the coaches for the Brown U. football team, went to work in the production department of the *Reader's Digest Magazine*. A mutual friend told me that he needed a lawyer because the people there had subjected him to painful racial slurs and other discrimination. In particular, they taunted him with a venerable and odious printer's term, "splitting the n****r's head," which meant stacking colors accurately on top of each other. Would I bring a racial discrimination suit against the magazine? Yes.

The case would be hard to prove because it would be Arthur's word against a bunch of the magazine's employees who might be inclined to say what they needed to to defend their employer and keep their jobs.

Reader's Digest hired the highly regarded firm of Paul, Weiss, Rifkind, Wharton & Garrison and specifically the well-known civil rights lawyer and one-time President of Brandeis University, Morris Abram. I took the depositions of quite a few of the magazine's employees, so I'd know what to expect at trial and maybe elicit a few helpful admissions. The *Digest* made a motion to get the case thrown out before trial, and the judge denied the motion.*

During the trial, I sat alone with Arthur at one table; at the other were Abram, two more Paul, Weiss lawyers, and the *Digest's* senior house counsel (internal lawyer) Martha Farquar, who acted as a sort of cheerleader for their lawyers and witnesses. The six-person jury consisted of two white women, three apparently minority people, and a man I can't recall. The first alternate juror was a bright-looking young man who worked for IBM.

Arthur testified well. Indeed, I thought the jury would now understand how deeply his fellow employees' racist taunts, which their superiors had done nothing to stop, had hurt him. Time and again, the *Digest* witnesses whom I called to the stand testified less helpfully than they had on their depositions, and I read their prior sworn testimony to show the jury how they'd changed it.

Trying the case lasted, I think, three days. The judge, who was the same one that had recused himself from Natalie's case, presided fairly. On the morning the case was to go to the jury, one of the jurors didn't show up, and I hoped the judge would fill her place with the first alternate, the IBM guy, who had been very attentive during the trial. As he was on the verge of doing so, the missing juror walked into the courtroom, the judge instructed them, and the alternates were dismissed. The jury did not take long. They found for the *Digest*.

The first alternate juror had waited for the verdict. He told us that he was convinced that Arthur had suffered terrible discrimination, and if he had been put on the jury, he was confident that he would have convinced the others. So that's how close Arthur and I came to winning the case against the *Digest*. Some months later against all possible odds, I ran into one of the two white women jurors in a crowded subway car. She told me that she and the other white wom-

---

* *Seymore v. Reader's Digest Association*, Inc., 493 F. Supp. 257 (1980).

an believed that Arthur had been presumptuous (i.e., uppity) and shouldn't have made so many suggestions to his superiors for improving their process. Which, if true, may have irritated them but has nothing to do with whether they inflicted racist pain on Arthur. These two women pressed the three minority jurors to agree with them, and the non-descript man said he'd go along with whatever the other five decided. So, two bigots gave the *Digest* the verdict. Arthur and Nancy and I remain friends to this day.

A teacher named Evelyn Harris, who lived in Easton, Connecticut, with her husband Mike, asked me to represent her at a hearing before the Westport School Board to try to persuade them not to fire her. We lost of course, but Ev and Mike and Nancy and I also remained friends. Shortly after Mike died a few years ago, the Fairfield police pulled Ev's driver's license when they shouldn't have—devastating for her because her home was too rural to walk to anything, and there's no public transportation nearby. I asked her local lawyer to phone the police. He declined, saying it would be too risky. I asked another local lawyer, who also declined. So I phoned the Fairfield police from my home in Vermont, and the captain I spoke with had Ev's license promptly restored. Sometimes lawyers are too cautious to do the obvious.

It was on January 23, 1976, that the prosecutor *nolle prosequied* (dropped) the criminal case against Barry Drayer. Three days later I flew to Costa Rica to discuss with a close friend named Bob Crawford and his partner Tim Reilly the possibility of suing the mighty Gulf and Western Industries, Inc., which liked to call itself Gulf+Western and I shall call G&W, and several other US and Canadian companies for cheating Tim and Bob's company, El Cid, Ltd., out of its contractual rights, known as the "Bolgol concessions," to mine gold in the remote, gold-rich Tipuani Valley of Bolivia.

There were two ways to reach the valley, by car on a narrow road along the edge of a lofty cliff off which cars and trucks regularly fell, killing the occupants, and by plane to an airport whose runway had a curve in it. There was no way I would ever visit the Tipuani Valley, but there was no need for any of us to visit it if we sued G&W et al., not to restore El Cid's rights to mine the gold, but for the money that El

Cid had lost by being wrongly deprived of the rights. The three of us decided that I would file a suit in the Manhattan federal court seeking money damages under the Sherman Act and Bolivian tort law against G&W, several related companies and individuals, and two Canadian companies, all of which Tim and Bob told me were part of the cabal that had stiffed them. Section 1 of the Sherman Act says:

> Every contract, combination in the form of trust or otherwise, or conspiracy, in restraint of trade or commerce among the several States, or with foreign nations, is hereby declared to be illegal.

A tort is an injury, and tort law lets injured people sue to be compensated by money damages.

Americans had a venerable tradition of cheating Latinos. When Kay and I had been visiting one of her college friends, the girl's father, who was the general counsel of a major corporation, regaled us with the ways that he and his colleagues had ripped off the locals in, I think, Colombia. Ugh! The title of Eduardo Galeano's highly regarded *Open Veins of Latin America: Five Centuries of the Pillage of a Continent* (1973, 1997) sums it up. The people who lived in the Tipuani Valley had reportedly been taking gold on and near its surface since the time of the Incas yet were living in poverty, and I would not have become part of a mining arrangement that did not deal fairly with them, but suing these US and Canadian defendants in New York for money damages avoided the need to work that out. The G&W companies never tried to mine in the valley. I don't know why.

We decided to call the case *El Cid v. The New Jersey Zinc Company*, which was the subsidiary of G&W that was most involved in the rip-off. Back in Connecticut, I did the needed legal research, drafted a complaint, served it on G&W and as many other defendants as I could, and filed it in the federal courthouse in Foley Square a few blocks north of the Brooklyn Bridge. Soon three New York City law firms were representing the defendants against my one-person operation. The case would continue for nearly ten years.

My first step was "pretrial discovery." Per the federal rules, I asked G&W companies' lawyers for all of their clients' papers that pertained to the case. They were more honest than I'd expected and gave me a pile that went far towards showing how the defendants had defeated El Cid's rights. Included were several G&W mining reports showing a fabulous amount of gold below the surface of the valley—a great help for proving the amount of the damages to El Cid.

The next step was to take the depositions of quite a few people who I knew from the papers had participated in the conspiracy. Plus, I had to submit Tim and Bob and their papers to similar discovery, a fairly quick job. All this took several years and was overseen by a federal magistrate (assistant judge) named Nina Gershon, who was tough but fair—"You're claiming zillions of dollars, Mr. Bell, you've got to show them more specifics."— and later became a federal judge. The actual judge on the case was Whitman Knapp, who had recently headed a City commission which, relying on two brave and honest cops, Frank Serpico and David Durk, produced an influential report in 1972 that exposed much corruption in the NYPD.

Two of the Canadian defendants made a motion to dismiss the case against them. Judge Knapp denied it August 1977—a victory that didn't matter much to the over-all case but may have increased my creds with the lawyers opposing me.*

During the pretrial phase of the case, Bob learned that he was at risk of being indicted in a criminal tax fraud and obstruction of justice prosecution of his friend and business associate Bill Kilpatrick in the federal court in Denver, Colorado. Bob asked me to represent him. After we discussed the facts, I decided that, not only was he innocent, but also that we had best take the risky step of trying to convince the prosecutors that this was true. Otherwise, he looked quite likely to face trial. I say risky because if they weren't convinced, everything Bob told them could be used against him before the grand jury to indict him and during the trial to convict him.

We met with the prosecutors in their office at seven o'clock on a warm summer evening. Four hours later, they gave us a letter granting Bob immunity from prosecution. But they planned to call him as a witness against Bill, and as we were leaving, a prosecutor named Snyder told me that if Bob "testified for Mr. Kilpatrick, all bets are

---

* *El Cid v. New Jersey Zinc Company*, 444 F. Supp. 845 (S.D.N.Y. Aug. 1977).

off." Bob and I took that to mean that the immunity he'd just received would be canceled and Bob would be prosecuted. Witnesses are often granted immunity in order to secure their testimony; I had done it in the Attica cases. The problem here was the informality with which it was granted. Which didn't matter to me; we weren't going to complain.

When I told Bill's lawyers about Snyder's warning, they seized on it as a reason to ask the judge to dismiss the case. I was called to the witness stand, where a government lawyer named Scharf, who was dismayingly disrespectful to the judge, tried to establish that I had fabricated Snyder's words. During a pause in his barrage of questions, I turned to the judge and told him that apart from Snyder's "all bets are off" remark, I thought he had conducted himself quite professionally. The judge did not rule on Bill's motion to dismiss but did grant him a new trial. In his opinion, he called me "a witness I found to be straight-forward, fair, convincing, and most generous to Mr. Snyder."* Thank you, your Honor.

When I had agreed to start the *El Cid* case, Tim and Bob agreed to pay me a share of any victory plus $1,000 a month while I litigated it. As it dragged on, they stopped paying, and I didn't complain. Transcribing the depositions plus traveling as far as Toronto and Minnesota to take some of them proved costly, and eventually they stopped paying these expenses too. I was using a court reporter named Fred Lorber to transcribe the depositions and once picked him up at his house in New Jersey on our way to the airport. Transcribing pays well; his house was much bigger than mine. He began saying darkly though correctly that he needed to be paid for his work. Finally, he sued me for, as best I recall, around $20,000—which I didn't have. New York law is quite clear that the client, not the lawyer, pays the reporter. Fred's lawyer tried to get me to settle. I refused. The judge ruled in my favor, the cleanest victory in my private practice. Fortunately, the case didn't need any more depositions.

Since it was nearly ready for trial, this was time to talk settlement. G&W's lawyers and I arranged for a meeting in Manhattan

---

* *United States v. William A. Kilpatrick*, 575 F. Supp. 325 at 335 (D. Colo. August 1983).

with them, some G&W business people, Tim Reilly, and me. Before the big day, Tim and I discussed our strategy and decided to tell them we'd settle for ten million dollars, take it or leave it, no need to decide right now. Then we'd exit the meeting—as we did, leaving a row of them sitting in their suits behind a wide table.

Their response was, not a counteroffer, but a motion for summary judgment on both the antitrust claim and the Bolivian tort claim. That meant they were asking the judge to rule that, looking at Tim's and Bob's deposition testimony and the facts I had uncovered during discovery in the light most favorable to El Cid, a jury could not possibly decide, under the law, for El Cid. A tall order, but I had a bad feeling that Judge Knapp would find a way to keep the case against G&W from going to a jury. That's what he did, in separate decisions on the antitrust claim and the tort claim.* I cannot say today that he clearly erred, but I'm fairly sure that if he had wanted to let a jury decide the case, he would have. The Court of Appeals gave my arguments short shrift, and in December 1985, the Supreme Court declined to consider it.

Since then I have often thought that Tim's and my approach at the G&W settlement conference was my greatest professional blunder, and that what I should have done was to sacrifice any elements of surprise and lay out precisely and in gory detail what our evidence showed, confronting their businessmen with the specter of what a jury would probably do about the dirty tricks by which their people had deprived *El Cid* of its gold mine. Of course, if G&W had accepted Tim's and my offer, I'd not call our approach a blunder.

One of the defense lawyers told me that G&W's law firm had devoted a whole room to their *El Cid* files. Those lawyers and the Paul, Weiss lawyers who defended the *Readers Digest* against Arthur Seymore might have thanked me for the huge fees I netted them, but of course they didn't. *El Cid* was the last major event in my private law practice.

In the fall of 1978, my old friend Dave Bender had gotten me a part-time position as an antitrust consultant with a major Manhattan

---

* *El Cid v. New Jersey Zinc Co.,* 551 F.Supp. 626 (S.D.N.Y. November 1982) and 575 F.Supp. 1513 (S.D.N.Y. December 1983).

corporation, just in time to replace my dying Chevy. I enjoyed the people and the work, which gave me considerable freedom for *El Cid* and my other cases, camping with Nancy, and writing much of *The Turkey Shoot*. The position lasted four years, until the defense against a large antitrust claim that Dave and I and several more of the corporation's full-time lawyers had been working on was handed off to my old firm, Dewey Ballantine, and my old boss, Len Joseph. It's quite common for corporations to hire outside lawyers to use their expert learning and skills, which house counsel don't have, for a significant case and to receive the blame if the case is lost. It's also quite common for these cases to settle, allowing both sides to claim victory. A bit tongue-in-cheek, I told Len at a Dewey alumni party, that defending this case was a piece of cake that he couldn't possibly lose. He looked uncomfortable. The case was settled. By the time the consulting job ended, my father had passed on and left me enough money to have a modest income and build Nancy's and my two-bedroom dream house in Vermont. The corporation had offered to hire me full-time, but I treasured my independence too much to even discuss salary.

During these years of private practice, nearly all my work came through friends. I am very grateful.

Beyond the Law

Doing Sanctuary

A train of life rolled northward through the 1980s. It started in mystery far below the Border and crossed into this country where the Rio Grande flows into the Gulf of Mexico and the Tijuana sewage ditch empties into the Pacific, at El Paso and Nogales and points between, wherever people swam the river, waded the ditch, scrambled under the barb wire, or otherwise eluded the Mexican and US *migra*, the immigration police. Without track or rolling stock, the railroad fanned out across the land, through most states and up branch lines into Canada.

The passengers were fugitives from carnage in Guatemala and El Salvador. Churches, synagogues, Quaker meetinghouses, and private homes served as stations along the way. The engineers and conductors lived much like everyone else, except they had brewed up a non-conforming view of our nation, laws, and God, and they dared to act upon it. As with the underground railroad that spirited slaves to freedom before the Civil War, no one was in charge.

We are taught to admire the crews of the first underground railroad, pillars of conscience who defied the Fugitive Slave Act and risked prison or death in order to help Blacks to flee the bondage in which most free, white Americans were content to let them languish. "Follow the Drinking Gourd" echoes down the years as a haunting song of hope. Harriet Tubman, Sojourner Truth, and Frederick Douglass are heroes in many history books, which is a safe place to keep them. Stations along that line still stand as shrines to courage, freedom, and a relatively few souls' defiance of what was then an integral pillar of the US economy and a profitable part of the American Way. Venerating the first underground railroad is as easy as recognizing that slavery was wrong, that is, easier today than it was at the time.

The new underground railroad strove poignantly to be heard, yet relatively few North Americans, as its Latino passengers called us,*

---

* Early in the movement, refugees pointed out that we of the United States are

166

felt the chill of its whistle in the night. Thanks to government and major media silence and deception, most of us did not have a clue that a dark slaughter, lit by dancing flames of torture, was eating like acid through the bustling cities and green countryside of Guatemala and El Salvador on the Central American isthmus. During the 1980s, scores of thousands of people fled their homes to save their lives. Many remained as refugees within their own countries. Others settled in Mexico despite too little work and too much official extortion, brutality, and risk of deportation back to the death squads, army sweeps, and American bombs they had fled. Still others continued north, often helped by people of faith, and crossed secretly through fence or river or in massed dashes at Border guards who waited to grab them as in a great game of "Red Rover, Red Rover, let everybody come over."

At first the fugitives sought lawful asylum; but when our government rejected nearly all of their applications and flew them back often to be killed, most of them stopped applying and tried to hide and survive in the US underground economy. Thousands were caught and sent summarily to their fate. Others found help from North Americans who rose up as quietly, though less abundantly, as the grass.

A simple definition of the Sanctuary Movement, as it came to be called, is a loose network of religious congregations, moved by faith and humanity, that stood with Salvadoran and Guatemalan refugees to protect them from their own governments and ours. Except as noted soon, the Sanctuary congregations I'm talking about went public with their stand, openly risking arrest as they appealed to the decency of the greathearted, if often inert, American public to press our government to cease enabling the mass torture and murder of civilians in those two little countries. The basic and often quoted Scripture was Leviticus 19:34: "The stranger who sojourns with you shall be to you as the native among you, and you shall love him as yourself; for you were strangers in the land of Egypt...." As movement dynamo Eileen Purcell put it,

---

presumptuous in calling ourselves "Americans" as though we own the term, and we remain oblivious that we actually share it with Central and South Americans. Technically, of course, Central Americans, Mexicans, and Canadians are also North Americans; but most of us in the movement took the refugees' point.

[T]he Sanctuary Movement was authentically born of
men and women of faith in a relationship with refugees who
turned to the church as one of the last institutions they felt
they could go to in a life-threatening situation.

The movement went public on March 24, 1982, the second anniversary of the assassination of Archbishop (now Saint) Oscar Romero
in San Salvador by a US-backed death squad. On that day, the Southside Presbyterian Church in Tucson, Arizona, and the University Lutheran Chapel and four other churches in Berkeley, California, proclaimed—in defiance of national policy and criminal statutes—that
they were offering sanctuary to these refugees. By the late 1980s some
five hundred religious congregations and other groups would similarly
declare. That may sound like many, but only about one parish in seven
hundred and seventy-five joined the movement. As to the refugees,
fewer than one percent of them entered the lonely, risky, nettlesome
life of public Sanctuary.

It is worth noting that the Sanctuary Movement did not seek an
open Border; that refugees from El Salvador and Guatemala were only
a small fraction of the Latinos who crossed it during the 1980s; that
by Immigration and Naturalization Service (INS) estimates, slightly
more than half the people who were in the US illegally then did not
sneak in but simply overstayed their visas[6]; and that of the people who
were here illegally, Europeans plus Canadians outnumbered Latinos.

When it came to the various denominations, Unitarian Universal-
ists had the highest ratio of Sanctuaries to their total number of congregations. Quakers were a close second, then Jews. While Catholics
were fourth, the seventy-three Catholic Sanctuaries were the most of
any denomination, and many of us saw their nuns as the backbone of
the movement.

I write about Nancy's and my decisions to break the law and join
the movement in "Inner Journey," below, because they marked a significant step along our spiritual paths. The present story sketches how
we actually lived out our decision to be amateur criminals following
the Wilton Friends Meeting's decision. Quaker meetings' decisions,
by the way, need not be unanimous but should reflect "the sense of

the meeting." In our Meeting, as in many others, one firm dissenter can block a decision. Ours decided to declare Sanctuary rather swiftly, and no one interposed a block, but afterwards several people silently left us. When we declared on March 23,1986, we were such neophytes that no one realized how close this was to March 24th, the anniversaries of Romero's murder and the public start of the movement.

The Meeting formed a Sanctuary committee and asked me to be its convenor, meaning its chair, to meet the needs of whomever we sponsored, solicit speaking engagements and expense money, and do whatever else was needed. We on the committee believed that if the feds indicted anyone, it would be us, not the whole congregation. Whether or not this was true, the belief forged a special bond among us.

As the convenor, I followed the recommended Sanctuary practice of writing to President Reagan, the State Department, the INS, and our Congresspeople, telling them what the Meeting had done. Only the State Department replied:

> Your claim that Salvadorans and Guatemalans deported from the United States to their home countries face death is false. El Salvador and Guatemala are governed by civilian democratic governments elected by a majority of the citizens of each country. Those governments do not victimize, abuse or punish those who attempt to enter the United States illegally and are subsequently returned.
>
> Harboring illegal aliens is against the law. We do not believe that the religious affiliation or humanitarian motives of sanctuary supporters can isolate them from the consequences of willfully violating the law. Thank you for sharing your views with us.
>
> [Signed:] William Walker, Deputy Assistant Secretary of Inter-American Affairs.

Walker's first paragraph was totally false as it stated our government's glaringly false official position. His second reminded me that we were engaged in serious stuff.

Two weeks after the Meeting declared, I flew to Chicago for a radio

interview with Studs Terkel about my recently published *Turkey Shoot.*
The trip enabled me to visit Rev. Michael McConnell at the office of
the Chicago Religious Task Force on Central America (CRTFCA),
which was the closest thing that the Sanctuary Movement ever had
to a leader. (The American Friends Service Committee provided its
offices.) The CRTFCA came into being in response to the rapes and
murders of three American nuns and a co-worker in El Salvador by
US-sponsored soldiers on December 2, 1980; and it had taken on the
task of matching refugees who were willing to speak out with congregations that were willing to host them. It also published the movement magazine, *Basta!* (*Enough!*); and invaluably, it published three
booklets on how to do Sanctuary: a blue overview of theory and practice, a green outline on "Sanctuary and the Law," and a brown "Nuts
and Bolts" guide to the day-to-day practicalities. Renny Golden of
the CRTFCA often quoted a poem by Antonio Machado: "Walker,
there is no road, the road is made by walking." She, Michael, Darlene
Gramigna, and the rest of the CRTFCA were among the movement's
early walkers, and these three booklets eliminated the need for each
congregation to reinvent the wheel.

Some of us also read Renny and Michael's *Sanctuary: The New Underground Railroad* (January 1986); James Chace's *Endless War: How
We Got Involved in Central America-And What Can Be Done* (1984);
and Jim Corbett's *The Sanctuary Church* (January 1986), which was
especially attractive to us because it was published as a Quaker pam-
phlet, was only thirty-six pages long, and Corbett was a Quaker as
well as being a co-founder of the movement. I regularly read the *New
York Times* (and still do online), and started subscribing to the *National Catholic Reporter* (and still subscribe) because it was so much more
complete and accurate than the *Times* about my new interests.

Soon after my talk with Michael about Wilton Meeting and maybe
partly because of it, the CRTFCA asked us to take on an outstanding
family. Though we weren't ready, we said yes.

On the warm evening of June 24, 1986, a fellow Quaker named
Woody Schempp and I drove a rickety station wagon along the high-
ways from Norwalk to the Newark Airport in New Jersey. We owned
more reliable vehicles but borrowed this one from a Meeting member

who accepted the risk that if the feds busted us for "transporting illegal aliens," they would seize it.

After all I had done to uphold the law in the aftermath of the 1971 Attica prison riot while New York State officials and police around me were breaking it, tonight I would begin several years of breaking it myself. Same conscience, opposite results.

The flight from Texas on which we expected Alma, Beto, and tiny Adrian Rodriguez (not their real names) landed late. Woody and I waited at the end of a long, brightly lit corridor as passengers from the flight straggled past us singly and in clusters. None of them looked like a Latino family. I was beginning to worry when we spotted them, a short, tan couple, she carrying the child, and he, a small bag with all their worldly possessions.

Alma and Beto had met and married in a church in Chiapas, Mexico, that they had fled to, she from El Salvador and he from Guatemala. His English was good and hers, understandable; they had already been in Sanctuary with a congregation in Texas for over a year. Tiny Adrian was born there and was thus a US citizen, meaning Woody and I were driving only two illegals that night. Beto, we understood, had been a sergeant in the army and had deserted rather that join a death squad. If arrested and sent home, he was certain to be tortured to death.

I forget whether it was at the Schempps or Bells that the little family slept that night. Thereafter it was in the Wilton Friends meetinghouse. Members had made one of the back rooms into a bedroom, and the ample kitchen across the hall soon gave off the aroma of Alma's delicious Salvadoran cooking. Since the restroom did not have a shower, members took turns driving the family to their homes. A back door in the bedroom opened onto a small lawn and large forest where we'd worked out a trail through the trees to the home of a Meeting family who agreed to take in the Rodríguezes if the feds came looking for them and they had to flee.

During the first weeks, one or two of us spent the night in the meetinghouse, and it was well that we did. One night when Meeting member John Perry was the chaperon, two or three Wilton police officers came to the front door and wanted to enter. John, standing in his underwear, refused to let them. He was right. It was the feds, not state or local police, who were empowered to enforce the immigration laws. The next day I visited the police headquarters and told their chief about our guests' plight. "If my men try to get in, don't let them," is roughly what he replied. "If they're overzealous, tell me about it." The Wilton police never bothered us again. Some months later, after we had found an apartment for the family and a car for Beto—back in Texas, Catholic Charities had managed to get him a driver's license— Beto ran out of gas. A Wilton cop picked him up and drove him home.

A well-publicized trial in Tucson resulted in the conviction of eight out of eleven Sanctuary worker defendants in May 1986, three-year and five-year sentences that July that were all suspended, and a PR disaster for the government for prosecuting people of conscience who had been saving refugees' lives from the despicable official conduct that most Americans hadn't known about. The spectacle that the trial staged by casting nuns, clergy, and other decent, dedicated people into the criminal dock dramatized the message of Sanctuary more vividly than any event that we in the movement ever carried out. The government had handed us what activists dream about: a perfect national action; and it never again prosecuted any other Sanctuary members. As time passed with no more indictments, we in the movement came to feel safer. Later I asked the INS spokesman, Duane "Duke" Austin, whether they had refrained from busting a certain family of undocumented refugees who were in Sanctuary with a religious community, in order to avoid bad publicity. He said yes.

Not that the feds overlooked us completely. Nancy and I were not alone in receiving mail now and then that had been torn open and crudely taped shut. We heard strange noises on our phone. One day I called a friend in San Diego who was more deeply involved in Sanctuary than I was, and instead of her live voice, I heard a conversation she had had a few days earlier with a Sanctuary person in Tucson. Apparently I'd tripped a recording device that most likely the FBI had planted. Eileen Purcell had a surveillance car and person parked outside her home in San Francisco for six months. Especially early in the movement, persons unknown surreptitiously and illegally forced their way into a large number of Sanctuary church offices and rifled through (messed up) their files but did not take anything of value—so theft was not the motive. Local police never caught the perps. Neither our Meeting nor any members suffered such a break-in.

Our members lived in two Congressional districts, and both our Congressmen (both Republicans) agreed to meet with our family, even though they were here illegally. I still recall walking the family to Rep. John Rowland's office on the second floor of a post office in Waterbury, down a hallway past a closed door marked FBI. Rowland was cordial but non-committal. Visiting Rep. Christopher Shays in his office in Bridgeport went better. After Alma and Beto and I told him what they had been through, he asked me to let him know if they were ever arrested so he could try to help them. But if I were arrested, he added, he would not help me. That was fine, I said, I understood the possible price of civil disobedience. We smiled.

Getting away with pranks in college stood me in good stead when it came to, say, flying to Chicago with Beto without arousing suspicion. At the same time, I remained mindful that if the feds wanted to bust us, they could, and if brought to trial, we'd probably be convicted. Later, I would write for my law school class reunion book that Nancy and I remained at large thanks to prosecutorial discretion.

She and I drove the Rodríguezes to represent Wilton Meeting at several gatherings of the New England Sanctuaries in Massachusetts. At one of them, Beto and I were chosen to represent the region at a nationwide gathering of Sanctuary communities that was put together by members of the CRTFCA, an activist named Margaret Swedish, and maybe one or two others (together, "the junta") to be held in July 1987 at Loyola University's impressive campus along Lake Michigan on Chicago's North Side. The people who attended felt nearly unanimously that Sanctuary could do the most good by inducing our government to stop enabling the terror in Central America. Three days of meals, meetings, and conviviality led to organizing the movement— or about half the nation's Sanctuaries that chose to join—into an Alliance of Sanctuary Communities and to choosing a National Steering Committee to run it. Beto and his sister Adriana were among the refugees chosen. I was among the North Americans thanks to the feminists who insisted on equality, meaning as many men as women.

I had spoken up enough during the meetings to be somewhat known and was one of the few men who had not left the gathering by the time the members were chosen.

A word about Margaret Swedish—Margie to those who knew her well—who became my sometimes mentor and Nancy's and my long-time friend; she appears in several stories hereafter. Her family, she said, came from Croatia, not Sweden. From 1981 to 2004, she was the director of the Religious Task Force on Central America and Mexico, and every two month, she wrote and published a newsletter that I, and I trust many others, found invaluable. Come 2005, she turned her attention to the ecological crisis. Maryknoll's Orbis Books published her *Living Beyond the "End of the World": A Spirituality of Hope* in 2008 and her and Marie Dennis's *Like Grains of Wheat: A Spirituality of Solidarity* in 2004. (More about Marie later.) She traveled considerably, speaking and conducting workshops about her concerns. I would see her in Washington, and she visited Nancy and me in Vermont, fairly regularly. She wrote a strong and insightful blurb for my novel *Roses in the Night*, though she had reservations about its explicit sex scene. One summer, she walked out of Nancy's and my front door and found herself face-to-face with a large moose. They both retreated. I admire her enormously for her devotion to bettering the lot of humankind.

Beto and I were to spend tonight in the apartment of Adriana and her family in the comfortable high-rise on the South Side where their Sanctuary sponsor, KAM Isaiah Israel, was lodging them. Though I did not start for there until well into the evening, I foolishly decided not to spring for a taxi but to take public transportation.

I am standing in a subway station under downtown Chicago. A uniformed attendant assures me that the L train I need will still be running after midnight. A woman who must be six feet tall and is blind, says no, it won't. I wonder what she is doing there, but she is right.

I am standing on an L platform looking back up the tracks at the towers of downtown. From a nearby group of Black women, I hear the words "ugly white face," and mine is the only white face in sight. It's Saturday night, and late as it is, it's party time on the avenue below —many people, much loud music. An enormous Black man wearing short pants walks down the platform and stops before he reaches me. I wonder whether he's strong enough to throw me across the tracks and down to the avenue, but he stands quietly. It's ironic, I think, that I've just spent three days trying to save Latino foreigners' lives, and here I am at risk in a Black ghetto that the System makes cruelly hard for the people around me to escape.

I am standing on a sidewalk waiting for a crosstown bus. The black iron mass of the L rises behind me. Across the sidewalk is a liquor store. Though it's well past midnight, people stream in and come out holding well-filled, brown paper bags. What a way to escape the ghetto! Which I eventually do on a bus and a long walk through quiet streets.

The Alliance put out a newsletter for its members. Louise Kaminsky was the editor, and I was the main contributor. Since she lived near Philadelphia, and Nancy and I were still in Norwalk, Louise and I met in one or another hospital cafeteria roughly midway in between and spent maybe two or three hours assembling and editing each issue. No one in a hospital cafeteria asks you to eat or drink or leave. Then Louise took it home and got it out. We didn't get much feedback about our efforts, though Rev. Gus Schultz told me that he found the newsletter "helpful and interesting "and kept him "in touch with some things going on that are far away."

The Alliance's annual meetings and more frequent Steering Committee meetings took Beto and me and sometimes Nancy to Washington, Milwaukee, Detroit, Chicago again, St. Louis, Philadelphia, Tucson, Cambridge, and Los Angeles. Nancy and I made many friends, some of whom remain close today. Two women who appear in later stories attended some of them: Sister Alice Zachmann, who founded and ran the Guatemala Human Rights Commission/USA, and Angie Berryman of the quietly helpful American Friends Service Committee. Someone at a conference asked Beto, if being deported was so likely to lead to his death, why didn't he go to Canada. "Because the CIA is here," he replied.

My good friend from college, Brown Meggs, and I had been in only sporadic touch for many years, until a Sanctuary meeting in LA opened the way for a delightful reunion with him and his dear wife Nancy in their home in nearby Pasadena. Another trip, another visit, this one very sad. A swiftly moving pancreatic cancer had taken Nancy and devastated Brown, as I describe in "Fans." My Nancy and I continued to see him after he moved to San Francisco and we were there visiting our sons Brian and Chris. Years of therapy and wine failed to bring him to terms with losing her, and he died in 1997 at the age of sixty-six. Doctors called it a stroke. I believe it was grief.

Jim Corbett and Rev. John Fife were clearly among the heroes of the Sanctuary Movement, of civil disobedience, and of Christian witness. But sometimes it is necessary to disagree with heroes, and most of the Sanctuaries in the Alliance disagreed with these two and their Tucson allies on a fundamental point: The Tucson people believed that the refugees whom congregations hosted should not denounce the terror they had fled. Sanctuary, they argued, was religious and making it political weakened it. That's fine, I thought, for Tucson, which had to contend with local rednecks. (For instance, Fife would set jugs of water out in the desert so that people crossing illegally would not die of dehydration, as many of them did, and local rednecks who found the jugs would shoot them with their rifles.) But for the Sanctuaries removed from the Border, meaning most of them, local threats were not a problem, and we of Chicago school, now the Alliance, felt that the best chance to end the violence that the US was enabling in the refugees' homelands was for them to tell people the horrors that they and their loved ones had suffered and for us North Americans to denounce the US complicity so as, we hoped, to mobilize public opinion against it. To us, denouncing the US role was both religious and political, and failing to denounce it, while it may have been prudent near the Border, would needlessly sacrifice a powerful tool for saving lives.

An unfortunate incident had fueled the Chicago–Tucson rift. In 1982, Fife sent a young Mayan couple to the CRTFCA. But because the couple believed that guerrillas had bombed and torched their village, the CRTFCA declined to place them with a congregation and sent them back to Tucson. They didn't get there and were not heard from again. Most of us considered that the CRTFCA was clearly sound for not giving the couple a platform to tell a story that was probably untrue and would surely harm the cause. But it should have seen them safely back to Tucson. The Tucson people, though, simply condemned the CRTFCA for the whole incident.

One of the Steering Committee's early efforts was to send three of its members, Terri English of Texas, Steve Hays-Lohrey of Berkeley, and me to Tucson for the weekend of February 26–28, 1988, to try to heal the rift, which meant convincing Fife and Corbett to stop urging Sanctuaries not to denounce the US-backed terror. It was a pleasant and memorable weekend. Hours of civil discussion with Fife and Corbett. Corbett's wife Pat drove the three of us down to Nogales, which straddles the border seventy miles south of Tucson, for a fine Mexican dinner. The waiter kept placing tiny paper cups of tequila before us. Outside the large window across the table was a chain-link fence that marked the US–Mexican border and had a large hole in it through which people used to cross into Arizona. On Sunday morning I attended Pima Friends Meeting and had a pleasant conversation with a member who wrote to me afterwards that she had discovered why I was there and I was "a wolf in sheep's clothing."

Our hours of debating with Fife and Corbett didn't change anybody's mind, though I'm glad we'd tried. The rift in the movement continued without noticeable effect now except in the history books. Most people who have written about the movement give due credit to the Tucson branch and its participants, but mention the CRTFCA briefly if at all, despite the fact that it, not Tucson, was the main coordinator of the movement and provided the main resources for it. They also fail to mention that Rev. Gus Schultz was a co-founder the movement along with Corbett and Fife, and that he and Eileen Purcell recruited, in the San Francisco Bay area alone, some eighty of Sanctuary's five hundred congregations. Ann Crittenden's 1988 book titled *Sanctuary: A Story of American Conscience and Law in Collision*, probably the most widely read book about the movement, has a few pages about the CRTFCA and nothing about Schultz or Purcell. The account of the movement in Jonathan Blitzer's 2024 book *Everyone Who Is Gone Is Here: The United States, Central America, and the Making of a Crisis* does well about Tucson, gives Tucson's perspective on the CRTFCA and the Mayan couple, omits Schultz, and says of Purcell merely that she "had been central to the earliest stages of the sanctuary push in the Bay Area."

Informal sanctuary had begun in the San Francisco area, largely for Salvadorans, back in 1979. In the East Bay it was modeled on the sanctuary that Gus Schultz had created in 1971 for conscientious objectors to the Vietnam War. Factors that led to the large number of Sanctuaries in the Bay area: Many of the people involved believed that they were not breaking the law, so they needn't decide whether to commit civil disobedience. Eileen Purcell says that "San Francisco was predisposed, because of our rich history, to come out very strongly in favor of the movement."[7] Then there were the recruiting efforts by Gus and especially Eileen. She told me,

> My conversion in El Salvador took place in my 1980 trip, and at that time I was touched by the people, and my own life was at risk at different points, and it makes you evaluate. (She laughed.) But to hold a woman in my arms who had witnessed her husband sawed in half and have her weep and simply to cradle her was a life-changing experience.

After that, with the blessing of San Francisco's Archbishop John Quinn,

> I became this kinda person on a horse that would go anywhere they would hear me and began telling this story. Anybody who wants to know, we'll go. I was not married. I had no children. So every night we spoke and showed the slides and told the refugee stories.

Gus Schultz, who often worked with her and once traveled with her to El Salvador, again at great risk, summed it up: "Eileen is probably the most underrated person in the whole movement. I think she had more to do with it than almost anybody."

In 2001, Jim Corbett died at age sixty-seven of a rare brain disease, ironic because his mind was brilliant. Gus Schultz died in 2007 at age seventy-two after a ten-year struggle with Lewy body disease. In 1992, John Fife became the Moderator of the General Assembly of the Presbyterian Church (USA). In 2023, now retired from his church though not from his human rights work, he graciously wrote a blurb for my novel *Roses in the Night*, which includes a fact-based description of him and his wife Mary Ann taking one of my heroines along with other desperate refugees into his Southside Presbyterian Church right after they crossed from Mexico.

Whether or not Sanctuary people saw themselves as breaking the law, they were clearly treating refugees more lawfully and far more humanely than our government was. The Reagan and first Bush Administrations applied the asylum law discriminatorily, cruelly, and illegally, causing probably thousands of innocent people to die, many horribly. In January 1991, the government finally settled a case that the American Baptist Church and several other churches had brought years earlier, by admitting, in fact if not in so many words, that the INS had been judging the asylum applications of Salvadorans and Guatemalans by illegal standards. It agreed to retry, under correct legal standards this time, some one hundred and fifty thousand asylum cases of refugees who had evaded or survived being deported to the US-backed death squads.

By the end of 1988, the Sanctuary work that Beto and Alma could do with Wilton Meeting had run its course, and it was time for the family to move on. Beto landed a job in Cambridge with Centro Presente, which served refugees, and in January 1989, the family moved to Boston. He and I stayed in touch, and once or twice I spent the night in their home, until Sanctuary rumbled on and gradually faded away.

By then, I was becoming involved other Latin America solidarity projects. From 1991 to 2013, I served as the corporate secretary and a member of the board of the International Mayan League/USA. From 1995 to 2012, I was a contributing editor and book reviewer for *Interconnect*, which was a quarterly created to serve the US–Latin America solidarity community by a wonderful pair of human rights activists and Nancy's and my dear friends, Peter and Gail Mott of Rochester, New York.

One day, after Nancy and I had moved to Vermont an old friend from Sanctuary times named Kathy Boylan and a Father Bill Bresotti—whom I think of as the "radical priest" in Paul Simon's "Me and Julio Down by the Schoolyard"—drove a van full of fifteen Salvadoran refugees up from Long Island for an event at the Weston Priory.

They asked the brothers if they could sleep on their floor that night. The brothers said no. What to do? Three hundred miles from home with all those passengers, one pregnant, and all illegal. So, they slept in our living room on the window seats and carpet, the most house-guests Nancy and I ever had.

In 2000 and again in 2001, Nancy and I participated in huge SOA Watch vigils outside Fort Benning, Georgia, against the School of the Americas, a.k.a. School of the Assassins,* which has trained tens of thousands of Latin American military and police offices in tactics and torture. In the vast crowd, we kept running into people we'd known in the Sanctuary Movement. In 2006, I attended again with my old friend Jim Keller. SOA graduates include a vast number of human rights violators and several Latin American dictators. At two of those vigils, Beto's sister Adriana was perhaps the most powerful of all the speakers. The vigils ended with a funeral march. Each of us carried a white wooden cross that bore the name of a person whose death was caused by SOA grads. The names of the dead boomed out reverently over the PA. After each name, we thousands of marchers shouted with one voice, "Presente!" It was very moving.

The fact that the soldiers responsible for shooting dead six Jesuit priests and two of their housekeepers on November 16, 1989, were trained by the SOA had moved a Maryknoll priest named Father Roy Bourgeois to found SOA Watch the next year. Its ultimate aim was to close the school. Roy had served for four years in the navy before becoming a priest in 1972. One night, he and an accomplice sneaked into Fort Benning with a boombox. He climbed an evergreen tree outside the barracks where the SOA's current attendees were sleeping and awakened them by playing loudly the last homily that Saint Oscar Romero gave before being assassinated. He later spent more than four years in federal prisons for several non-violent protests. In 1994 he re-

---

* In 2001, the school changed its name to the Western Hemisphere Institute for Security Cooperation (WHINSEC). An SOA Watch slogan put it, "New name, same shame." In 2023, Fort Benning, which had been named for Confederate Brigadier General Henry L. Benning, became Fort Moore, for Lieutenant General Harold Gregory Moore Jr., who served in Vietnam. Once again, "New name, same shame."

ceived Gandhi Peace Award and in 2011 the American Peace Award. He is one of my heroes, and I remain grateful to him for writing the foreword for my still-unpublished book *Sisters in the Storm*. But Rome defrocked him and dismissed him from Maryknoll for advocating that women should be able to become priests.

To bring Nancy's and my Sanctuary story full circle: In 2013 in Gig Harbor, Washington, a Catholic Tacoma Dominican Sister joined together in holy matrimony our dear friends and former Sanctuary committee comrades, Betty Devereux and Diane Dilley. Nancy and I were privileged to participate in the ceremony. Rome was not consulted.

Border Witness

Ever since joining the Sanctuary Movement, I had been hearing about events in the Rio Grande Valley of Texas, but I did not have a clear idea of what or where it is. In September 1994, I finally flew there for a program called "Reflecting on Border Realities," which was run by Sister Ellen Lamberjack of a Franciscan community in Tiffin, Ohio. The Valley does not slope down to the river except at the riverbank itself. Rather, it is a vast flat plain at the east end of the Rio Grande—called the *Rio Bravo* in Mexico—which begins nineteen hundred miles northwest in Colorado and isn't very grand by the time it reaches the Valley. In many places, it's an easy stone's throw across. Only two good roads led north out of the Valley, and they were heavily patrolled to keep "illegals" out of the greater USA.

That September's program—which began on the 9/11 five years after my flight to Guatemala City related in "'Keep It Handy'"—consisted of Sister Ellen, who did the coordinating, cooking, and driving, Sisters Carolyn and Rita, and me. We didn't use "Sister" while talking with each other, so I shan't use it hereafter. Carolyn directed La Posada Providencia (The Inn of Providence), a temporary shelter in nearby San Benito for refugees who had asylum, or had applied for it, and were on their way north out of the Valley. Sister Rita was the peace and justice coordinator for her community in St. Paul, Minnesota. Besides running Border Witness, Ellen coordinated her community's Sanctuary work in Tiffin.

Sunday: Arrived Harlingen and lodged with Carolyn and Rita at peaceful, comfortable Casa de Vida (House of Life), a small retreat center on the plain near Brownsville. Except for occasional palm trees and fields of sugar cane, which looked like tall, skinny corn stalks, this southern tip of the Midwest could have been Ohio or Illinois in July-like heat. Ellen went over the week's program and gave us packets containing an agenda and map, daily worship programs and readings, and background readings about the places we'd visit. We were to be on our own until worship and reflection at ten in the mornings.

Monday: Today we glimpsed local labor and poverty just south of the Border. In McAllen, about fifty miles west, an ex-priest, ex-worker for Cesar Chavez, and now CEO of a local corporation whose named was Mike Allen explained *maquiladoras*, which are factories or assembly plants that US and foreign companies set up in Mexico for the cheap labor and low taxes. He drove us across the Rio Grande—a tiny river here considering the millions of gallons of human and industrial waste that flowed into it every day—to a showcase maquiladora that made antilock brake parts, parts for Audi car horns, air and water switches, gold-plated jewelry, expandable file envelopes, and more.

We were shown around the big, windowless, fairly clean and quiet, air-conditioned plant. Worker turnover was 48-60% a year. The workers, 70% of whom were women, did 48-hour weeks—$9^{1}/_{2}$ hours a day with two twenty-minute breaks and thirty minutes for lunch—for around $30–50 (US) a week. That was often enough for them to survive on in squalor. A mother who needed money might work two 9 1/2 hour shifts a day for three days a week, which was unlawful to do.

In the city of Rio Bravo a few miles east of Reynoso, we met with Ed Krueger, who worked with the Border Committee of Working Women. A red volume of Mexican labor law served as his bible. He explained to dozens of little groups of women the legal rights that the maquiladoras routinely denied them. The local unions helped managements more than workers. He thought that only about 5% of the maquiladoras could pass an OSHA safety inspection, and cited methyl chloride that causes cancer, methyl ethyl ketone that causes birth defects, and other poisons that maquiladoras exposed their workers to with no protections.

The maquiladoras provided jobs that didn't pay particularly well even for Mexico but beat the unemployment and even worse squalor in which the prevailing system kept most Mexicans. Besides supporting that system, they drew hundreds of thousands of workers to the area, profited greatly from them, but failed to put in the roads, sewers, and water pipes that these people needed. They flouted environmental and safety laws, hurting workers, making them and their neighbors sick, and creating a high incidence of brainless babies who did not survive.

Ed guided us through a nearby colonia of rutted, muddy, dirt roads, homes built of odd boards, with corrugated roofs and dirt floors. They had no electricity, no sewage, and no running water except a rushing, stinking, gray stream full of you know what. We visited an incredibly affirmative and hearty woman named Adriana, who told us about Zenith's shabby treatment of its workers in a nearby maquiladora. Its cafeteria served spoiled meat and cockroaches in the food. Women job applicants had to submit urine samples, and if they were pregnant, they weren't hired. Maquiladoras often dumped workers before Christmas bonus time and paid holidays.

The lower parts of Adriana's uneven dirt floor were muddy from recent rain that ran in. Her family had raised the floor with truckloads of dirt when they could afford to. A $20 load cost more than half a week's pay, and anyway, they couldn't add more dirt to the floor now, until they raised the roof, whose rusty nails pointed downwards an inch or so above my head. A dilapidated car seat, resting on cinder blocks and draped with blue floral cloth, served as a couch. There was a nice-looking boombox by a big mirror on one of the walls. Wisps of cloth hung down to supplement the ill-fitting screen doors. Winters were windy and in the forties or thirties, and the mostly plywood walls sported many cracks. In spite of all, Adriana said she found life here better than it had been for her in nearby Durango. It pleased her that we cared about peace and justice and came to visit, and she touched her hair into place before I took her picture. A pure white streamer of toilet paper twisted from a roll on a table between her house and an outhouse.

Tuesday: A woman named Lisa, who was in her twenties and ran Mano a Mano (Hand in Hand), which helped pregnant women in Brownsville and across the river in Matamoros, guided us for about forty minutes across the vast, flat Matamoros city dump, through its awful stink and loud swarms of flies. A few hundred Mexicans—many of whom dwelt in shacks on the edge of the dump or parts of it that were no longer used—competed with sea gulls, crows, vultures, and lively hogs to eke a living out of the garbage. Now and then a human fetus turned up. Picture dark-skinned, solid gleaners in dull, grungy garb and delicate, blue-eyed, blond Lisa in a red floral dress embracing each other as she gave them bags of vitamins.

A van stopped near us, and several Evangelicals got out. Their ministry to the dump-dwellers was obviously popular, and they were immediately surrounded by nearby gleaners. Lisa told us that when a woman would ask them how to stop having babies, they would tell her that if God wanted her to have another child, she would have one. It was Catholic sister who told these women how to stop conceiving.

The Cameron Park colonia, which had existed on the outskirts of Brownsville for thirty years, still lacked sewers and regular water. There Lisa introduced us to an undocumented woman who had crossed from Mexico to birth each of her three children and now lived on almost nothing. The woman said proudly that her oldest son had just gotten a 97 on an English exam, and added that she wants her kids to become "the three biggest liars: a doctor, a lawyer, and a preacher." All eyes turned to me, and I agreed. She served us huge glasses of Coke with ice and asked us to let her know if she could help us later on. As we left, she thanked us for coming.

Wednesday: Project ARISE was sort of a Head Start, English teacher, and general helper for twenty-seven *colonias* totaling at least ten thousand people ("illegals" often aren't counted) around the city of Pharr. As we sat in a circle, three young women who work there told us about coming from Mexico. Each of them wept as she related the ways that some Texans had humiliated her for not knowing English. The young woman named Virginia was so beautiful that I somehow didn't expect her to be so affected, but as she talked to us, tears rolled down her lovely cheeks. All three women were gracious about my ignorance of Spanish.

In a cavernous room adorned with huge, Orozco-type murals at the United Farm Workers building, a lawyer named Ray Gill, who was so spirited that I kept forgetting he was wheelchair-bound and could barely move his arms, talked about the UFW's on-going legal battles to stop growers from cheating workers on the minimum wage, to force growers to obey various laws, and to start providing toilets in the fields—many women got bladder infections because they were too embarrassed to pee where there weren't any bushes—and other amenities (necessities) that nearly all American laborers except our farm workers receive. My wife Nancy's eyes were opened to these realities—and what they say about America—during two high school summer vacations that she spent with migrant farm workers in Pennsylvania caring for their children.

Since the 5:30 mass at the nearby Shrine of the Virgen de San Juan del Valle was in Spanish, Ellen and Carolyn, who were quite fluent, attended. Rita and I, who were not, walked our separate ways along a Stations of the Cross around a big, flat park behind the shrine. Beautiful statues adorned each station. Jesus had the long, white, northern European face.

Thursday: From a little park near the bridge between Brownsville and Matamoros, the sisters and I watched several men, naked except for one in white briefs, wade and swim across the little Rio Grande holding aloft their clothes in bags. Women usually stayed clad as they crossed, changing into dry clothes in the bushes on the US riverbank. We didn't see any women crossing, but many colorful articles of clothing hung in those bushes. Border Patrols on foot or in white or pale green suburbans missed some crossers and caught some, whom they would return to Mexico now and maybe other times today.

A pleasant young officer in a well-pressed green uniform told us she understood that they would catch maybe 10% of the crossers, mostly Mexicans. (It was closer to 50% while we were watching.) The officers got to know the names and birthdays of some frequent crossers. It looked like a big game, not serious or dangerous, though an estimated two hundred bodies a year were washing up along the river. Around a quarter of those dead people had been victims of foul play.

Poignantly close to a wildlife refuges sat the Port Isabel Service Processing Center, a.k.a. the Bayview Detention Center, commonly known as El Corralon (the big corral). Since the INS returned nearly all Mexicans it caught to Mexico, its 750 detainees (prisoners) were mostly OTMs (Other Than Mexicans). They called each other *zanahorias* (carrots) on account of their bright orange garb. A civil but impatient lieutenant gave us a short tour. No, you can't see the barracks, you can't see the library. Yes, this is a minimum-security prison. Married prisoners could not stay together because, he said, "Population is already a problem and we don't want it increasing in here." Some child prisoners (not in carrot clothes) were with their mothers. Most of the prisoners merely stood around in the sun. Their crime was coming here as our forebears had come. It wasn't their hopes and needs that had changed, but US receptiveness.

Friday: Ellen picked me up at 8:00 to interview Brenda, a refugee who had received asylum, for a book I was writing about the Sanctuary Movement. She had worked for a Lutheran Church in San Salvador. One day a squad of security forces pursued a group of her, her fellow workers, and their children. They barricaded themselves inside a garage. The pursuers opened fire through the door, and Brenda and her little girl survived only because she fell beneath the bodies of people who were shot. As she related more of her story, she wept for her many "friends who have passed away." These murdered friends were with her constantly, and she named her children after two of them. She was so grateful that this gringo cared about her story and her people that she told me I could stay in her home any time I was in the Valley. It is for her that my novel *Roses in the Night* has a heroine named Brenda.

I had received a similar offer of hospitality in 1975, when I became a regular at the Stamford, Connecticut, unemployment office. A staff person told me that after she and her husband moved to Boston, I could stay with them any time I came there. Had I stuck to my career path, I'd have made more money, but money could not have bought these deeply moving offers.

Saturday: The sisters and I walked on the beach on South Padre Island sharing our reflections on the week after we'd eaten huge fish sandwiches. Then a good dinner at a Mexican restaurant. Then a fiesta, in San Benito. Down to eighty-five degrees by 9:00 p.m. Home on Sunday.

The impoverished Mexicans I met this week seemed as intelligent and were often more hard-working than the middle-class gringos I have nearly always lived among. The physical squalor, which was all that their long dull workdays earned them, said much about the System that kept the unions flaccid, unemployment high, and most people uneducated and focused on rewards in Heaven. Once again, the Christian promise of eternal life served godless exploitation.

The treatment of Latinos seeking asylum or a better life in America in 1994 seems benign compared to recent years when our officials have crowded large numbers of them into frigid caverns with little or no bedding, inadequate toilets, toilet paper, and tampons, and no privacy; deported prisoners sick with Covid back to infect the cities and villages they had fled; forced asylum seekers to live and sometimes be killed in Mexico while their cases dragged on in the US; and kidnapped more than five thousand children from their parents, inflicting agonizing traumatic damage on the children and parents alike. What has this nation descended from immigrants become?

"Keep It Handy"

I had grown to like and respect Beto's sister Adriana as we worked together on various Sanctuary projects. Beto and I had stayed with her, her husband Jeff, and her girls Stella and Olivia in Chicago when the work took us there, and I knew them as a lively and loving household. Jeff was slender, blond, bespectacled, thoughtful in both senses, and a practical idealist. The first thing that struck me about their apartment was his magnificent wall of paperbacks—Kant, Spinoza, Dostoyevsky, Freud, classics of literature, and more. Stella, who was dark, attractive, and about to be fifteen, tended to be reflective and quiet; when she applied to private schools in Chicago, four of them accepted her and offered her scholarships. Olivia was twelve, tiny, and impatient to start growing, a fun-filled imp. The times I see her in my mind, she is laughing. Adriana was like them both; her pain lurked behind her laugh. She seemed so sensible, vivacious, and good-humored that it took me a while to appreciate that she was surviving a torture that never ceased. After many false leads, nightmares, and dashed dreams, she still harbored the hope that somewhere her other two girls, Rosaura and Glenda, who on 9/11/81 had been disappeared along with her father and several other loved ones, were still alive.

I asked Jeff one time how he and Adriana happened to get together. He said that back when he was working in a school in Fort Worth, Texas, he read a paper that a student named Adriana had written, and saw that she "had a gift for connecting images and really seemed to have a capacity to convey the world as she saw it in a language that she didn't know that well at that time." Several months later when he was the coordinator of the night program, he would talk with the students, and he "liked her, and to engage her, because she was fearless and really enjoyable to talk with. She was not falsely deferential and was willing to talk about ideas larger than what people normally would see in their own immediate self-interest. Some of the other students were shy and very, very deferential. She was shy, but it didn't keep her from talking." (We laugh.)

So it was Adriana's mind that first drew Jeff to her. Several years later the mind of a Mayan guerrilla would draw Jennifer Harbury to him. In my brief conversations with an attractive guerrilla named Emma later on, it was her mind that I found fascinating.

One thing leads to another, and conscience may lead to trouble. Adriana's decision of conscience to speak out in the United States on behalf of her people make it imperative for her, Stella, and Olivia to visit Guatemala. They were living in constant peril of being arrested and deported to the death squads. The great majority of their compatriots who fled here hid out as best they could in the underground economy or went on to Canada, which was actually providing the humane, lawful asylum that the United States touted but was in fact refusing to grant to nearly all Guatemalans. Adriana and Jeff had married in September 1987. That placed her, Stella, and Olivia at the start of a bumpy road to becoming legal US residents. Residency would lift the shadow that had darkened their lives and free them to obtain green cards (work permits, which were not green), to travel, go to school, and just to walk down the sidewalk openly and without the constant fear of federal agents. But before they could become "legal," the State Department required them to leave the country and be processed at an American embassy or consulate abroad. It was the choice of the

US Embassy in Guatemala that they should return to their homeland, the place they dreaded the most, from which they had fled for their lives—a choice that Jeff and Adriana had challenged without success during nearly two years of bureaucratic back and forth, that is, ever since they married.

I understood the State Department's interest in requiring foreigners who had entered illegally to exit and return through official channels. But why subject Adriana and the girls to the danger, not to mention the inconvenience and expense, of returning to Guatemala of all places, when US consulates in Juarez Mexico or Montreal Canada would serve as well?

No official answered Jeff directly. One of them assured him that they'd all be safe in Guatemala because the noted dissident Rigoberta Menchú had recently made a safe visit. In fact, Ms. Menchú had recently made two visits. The second one had gone safely enough, but not the first—as the official did not disclose but Jeff knew because he had helped to keep her safe. She and another member of her group had been kidnapped in the Aurora Airport outside Guatemala City as they arrived. Jeff was one of the internationals who awaited her there in vain and then gathered at the Camino Real Hotel for the hue and cry that pressured the regime into releasing her.* And so Ms. Menchú survived and went on to win the Nobel Peace Prize four years later.

In May 1989, Beto asked me to accompany Adriana and her family on their required trip to Guatemala. We'd arrive on Sunday, September 10th and leave on Friday, the 15th. He assured me that others would be going too, Jeff of course, Sidney Hollander, who headed the sanctuary committee of the synagogue that was sponsoring Adriana and her family, and Dr. Antonio Martinez, who facilitated a group of survivors of torture that included Adriana.

I did not want to go. Time and money were factors but not the problem. Honored as I felt to be asked, fond as I was of Adriana and Stella and Olivia, and clearly as I saw that they needed Americans at

---

* Also part of Jeff's group were Sister Judy Stephens, who kindly wrote an epigraph for my novel *Roses in the Night*, and Father Joe Nangle, who took considerable risks in Guatemala on behalf of Sister Dianna Ortiz following her kidnapping and torture there in November 1989.

their side, I was scared. I told Beto that I would talk it over with Nancy.

Guatemala made a fascinating tourist destination if you were not accompanying a perceived subversive. In the '70s a friend who lived in Costa Rica had warned me not to visit Guatemala even as a tourist because the bodies of dissidents often ended up on the streets, and I might be kidnapped or shot. I knew that Guatemala had the most brutal army and worst human rights record in the Hemisphere, making Cuba look nearly as innocent as Sweden.

Respected media had been assuring us that Guatemala was no longer a military dictatorship but a democracy or "fledgling democracy" since a civilian, Vinicio Cerezo, became President in January 1986. The *New York Times*, which I read faithfully, said this repeatedly. But I knew that such reports painted a false picture. Those of us who paid attention knew that the security forces still ruled by violence and killed with impunity.

But Adriana needed protection. The authorities down there had found cause to kill much of her family and likely knew that she had been denouncing them in the United States. But if Americans stick physically close to an imperiled Guatemalan, this reduces the chances that such will befall them. My value lay in my US passport and Anglo-Irish skin.

I knew that the young Americans, Canadians, and Europeans of Peace Brigades International, armed with only notebooks and cameras, were continuously accompanying Guatemalans whom the authorities wanted to kill. Over lunch, Jean-Marie Simon, an American who had recently compiled a powerful work of photojournalism, *Guatemala: Eternal Spring, Eternal Tyranny*, told me about roaming through the highlands to take her photos. Yet here she sat full of life. If Jeff, Jean-Marie, the people of Peace Brigades, and other Americans could accompany people at risk and emerge unscathed, why not me? I feared that my grim view of Guatemala was making me unduly reluctant to accompany friends in need. The trust with which Olivia and Stella hugged me as I'd come and go in Chicago mattered. Nancy and I did not know that Guatemala was in the midst of the renewed violence against Americans. Nor that death threats had driven an American named Sister Dianna Ortiz back to Kentucky in July. Nor that the bloodshed and atrocities during the month of the planned visit would make it known as Black September.

Armed with my information, shielded by my ignorance, and moved by my feelings for Adriana and her girls, I let the question marinate until it felt right to go. Nancy agreed. When we had decided to join the Sanctuary Movement, we thought the worst that could befall would be that we might spend a few years apart in federal prisons. We'd hate that, but thought we could live with the risk. Now the diminishing prospect of a US slammer was the least of our worries.

If a death squad pounded on your door, you'd probably dial 911 and ask the police for help. In Guatemala, the police were in league with the death squads. Having decided to venture beyond 911, as it were, I took the precautions that came to mind, wondering whether I was overdoing it and feeling a bit foolish. Congressman Christopher Shays (R, CT), gave me a note bearing the blue-and-gold-embossed letterhead of the United States House of Representatives to carry in my pocket. I phoned the US Embassy in Guatemala and was advised to register with them when I arrived, check with them before going into the countryside, and watch out for pickpockets. I alerted my brother Richard, who lived in Costa Rica, and asked Peace Brigades volunteer Janey Skinner in Guatemala City if I might call upon her if a need arose. She graciously said yes, though she did not mention that her office had just been bombed.

Sunday, September 10th, the Day of Departure, came on too fast. Searching my luggage in the Newark Airport, a security guard found a big green valentine that Nancy had tucked away.

I met Adriana, Jeff, the girls, and Sidney in the Houston airport and was so happy to see them that I forgot my misgivings for the moment. Sidney, whom I had not met before, had black wavy hair laced with gray and was taller, younger, and gentler than I. Dr. Antonio Martinez was not to join us until Tuesday.

Jeff drew Sidney, Adriana, and me aside. When he had accompanied Rigoberta Menchú's group to Guatemala City last year, he explained, the airport was set up so that Guatemalans had to go through passport and visa inspection on one floor while everyone else went through on another, leaving foreigners none the wiser when officials disappeared

Guatemalans at the airport. Jeff, who looks very gringo, said he was going to stick with Adriana and the girls no matter what. Sidney and I were to hurry though on our floor and wait for them at the far end of theirs. If they did not emerge, we were to ask why and call for such help as we could. Not perfect, but no one could think of a better plan—my first taste of the relative helplessness we were flying into. Jeff handed Sidney and me letters from Senator Paul Simon of Illinois like mine from Rep. Shays. They said nearly nothing but bore the gold official letterhead.

At last our jet roared down the highway to nowhere and rose like a javelin flung at the sun. What memories, I wondered, stirred in Adriana as the snug plane reversed the tedious, perilous journey that she, her then husband, and Stella and Olivia had made across Mexico and the parched, frosty desert to enter the US in secret?

Eight years ago, she and her sister-in-law, Lucia, each carrying a very small child, were going to her father's house for a family picnic. Her daughters Rosaura, ten, and Glenda, nine, were already there. But as the women approached the house, they saw twenty or thirty armed men, some in uniform, milling around. The door to the house was open. Adriana saw two or three men inside. One had a hose and was washing the floor.

Men surrounded the women, holding their cold gun barrels against their backs and the backs of their heads while their leader, whom Adriana called "very handsome [with] kind of green eyes and glasses with golden metal frames," questioned her for what seemed like a long time. He kept urging her and Lucia to go inside the house to see their family. Adriana kept refusing. Finally she said, "Well, thank you very much, I guess now I should go." They left. Half a block away, she realized the reality. "It was what every Guatemalan fears is going to happen. We started running. They realized that they made a mistake letting us go, and they started running."

There was a taxi stand about two blocks away. One of the driver saw what was happening, started his engine, and opened the doors of the cab. The women jumped in, and they took off. Did the pursuers get the cabbie's license number? Did he survive the terror? Adriana does not know. She has never again seen Rosaura or Glenda or the others who'd come for the picnic.

She and her husband and surviving daughters stayed in Guatemala for three more scary years, until they learned that they were on a death list. They took a bus to the Mexican border, crossed into Tapachula for "Christmas shopping," and bussed northwards, losing most of their money when Mexican officials shook them down at several bus stops. Sister Beatriz Zapata and a woman from Tucson crossed them into Arizona via a route that Beatriz, Sister Judy Stephens, and another nun had recently worked out. Adriana fell in the dark, broke her wrist, and passed out before they reached the wire fence marking the Border, which they crawled under. Then a three-day, three-night trek through the Sonoran Desert, hiding under bushes when INS planes flew over, sleeping on the ground, and waking to find ice in their water bottles.

The trek was so arduous that at one point Adriana's husband sat down on a creek bed and said "I want to die." After about an hour, Beatriz told him, "We have to leave, and if you want to die, fine, go ahead and die. But I don't want to die with you, and anybody who doesn't want to die needs to come." They left him but went slowly along the creek bed. An hour or so later, he caught up with them. They made it safely to Rev. John Fife's Southside Presbyterian Church in Tucson, and from there went into Sanctuary with a small church in Texas, where they displaced Adriana's brother Beto and his family ("Once we got there... people wanted to see a crying woman who had lost children."), making them available for us at Wilton (CT) Friends Meeting.

Five sleek but elderly jet fighters and eight helicopters lined the runway, which has a dip in it, as we bounced along at the Aurora Airport on the outskirts of Guatemala City. Jeff: "I was watching Adriana and the girls' emotions, their faces, when we got off the plane. She was so happy she was crying. I sensed a real strong emotion of, *I'm here.* Once you leave for that long, coming back must be an enormous feeling."

Inside the airport we were able to stick together, all on the same floor, through passport inspection and into a lofty, gloomy cavern to await our luggage. We had assumed that the Guatemalan security forces knew about our trip from the FBI or the Embassy. Now we wondered whether we, in particular, were being watched by any of the people gazing down from the railings above us. After what seemed like a long time, we crowded into a big, dilapidated, US-made cab, laughing in relief as it carried us off through the wet twilight.

As the cab turned from the broad *Avenida Reforma*, the off-white facade of the Camino Real, curving up behind a semi-circular driveway, loomed over us. Palm trees and flower beds filled the crescent between the driveway and the sidewalk. It was an ultramodern Westin hotel, tall by local standards, about a dozen stories. I forgot that the hotel would tap our phone calls.

Busy lobby. Cheery, touristy check-in. Lots of bellhops and security men with two-tone brown uniforms and little two-way radios. An iridescent green and crimson quetzal brooded in a glass case by the elevators. The quetzal is Guatemala's bird of freedom and adorns its blue and white flag. It is said to die in captivity. This one was stuffed.

We accepted the clerk's offer to put us in two rooms across the hall from each other on the fourth floor. It did not occur to us that these rooms might be bugged. Sidney and I looked down on the front entrance of the hotel from a big, heavily draped window. The Bartows overlooked paved patios, lawn, and a swimming pool out back. Each door to our rooms had one of those glass buttons that let you see anyone outside. The view was 180 degrees. I looked through ours often. The carpeted corridor was always deserted in both directions.

After we stowed our luggage, Sidney, on a sudden impulse, strode down the hall to the fire stairs and surprised a security guard talking into his radio. Flustered, the guard vanished down the stairs. "We exchanged glances," Sidney told us, "and I retreated. I was glad that he knew he had been seen, but I was also a little worried."

So was I.

Supper in the dining room was fun, and the local Monte Carlo beer tasted good. Most of us ordered the Guatemalan combo special, which gave us a tourist's sampling of local fare. I was enjoying being a tourist, yet trying to stay alert. After supper, we bought a local newspaper, and Adriana read it on one of the Bartows' double beds while the rest of us relaxed in their room.

Suddenly she exclaimed. A news item said that a bomb had gone off in front of our hotel at 10:20 the night before, exploding among the flowers between the driveway and sidewalk. We wondered jokingly whether the explosion could have been to welcome us.

Adriana returned to her reading and the rest of us to relaxing. Now she exclaimed in horror. Another news item said that a man named Carlos Cabrera, who taught at San Carlos University, was washing his car outside his home yesterday morning when eight men with guns and walkie-talkies pulled up in two vehicles, hustled him into one of them, and drove off.

Carlos Cabrera and his wife, Amparo, were Adriana's dear friends and former in-laws. Adriana and her first husband had lived in their home. There she had borne her lost daughters, Rosaura and Glenda. Carlos, she said, had been like a brother to her. Earlier that day she had been radiant when she talked about seeing Amparo and him at a family reunion tomorrow.

Her face dark with apprehension, she phoned Amparo. A few words in Spanish. Adriana screamed. Her sobbing shook her body. Carlos's corpse had been found this morning in some bushes beside the university, along with three other bodies. They had all been knifed, though apparently not tortured. All of them had been among the leaders of a failed teachers' strike for higher pay that June and July. Eight other strike leaders had also been disappeared, but these were the first bodies to turn up. Any union activity that threatens the status quo or the miserable level of workers' wages in Guatemala could be a capital offense.

We decided that our visit had almost certainly not caused Carlos's death, but the timing alarmed us. During the past few weeks Adriana had been talking with Amparo on the phone about our plans. Given Carlos's role in the strike and the fact that he was soon to be killed, their conversations had almost certainly been monitored. As noted, our government may have told the security forces about Adriana's trip. Then there was the security guard whom Sidney surprised on the stairwell. We assumed that the security forces almost certainly knew the particulars of Adriana's trip. That night we did not doubt that it was they who had murdered Carlos.

If it had been only Carlos's murder that coincided with our arrival, we might not have felt as threatened as we did. But the murder plus the bomb gave us, as we supposed they were intended to give us, a very strong feeling—it seemed almost a certainty that night—that they were not coincidental. The peril that I had felt I exaggerated in Connecticut seemed to be staring us in the face. Jeff: "I don't think that I rested on the trip from that point forward."

Sidney and I gathered up the pillows and blankets from our beds and bundled them across the empty hall into the Bartows' room. We checked the bolt on the door to the adjoining room and dragged a heavy dresser across it, then bolted and chained the door to the hall and wedged a chair under the knob. Jeff phoned our plight to Beto in Boston. Stella and Olivia played cards on their bed, cheerfully oblivious of their elders' tense, tedious efforts to get us through the night.

Back in the States, Beto phoned Nancy and told her about the bomb, though not about Carlos's murder, and said that he was trying to phone us and couldn't get through. Frightened, Nancy was able to reach the hotel but was told that all lines to our rooms were busy, though in fact they were not. "I never got through to you," she said later. "I tried all evening."

(One evening three years later, another American wife would try without success to get through on the phone to her husband, Peter Tiscione of Queens, NY, who had locked himself in his hotel room in Guatemala City after telling her he feared for his life. She persuaded the hotel clerk to go to his room where he found him stabbed to death in the bathtub after an apparently violent struggle. The US Embassy accepted the police conclusion that he committed suicide.)

At 10:30 Jeff and I phoned our Embassy. A Marine sergeant named Schultz was the ranking person we could reach on this Sunday evening. We asked him if he would send a car to bring us there, or otherwise provide us with a safe place to pass the night. No, he would not. He told us to come to the Embassy in the morning. That sounded too late. He did give us some sensible advice: "Stay out of the hotel bar. Lock yourselves in your room. Don't let anyone in you don't know." And, "If you have anything available, if you know what I mean, keep it handy."

Apart from the fact that our Embassy had just refused to help us, I felt oddly reassured that this Marine sergeant took our plight seriously. Never before had I felt the claustrophobic isolation of knowing that there'd be no point in calling the police. Consider this Marine's advice: if you have a gun, be ready to use it, to shoot it out with a death squad!

All was calm, all was dull. I felt myself growing tired to the point that our peril seemed to be fading off in the quiet, comfortable, boring hotel room. I did not trust that feeling. At about 11:30, I phoned Janey Skinner, waking her up at the Peace Brigades house. She took our situation as seriously as the sergeant had. I asked her whether she thought we'd be safe using a cab to go to the Embassy in the morning, as I did not want us to be driven away by a secret policeman.

"Ye… Yes." Good. "It's best not to discuss plans on the phone," she added. Point taken.

"Do you think anyone would be stupid enough to try anything in this hotel?"

After a long pause she said slowly, "I have no idea."

Back in the Bartows' room, Stella and Olivia had long since finished their card games. How trusting they looked asleep in the bed they shared. What could I do if someone broke in? Maybe shout, "We're Americans! You must have the wrong room!" Do death squads understand English? Later it occurred to me to set a fire in a wastebasket and raise a ruckus. Jeff went to the small refrigerator and armed himself with two large bottles of soda. We sensed that if *they* wanted to get us, *they* probably would.

My mind knew our danger. My body felt it had been a long day. Around midnight I set two pillows end to end on the carpet between a bed and the draped window, pulled up a blanket, and slept more soundly than I'd expected to. Sometime in the early hours I got up in the hot, quiet room that was softly shadowed by the light we'd left on in the bathroom. Adriana slept. Jeff, lying beside her, was gazing at the ceiling. "Strange," he muttered. "Very strange." He told me later that he had not slept at all, but had no recollection of saying those words and no idea why he'd said them. Perhaps he felt the strangeness that I was feeling at not being sure we'd live through the night.

Reunion

Suddenly the warm light of Monday morning filled the room as Gua-

temala City bustled in the sunshine. From the random way that people were lining up for cabs, and cabs for people, at the hotel's front
entrance, it seemed unlikely that our driver would be a secret agent
unless they all were. We crowded into the rickety hack that reached us
as we reached it, and sped beneath the trees that lined the busy *Avenida Reforma*, now and then passing purple bougainvillea or a fire tree
decked with bursts of vermilion like a Christmas tree on a spring day.

The great white United States Embassy rose behind massive concrete flowerpots that sprouted green bushes along the sidewalk and
were presumably designed to stop a bomb-laden truck. Four short,
swarthy men, who wore the blue uniforms of the Wackenhut security
company and had short-barrel shotguns slung on straps across their
chests, roamed the sidewalk between the flowerpots and a high fence
whose spikes rose like skinny black teeth at the foot of the wide, empty Embassy steps. A Wackenhut told us we had to use an entrance in
the side of the building. I started to take a photo of the Embassy. Two
of them motioned NO. I lowered my camera.

At the side of the Embassy, we passed through a little security house
where I had to check my camera while a man beside me checked a flat,
black automatic pistol. A man in civilian clothes behind the counter
inspected it and thrust it under his belt.

You never really entered the Embassy, but merely a cul-de-sac con-
sisting of two lobbies joined by a short hall, like a double abscess in
the side of a great white body. Two windows in the first lobby were
like those in a movie theater that do not open but have space under
the glass (bulletproof, I supposed) for passing papers in and out. The
Bartows checked in at one of the windows, then sat in white plastic
chairs and waited to be called back to a window. The chairs were arranged in rows as if for watching a movie that never began. I wandered
into the short hall. Tacked to a bulletin board was a State Department
travel advisory (warning) dated August 31 for all of Guatemala that
no one had mentioned when I'd phoned the Embassy on September 8.
Similar warnings hung there for Nicaragua and El Salvador. From the
wall of the other lobby that faced me, huge color photos of President
George H. W. Bush and Vice-President Dan Quayle smiled down like
Big Brothers.

Eventually Jeff was able to talk through a window to an immaculate young vice-consul named William Silkworth. Jeff described the bomb at the hotel, the murder of Carlos Cabrera, and our surreal night. Silkworth assured him that Guatemala had grown safer in the last three weeks—safer than what, he did not say. The most he would do for our safety was to expedite the processing by one day, so we would finish by Wednesday instead of Thursday, *if* we could persuade the Guatemalan doctors and medical lab to work that fast. We did and they did. By leaving us in whatever danger we were in, the Embassy stuck to the official position—apparently not shared by Marine Sergeant Schultz or Janey Skinner last night—that we were not in danger.

Standing on the sidewalk in the sunshine again, we made two decisions: If we found ourselves in palpable peril, we would try to flee, not to the US Embassy, but to the Canadian Embassy. And if the US Embassy refused to give Adriana and the girls the papers they had come here for—making it impossible for them to re-enter the United States legally—we would go to the Canadian Embassy and place ourselves at their mercy. From what we knew of the Canadians, we didn't think they'd let us down. Our ease in reaching this consensus was to prevail throughout the trip.

After a late breakfast at a nearby McDonald's, we began the rounds of the doctors and labs that the Embassy had designated. It was pretty snug for the six of us when our cab happened to be a subcompact, but we refused to separate even to the extent of taking two cabs. The times we walked somewhere, we would pass fierce-looking men standing in the doorways of banks and shops holding shotguns on their hips, forefingers near the triggers. Hiring them was cheaper than buying insurance. I would say, "Buenos dias," and they would smile.

Later that morning Sidney and I walked the girls to the McDonald's for cokes and orange juice and to read today's *Prensa Libra*, with the girls translating. The banner headline announced the murders of Carlos Cabrera and the other three. Their arms bore needle marks. Apparently they had been interrogated with drugs rather than the less reliable torture. In those days, I still thought that the main purpose of torture was to extract information, unaware that it was primarily to terrorize the populace into passivity. As the girls read the paper, a jeep full of soldiers, their assault rifles pointing skyward, bounced past on the avenue.

"That's our uncle," Olivia said, pointing to a photo of a body on a stretcher borne by four firemen. It was firemen who removed bodies at that time and place.

"I've heard worse. I've seen it," Stella said.

"We've seen eight bodies," Olivia said.

Back in the Bartows' room, Adriana wept again as she read the newspaper and studied the pictures. "Tell Beto all we went through," she said to me. "He has no need to feel envy"—because she had gotten to return to their homeland while he could not.

Lunch at the Camino Real featured a Honduran buffet. The elegant spread ended with an enticing array of fruits and dishes of sweets. Olivia's face lit up. "Let's take advantage of the desserts," she said. That afternoon we all took long naps. Then I phoned Nancy and was distressed to hear that she had tried so hard yet failed to reach me. Last night had not been easy for her. Nor was today as she taught her third grade class in Ridgefield, Connecticut.

The AEW (teachers' union) accused the government of kidnapping and killing the four universitarians, according to the huge headline in Tuesday's *Prensa Libra*. I was pleasantly surprised that the paper would print that. We feared for the life of the union man whom it identified as making these charges until we heard that he had fled into the Swedish Embassy and was presumably well out of the country before the paper reached the streets.

Happily, Dr. Antonio Martinez, Adriana's therapist who had traveled through the night from Chicago, joined us for breakfast. From time to time, he muttered angrily about the Guatemalan security forces who gave him so much business—and who would give him Sister Dianna's shattered self the next year.

I phoned Janey Skinner at Peace Brigades. She told me about the August 15 bombing and said that their windows whose shattered glass was blown across their office—they were saved by being in the kitchenette behind a partition—had now been replaced. She added in a not unfriendly way that I should not have used people's names when I'd phoned her from Connecticut or Sunday night. I took that to heart, realizing as she said it that she was right.

Later I learned that shortly after our harrowing night in the Camino Real, a Peace Brigades member named Meredith Larson spent a day and far more harrowing night in another hotel with two Guatemalans who were being pursued by a death squad and had to flee the country. Her team was "really afraid that they were not going to get out alive," she told me, "and at points during that 24-hour period, I wasn't sure if I was going to either." (The couple received asylum in Europe.) Meredith had started at the PBI office in August shortly after the bombs went off. In December, she would be stabbed in the chest and arm near the PBI office by a man who ignored her purse. She would returned to the US for medical treatment and become an activist in Washington. She reappears in later stories.

Adriana and her family had been looking forward to renting a car and driving to Adriana's hometown today and Wednesday, and I looked forward to seeing the great green countryside of Guatemala,. But after Sunday night, we decided to forego those rural roads with their army checkpoints and instead to stay in the city and mostly close to the hotel.

This afternoon, though, we chose to feel that we'd be safe going downtown to the Central Market and to split up to the extent of taking two cabs, as we had to now that Antonio had arrived. Creatures of our culture, we wanted to shop. On a side street off the Central Plaza, we descended a wide flight of stairs and entered an underground labyrinth of narrow passages jammed with booths full of brilliant Mayan weavings, redolent leather belts and bags, clothes, luggage, woodcarvings, and other crafts. Prices were low, and if you hesitated, the vendors dropped them lower.

Antonio: "I felt very scared in the craft market because it was a perfect place for somebody to come in the back and stab you very easily. I was very much aware of the children."

Adriana: "I was so happy, so excited with this stuff that I wasn't thinking of being kidnapped or killed or anything there." Did she think the security forces would have moved on them there? "No. It would have been between the hotel and the Embassy, or in the hotel."

Antonio: "We rushed back to the hotel, and there we had food.

Those were the relaxing moments, the moments when we had breakfast, lunch, and dinner. They were nice moments that we were all together and we didn't feel that oppressivity."

Nancy tried a dozen or more times to phone me that evening. The times that she reached the hotel, they told her that our line was busy. In fact, we spent a quiet evening in the room. The phone sat silent on the table.

The banner headline in Wednesday's *Prensa Libra*: "For Violence USA Imposes A Travel Advisory." I was the first one down for breakfast again, and asked the vivacious hostess to translate the story. "A beautiful country," I said as she finished putting the Spanish into English, "I hope I'm okay."

"I think tourists are safe." Her eyes twinkled as she laughed. "They are only killing students."

Anger went off inside me like a flashbulb though I doubt it showed, my years on Wall Street having trained me to look placid on most occasions. In that moment, I felt disgust for her and everyone like her, then wondered how many Guatemalans this bouncy young woman spoke for. Many, I supposed. She was the first Guatemalan I'd met who got along by going along, cultivated her tolerance of the intolerable, suppressed any compassion for the victims—"only killing students"—and so survived. The terror touches others. Real people like her and me are safe. Except that everyone is real and no one is safe. Already I was beginning to feel the embrace of an invisible straitjacket, fetters that bind tongue and mind and you can only resist at your peril here in the *New York Times's* "fledgling democracy."

Back in the hotel room, I phoned Phyllis Speck at the Embassy. She said it was "well-established" that the bomb that had gone off in front of our hotel was a grenade. That sounded likely. As bombs go, it had not been large, though it was apparently the same size as the two grenades that had nearly killed or maimed Janey Skinner and her companions at Peace Brigades.

After breakfast, we cabbed once again to the Embassy. Inside the cul-de-sac, William Silkworth interviewed the Bartows through a window and told them to return late that afternoon because the papers they had come for might be ready by then. No promise, but it sounded encouraging. When they emerged and told us this, we all felt a euphoria that was the opposite of Monday's dismay, though little had actually changed.

There was a hitch. Adriana and the girls had sent passport-type photos of themselves to the Embassy as required. Now Silkworth told them that the Embassy did not have the photos. No photos, no documents. Silkworth directed us to a pricey photographer a short walk away—problem solved, though a question lingered: At the time we attributed the absence of the original photos to error or incompetence at the Embassy. Later I pondered the links between US and Guatemalan intelligence. Those photos would certainly have helped the security forces to keep track of Adriana and the girls at the airport, the hotel, wherever they went. Paranoid? In this fledgling democracy, you never knew.

Later that morning a wrinkled Mayan woman set out her gaily colored weavings in the sun along the side of the hotel.* While Adriana talked and talked with her and bought some things, a young security guard and I managed to have a pleasant conversation even though his English was little better than my Spanish. We gestured, smiled, used what words we could, and exchanged more information than I'd thought possible. Another man in two-tone brown took him aside and whispered to him. From then on he didn't know me.

The Maya had borne the brunt of the repression. It threatened their venerable culture. While the term *genocide* is sometimes used, the Maya did not face physical extinction overall. Even though the security forces had slaughtered scores of thousands of them, their numbers had actually increased during the US-backed terror. But consider El Salvador: After the *Matanza* (Slaughter) of perhaps 30,000 people in 1932 in what was then a nation of one-point-four million, fear and prudence drove those Native Americans to put aside their traditional ways and clothes and become anonymously Western. Lost as the Lost Tribes of Israel.

Our plight this week had an excitement that was not entirely unpleasurable. All the same, I wanted to get the hell out of there. Since it looked as though the rigmarole with the Embassy would really end

---

* She becomes Maria's aunt Sara in my novel, *Roses in the Night*.

this afternoon, we phoned the airline to try to change our return flight from Friday to tomorrow. But this morning's headline about the travel advisory had caused a run on tickets, and we could get only four confirmed reservations and three standbys. The flight originated in El Salvador, a short hop over the mountains. We might not know before it actually left there tomorrow morning whether it would have seats for all of us.

The reunion of Adriana's family that was to have occurred on Monday took place this afternoon. Half a dozen or so relatives and friends drove up in a Toyota pickup truck and parked across the street from the hotel. Amparo wore widow's black. Adriana's ex-husband and his wife were there. As they started up the crescent driveway, Adriana and the girls rushed down to them. Weeping, they embraced, moving those of us who were watching to fight back tears of our own. They all went up to the Bartows' room while Sidney, Antonio, and I hung out in ours.

Antonio: "It was a very emotional moment when the family of Adriana came to visit her. They were very beautiful people, all dressed in black. When Adriana saw them, they began to embrace, and they began crying and holding each other right there. It was like suddenly the realization of pain was bigger than the fear. Except me, I was really very afraid."

Standing at our large window with Sidney and me, Antonio studied a pale green 1989 Volvo that had parked below us soon after the Toyota pickup arrived. A young man lounged beside it while a second young man lay on his back across the front seat, the door open, his feet out on the sidewalk. "How do they afford that car?" Antonio demanded. "How can they loaf like that?" He was convinced that they were secret police who had tailed the family here and were waiting to tail them when they left. That sounded likely to Sidney and me. Antonio left the room, and Sidney and I watched him walk out below and speak with one of the men.

"I went outside," Antonio told us back in the room, "and I pretended I was looking around at different stores in front of the hotel. I was like having all this bottle of anger from the whole trip, fear and anger. We talked about his car and my car in Chicago. I wanted him to know that we'd spotted them."

More time passed. At the window Antonio continued to mutter Anglo-Saxon expletives in his Spanish accent. At last Adriana's party were once again in the driveway. More tearful embraces, and the visitors drove off. Antonio bolted out the door. Again Sidney and I watched him stride out below and talk with the same young man. "I told him we knew who they were, we had their license number [CD 13], and if anything happens to that family, we'll come back and testify against them," Antonio said a few moments later. "He said they were in the diplomatic corps and had driven somebody here for a meeting in the hotel."

Jesus, I thought, you're a braver man than I am, Antonio. I was in no hurry to come back to Guatemala for anything, let alone to testify against secret policemen. Fervently I hoped, for this family's sake as well as my own, that I would never have to face that decision. Antonio's concern for the family and his anger at torturers had overcome his prudence and moved him to challenge likely agents of the terror. I envied him his courage.

Sidney: "I thought he was out of his mind. I guess I had some admiration for him, but I was very, very scared."

Antonio: "In Guatemala you get the sense that all these injustices are done and that you don't have any say, you have to shut up. I'm not trained to be shut up, I'm a very vocal person. So I confronted the man. I said, 'If you're really thinking of hurting these persons, let me tell you, I know your face, I remember this car very much, and I'm going to find you any place that you are and denounce you and will really make your life very impossible after this, so be careful because I'm here observing you.'

"He told me, 'I'm the chauffeur of the Ambassador of El Salvador.' Later on, I learned that CD means *Cuerpo Diplomatico*, Diplomatic Corps. My Guatemalan friends told me that all the chauffeurs, all of these people working for them, are secret police."

He told Adriana and Jeff what he'd done. "I wanted not to tell," he said afterwards, "because I got a gut feeling that I did something that was very stupid. They told me that I could really get killed by doing that. At that moment, like a cold shower came through all my body, and really I realized how stupid I was."

"It was very courageous, Antonio," I said.

"Yeah, but it was foolish because it was something inside that I could not hold."

When he told me some years later about the ways that torture had marked scores of his patients, I was better able to appreciate the anger that had driven him to confront the men at the green Volvo on that Wednesday afternoon.

"It was a very dangerous thing for him to do," Adriana said. "We were lucky that the guy was not a *Judicial*. If he was, Antonio wouldn't have left the place alive. We don't have the right to do those things to this kind of people. They have the power. They have the guns. It was something very courageous of him to do. It could have been a tragedy for everybody."

Time dragged by inside the Embassy cul-de-sac. Finally, a clerk slid under a window to the Bartows three visas and three maroon file envelopes, sealed with scotch tape and official imprints in the pale crimson ink that our post offices used. Eureka! These were what we came here for! Jeff told me that he found these Embassy people to be "human within the machine."

Around 4:00 the next morning a knock on the door awakened me. Jeff wanted to work out what we'd do if things went against us today. Sitting on the beds, he, Sidney, and I agreed that Antonio and Sidney would take a cab to the airport at 5:15 and try to change the three standbys to confirmed seats. The Bartows and I would follow at 6:30. We thought it would be too risky to send the Bartows to Texas in the four seats already confirmed. If the INS in Houston sent them back here—as they readily could, despite the visas and maroon envelopes and pale crimson seals—they'd have lost three-fourths of their gringo escort. So the seven of us would leave Guatemala together or none of us would leave; if the INS in Texas sent anyone back, we'd all come back. We didn't want to try, at this late moment, to fly on another airline to another country. I hated the prospects of staying here or returning, but saw no other sensible way.

Pink gray day was breaking as the cab rattled up the hotel driveway that curved around the flowers where the bomb had gone off. In

I climbed with this family who had survived so much so far. As the tall hotel shrank behind us, we joked that we might be checking back into it for breakfast. The cab swung around the road to the terminal. Antonio and Sidney were standing on the sidewalk smiling—seven seats confirmed on Continental's 8:35 flight to Houston.

At last, the plane gathered speed down the runway with the dip in it. All but one of the jungle-splotched helicopters that had been there four long days ago were now somewhere else. The city fell away, and the volcanoes rose above scattered clouds, dwarfing the other mountains. I felt buoyant as I snapped photos through the window. Soon rugged green Guatemala grew hazy below us. To our relief, we all passed smoothly through immigration. I could not help telling the woman in an INS uniform, as she looked at my passport, how good it was to be back here in the USA. It truly was.

Each Embassy envelope had contained a visa and, as Adriana put it, "a sealed envelope that we never learned what was inside. The INS officers opened the envelope. They made some comment like they have never seen anything like that before, and they just gave us the stamp we needed to enter the United States."

"I had nightmares for a little while when I came back," Antonio said. "What we didn't conceptualize is, all of us were tortured. We think of torture in terms of the physical aspects, but that was psychological torture." If so, I thought, it was trivial beside so many.

Back in Connecticut, I told Rep. Shays about the trip and mentioned that our group's decision to flee to the Canadian Embassy if need be. "Not to the US Embassy?!" His face and voice showed shock. I looked at our decision afresh. Yes, I agreed, it *was* shocking. I sensed that what upset him the most was how logical and prudent it had also been.

Adriana had barely survived the terror during her final years in Guatemala. By publicly denouncing it during the past four years in Texas and Chicago, she had risked being deported back to it. When she sought to make herself and her girls legal, the Embassy, to further the fiction that they were safe in Guatemala and perhaps for darker reasons, had caused them to place themselves within the terror's grasp again, as the price of making their haven safer in the United States, where she would keep on denouncing US complicity.

One thing had led to another. The 1954 coup and US subsequent complicity had launched and fed a reign of terror that, among its manifold accomplishments, disappeared and presumably murdered much of Adrian's family (along with 200,000 or more other Guatemalans), drove her and her surviving girls to flee, murdered Carlos Cabrera when she returned, and threatened us while we were there, not least because she had the courage to denounce, for the relatively few Americans who cared, the mass murderers in her homeland and to expose their lanky partner in his blue coat, red and white striped pants, and star-spangled hat.

Several years after the visit to Guatemala, I asked Adriana why she had taken the risks of doing Sanctuary. "I wanted to work in the Sanctuary Movement because Sanctuary was a platform for me to speak out," she replied. "I knew that through Sanctuary I could have access to churches, universities, different sectors of the United States population, and I could talk to them about the situation in my country. I was very naïve then, very, very naïve. I thought that all I had to do was talk to people and tell them what happened, and then a year later I would take my family back with me to Guatemala. Because the United States was this powerful nation, and I believed that the people of the United States had control and power. I know better now."

The date September 11 means different things to different people. For Americans, 9/11 of 2001 is a day of infamy that changed the nation's course. For the people of Chile, 9/11 was the day in 1973 when a US-abetted coup overthrew the elected government of Salvador Allende, left him dead, and launched the murderous dicta¬torship of General Augusto Pinochet, as Chileans looked for loved ones among the battered cadavers under the National Stadium or in various morgues. For Guatemalan anthropologist Myrna Mack, 9/11 of 1990 was the day that security forces took her life. For Adriana, 9/11 meant the sleepy day in 1981 when secret police seized her loved ones, surely killing most or all of them, and she barely escaped. Each September 11, she told me some years ago, "I spend all the day crying, giving myself fully to the pain. I want to get rid of what I'm feeling in one day, but I can't."

On that morning in 2001 that marked the 20th anniversary of her loss, her anguish and the anguish of other loved ones of disappeared people came home to America. Until then those agonies had been almost entirely a US export product; but that morning nearly three thousand of *us* vanished, the most when the Twin Towers plunged into their own stone crypts. Even before the dust had settled, New Yorkers were walking the canyons of lower Manhattan looking for wives, husbands, children; and during the days that followed, many of them put up small, colorful shrines that quickly tattered on the sidewalks and iron fences near Ground Zero. However surely their intelligence told these people that virtually all of the "disappeared" were entombed in the rubble, they, like Adriana, hoped that *their* loved ones had somehow survived. Many of them posted photos of the missing on nearby walls and fences. Some may, like Adriana in Guatemala City, have searched from their windows as they rode bus after bus through the boroughs of New York to the end of the line.

The shock of America's 9/11 led Adriana to a breakthrough that came strangely yet naturally out of the attack. "On September 11th, 9/11, when I was at home and saw what was happening," she told me, "I felt this horrible pain for my own loss, but also for the horrible thing that happened, and I realized that even if it is against my will, I do love this country. This is a beautiful country, and has a beautiful people."

Cuernavaca

Among the lay community of the Weston Priory were Bill and Patty Coleman. He had been a priest, and while living in Weston, he wrote homilies for liberal priests who didn't write their own. Patty told me that if he stopped writing, the left wing of the Catholic Church would be that much shorter. In the late 1980s, they felt called to go to Cuernavaca, Mexico, which is about an hour by bus south of Mexico City, to see what they might do for its very poor people. With help from the brothers of the Priory, they founded VAMOS! (Vermont Association for Mexican Opportunity and Support!) to educate children who were too poor to pay for the transportation, uniforms, and books needed to attend Mexico's free schools. The result became ten projects in and around Cuernavaca that provide education, computer training, medical, dental, and psychological services, and nutritious meals to about seven hundred and fifty youngsters and two hundred of their mothers. The ultimate goal was and is to help the kids break out of the cycle of poverty to which most of them were otherwise condemned.

Nancy and I joined the VAMOS Board of Directors, she in the late '90s and I in the early '00s. Until well into the 20-teens, we joined the other directors on yearly visits to Cuernavaca to visit the projects and show the staffs, students, and mothers that we cared. We'd usually stay at a gated motel with a sprawling lawn and ample breakfasts on a patio—being careful not to take any water in our mouths when we showered. Then we'd be driven to visit the projects where the kids and mother were being educated and fed. Then we'd share festive dinners at one of the fine restaurants around town. Nearly all the children in the projects we visited year after year seemed happy. No matter how little water their families had, their clothes always looked clean.* Some of the directors really got into what the kids were doing at their tables. Being more reserved (shy), I would stroll from table to table with my hands clasped behind my back and look down at what the kids were up to with as interested an expression on my face as I could muster, in the manner, I hoped, of Great Britain's Prince Philip.

While the VAMOS operations were shut down during the Covid pandemic, we continued to pay the staff and provide food for the needy participants.

The trips had their perils, most immediately from crossing streets full of exuberant traffic, but also from being kidnapped for ransom—which your loved ones paid or you died. A VAMOS person would always meet us at the airport and shepherd us to one of the luxurious busses that shuttled between Mexico City and Cuernavaca. Tourists had been kidnapped right outside the terminal. We actually benefitted from the local drug trade. The restaurants gave very good value and seemed to thrive even though they were often nearly empty except for us. We understood that the next morning, they'd go to the bank and

---

* Many communities had no running water. Trucks came by to fill up 55-gallon drums for everyone to dip into. In communities that had no electricity, daring souls often climbed the poles to tap into the power lines passing overhead.

deposit the large amount of money that a full house would have netted them, most of which was drug money being laundered.

One day Nancy, a friend named Ruth, and I were walking from dinner back to the motel along one of the city's main avenues. It was still daylight. Nancy got maybe twenty feet ahead of Ruth and me. A black sedan pulled over to the curb beside her, and a young man jumped out of the rear door. Ruth and I speeded up. He saw us and jumped back in. The car sped away.

The brothers of the Priory had a close relationship with *Las Misioneras Guadalupanas de Cristo Rey*, a community of Benedictine sisters whose large Mother House was within walking distance of the huge Metropolitan Cathedral in Mexico City. The sisters also had a fenced-in, park-like compound in Cuernavaca. The brothers would organize interested people into ten-day retreats with the sisters "to introduce participants to the present-day reality of the Mexican people and to give some understanding of life and faith lived in Latin America."[8] One year, Nancy and I joined a retreat that was comprised mostly of members of a Catholic congregation and their priest from Pennsylvania.

We all lodged in motel-like units in the Cuernavaca compound, dined with the sisters—I happily found hot sauce on the buffet line even at breakfast—and experienced far more of the harshness of the life of Mexico's poor than we had even during our VAMOS visits. The sisters drove us around in two large white vans and impressed me with their ability to muscle their way into the traffic at the rotaries. One morning, the priest led a Eucharist with all of us standing in a circle. Since Nancy and I did not partake of the bread and wine, he placed his hands gently on our heads and blessed us. To my surprise, I wept. So did she.

I'd often feel on returning to the States that we were leaving the real world with its bustle, filth, vitality, and poverty, and reentering a cocoon.

Sister Alice

Alice Zachmann, of the School Sisters of Notre Dame, founded the Guatemala Human Rights Commission/USA (GHRC) in 1981 to serve as a font of specific, reliable information about the massive human rights crimes in Guatemala that our government was fueling and our responsible media were largely ignoring or distorting. With talks at schools and universities, personal contacts, newsletters she called *Updates* that she started publishing twice a month in 1989, and other work, Alice was telling hard truth to Congresspeople, officials, and everyone else who cared to hear it. Predictably few believed it or cared.

During the 1980s she worked with the Sanctuary Movement and sheltered several "illegal" Guatemalan refugees herself. In 1989 she organized a student exchange program, but it collapsed when the students' leaders in Guatemala were kidnapped and murdered, leaving her to wonder whether she had provoked any of those deaths.

She had grown up on an eighty-acre farm that lay a few miles outside of St. Michael, then a town of 350 people, on the flat plains of Minnesota. Like other nuns, she possessed the faith and moxie it took to choose poverty, chastity, and obedience in a society that stresses consumerism, sexual permissiveness, and individualism. She taught grade school and was a school principal for twenty-two years, spent three years with a center for low-income families in St. Paul, then moved into pastoral ministry with senior citizens. Why she had become a nun, she told me, "continues to be a mystery. I did have School Sisters of Notre Dame as teachers, and I can't describe it otherwise. It was just a call that I received and felt that this is what I wanted to do with my life."

Two decisions of conscience placed her where she could support Adriana and two other valiant women whose stories I participated in to a small extent and include in this memoir, Sister Dianna Ortiz and Jennifer Harbury.* The first of Alice's decisions came one frosty morning in the 1970s when she and five other nuns who were supporting the United Farm Workers confronted several Gallo wine trucks outside a warehouse: "We wouldn't let the wine trucks out," she said. "We grasped hands and stood there. It was a real cold, icy day, and the truck drivers were very angry. One truck kept on coming and coming and coming. We made the decision we were going to stay there. If he runs us over, that's it. We knelt down, and the truck was so close it was literally touching our chests before it was able to stop. That's when

---

* I write about all three at much greater length in my yet unpublished *Sisters in the Storm: Life and Death on the Receiving End of US Power.*

I made a decision: it was either life or death for the cause of peace and justice. We were the first religious women that had ever been arrested in St. Paul, so that was the talk of the town."

Alice's second decision evolved during six years beginning in 1975 when she visited a friend in Guatemala and was, she said, "smitten by the beauty of the people and the country, but appalled by the oppression and extreme poverty." Back in Minnesota she "couldn't let go of Guatemala," so she started sending down supplies for clinics and schools. Returning in 1979, she felt "a really quite strong desire to become a missionary." She didn't become one, but by 1981 it seemed time to leave her job with the seniors in Minnesota. She went on a silent retreat for thirty days during which "it became very clear to me that I needed to do something for peace and justice, but I didn't know what." Providentially, as some people would put it, several American and Guatemalan friends promptly asked her to consider forming a commission that would work for the human rights of Guatemalans.

"It was sort of a shock," she says. "I hardly knew what human rights meant or what that work would involve." She consulted people at Amnesty International, the Washington Office on Latin America (WOLA), and Americas Watch (a predecessor of Human Rights Watch). "The first question they always asked was, 'Do you know Spanish?' and I said, 'No,' and they said, 'That would be difficult.' Then they asked, 'Do you have money to get this started?' and I said, 'No, but I do have a lot of faith,' and they kind of looked at me and said, 'It's going to be very hard.' I accepted that."

She told her community at the Mother House in Mankato, Minnesota, that she "really felt that this was the work of Jesus and what our community had given us a mandate to do, to make the concerns of the poor our own and also to educate in order to bring about systemic change. Having laid out the best-laid plans I had at that time, I received the community's blessing and came to Washington and started the Commission."

And so, from teaching school in the heartland, Alice came to strive in Washington on behalf of the largely voiceless majority of a small foreign country whom the US-backed security forces were torturing, raping, and murdering by the thousands. Finding the money, office space, legal and accounting advice, and above all, the information she wanted to disseminate was a scramble, but she persevered. The Reagan Administration took notice; but with the pro bono help of a large law firm, she got through a meticulous Justice Department investigation into whether "this one-woman office" was a foreign agent. She soloed for three years, before becoming a three to five employee concern, plus interns who included for a time a daughter of the Canek family in Sanctuary in Weston, Vermont.

It was while the principal massacres were happening that Alice began her efforts, she said, "to research and document and educate the US people about the human rights situation and help victims of the human rights violations in Guatemala. We tried to tell the Congress, and we tried to tell people, and it was just like a dead silence at the other end. We couldn't get them to believe what was happening, particularly in Congress. It was a *shut book*. 'It couldn't be happening.' And, 'How do you know?' And, 'Have you been down there?'"

In fact, she returned to Guatemala at least nine or ten times after starting the Commission, though she never learned Spanish. Her primary source of information was the Guatemala Human Rights Commission in exile in Mexico, which got it from inside Guatemala. She also relied on US missionaries, a justice and peace group working in the countryside, and the Archdiocesan human rights office in Guatemala City.

"We always had to be very careful," she said, "that it was very accurate, so we checked it out with groups like Amnesty, Human Rights Watch, and the Washington Office on Latin America. Often we would have the information before they did, so it was a mutual sharing."

The Administration was painting an opposite picture—for example, that most slain civilians were caught in crossfires that never happened—while the media mostly peddled this Official Version ("echo journalism") or held their peace. Years later, reports of Archdiocesan and UN truth commissions would establish conclusively that Amnesty, Alice, and the others had been right all along in attributing the vast bulk of the carnage to the US-backed forces and very little to the guerrillas.

Alice cared not only for her Commission's projects, but also for the efforts and often the plights of other people caught up in the Guatemalan terror. One of them was Jennifer Harbury, Harvard Law School '78, who had gone to work, not for the big money, but for impecunious and abused migrant farm workers in the Rio Grande Valley of Texas and had improbably married a Mayan guerrilla whom the army had captured and presumably was torturing for his guerrilla secrets, if it had not already killed him. Jennifer determined to do whatever she could to save him and went to one human rights group after another seeking support. But because they didn't want to appear to be siding with the guerrillas, none of them would help her. Except Alice.

Alice's concern for Sister Dianna Ortiz, like that of many other activists, began on the day she was kidnapped, November 2, 1989. "As soon as we heard," Alice said, "we let people know that she had been disappeared and asked them to let other people know or call the State Department—what we usually do when we hear about an urgent action." Alice's concern for Dianna, like that of the others, turned to relief on hearing that she had escaped, then to horror as the details emerged. But being Alice, she would not simply remain horrified; she would do what she could to help Dianna.

I relate, too briefly, what Jennifer and Dianna did and what Alice did to support them in stories that follow. It was my privilege to help out from time to time. Little as this was in their overall efforts, it's one of the most useful things I've ever done; and I treasure the friendships that resulted, particularly with Alice, who is in her late nineties and largely retired with her community in Minnesota, and with a man named Harold Nelson, a college professor who became her assistant and whom you'll meet in the story called "The Vigil."

Tour

Soon after I accompanied Adrianna Portillo-Bartow and her girls to Guatemala in 1989, stories began to circulate in the Sanctuary community—though not in the US media—that an American missionary from Kentucky named Sister Dianna Ortiz had been "disappeared" (kidnapped) and tortured in Guatemala seven weeks after we had flown back to Texas. A nun at a Sanctuary conference gave me a copy of Dianna's sworn account of her shocking ordeal.

In October of 1994, five years into Dianna's never-complete recovery and three years after she felt able to speak about the ordeal to an audience of strangers—at a large conference in Washington, DC that Sister Alice organized and Enrique Canek and I attended—he and his wife Sophia invited Dianna to Vermont for a weekend of talks that they and a group of their supporters had arranged. It was my good fortune to drive her and the Caneks to the venues around the state.

Although the red, orange, and yellow leaves had already fallen from the slopes, autumn was lovely the afternoon we rolled along the gray Green Mountains from Weston north to Burlington on Lake Champlain. During supper at a McDonald's, I worried that Dianna was not eating much; I didn't yet know that she usually didn't. It embarrassed me that only nineteen people showed up that evening at the University of Vermont to hear her and the other speakers who had gone through so much and come so far, and I apologized to her for the rotten turnout. She quickly said how enthusiastic those few people had been and what good questions they'd asked. She tried to make you feel okay when you didn't. She would speak, she added, any time there was any chance of saving a single life in Guatemala.

Apart from reading her affidavit and seeing her at Sister Alice's conference, I knew very little about her. Paul Soreff, the attorney who helped her write the affidavit the month after her ordeal, would tell me later, "She was very emotionally fragile, still extremely shaken from what she had endured, very thin and frail physically. The interviews were excruciating for Dianna and for me."

Seeing her at Alice's conference stood out in my mind as I chauffeured her that weekend; it stands out as I write this today. I am sitting in a steep amphitheater with several hundred others at Catholic University of America in Washington. At the podium below is this slender young woman with black hair. She holds up a small object that I can't make out and says:

On behalf of other survivors of torture, I have the "honor" of introducing to you a rather unique friend, a friend who is a frequent visitor of ours, a friend who journeys with us wherever we go, a friend who comforts us in our darkest moments. What makes our friend unique is that she is a razor blade. With a little help from our friend, we know that we can put to rest the violent memories of torture that have been embedded within us. Yes, with the help of our friend, we can say goodbye to yesterday.

I feel a chill sweep the room. My friend and sometimes mentor Margaret Swedish tells me that she feels it too.

It all began when Dianna was six years old and living with her family in the small city of Grants in the sun-drenched vastness of New Mexico, and she announced that she was going to become a nun. She did, earning a degree in elementary education and early childhood at Brescia College in Owensboro, Kentucky, and joining the near-by Mount Saint Joseph Ursuline Community. She was comfortably teaching preschool and primary grades, when she felt called to teach Mayan children in embattled Guatemala. Which she did in 1987, joining two other nuns in the small city of San Miguel Acatán in the remote, green, western highlands where the then "most brutal army in the Hemisphere" held sway. No problem at first, until for no discernible reason, she began receiving threats, mild at first but increasingly dire: "Eliminate Dianna, assassinate, decapitate, rape"; and leave the country. Her friends and advisors urged her to go back to Kentucky, and for a time she did, but her feeling of commitment to the Maya overcame their arguments and her fears, and she returned for them.

On November 2, 1989, three secret policemen kidnapped her from a garden at a retreat center. They repeatedly burned her with cigarettes, gang-raped her, and otherwise tortured her until their boss, whom they called "Alejandro," a tall, fair-skinned man who spoke American English and bad Spanish, entered the torture chamber, which was in the old *Politécnica* Military Academy, a Guatemala City landmark that had become a well-known torture center. He declined their offer to join them in raping her yet again, but instead ordered them to bring her her clothes and some water and then leave the room. They obeyed his every order. He helped her dress and led her to his car to drive her, he said, to the US Embassy. When they stopped in traffic, she fled to the travel agency that was holding her passport. Friends brought her to the city's Maryknoll House.

Embassy officials and local police who had been searching for her naturally wanted to question her, but her friends refused to let them because she was a physical and emotional wreck. Maryknoll Father Dan Jensen, who had led the retreat from which she was disappeared:

> She looked like a ghost. She looked transparent, as if the person wasn't really there. She was a shell, that's all I can say. I went up to give her a hug, and she screamed and backed off into a corner, kind of like a cornered animal. She'd known me and knew she could trust me.

Her comrade from San Miguel Acatán, Sister Darleen Chmielewski:

> Dianna was very clear that a uniformed Guatemalan policeman kidnapped her and tortured her and that a North American came to get her out of the torture center. We were so fearful that the Guatemalan police would take her again. I just wanted to protect her. I didn't want her to have to go through anything again.

Finally, they allowed US Ambassador Thomas Stroock to see her but not to question her. Though he admitted that she "appeared severely traumatized," he cabled Washington his concern that Sisters Dianna and Darleen, Father Dan, and other nuns and priests were all conspiring to block the renewed funding that Congress was considering to help the Guatemalan security forces continue their reign of terror in the name of quelling a non-existent Communist threat.*

Her friends, fearing that the police would return with an order to seize her, asked the Apostolic Nuncio (the Pope's ambassador), Archbishop Oriano Quilici, for sanctuary. He promptly sent his car to bring her to the Nunciature. The next morning, he escorted her and two of her sisters, who had come from Kentucky when she vanished, to the airport, through customs, and to their seats on the plane to America.

---

* Guerrilla leaders, who had no chance of winning the civil war, espoused Communism in principle, until the State Department's Dr. Richard Nuccio met with them and talked them out of it. Marxist and Leninist principles do not appear in the 1996 peace accords that ended the conflict.

I couldn't help reflecting that Dianna and her sisters must have felt a relief that was far greater than mine had been two months earlier when Adriana the rest of us had flown from the same airport after our far milder, physically harmless ordeal in that bustling city of nightmares.

To its credit, the Embassy had prevailed on the Guatemalan police to let Dianna leave the country rather than take her into custody. It is not hard to imagine the effect upon the raw gashes in her psyche if they had seized her and interrogated her even briefly.

On reaching the United States, she went to her family in New Mexico and did not recognize them. The family doctor counted a hundred and ten cigarette burns on her back alone. Returning to Kentucky, she did not recognize her Ursuline sisters. The four torturers had wiped out most of the memories of her first thirty-one years. What she said now about those years was what her family and friends told her about a Dianna she barely knew.

Soon, she and her community tried to resume her life as though she were back to normal. It didn't work. Her trauma went deep, and the hospital they eventually put her in, clueless about treating survivors of torture, made her worse. Finally, Sister Alice Zachmann, who had been following her progress, put her in touch with Dr. Antonio Martinez and Dr. Mary Fabri of the Marjorie Kovler Center for Survivors of Torture in Chicago; and they started her on the path to as much recovery as she would ever achieve.

Dr. Martinez: "We see the minority, the ones that survive, because the majority of people that go into a torture chamber in Guatemala or El Salvador will never come out of it. [Dianna's] are normal reactions to an abnormal social situation. We try to rebuild people again, little by little. Rehabilitation is not the absence of symptoms. Rehabilitation is the working on the strengths so they will be able to take care of themselves again."

Dr. Fabri: "Torture is a wound which remains with someone forever. Even though there are times where it's not throbbing or inflamed, it's still there. Any bump to it reactivates it. Cigarette smoke. The smell of alcohol. Security guards. Bus drivers wear uniforms. It's not just sight, it can be sound or smell."

Many well-meaning Americans believe that torture, while horrible, is sometimes necessary in order to extract life-saving information. Though Dianna and a great many others were tortured in Guatemala, not for their information, but to induce terror, it is worth noting that, counter-intuitively perhaps but according to the experts I have studied, torture produces less truth and more false information, and produces it more slowly, than the lawful and non-violent methods of the FBI and other experienced law officers. In September 8, 2006, Robert Mueller III, then the Director of the FBI told NPR that even in the "ticking bomb" case—where you need the suspect to tell you where the bomb is hidden before it explodes—he would rely on the FBI's non-coercive methods. It follows that, by relying on a second-rate method (torture), many US personnel have inevitably goaded suspects into withholding valuable information and confessing to false information; and they have failed to learn stuff that, if sought by sounder methods, would have saved American lives.

Why did the geniuses who ran the terror, pick on this ordinary nun? The leading theory was that if torture could happen to *any* missionary, it would scare off *all* the missionaries who were standing with the people the geniuses wanted to keep terrorized and passive. But, I was told, torturing Dianna backfired. For the most part, it strengthened the resolve of other missionaries. Plus, Dianna was not ordinary, and her courage, conscience, and determination generated much publicity and hope among Guatemalans, which was the last thing the geniuses had wanted.

I asked Janey Skinner of Peace Brigades whether Dianna's was kidnapping was a big story in Guatemala. "Very big" she said. "As I recall, it was front page news. It was obviously hard to get straight what had really happened because neither the Embassy nor the Guatemalan government was giving any straight information."

Justice for the people of Guatemala—particularly an end to the bloody violence against suspects, dissenters, and Maya who might be helping the guerrillas—was precisely what their government and ours did not want. Nor did they want justice that would expose and incriminate themselves. So they impugned Dianna's account of being tortured by Guatemalans who obeyed an American, and they tried to drive her into silence. "She is lying, hallucinating, or crazy." Two weeks after her ordeal, the need for damage control must have looked more pressing than ever, after the US-sponsored Atlacatl Battalion shot dead six Jesuit priests and their two housekeepers over in El Salvador.

Officially disbelieving Dianna, though, was not sufficient. Officials of both governments also accused her of hindering the investigation of her ordeal, which she so desperately wanted to succeed. And since her burns, bruises, and emotional trauma could not be denied, these officials spread a bizarre story, which each blamed the other for starting, to both explain the injuries and smear Dianna, to wit, that she had received all those burns and so on during a "lesbian tryst."

The next April, a small group went to Guatemala to try to convince the Embassy that the official versions were wrong on all counts. Included were a nun from leadership of Dianna's Ursuline community; Father Joe Nangle, who had been a missionary in Peru and now worked with Franciscan missionaries; Marie Dennis, who worked with Maryknoll missioners (and would become Co-President of Pax Christi International and the Director of the Catholic Nonviolence Initiative); and lawyer Paul Soreff who had helped Dianna with her affidavit. Joe and Marie had risked their own lives by accompanying people at risk in El Salvador, and they were senior members of the Assisi Community of activists in Washington. The group succeeded in varying degrees. Ambassador Stroock agreed "to send Soreff a letter, which Soreff could make public, stating the Embassy had no reason to doubt Sr. Diana [sic]." Defense Minister Hector Gramajo—who was one of the great butchers of the era, had honed his skills at the US School of the Americas, and would later earn a degree at Harvard's Kennedy School—dictated and gave to Paul, Joe, and Marie, a note on official letterhead that scotched the false rumor.

It strikes me as very unfortunate, especially for actual lesbian nuns, who do God's work as selflessly and well as heterosexual nuns, that the canard against Dianna was made more effective by claiming that her nonexistent tryst was with a woman.

Two years later, in April 1992, Dianna herself returned to Guatemala in order to advance her lagging case by testifying before a judge and physically retracing the steps of her abduction in a "judicial reconstruction." She rightly feared revisiting "the place where my body and soul had parted." But, she said, "I either sat by and watched others being tortured, or I risked torture myself to save them. I had so many people to fight for my life—my family, my Ursuline sisters, my church family, the international community, etc., but what about the people of Guatemala? Who will speak on their behalf?" And so once again, her conscience overcame her fear, and she would do her best to "hold the Guatemalan army accountable for the first time in history for the crime of torture."

(Would that someone would do the same for the CIA and other Americans who have tortured suspects with impunity for many decades in many places!)

Her testimony was cleverly arranged to be as painful as possible; and as she retraced her abduction, she often stopped and sat down and sobbed. According to a report that Stroock sent to Washington, she "had a serious flashback and appeared to be hallucinating that she was actually experiencing the kidnapping." She began flailing and screaming. Then little later, Mary Fabri said, "She was having a very severe flashback, and they told me to get in there and get her oriented. I jumped in the van, and I got incorporated into her flashback. She attacked me. I had scratch marks down both my arms, and she has no recollection of that. The next morning when she saw my arms, she wanted to know what had happened."

During the trip, Ambassador Stroock won their praise for the hospitality, transportation, and security he provided on the condition that they not ask about Alejandro! Dianna received constant help from the archbishop and her other supporters in the Catholic Church; they stressed that her case "represents a major battle by the church in its role as advocate on behalf of the people against the impunity of corrupt military and government officials." Before flying home, she held a press conference at the archbishop's palace (Mary: "It's not a *palace* palace.") in which she addressed the people of Guatemala:

> I return to Guatemala for you. I pursue the investigation
> of my abduction, interrogation, and torture not just for
> myself but for all of you who have been tortured or disap-

peared or forced to flee your homeland...and for all of you who carry in your hearts the pain of the hideous crimes that your loved ones have suffered and continue to suffer.... I pursue the investigation because the *truth* of your oppression must become known to the rest of the world, and because *the torturers and assassins must be stopped!*

Guatemalan TV broadcast the entire event, and the newspapers quoted her at length. Many Guatemalans and members of Dianna's group agreed that the media coverage may have been more significant than her legal testimony, since it brought the public face to face with the human rights crimes, official impunity, and the fact that an American survivor who cared about them had returned to challenge their oppressors. Another nun: "Many humble street people in Guatemala, recognizing us from the ... reports, stopped to thank us for what we are doing."

During the seven-day trip, Dianna had eaten and drunk nearly nothing, slept very little, had nightmares when she did sleep, and lost fifteen pounds. Mary: "Back at Su Casa [a home for survivors in Chicago], she was totally shut down—dehydrated and almost in a state of shock psychologically." She was on an IV for two days and suffered flashbacks for about ten days and nightmares that continued longer.

When her progress allowed her to leave Chicago, Sister Alice took her under her wing in Washington, hiring her to work on a project called "Coalition Missing," which served loved ones of the disappeared, and included Jennifer Harbury, who soon became like a sister to her. The job allowed Dianna to be useful, and Alice to nurture and protect her. And she moved into the Assisi Community, the home of Father Joe, Marie, Jennifer when she was in town, and other like-minded activists who would help her through what lay ahead.

I knew very little about all this, or how heroic Dianna had already been, beyond what she had sworn to in her affidavit, during the weekend I drove her around Vermont. Yet as I watched her before one hushed audience after another, my heart went out to this slender, shy woman who looked, in spite of what she had been through, far younger that her thirty-six years. Each time she described her abduction and, briefly, the torture, I sensed that she was reliving them.

The church in Montpelier where the panel spoke on Saturday was nicely full, and the day passed smoothly. Sunday morning saw Dianna and the other speakers facing another audience, who sat on folding chairs in the low-ceilinged, cheerful basement of a church in Brattle-boro at the south end of the state. Worried that speaking three times in three days would be too much for Dianna, I told her that she didn't have to do it if she didn't want to. But she did, and got through it fine, I thought.

A few minutes later she left the room. When she hadn't returned after what seemed like a long time, I went looking for her. She was sitting on the stairs with no expression on her face.

The words of a Salvadoran refugee named América Sosa came to me: "We were taught to resist torture.... The members of the Christian communities...taught us that when we were blindfolded and all our strength and identity were gone, we should think of beauty. We had a mental exercise to think not of family or children but of beauty."

I asked Dianna to come outside. We walked across the parking lot behind the church and stood on the lip of an embankment. The broad Connecticut River flowed below, and a mountain studded with out-croppings of gray granite rose from the far bank. The gray sky muted the beauty, but it was the best I could offer her. After a few minutes she seemed to return from wherever she had been, and we walked back inside to the speakers' table.

Driving to Weston afterwards, I assured her once more that she need not speak again. Again she persisted, that evening to a group of friends of the Weston Priory, which was comfortably larger than the crowd in Burlington had been, and yet again the next day to the monks of the Priory. She told me later that the weekend had taught her not to speak so often in so short a time.

What struck me most as I watched her was the silence while she spoke. The audiences were more silent for her than for any of the other speakers, more silent than I remember any audience for any other speaker anywhere. They seemed not only to know but to sense that this slender, soft-spoken woman was reliving it as she told it. Will her effectiveness wane, I wondered, if it becomes less painful for her to tell people about the agony inflicted upon her?

And so she helped maybe two hundred Americans in remote Vermont to understand what our government was doing in a small nation not far away but off most media's radar. Very soon after leaving us, she and several other members of Coalition Missing flew to Guatemala City to support Jennifer, who was fasting in the Central Plaza, exposed to the elements and the many people who wanted to shoot her, as she was taking another bold step on the slim chance of saving her husband's life.

"More and more friends begin to arrive from the United States," Jennifer wrote later. "Then the Coalition Missing members arrive, and I awaken to see them rushing across the square to give me hugs and encouragement. Meredith reaches me first, then Josh and Trish and Peter, and then beautiful Dianna Ortiz. She sits down on the edge of my chair and puts a slender arm about my shoulders, bringing tears to my eyes, for I know what it cost her to return here, what memories haunt her in the night. Yet her presence gives me strength because she survived. She survived and came back home. It is not impossible."

Jennifer Harbury

Sophia and Enrique Canek and two of their daughters gathered with Nancy, me, and six more of the Caneks' supporters in their snowy driveway early on a wintery morning in Weston, Vermont. We loaded our stuff and selves into a big, blue, rented van and rolled down the Interstates to springtime in Washington. The next morning, Sunday, March 12, 1995, we betook the van to the simple frame house that contained the offices of the Guatemala Human Rights Commission/ USA (GHRC). Grandmotherly Sister Alice was bustling over the final details of the celebration that would launch Jennifer Harbury's third fast to try to save her husband, the Mayan guerrilla leader whose *nom de guerre* was Everardo.

Jennifer was there, intense as she had been when Nancy and I first met her at the Caneks' last summer, but now ominously slender. Sister Dianna was there, radiant as she sometimes was, working on the speech she would give. Nineth Montenegro, who led the GAM (Mutual Support Group), and Amilcar Méndez, who led the CERJ

(Council of Ethnic Communities), were there. Both were heroes of the non-violent resistance in Guatemala, remaining alive only because Peace Brigades volunteers accompanied them 24/7. What a tribute to Jennifer and her mission, I thought, that they came here for her.

Alice would provide the support base as she had for Jennifer's 1994 fast in Guatemala, and as she would for Dianna's vigil here in Washington, DC next spring. Today's event would also commemorate the anniversary of the army's massacre of one hundred and seventy-seven unarmed civilian Maya at Rio Negro in Baja Verapaz on March 13, 1982. A survivor of the massacre would join the speakers this afternoon.

Alice had had a stage erected on the grass of Lafayette Park opposite the White House. A crowd gathered—the Park Police estimated three hundred people; a civilian crowd estimator said fifteen hundred—including many alumni of the Sanctuary Movement. Hank and Dorothy Harbury, who had driven down from New Hampshire, were plainly proud of their daughter yet worried about her health. Her fast last fall had devastated her physically, and she was far from recovered. Many of us carried white wooden crosses bearing the names of people, including the one hundred and seven children, whom the US-backed soldiers had killed at Rio Negro. Near the stage, I spotted a friend I hadn't seen in over two years. She saw me. We hugged. Adriana! She had come from Chicago for Jennifer, as she would for Dianna's vigil the next year.

There they were, Jennifer, Adriana, and Dianna. Not tall or blond or young. If you didn't know their stories, you might think they were just three more middle-aged women enjoying a sunny Sunday afternoon.

The sun cooked the park. The stately White House across Pennsylvania Avenue looked more benign than did the black silhouettes of several figures on its roof. People strolling along the walkways paused on the fringes of the crowd, some lingering for the event, most vanishing into their lives. Too bad, I thought, that most of them haven't a clue about the courage and purpose represented on that stage. Occasionally I looked up at the black figures on the White House roof who, I supposed, sometimes looked down on us.

Dorothy Harbury had sketched Everardo's face from photos and Jennifer's memory. Dianna had the sketch printed onto yellow T-shirts that asked, "Where Is Everardo?" Now these festive accents dappled the crowd as we listened to grim talks by Nineth, Amilcar, Dianna, and the survivor of the massacre—fewer Native Americans than died at Wounded Knee, but this army had wiped out more than four hundred and forty Mayan villages.

The celebration ended when the Canek family, in their many-colored Mayan clothes, performed a Mayan sun ceremony to the taped music of a marimba. There weren't enough of them for the ceremony, so Nancy became the tallest and blondest Maya on the stage. Then came a reception in a nearby hall. Everybody nibbled on the simple hors d'oeuvres, except for Jennifer who walked among us carrying a small bottle of mineral water. Her fast had resumed. Another year and venue, same tactic, grit, and poignant hope.

This afternoon's celebration had begun for Nancy and me around the pond at the Caneks' home on a warm summer afternoon the previous year when the Caneks gathered maybe twenty or thirty of their supporters for a corn roast and a talk by a rapid-fire speaker, Jennifer, whom I knew little about and who struck me as being attractive though zaftig. Actually, she was bulking up for the long hunger strike before the Guatemalan National Palace, but her plan was secret lest the Guatemalans hear about it and bar her from their country.

She told us that the army was holding her Mayan guerrilla husband in a clandestine prison and torturing him for his "treasure trove" of information, and she asked us to phone the Guatemalan Embassy in Washington to urge that he be treated like a prisoner of war if they hadn't already killed him. Her plea moved me to talk on the phone with a bemused-sounding official in the Guatemalan Embassy a few days later. Nancy and I wondered, like many others, how Jennifer, a fellow graduate of the Harvard Law School, came to marry an unschooled Mayan guerrilla.

She was born to privilege, but it did not slow her down. She grew up in New Haven, Connecticut, where her father taught biochemistry at Yale. He had lost family to the Holocaust and used to tell her that if she ever saw another holocaust coming, she should try to stop it. She went to prep school, then Cornell, during which she took time out to work on a farm in Switzerland and backpack across Turkey, Yugoslavia, the Greek Islands, and Morocco.

"In North Africa," she told me, "I was stunned by the colossal scars left by the colonial era. The world was not what my schoolbooks had taught me. I did a lot of thinking...."* Thinking with an open mind is, of course, subversive. Then to law school.

On a crisp October morning in 1988, Professor Arthur Miller, who used to explain the infamous O. J. Simpson murder trial and other matters of legal moment on ABC's *Good Morning America*, told the alumni of his reunion class and mine, the Class of '58 at the Harvard Law School, "Once today's seniors get the chance to earn $72,000 a year (real money back then), you can't even talk to them about going into public interest." Jennifer, of the class of '78, was an exception. Miller remembered her well. "She was intense, involved, inquisitive," he said, "always worrying about the underdog. It was clear she wanted to use the law as an instrument of social policy. She was headed for a public interest career and was not to be seduced by big-firm practice." As I had been.

During a summer break, she had clerked for Legal Services in the Rio Grande Valley of Texas on projects like obtaining clean drinking water for *colonias* (immigrant settlements) near Brownsville and getting ailing immigrants admitted to hospitals. "That summer in Texas was a *great* program," she recalled. On obtaining her degree, "There I went. It was a lot of fun, very invigorating, very challenging. I was working on cases that I really enjoyed." How had she made her choice? "It just always felt like what I wanted to do. The only reason I went to law school was to be able to do stuff like helping farm workers."

Many of those workers were undocumented refugees from Guatemala and El Salvador, which were both beset by "civil wars." In order to improve their slender chances of obtaining political asylum, she visited Guatemala in 1985 to gather evidence about the violence they had fled. "I went down there thinking I'd be gone for a couple of months, and instead I stayed a couple of years, except I came home for

---

* My quotes in this story are from either my interviews or Jennifer's 1997 book, *Searching for Everardo.*

Christmas. I'd go up to Texas by bus and work for a couple of weeks to make a little money and come right back." If she had stuck to her plan to be gone only a couple of months, she would have missed the heart of her life.

In order to learn about the guerrillas, she managed to spend a month visiting a large encampment, which the far bigger and better equipped (mainly by the US) army had been unable to destroy, high on the slopes of the vast volcano Tajumulco in the western highlands near the Mexican border. Her tent mate was a lithe, attractive *ladina* named Emma who had survived nearly fifteen years of fighting and walked with a limp after one of her feet had been partly shot away. Jennifer was soon taken with the humility and effectiveness with which the battalion commander, Everardo, led the fighters. Gradually at first, they grew to know each other. "His mind is like an enormous vortex, spinning everything inward toward his hungry center," she wrote later. One evening he asked her, "about my experiences in Guatemala, where I traveled, what I saw, and what I thought. What did I like about the people? Why? What else? By the time I reach the tent, I know I am falling in love with this extraordinary man and I curse myself for being a fool."

(A few years later, I would drive Emma around Vermont. "When I met her," I said, "I was fascinated by her mind. She was so inquiring, wanted to know what was going on, was just a dry sponge eager to soak up all the information she could. Was Everardo anything like that?" "Yeah," Jennifer said, "he wanted to know about absolutely everything. It was quite amazing.")

Emma saw that Jennifer was fighting her feelings and told her that he felt the same way about her. Like lovers everywhere, Jennifer had not seen it. Walking her back to Emma's tent after a dance one night, he kissed her, "shattering forever my intended self-restraint." He said that he loved her, but that they could not possibly remain together. But they did. And they married without benefit of clergy (as Nancy and I had) in her home in Texas and honeymooned locally where he did not stand out among other Native Americans. He returned to the volcano to lead his fighters, and she could not follow. Then in January 1993, she received the devastating news that he had been killed in a firefight. In her grief, she miscarried the child she did not know they had conceived. While the army insisted that he was dead, she learned more reliably some time later that he had been captured and was being interrogated—meaning tortured—to extract his guerrilla secrets.

Knowing that once the army learned all they could, they'd kill him, she began a campaign against the odds to compel the rulers of Guatemala to cease the torture and treat him as international law requires for prisoners of war. She talked with as many officials of both governments and US Congresspeople as would listen, pursued every legal remedy she could think of, inspected cadavers in remote graves that were not Everardo's, and sought help from American human rights groups. Which was hard because the rights she was asserting belonged to a guerrilla. It wasn't hard, though, for Sister Alice, who heard her story and committed to doing what she could to help her. Pat Davis, an activist on Alice's staff, soon accompanied her to Guatemala and became, she said, "my most trusted advisor and companion."

Still stymied the next September, she took the bold and bizarre step of fasting for a week on a traffic island in the busy *Avenida Reforma* which lay opposite the colorful, castle-like old *Politécnica* Military Academy, where Sister Dianna among many others had been tortured and she suspected that Everardo could be being tortured as she sat there.

The sight of a well-dressed *gringa*, surrounded by posters that said "Where Is Everardo?" and so forth and accompaniers who included a man poised to film of any attempt to remove her, attracted enormous attention—from soldiers outside the academy who did nothing, from the police and US Embassy (which was three blocks up the *avenida*) who periodically checked on her safety, from motorists who waved, honked, and otherwise wished her well, from a few brave Guatemalans who risked visiting her, and from the local media. Immediately the Guatemala City newspapers and TV carried her convincingly documented story that the army had Everardo alive and was lying when it denied it. Now her efforts to save him were very public knowledge, not known merely by the people she'd told one-on-one, who included the many officials who'd been unhelpful in varying degrees.

That same September of 1993, Maine's Common Courage Press

published her book *Bridge of Courage: The Life Stories of the Guatemalan Compañeros and Compañeras.* In it, guerrillas whom she met during her time in their encampment, tell their stories. Reading it gives one considerable insight into why they had taken the dangerous step of leaving their homes and joining the fighters. The next January, the head of the army's G-2 military intelligence told her that he had read the book and found it "quite shocking and offensive," and clearly she was a "subversive."

The following July 24th brought Jennifer to the gathering at Enrique and Sophia's where Nancy and I first met her. Her second fast for Everardo—the one that Sister Dianna and others of Coalition Missing visited at the end of "Tour"—would begin something over two months later. She tried hard but to no avail in the US and Guatemala to save him without needing to resort to it, and she studied up on how to preserve herself without eating. The keys, besides her grit, were body fat and Pedialyte, which she called "basically Gatorade without the calories." The Embassy's "1994 Country Human Rights Report for Guatemala," which it cabled to the State Department on October 6th—nearly nine years after our government and responsible media hailed Guatemala as a democracy—confirmed what Jennifer knew she was flying into:

> [S]ecurity forces…are believed to have committed numerous serious human rights violations in 1994…. Human rights violations continue at an alarming rate…. As in past years, many bodies were found throughout Guatemala bearing signs of severe dismemberment or postmortem mutilation.

In the broad Central Plaza on October 11th, it began. There were sun lotion, rain ponchos, candles in glass wells so they wouldn't blow out, chairs for the observers, and a placard of Everardo's face that she constantly held in front of her. Big signs said in Spanish: "EVERARDO, I LOVE YOU, I WILL WAIT FOR YOU HERE UNTIL THE END" and other brief messages that she considered key.

A crowd gathered. Reporters appeared. US Ambassador Marilyn McAfee came by and promised to send a patrol car regularly to check on her safety. Cars with dark windows parked where she and anyone with her could see them. She watched men at the parapet atop the National Palace watching her. As they looked down on the small figure below, they must have known that it would be bad PR to shoot her; but they had incurred bad PR before, and would again, to eliminate troublemakers.

"People came out and circled me all day twenty-four hours a day," Jennifer wrote, "and brought me poems and flowers and water and told me about who'd been killed in their family and how I should keep it up and talked to me about the case. It was a very, very supportive reaction."

A drunk told her to go home, eat, and find another man. Embassy people and the police kept checking on her. Americans, including me, were phoning the Embassy; and the White House was reportedly receiving around a hundred calls a day. As time passed, it grew harder for her to walk the five blocks to her hotel each morning to shower and change. After two weeks she could not concentrate well enough to read. Conversations exhausted her. Like the Everardo who talked with her inside her mind, she was always cold.

Back in Washington, Sister Alice said, "We got hundreds of people involved in actions and in demanding that the State Department request the Guatemala government to disclose where her husband would be, and tried to get Congress involved." Jennifer considered Alice, Pat, and Dianna "a veritable mission control center, organizing the telephone campaigns, speaking with officials, working out strategies, and answering the endless calls of inquiry." Alice would catch a few hours' sleep on her office floor while Jennifer slept on a foam pad across two wooden crates in the Central Plaza. The Guatemalan newspapers and TV continued to endanger themselves by carrying her story.

As the last red and yellow leaves were falling and the night air chilled in New Hampshire, Dorothy and Henry Harbury grew more and more concerned about their distant daughter. "We're hoping her health and life will be spared," Henry said on Day Fifteen of the fast, "but that's not in our control." By then Jennifer was growing increasingly tired and afflicted by dizzy spells. She had not told her parents about the fast before it began; they learned about it from a friend who heard it on the news. "She's like that," Henry said. "She wanted to spare us the news. She's very brave and we love her with all our hearts. We have great admiration for her and for what she's trying to accomplish."

She knew that the women of the GAM, who's loved ones had been disappeared and who had even less reason to hope than she did, kept on trying. To support her, Nineth Montenegro, the GAM's leader, was sending several women to sit near her every day. Some people who stopped at her encampment left coins to help pay for her needs. You must live so you can speak for all of us, they told her. A young Maya came up and handed her a poem, which ended:

> You are not alone in your struggle,
> You have the suffering Mayan peoples
> Supporting your courage, your love, your life,
> Your hope for a new dawn.
> Our minds and our hearts are with you....

Apparently the army recognized that though they could not force medical care on her, they were within their rights to prevent her suicide. A forensic doctor came up and said he had a court order to check her health. Finding him likable and not wanting him to get into trouble, she let him examine her at her hotel. He concluded that she should be fine for a while if she kept on drinking the Pedialyte and plenty of water. He told other people that she was "bionic."

Marie Dennis and Father Joe Nangle arrived at her encampment, followed by her friends from Coalition Missing, as noted in "Tour." Some Guatemalans got her hope up by saying they'd seen Everardo, but they were mistaken. Officials did all they could do to break her, with some care since she was so public, even getting her in her weakened condition to travel to another distant exhumation. Some citizens and, she is sure, soldiers masquerading in street clothes, called her a Communist (of course) and otherwise insulted her.

Her blood sugar level dropped to 42 milligrams per deciliter. The normal range is 80 to 110. If it went much lower, she was told, she could suffer organ damage and fall into a coma. While her kidneys were still strong, one eyelid was drooping, and she could not keep it raised. Her blood pressure was falling; her heart beat fast each time she stood up. October 27 was her forty-third birthday, "the best birthday of my life," she told a reporter for *People* magazine. "I'm not afraid," she added. "I think it's because I'm totally at peace with what I'm doing."

A crew from *60 Minutes* arrived, and soon, their ace reporter Mike Wallace. She found him "fully familiar with every fact of this case, which wins him my prompt respect and trust." He told her that he had learned from a confidential source that the Embassy had a CIA report that confirmed that Everardo was indeed captured alive by the army in 1992.

This news, she wrote, "hits me like a sandbag." She thought of all the times that US officials had told her they raised her case with the Guatemalans and what more could they do. "So they have known all along," she thought. "They have been watching me go through this hell, knowing all along and saying nothing. They are covering for the army. And now? My heart lurches. Is it too late, Everardo, or do we still stand a chance?"

It was natural for Jennifer to conclude this, though declassified documents suggest that some officials knew all along and some did not. It often seemed that the CIA knew but didn't talk while the State Department talked but didn't know. All the same, Ambassador McAfee et al. could surely have informed her at least a few painful days sooner without compromising their sources. That McAfee did not may have been due, not to ill will, but to her primary duty to preserve our government's alliance with "the worst human rights violator in the Hemisphere."

Jennifer continued to weaken. The times she felt dizzy, she would bend over and pretend to tie a shoelace. Her upper lip became hard to control, slurring her speech slightly. A doctor told her she had maybe another ten days before serious damage set in. On October 30, the Reuters news service reported:

> She is growing progressively weaker. [Guatemalan Ambassador] Edmond Mulet...told reporters he feared Guatemala's preferential trade benefits with the US may be threatened if the situation is unresolved.... "The case is very important

to the US government because of the involvement of a US citizen and because it addresses fundamental issues of human rights".... Guatemala's army, which has spent the past year trying to revamp its image as Latin America's human rights pariah, insists that [Everardo] ... killed himself to avoid capture two years ago.... The case is embarrassing the army, which pledged to respect human rights as part of peace agreements signed in March.... Harbury's campaign is backed in Washington by an impressive array of establishment figures, including former President Jimmy Carter and dozens of Congress members.

On the evening of Sunday, November 6th, Nancy and I had Enrique and Sophia over for supper, and we joined millions of Americans, as well as people in Guatemala who could access TV, in watching Mike Wallace interview Jennifer. There was her little camp with the National Palace rising behind it. There was Dianna. Wallace, wearing khaki pants and jacket over a blue shirt, leaned forward on a folding chair. Jennifer wore a red cardigan sweater in the bright sunlight, while several men stood behind them in shirtsleeves. Holding her big photo of Everardo before her, she told her story. "He's somewhere here in Guatemala," she said, her words burning like a blowtorch, "and I don't plan to leave without him."

As she had hoped and others feared, the *60 Minutes* report heightened officials' and many other people's concerns about her and Everardo in both countries. The *New York Times* wrote under a headline, "US Wife's Resolute Quest Shakes Guatemala":

> Supported by a network of volunteers in Guatemala and efficient publicity in the United States, she has brought so much attention to human rights violations in Guatemala that the country's relations with the United States are being tested.... Guatemalans are uneasy with the increased attention their country has received because of Ms. Harbury...

So, relations between these democracies were secure only as long as the lid covered the cesspool.

Her fast gained great publicity and caused more turmoil, posturing, honest efforts, and mendacity among more officials than she could know, but it produced neither Everardo nor reliable current information about him. On Day Thirty-Two of the fast, while many Americans were reading her op-ed in the *New York Times* entitled "The Death Squads Have My Husband," she told the reporters that she was ending the fast. Her reasons: she had to talk with high officials at the White House if she wanted to save Everardo, and she couldn't help him if she were disabled or dead.

The winter passed with many talks and no Everardo. Though Jennifer's body had far from healed from the injuries that starving for more than a month had inflicted, she knew that time was running out, if it hadn't already, for the slim chance of saving her husband. Hence the festive March 12 launching of her third fast that the Caneks, Nancy and I, and the other Vermonters drove down for. Incidentally, Everardo's real name was Efrain Bamaca, and we all knew it as we wore those snazzy yellow "Where Is Everardo?" T-shirts.

"We just kept on sending out faxes and letters," Sister Alice said as Jennifer continued her vigil opposite the White House, "and pressuring Congress to go visit her, to talk to her, and get news media. We did everything we possibly could, making banners and all the fliers that were needed to be handed out to people. She's very articulate and very strong, and she kept on saying what was happening."

This time, though, she was not bionic. After only four days, her upper lip began to stiffen. By the end of the first week, her heart was pounding, her blood pressure was dropping, and she was cold in the rain and sun alike. "Perhaps I will die," she thought, "or perhaps I will awaken in a hospital with permanent injuries. I no longer care at all. In fact, I almost yearn for my stubborn body to break down and finally set me free. I so long for this to be over."

On March 21, NPR's Diane Rehm interviewed her. A State Department summary included the following ominous exchange:

Q: What proof do you need to believe that Bamaca's dead?

A: His body.

Q: Are you prepared to die?

A: I hope it's not necessary but what choices do I have?

Q: You're asking for a lot—for the USG to change its entire policy.

A: No. I just want them to enforce existing policy on human rights [and] peace.

That day, too, I talked with Jennifer on her cell phone as she sat on the curb. After about twenty minutes, she said she wanted to stop and resume the next day because she was too weak to continue now. But when I phoned the next day, Day Eleven, she did not answer. An aide of Congressman (later Senator) Robert G. Torricelli, Democrat of New Jersey, had already invited her to his office. She told me later:

> Torricelli asked me to come in and see him. His clerk said he wanted to see me immediately. I went in, and he sat me down and wanted to know what I had been told. I went through everything the Embassy and everybody had told me. He was just absolutely, visibly furious, and I wasn't sure why.
>
> He said, "What's happened is your husband was ordered executed by Colonel Alpirez sometime in 1992. Alpirez also ordered the killing of [an American innkeeper] back in 1990. He was a CIA contact. They've known this all along. Why haven't they told you?"
>
> It wasn't clear how long all of the US officials had known it, but it was clear that while I was sitting out there in front of the White House, they knew it very, very well. He was livid, really really upset about it.

This word from this Congressman that Everardo was dead shattered whatever it was that had been holding her together, yet she remained composed, and he did not seem to notice. "Torricelli is still speaking," she wrote. "I know this because I can see his lips moving, and yet I hear nothing at all. I cannot hear his voice because my ears are filled with the terrible roar of a bullet as it smashes through flesh and bone—your flesh and bone, Everardo—and stops your fierce, clean heart forever."

Jennifer returned to the Assisi Community and found a birthday party in full swing for Marie Dennis's son Matthew. "Jennifer did not want to disrupt the birthday with this bombshell," Father Joe Nangle told me, "so she kept it quiet and said to us, 'Tune to the *Today Show* tomorrow morning, it's going to be interesting.' We said to her later, 'Why didn't you tell us?' She said, 'Well, it was his birthday.'"

"Guatemalan Agent of CIA Tied to Killing of American," blared a front-page headline in the Thursday, March 23rd, *New York Times.* The story, datelined the 22nd, began:

> A Guatemalan military officer who ordered the killings of an American citizen and a guerrilla leader married to an American lawyer was a paid agent of the Central Intelligence Agency, a member of the House Intelligence Committee said today.
>
> The intelligence agency knew about the killings ordered by the Guatemalan colonel on its payroll, but concealed its knowledge for years, the committee member, Representative Robert G. Torricelli...said in a letter he sent to President Clinton today.
>
> Moreover, the State Department and the National Security Council learned the facts months ago but did not tell the guerrilla's widow, Jennifer Harbury, who has been petitioning the White House to disclose her husband's fate, the letter said.
>
> A member of the Senate intelligence committee who had been briefed on the two killings, confirmed the gist of Mr. Torricelli's statement....
>
> The Congressman said Ms. Harbury, a Harvard Law School graduate, wept when he told her that her husband, a leftist guerrilla named Efrain Bamaca Velasquez, had been killed while a prisoner of the Guatemalan military since 1992....
>
> Ms. Harbury said tonight that "they say 'the truth shall make you free,'" citing the inscription from the Gospel of John engraved on the wall of the CIA's lobby.
>
> "And now I feel free," she said. "At least I know my hus-

band is free of torture, and I am free of the nightmare that he's suffering somewhere."

She added: "I was told nothing except lies for two and a half years. There is no way out of this for the Guatemalan Army and the State Department and the CIA They've been caught, for once and for all...."

A few days later in Mexico City, the Guatemalan government and the URNG [coalition of guerrilla armies] signed an agreement that provided for the rights of the Maya—rights that Everardo had fought for on the volcano and worked towards during the interlude so long ago when he and Jennifer had been happy together—rights that would largely not be implemented after peace finally came.

The *Times* and other US media continued to report one more revelation after another about US support for the terror in Guatemala. The publicity that resulted from Jennifer's fast the previous fall had mentioned the human rights violations but focused on the romantic story of a valiant wife risking her life to save her husband. Now, though, the focus was United States complicity in mass torture and murder.

Torricelli had received his information about Bamaca's death from Dr. Richard Nuccio, who had previously worked for him and was currently the State Department's Guatemala expert and was making considerable progress towards ending the civil war. He believed that Jennifer's quest was impeding that progress, as he told her during her second fast.

It was my pleasure to interview him about all this in March 1998 over lunch at the Harvard Faculty Club; he was a Visiting Fellow at that university after leaving the government. Energic and intense, he salted his talk with humor and irony. He was called a "whistle blower," but he wasn't one. Whistleblowers go public to halt wrongs, yet they, not the wrongdoers, often pay a price. Nuccio did not go public but to a Congressman.

It started October 19th, 1994, when the Guatemala desk officer brought me a report that wasn't supposed to exist—a report about Efrain Bamaca that made it clear that the US government knew quite a bit about him, even though I and other State Department officials had been telling Jennifer and members of Congress that we didn't have any information about him. From October 19th of 1994 until March 17th of 1995, I was in a highly agitated emotional state.

Pain danced behind his eyes as he said this. I asked him what his position in the peace negotiations had been up until that October.

It was me and pretty much no one else. I kept my boss, the Assistant Secretary for Latin America informed of what I was doing. Within a month it was a flood of information: Bamaca was alive and captured and held by the Guatemalan army for some period of time. We don't have reports about him after June or July of '92. What we gave Jennifer on November 10th is a fair summary of what those reports said. She ended her hunger fast the next day—because of that, plus the offer of [National Security Advisor Anthony] Lake [to meet with her].

You told Mike Wallace that you rarely slept a full night in those days.

It was rare from October '94 until quite recently that my wife could count on seeing me in bed when she went to sleep and still there when she woke up in the morning. She would usually find me at my computer or reading the newspaper or watching TV to try to while away the hours until I could go to work again.

Why did you go to Torricelli when you did?

In early February 1995, a report came in that indicates we knew things about the Bamaca case because a person identified as being a CIA asset involved in both the Bamaca and the [American innkeeper] Michael DeVine murders was reporting them. That changed the nature of my emotional distress. It was one thing to have misled—unintentionally, but still misled—Congress about Bamaca. I now came to believe that

I had stumbled across a conspiracy inside the CIA to cover
up their involvement in the murder of an American citizen as
well. The fact that one of our own people was involved had
been hidden from the Congress, I believe, deliberately—because they knew that if they told us that and we started to
pull on the string, the string would eventually go to DeVine,
and that would get some of them in trouble. The CIA station
chief had lied to the US Ambassador, who was conducting
an investigation at the time, and had never told the Congressional Oversight Committee that one of their guys had gone
bad and may have been involved in a crime against an American—which is what they have to do under the law.

Over the next six or seven weeks, I grow more restless,
have more sleepless nights. I see Torricelli. I go to his office
and say, "Remember that case you asked me about a couple
of times? Remember I told you we didn't know anything
about it? Well, that's not true."

Torricelli exploded, though it was a few days before he called Jennifer in. Rick continued with what he saw as being at stake:

After we had signed a human rights accord in June of
1994, the CIA continued to hire Guatemalans who engaged
in murder, torture, and kidnapping in Guatemala. While I
was at a peace table representing the President of the United
States and signing for the US government saying, "We are
working to end human rights violations," another part of my
government—literally perhaps at the same moment—was
handing over thousands of dollars to someone who was
committing those violations. That meant that my attempt to
create a role for the United States as an honest broker was
itself a lie. We were not trying to achieve peace. Part of us
was trying to murder people in Guatemala.

Jennifer's case unmasked that betrayal at the center of the
policy, a betrayal by the CIA of our own government. Yet
they have largely escaped with impunity. Thank goodness
the peace process was stronger than the United States and

could overcome that betrayal.

About Jennifer, he said:

> I was worried because she was giving every indication that
> she was going to stay there till she died or they dragged
> her away to a hospital. I suspected that the Park authorities
> wouldn't have let her die, but she might have done perma-
> nent damage to herself, her liver or one of her vital organs.
> This was less than six months from her last hunger strike.
> She says in her book that getting her out of the plaza with
> the information that Torricelli gave her saved her life. I
> think that's probably right.

The CIA, which expects secrecy and impunity when it commits
crimes in the perceived national interest, vengefully pulled Nuccio's
security clearance after a Justice Department lawyer had proved unable to prosecute him—because providing truthful information to
Congress is not a crime. "They just took away my career instead of
sending me to jail," he said. "When the CIA took my clearance away,
that effectively ended my career in government."

Father Joe Nangle told me some years later, "I felt sorry for him. I
think I still do. Nuccio was caught in an intolerable situation, and he
finally came forward and sacrificed his career for the truth."

Most of what Jennifer had felt about Nuccio along the way had
been negative. In the end, though, she felt gratitude. "This act of courage and honesty has not gone unpunished by US officials," she wrote
in her memoir. "I can only say, Richard Nuccio, that you did the right
thing and that it probably saved my life. You have my respect and
thanks."

Two people of conscience clashed, and truth was a two-edged
sword. Telling it inside the System cost Rick his power; seeking it
from the outside gained Jennifer hers. Having worked for peace, followed his conscience, sacrificed his career in our government, and kept
his integrity, he returned to college teaching and found other ways to
serve the public. In our society, heroes like him are too rare.

The September after Jennifer's final fast, Meredith and Dianna were attending a conference on US relations with Guatemala, mainly to support Jennifer, who was on a panel with former Ambassador Stroock. During a hot exchange with Jennifer, Strook suddenly said, "I see you out there in the audience, Meredith Larson and Sister Dianna," and went on to challenge Dianna. She walked to a microphone, and the bottled anger from years of his betraying her poured forth. "Everything you said, Mr. Stroock, is bullshit!" She continued to tell him off, and as Jennifer told me, he "was attacking her in this very snide, loud, aggressive voice. She was still extremely fragile, but she was standing up for herself, and she did very, very well. But he was submitting her to unbelievable levels of pain."

Dianna received huge applause, but back in her seat, she collapsed in tears. As Meredith told her later, "You had entered your own space, crying, and literally seemed to be elsewhere. I so wanted to comfort you, I tried, and you didn't respond." Dianna felt intensely humiliated. She wrote later that "People had seen my weakest side. I was so ashamed and at that moment all I wanted to do was die—to undo that scene where I had become like my torturers."

Back at Assisi, she said she wanted to be alone and went up to her room. When Meredith knocked on her door later, she did not respond. Mindful that she sometimes needed space, Meredith withdrew. When Dianna did not appear for dinner, though, Jennifer worried. She heard the water turn on upstairs. Thinking it was the shower, she was surprised to hear it turn right off. She left the table and hurried up the stairs.

"Dianna, Dianna," she called. Dianna opened the door. Blood was flowing from one of her wrists, and she was holding a bottle in which she had been saving Halcion and Valium pills. It was empty. Jennifer, joined by Marie Dennis, tried to convince her to rush to an emergency room. Weeping and still terrified from her experience in the hospital in Kentucky, she pleaded with them not to send her to one. So, Jennifer and Marie summoned a doctor who bandaged her wrist and fed her charcoal pills to absorb as much of the deadly drugs as was still possible. Dianna's friends stayed up with her through the night, kept check on her breathing, and awakened her every time she dozed off lest she never wake again.

Later the same month, as a direct result of the information that Jennifer's quest had brought to the fore, CIA Director John Deutch fired the former chief of CIA operations in Latin America, Terry Ward, and the station chief in Guatemala from 1991–1993, Frederick Brugger. He demoted a second former station chief, and reprimanded a third plus six more present and former CIA employees who held posts as high as deputy chief of Latin American operations. This was reportedly the most severe internal CIA discipline since several senior officials were fired or demoted over Iran–Contra in 1987. Deutch said that he had also imposed new rules to avoid future failures to tell the truth. Significantly, he imposed a layer of supervision over the hiring of local "assets" like Colonel Roberto Julio Alpirez. President Clinton called Deutch's actions "forceful and fair." In reporting Deutch's disciplinary steps, the *Times* told its readers:

> Scores of senior officers in the Guatemalan Army, which has killed tens of thousands of civilians and tortured thousands more in a long campaign against a small guerrilla force, have served as CIA agents.… The CIA's station went to great lengths to protect many Guatemalan military officers on its payroll from reports that they were involved in human rights abuses—in some cases suppressing its own reports, according to senior CIA and State Department officials.… In 1991–92, while the United States pressed Guatemala to find the killers [of US innkeeper DeVine], Mr. Brugger failed to notify Ambassador Stroock that colonel Alpirez, a prime suspect, was a CIA agent. "Not only did they not tell me," Mr. Stroock said in an interview.… "They did not tell my boss, the Secretary of State or the Congress. That was stupid." … A 1980 law requires the CIA to keep Congress "fully and currently informed" about its activities abroad.…
>
> [T]he Guatemalan Ambassador to the United States Edmond Mulet—who said his father had been killed by leftist guerrillas—said the CIA should stop spying on his country.… "The CIA has been supervising military operations

and treating Guatemala as if it were a national security matter for the United States, which it is not," Mr. Mulet said.
The agency has also been pitting Guatemalans against one
another, whipping up popular sentiment against a vanishing
leftist threat, he said. Except for operations against cocaine
trafficking, he said, "I don't think the CIA has any business
in Guatemala."

Years later, the CIA would blame Jennifer, and Deutch's modest
supervisory steps, as a reason for its failure to prevent the horrendous
9/11 attack on the Twin Towers and Pentagon. Better to blame an
alleged lefty than their own incompetence.

One very rainy Saturday in October of 1995, three weeks after Jennifer had saved Dianna's life, she, Margaret Swedish, and a scholar of
the Maya named Daniel Matul gathered to speak about Guatemala at
Dartmouth College in Hanover, a few miles from the home of Jennifer's parents, at a symposium arranged by Sophia, Enrique, and their
friends. The next afternoon, which was dry and brisk, they spoke to
a smaller crowd at the Weston Priory. Afterwards, Jennifer and her
mother wanted to attend the vespers that the monks sang in their
stone chapel to the music of their guitars. But Jennifer hadn't brought
anything to wear on her head. Would it be all right, she asked, to attend the service? Nancy and I assured her that the brothers welcome
everyone, and most women worship uncovered.

That's the real Jennifer, I thought: sensitive, respectful, and humble,
so different from the tightly focused, highly articulate lawyer that the
public sees when she packs everything she can into a brief interview on
TV. It was these gentler qualities that had permitted her to draw close
to Everardo and other Maya in the forests on Tajumulco. Here were
the same qualities today among the Green Mountains of Vermont in
the presence of a faith that she did not profess.

Standing in the chapel in the row behind her, I looked down and
thought how much those shoulders, still slender from her last fast, had
borne since Nancy and I first met her at Enrique and Sophia's a year
ago that summer.

A report of the Intelligence Oversight Board said, "We...believe it plausible that [Bamaca's] execution would have been ordered at the highest levels of the Guatemalan military and that his interrogation at times included torture." How forthright! While not persuaded that Colonel Alpirez had killed Bamaca, the IOB believed "Alpirez participated in at least part of Bamaca's interrogation." Significantly, the IOB found that

> while the State Department went to great lengths in pressing the Guatemalan government on the issue [of Bamaca's fate] ... [w]e found no indication ... of any request by the State Department for a search of past intelligence on the case until [Nuccio's request in] October 1994. If it had done so in early 1993, when Jennifer Harbury first raised the issue of her husband's fate, the Department might have been able at a much earlier date to provide her with useful information about her husband's fate—that is, a report that he had been taken alive.

In other words, Jennifer might well have succeeded in saving Everardo if US officials had been more diligent. Their failure cast a tragic and infuriating light on her story.

One night in January 1996, someone torched the car of Jennifer's lawyer outside the home in Washington where he and his family were sleeping, the flames melting the nearby plastic garbage cans. Across town the next night, someone fired a pistol bullet from down the street that pierced a side of the bay window below the room where Jennifer was asleep in one of the Assisi Community's two houses. The bullet slammed into the wall across the room, knocking coats off their pegs in the hallway on the other side. Recall that in Guatemala, attacks intended to send a message often came in pairs. A Salvadoran refugee who was staying at Assisi sometimes stood in the bay window late at night holding her baby, fortunately not when the bullet passed through that space.

In 1997 Jennifer published *Searching for Everardo: A Story of Love, War, and the CIA in Guatemala* (Warner Books). The memoir tells her story, fervently but modestly, and discloses more than the media had about the extent of US complicity. In it, she sets aside her psychic armor and lets us see her private self in love, sometimes in doubt or fear or pain. The *Washington Post*: "There are heroics here. There is a bold reach for truth. And, most memorably, there is a clear-eyed gaze into a labyrinth of lies." The *Washington Times*: "Extraordinary.... poignant.... a staggering book." The *National Catholic Reporter*: "...a heart-wrenching story of love, hope, dreams, determination, commitment. Beautifully written, a classic." The *New York Times* review was hypercritical.

After she learned that her husband was dead, she searched for his body, sometimes at great risk, in order to give it a proper burial, even though she knew that the army may have dropped it into a volcano or the ocean or buried it in a zillion pieces. Finally, from additional declassified documents—and tips from army people "who do want me to hear a little bit more"—she concluded that "he was alive probably till the summer of '94 and was dismembered and scattered across a sugarcane field so that no one would ever be able to identify his body. I think that, unfortunately, is the right story."

Though she never found Everardo's remains, she did find his father, sisters, and their families, and invited a number of them up to Texas for a month's visit. "That was real fun." With money from a judgment that the OAS court awarded her, she set up a trust to offer college to all twenty-eight of Everardo's and her own nieces and nephews. "All of them are *campesinos*, so they've had very little formal schooling. They're real bright and they want to go to college, so they're going to go." Although her nieces and nephews, and the daughter of her dear friend and onetime tent-mate Emma, did not replace the child that she and Everardo could not have, those children have delighted her.

I asked Adriana if she thinks Jennifer is a survivor of torture. "Absolutely," she replied. "Disappearances are the perfection of torture because they involve not only the disappeared but the relatives. For the relatives, not knowing what happened has the same effects as the other kind of torture: not sleeping, the fear, the anger, the despair, feeling impotent, not being able to do anything, just the pain. There is no end, no resolution to that pain, the nightmares, the distrust. She is a survivor of torture."

"I don't think people think of her that way," I said. "She's always so competent, and she's so tough."

"That's what makes her a survivor," Adriana replied.

In 2004, she visited her old teacher, Professor Arthur Miller, at the Harvard Law School. "She hasn't changed a bit," he told me, "in spite of the hell she's been through. She's going to hang in there forever. It sure makes law teaching a lot more interesting when you run into people like that."

Where, I asked Jennifer, had she found the courage to take on the most brutal army in the Americas and its sponsors in the US government? She laughed and said, "I think I was just desperate."

Many people saw her and Everardo as an odd couple. While the media wondered how an American lawyer could marry an unschooled Maya, I wondered how a disciple of non-violence could accept a man who felt called to kill. "You marry a warrior, yet you fast like Gandhi," I said and she laughed again. "How do you feel about non-violence?"

"Non-violence is very wonderful if it can be done," she said. "In India it was obviously an incredible and courageous and strong thing to do. Unfortunately, the Guatemalan army in all these years was killing everybody like Gandhi."

In an age where self-interest is in favor, families falter, and roughly half of all marriages fail, Jennifer set an example of invincible devotion to her spouse. An unlikely paragon of family values perhaps, she repeatedly risked her life and injured her body for his sake. Though she could not save him, she probably did more than anyone else to make the public aware of United States participation in barbarity in Guatemala, thus giving the public the opportunity to take the steps that human decency seemed to require. But as usual, the public remained largely passive.

At first blush, she and Everardo could not seem more different, yet at heart they were much alike: gentle and considerate where circumstances permitted, fiercely determined, and ready to lay down their lives for each other, their comrades, and the oppressed Maya. They met on a volcano, fell in love, marveled at each other's ways, adjusted to them as best they could, and married. She was drawn to his brilliant and voracious mind (and vice versa) much as Jeff Bartow had been drawn to Adriana's. Though Everardo killed people in battle and from ambush, Jennifer admired his humility and gentleness. They were not impervious to fear, but did not let it deter them. In courage, resourcefulness, determination, and respect for other people, they were well-mated indeed.

Everardo told Jennifer during a halcyon summer when they lived together in Mexico City that she has the eyes of a hawk, causing her to reflect ruefully that the remark said more about his honesty than his tact. Neither of them could have known that, trying to save him when he seemed beyond saving, she would plunge like a hawk upon the official beast time after time, swooping up to plunge again. Nor did he live to know that she did this, but he knew her spirit. If in some hereafter, we learn the deeds of the loved ones we leave behind, I suspect that he was gratified by what she did for him and his people— gratified but not surprised.

In *Searching for Everardo,* she spoke to the man who lived in her memory as though he were there beside her. While they came from different worlds, she wrote that, "we understood each other on some deeper level from the very beginning. We were never equals, for you were always far ahead of me in wisdom and in vision, yet this didn't trouble either one of us. You always treated me as an equal in every way and you were always proud of my independence. You took the time to really listen to me, to understand me down to my very bones. Even now after all these years, I still miss you. I am proud, so proud to have known you."

Confession

"She is our voice," Sophia Canek said, meaning that Sister Dianna Ortiz was the voice of the Maya of Guatemala.

Sophia, Enrique, and I were sitting at their long wooden table beneath the vault of their converted barn on the evening of March 31, 1996. They had fled for their lives from Guatemala and had been living for the past twelve years in Sanctuary with the monks of the Weston Priory. Sophia's remark referred to a quest that Dianna commenced that afternoon in Lafayette Park across Pennsylvania Avenue from the White House. Standing there before a throng of maybe five hundred supporters and passers-by, she proclaimed:

"Today, on Palm Sunday, I begin my silent vigil for Truth—the truth about my own case, and the truth about all those Guatemalans who have suffered and died at the hands of the officially sponsored death squads. For those of us who know and love Guatemala, it is painfully clear that our own United States government has been closely linked to these death squads, and has a great amount of detailed information about those of us who have survived as well as those of us who have perished. On behalf of all of us, I demand that President Clinton declassify all US government information related to human rights abuses in Guatemala, from 1954 to the present."

Dianna would be out on that grass and a candle would burn day and night beside her for as long as it took, she said, to remind the President of "those victims and survivors whose flame will never die. She asked the crowd about a tall, fair man called "Alejandro," who had commanded her own torturers, "Was he a CIA agent? Why is the US government protecting him? How many other Alejandros are there out there, supervising the torture of innocent people?" If not an actual CIA agent, she asked the crowd, was he working for the CIA, like the man who had tortured the husband of her friend, Jennifer Harbury?

Dianna had not embarked on this vigil lightly. A year ago, in the wake of revelations that Jennifer had elicited about CIA ties to torture and murder in Guatemala, Clinton had directed the Intelligence Oversight Board to investigate several human rights cases including hers; it was to finish in three months. The previous April, Dianna herself had filed a request for documents about her case under the Freedom of Information Act. In August, the Justice Department finally began its own investigation of her 1989 abduction and torture, "six years too late," she said. So far she had seen zero results from the two investigations and her FOIA request. "Even after Jennifer had risked her life and gotten a firestorm of press," she explained later, "things had gone back to normal. It seemed that the CIA and the US government were going to get off the hook. The Guatemalan people would never have the rest of the story, and neither would we."

Sophia Canek was right. This evening Dianna was speaking through her silent vigil and flickering candle for all the Maya of Guatemala, a bright star in their long night that had begun when Spaniards invaded their land nearly five centuries ago. Launching the vigil was very hard for Dianna. She was shy and so private that she often retreated into her bedroom at the Assisi Community and shut the door. Now she would be sitting across a few feet of grass from a sidewalk flowing with strangers. Was she up to it? Jennifer had put herself through three public hunger strikes, "but I wasn't Jennifer, and I couldn't be Jennifer. I wasn't that strong."

And a heavier burden was weighing her down. To seek the truth in public, she felt honor-bound to purge herself of a truth she had hidden from everyone except her closest confidantes. She had tremulously tiptoed up to this revelation at a Congressional hearing last September when she testified, "I am prepared to share aspects of my torture that before were too painful to bring to light. One of these is that my torturers forced me to commit some horrible acts, and they videotaped and photographed me committing these acts. Since the day I escaped, I have been afraid that if I continued to struggle for justice, my torturers would distribute those videotapes. I was afraid I would be held responsible by people like you. So I opted to lock these dark secrets in the depths of my soul where for years they have been dragging me slowly to my grave."

Melodramatic as that may have sounded to her listeners, it was the truth; and the grave lurked closer than she knew. She carried a "special friend" (a razor blade); a confrontation later that month with an old antagonist, former Ambassador Thomas Strook, would drive her to use it. She was not, in fact, prepared to share her secret with those Congresspeople that nearly fatal September; but today she forced herself to share it with the throng in the park. The Caneks' daughter who was interning at Sister Alice's GHRC, where Dianna worked, had faxed them a copy of her talk. Now it was depressing our mood. Enrique, Sophia, and I were thrilled that Dianna had begun the vigil, and we should have felt jubilant; but a deep sadness for our brave, tormented friend hung over us. For this afternoon she laid bare the dreadful deed that had been tormenting her, unfairly but effectively, through the years:

"I cannot forget those who suffered with me and died in that clandestine prison. The memories of what I witnessed and experienced that November day haunt me day and night. Even to this day, I can smell the decomposing of bodies, disposed of in that open pit. I can hear the piercing screams of other people being tortured. I can see the blood gushing out of the woman's body as I thrust a small machete into her body. For you see, I was handed a machete. Thinking it would be used against me, and at that point in my torture, wanting to die, I did not resist. But my torturers put their hands onto the handle, on top of mine. And I had no choice. I was forced to use it against another human being. What I remember is blood gushing—spurting like a water fountain—droplets of blood spattering everywhere—and my screams lost in the cries of the woman."

In the crowd facing Dianna stood my friend Margaret Swedish. "When she started reading her statement—I'm sure we'll never experience anything quite like it again—I've never heard a group of people whose silence was palpable. And she fell apart. I think one of the most remarkable moments in that whole vigil was that she was not able to go on as she was approaching this final admission about participating in murder. She broke down. She stepped away from the microphone and was being embraced and supported. Pat Davis went up and started reading from her statement, and it was incredible to watch what was going on right over here on the side because this woman pulled herself together and got back up to that microphone and was able to say it herself. She needed to say it. This cleansing act had to happen. And the horror of it! When you think of all the terrible things, the multiple rapes and the pit with the bodies and the rats and the whole thing, that should be enough to explain her brokenness, but to think that in that moment of complete breakdown, they would force her to participate in something like that! I thought I'd heard it all until that moment. The courage of being able to stand in front of a crowd of people and media and say, 'This is what they made me do!' I will never forget it as long as I live. And I think one of the things that brought so many people to her in those weeks of the vigil was this need that many of us had to say, just by being quiet with her in the park, 'Dianna, it's okay, you are not responsible.' There was something that really bonded the community in wanting to lift that burden finally from her heart."

This day of public breakdown, recovery, confession, and release in Washington came eight and a half years after she had left her safe, comfortable Mother House in Kentucky to answer what she discerned as God's call to teach Mayan children in the vast, green highlands of Guatemala. Some say that bad luck and mistaken identity shaped her journey since then, yet when she asked the crowd whether Alejandro worked for the CIA, she had considerable cause for believing that he did.

Sophia, Enrique, and I agreed at once that Dianna was not a murderer, that she had done nothing wrong. To heighten her agony and plant festering seeds of guilt and shame, the torturers and they alone killed the poor woman, then pounded the lie into Dianna that she had played a part in it. That's Dianna, I thought. What courage it took to tell her unsuspecting supporters this secret that's been gnawing within her like one of the torturers' giant rats! How far she's come, since escaping from Alejandro's car as he drove her from the torture chamber towards, he claimed, the US Embassy!

Later, Dianna would reveal more particulars: After the torturers had burned her with their cigarettes and done other horrible things, they shut her in a room whose walls were splattered with blood and feces. On a cot lay a woman who had already been gruesomely bruised and sliced. They held onto each other. They wept. "Dianna," she said, "they will try to break you. Be strong." The three torturers burst in and handed Dianna the machete. The one she called the Policeman got behind her. Suddenly he clamped his hands over hers and thrust the machete into the woman. This was the man who had first forced himself into Dianna. She had resisted then as fiercely as she could, but he was too strong for her. With the machete, too, he proved too strong. Even after she overcame her surprise, she could not halt his repeated thrusts. She saw another man filming the grisly scene with a video camera. She was never certain that the woman died, though with all that blood spurting from her vitals and no one trying to stop it, she must have. The torturers in their diabolical way convinced Dianna that she had participated in murder. "If I refused to cooperate," she said, "their boss, Alejandro, would have no choice but to turn the videotapes and the photographs over to the press, and everyone would know about the crime I'd committed."

So she was even braver than we knew, or than Alejandro and the superiors who commissioned this agonizing torture had probably expected, when she spoke out again and again, most forcefully today as she disclosed her ravenous secret, in defiance of his threat and regardless of the consequences to herself.

As a onetime New York State prosecutor, I was clear that her hands, crushed as they were between the hands of the Policeman and the handle of the machete, did *not* make her a participant in that murder. She had no intent to cause harm. She did no act that caused harm. She did not participate any more than his glove did if he was wearing a glove, but once torturers take away their victim's *self*, they gain the power to instill just about any notion, however false. Even years later she insisted that she participated in the murder, rather than being simply a spectator who was held far too close to it.

Even if Dianna had done something criminal, it is very hard to imagine (impossible under US laws) that she could have been convicted of anything at all solely on the basis of a free-floating videotape, i.e., without a torturer testifying that the tape gave a fair and accurate representation of the event and was not simply a Hollywood-type concoction—and it was most unlikely that a torturer would come forward and inevitably incriminate himself by testifying against her. It was unlikely, too, that there was film in the camera. Why would they make a movie of the Policeman committing the murder?

As Dianna had told the Congresspeople the previous September, she felt shame and guilt that March afternoon and the fear that the crime, which in fact and in law she did not commit, would be exposed and turn people against her. She wondered if she could still be a nun. The morning after her confession to the crowd in the park, word reached her that her family and her community of Ursuline sisters still supported her without reservation. In fact, the news of this horror brought people everywhere closer to her.

The Vigil

The vigil for truth that Sister Dianna began, as we have seen, on

Palm Sunday of 1996 when she revealed her own terrible truth, which was actually a falsehood that the torturers had driven like an iron spike into her brain. The vigil was duly heralded by the *Washington Post* and *New York Times*. It would last for thirty-seven days through sun and snow and rain in Lafayette Park, where Jennifer had held her final hunger strike a year ago, as spring came forth and the information that Dianna sought about her case did not.

She would be out there from eight in the morning until five the next morning when she would leave to grab a shower and an hour or so in her own bed at the Assisi Community before returning for the next long day of facing the weather and the people and, across Pennsylvania Avenue, the White House with silhouetted figures moving about on the roof. "Whether I am in the park or out of the park," she said, "the darkness of the blindfold is with me. This time, it is not my torturers who conceal their identity from me. It is the US government."

Always, a blue and white Guatemalan shawl lay around her shoulders or across her lap or beside her. When the air was cool, she put on a dark blue, maroon-trimmed ski jacket and sometimes tucked her legs into a sleeping bag. Or she tilted a large umbrella on the ground by her head to block the sun or wind or gaze of the endless stream of strangers. Around nine in the evening she would retire, more or less, behind the umbrella, and several of her accompaniers would unroll their sleeping bags on the grass close by. She said she was never comfortable on her pillows; an air mattress proved too rigid to sit on; and as she lost weight, the pain of sitting worsened no matter how she arranged herself. When she lay down for the short nap at Assisi, she had to place a pile of pillows beneath her. She wasn't fasting but wasn't eating much either and lost ten pounds during the first three weeks in the park.

Signs on either side of her encampment told passersby: "SILENT VIGIL FOR TRUTH, SR. DIANNA ORTIZ" and "VIGIL FOR TRUTH, THE GUATEMALAN PEOPLE AND SR. DIANNA ORTIZ SEARCH FOR THE TRUTH, SUPPORT THEM!" and "WHO IS ALEJANDRO?" Ranged on a dark plastic sheet before her were vases of well-wishers' flowers, plastic water bottles, and a candle flickering inside a tall glass jar that she scrambled to relight whenever the wind blew it out and to replace when it burned low. There was a guest book that people were asked to write messages in rather than break the silence by talking to her. Their messages were sometimes long, and often moving, showing as they did how Dianna touched the writers. John, age eight: "I hope someone will tell her the truth." And piles of handouts that accompaniers offered passers-by and her GHRC supporters kept replenishing. A box for flashlights, first aid stuff, and the unsolicited money that passers-by kept leaving. Bricks to lay along the edges of a big bright blue rain tarp when it was pulled over the whole encampment from back to front. When that happened, Dianna and an Ursuline friend from Kentucky, Sister Suzanne Sims, or whoever else was inside with her, would open umbrellas to raise the tarp and create space inside. Now and then, Dianna would tidy up her little patio. When Nature called, one woman or another accompanied her to the fancy Hay–Adams Hotel across the park behind her encampment.

When Nature called the rest of us, there was a McDonald's a few blocks in one direction and a Starbucks a few blocks in the other. Sometimes we'd use the Hay–Adams, which seemed silently sympathetic to Dianna's cause. Back in the day, I had stayed in that hotel two or three times along with lawyers Len Joseph and Len Boehner when Dewey Ballantine sent us to negotiate with Securities and Exchange Commission lawyers over stock fraud charges that the Commission had brought against one of the firm's clients.

Stretching back from behind Dianna was a mound of stuff under the blue tarp: sleeping bags, backpacks, umbrellas, folding chairs that the Park Police would not allow anyone to sit on so as not to violate a rule against erecting a "permanent structure" in the park. Many people, including me at first, assumed the mound was a tent that Dianna could retreat into. Unfortunately not. There were trees near the encampment and plenty of lawn that was open to the sky. Traffic was banned from the block of Pennsylvania Avenue that separated the White House and Executive Office Building from the park; its broad black pavement lay empty except for Secret Service men in black shorts, shirts, and helmets who pedaled slowly around and around on Trek bicycles that had little pouches on the handle bars (containing short Uzi machine guns, I supposed but did not ask). Until late evening, the sidewalk streamed with government and business folks who tended to walk fast and tourists who didn't, the passing parade across the capital of the world.

The Friday before the vigil began, someone had left a box of shit at Assisi for Dianna. Early in the vigil, a park policeman taunted her that rats the size of cats would surely snuggle up to her for warmth while she slept. Thereafter she fought to stay awake, while her accompaniers stayed alert to shoo any rats away. I never saw one near her. The policeman's taunt was perfect for thrusting her back into the torturers' pit with huge rats "amusing themselves," as she put it, on her bruised, burned, raped, naked body where she lay among other naked bodies, some moaning, some dead. I wondered whether the policeman's words came from his own nastiness or official prompting.

The first Tuesday of the vigil, a tall man with short blond hair, a suit, tie, and sunglasses confronted her from the sidewalk. "Sister Ortiz," he said, "I just want to tell you that at least one American doesn't believe you." Jennifer Harbury, who was sitting beside Dianna, challenged the man, and to their surprise, his retorts showed that he was fully familiar with both women's cases. He seemed to know, too, that being disbelieved upset Dianna. The Guatemalan G–2 (intelligence) reportedly kept a presence in Washington, and of course CIA headquarters was right across the Potomac. If their unholy alliance did not fear Dianna, why would they harry her?

Sister Alice served as the base captain for the vigil. Sister Suzanne Sims had charge in the park—a southern lady as top sergeant. A homeless man showed Suzanne how to fold the big tarp so it could be pulled easily over the encampment when a rain shower rolled in. Several homeless men took up Dianna's cause and befriended her and her main accompaniers. A Native American named Tony told us that she had "the support of the drinking community in the park." Several homeless men slept between plastic sheets on the grass beside the encampment along with other accompaniers, or on nearby benches, to help guard her through the night.

"Dianna is very thin but smiles warmly and is agile when she does things and then subsides within herself," I wrote in my notebook, my first impression on reaching the vigil the evening of April 25. Though

I was there most of the time thereafter except late at night, the only time I saw joy on her face was when little children climbed onto her lap, they and she heedless of their weight.

Like other new accompaniers, I received an instruction sheet: "Keep police away from Dianna.... If conversation becomes necessary, please move away from her area.... Encourage people to sign the book. If they absolutely must greet her directly, ask them not to touch her.... Give her room.... If tourists stop and stare, hand them brochures and/ or walk away from Dianna's area to explain her story. If Dianna becomes sick or weak, do not call an ambulance. Call the Assisi Community or GHRC/USA. She should be taken to the Assisi House...."

That last instruction startled me until I learned the frightful experiences that Dianna had endured in a hospital in Kentucky where her well-meaning sisters put her to try to cure her trauma, and the staff were both overconfident and clueless about the ways to treat survivors of torture. Another patient gave her a key to peace, the razor blade she always carried.

Looking at Dianna, I always found it hard to believe what she survived, physically at least, between her abduction from the retreat garden, and her escape from the car of the torturer's gringo boss "Alejandro" as he drove her, he said, to the US Embassy in Guatemala City. She smiled her warm smile whenever people engaged her attention. Though the vigil was "silent," she sometimes whispered with her friends and advisers or wrote notes to them. Sometimes she stared vacantly. For long periods, she looked as though tears were about to flow from her eyes to the downward curve of her mouth. She passed many hours listening to a Walkman and now and then read the messages in the guest book. Some people refused to write in it but went directly to talk to her. She listened patiently to the devout, the devoted, and the demented, and usually motioned me off when I walked over to ease them away.

Earlier that year, I had decided to write a book about three valiant women, Adriana Portillo-Bartow, Jennifer, and Dianna, who took on the murderous US–Guatemala alliance and survived. But Dianna struck me as being particularly vulnerable, and I wasn't going to inflict my version of her life on her unless she agreed. One day, I knelt on the grass beside her to ask my question. I barely started when she whispered, "I trust you." How beautiful, I thought, and what a responsibility! The stories in this book about her, Jennifer, and Adriana come largely from that yet unpublished book, *Sisters in the Storm: Life and Death on the Receiving End of US Power.*

One night an actual thunderstorm stationed itself over Lafayette Park. All was quiet where Dianna was sleeping, or maybe trying to sleep, under her end of the big rain tarp. Though Alice feared lightning, she wouldn't leave. Since her umbrella was missing half its fabric, another guy and I tried to hold our umbrellas over her, but, restless soul that she was, she'd roam out from under them to check on the rain tarp and whatever. Around she went, drenched but free, (*pace* Shakespeare) a touch of Alice in the night. The people who were due to relieve us at eleven didn't show up. About one o'clock, an angel in a long red plastic poncho materialized through the mist, a Carmelite named Sister Maureen. At last Alice could go home, dry off, and maybe catch a few hours' sleep before driving her little red car back through the rush-hour to attend to the next day's support for Dianna. Alice had invited me to sleep at her place. Sometimes I'd come down for breakfast, and she walk in the door after pulling an all-nighter at her office after dropping me off late the previous evening.

A very hard part of the vigil for Dianna was being on endless display. Though most passers-by didn't gawk or take photos, a few did, thrusting her back to the torturer appearing to videotape the murder. A young man remarked as though she couldn't hear him, "She looks like a queen on a throne!" As she sat on her pillows amid her loose entourage, I saw his point, though he hadn't a clue how it pained her to sit there or why she was subjecting herself to people like him. Some passers-by supported her, most meant no harm, and a few sounded loutish or hostile. A number that surprised me seemed unbalanced. Most did not know her story or what the US had been doing in Guatemala. Trying to remedy that, Alice provided, and we accompaniers handed out, some 38,000 fliers—orange, yellow, or blue, packed with information. Did people simply throw them away? I sometimes looked into the Park's trashcans and seldom saw one.

Dianna's vigil formed an incongruous island of almost monastic peace at the edge of the busy park by the busy sidewalk in this self-important, insecure city of monuments and decay. As time passed, it seemed that the Park Police came to respect Dianna and maybe even her cause, and to appreciate the calming effect she was having on the park's population. Besides the park's homeless men, her accompaniers included nuns, human rights workers, members of the Assisi Community and GHRC, people from a Catholic Worker house, and several government employees, all radiating protection for Dianna. While the White House had ignored Jennifer during her fast last year, it chose to notice Dianna, partly perhaps, as a result of Jennifer's breakthrough in the face of its silence. National Security Advisor Anthony Lake occasionally stopped by to check on her when he finished work late in the evening. So did Nancy Soderberg of the National Security Council. Massachusetts Congressman Joe Kennedy drove up several times in a huge yellow convertible, top down, the only civilian car ever I saw on that block. Once he brought his mother, Ethel Kennedy, to be photographed with him and Dianna.

One day Hillary Clinton invited Dianna into the White House, and they talked for twenty or thirty minutes on a small bench. The First Lady listened attentively and assured Dianna that she would push the Justice Department to identify Alejandro and do all she could to see that she received all the information she was entitled to. Dianna did not rule out the possibility that Clinton's words were calculated to lull her into stopping the vigil: "Hillary Clinton inspired more trust than the National Security Council officials Jennifer had dealt with, but who knew what kind of forces Hillary Clinton was up against? If she was fighting an old boys' network of secrecy, publicity and public pressure could only help her. I wasn't leaving my spot."

The week after the meeting with the First Lady, NBC's *Today Show* flew Dianna and her close friend Pat Davis to New York, treated them to a hotel infinitely more comfortable than the pillows on the grass, and drove them to the studio the next morning for Katie Couric to interview Dianna. Waiting to go on, Dianna watched a monitor as a glamorous, blue-eyed blond from California named Jeanne Boylan, who happened to be a premier forensic artist, described how she had made an accurate sketch of the Unabomber by talking with witnesses who had only glimpsed him. "With eerie accuracy," the *Reader's Digest* would write, "Jeanne Boylan's drawings have helped bring to justice some of the worst criminals of our time." When her own turn came, Dianna was relieved to find Couric to be "understanding and gentle." Couric: "You had a lot of courage to come here and tell us [your story]."

Back in the waiting room, Boylan watched the interview. When Dianna came out, she introduced herself and offered to work with her to make sketches of the torturers. On the plane home, Dianna realized that meeting Boylan, wholly by chance it seemed, was even more significant than putting her story onto national TV had been. She phoned her. Later I asked Boylan if she believed Divine coincidence had brought her and Dianna together at the *Today Show*. "Absolutely," Boylan replied. "I didn't know why I was there until I met her."

A two-page spread on the vigil appeared in the April 22 *People* magazine. Its photo of Dianna, which took up twice as much space as the story, showed her bundled up in her blue and maroon parka, looking as cold as a spectator at a football game that never ends.

It was raining hard the afternoon that Sister Helen Prejean, the crusader against capital punishment whom Susan Sarandon portrayed in *Dead Man Walking*, visited the vigil. Sister Helen, dressed in a neat blue suit, asked me to hold her umbrella, got down on her hands and knees on the muddy grass, and crawled under Dianna's tarp.

"I had gone to give a talk in Washington," Sister Helen told me later. "I didn't know very much about her. It was raining, and I still had on my suit because I had given a talk to about a thousand people in this huge ballroom. I was struck by the contrast of what I had just done, which is basically to help people to understand that the death penalty is wrong and we have to do away with it, and then crawling into that tent, and there she was fasting. I remember how warm she was, almost like she had a fever, this woman almost alone with just a few friends to help her, standing up to the US government. It was a profile in courage that deeply touched me. I sat with her and held her hand. Her voice was so soft and her face was so gentle, it was hard even to think of how they had tortured her. She was using her energy, not to seal it over and go on with what's called a normal life, but to make the US government accountable and get them to speak the truth. I was very struck by her courage and integrity. The complicity of our government in Latin American regimes has been one of the most brutal and scandalous things that our government has ever done. When the Church, Dianna among them, took the side of the poor, that is what made her a target. She suffered because she aligned with the poor and with their rights and their struggle. We need to tell the story because people generally are so oblivious. And here she was, as Jeremiah says, with her incurable wound standing before the power of the US government. It touched me deeply. I crawled out of the tent and tried to support her after that."

The longer Dianna sat in silence before this center of US power, the stronger grew her voice for the Maya and for tortured people everywhere. On April 22, she issued a statement saying that because she had endured six years of official runarounds and the first three weeks of her vigil had failed to educe the information she sought, she was now upping the ante.

You may think this strange; but even at this moment, I can sense the presence of my torturers. I can smell the torturers. I can feel their monstrous hands on my body, I can hear them hissing in my ear that I am the one who killed the woman. I can see them blessing me with the blood of the woman. Will it end? Jean Amery, an Austrian philosopher tortured by the Gestapo, said, "Anyone who has been tortured remains tortured.... Faith in humanity, already cracked by the first slap in the face, then demolished by torture, is never acquired again." It is with great horror that I repeat these words. Torture, for him, was an interminable death. Amery took his life in 1978. I want so desperately to live. I want so desperately to believe in humanity again...to be free of Alejandro and all my Guatemalan torturers. Thousands of Guatemalans who have been tortured by the security forces also want to live and to believe in humanity again. Only the truth will set us free. Because I am still barred from knowing the truth...still in a prison of silence..., I will now begin a fast of bread and water, continuing my silent vigil in front of the White House and daring to place my life in the hands of the US government....

I and, I'm sure, others found her reference to survivor Jean Amery's suicide more than twenty years after being tortured unnerving.

Thereafter Marie Dennis baked the three slices of daily bread that Dianna was allowing herself, filling them with all the nutrients she could mix in. Often Dianna did not finish eating them. Her frailty must have dismayed her mother Amby and sister Barbara when they journeyed to the vigil from their homes in New Mexico. Dianna saw them coming up the sidewalk and ran to embrace them. Having hugged her lightly when I arrived, I thought how shocked they must be to place their palms on the back of their beloved Dianna and feel only bones.

It cheered Dianna to hear that people were holding vigils in El Salvador and Honduras in solidarity with her. Joseph Cardinal Bernardin of Chicago and thirty or so Catholic bishops wrote to President Clinton asking him to release the information she was seeking. Perhaps best of all, the Inter-American Commission on Human Rights, which had been investigating her case for five years, recommended that it be forwarded to the Inter-American Court; this meant that the Commission believed her and not what the government of Guatemala was saying about her.

Jennifer attended the vigil from time to time. How much safer and more comfortable tonight will be, I thought as I watched her lay out her sleeping bag neatly on the grass, than all those nights had she risked being shot as she slept on her pallet above the stones of the Central Plaza in Guatemala City. Now she spent much of her days revisiting the members of Congress and staffers she had once asked to help her to save Everardo. This time, she and several other people obtained the signatures of 103 Congressmen for a letter to President Clinton which concluded, "Mr. President, Guatemalans need to know the truth about the crimes committed in their country. US citizens also have a right to know what their own government knew about these crimes." Not to overburden any Congressman's courage, the letter did not mention Americans' right to know about US participation in these crimes.

The vigil seemed to move everyone who spent any time at it, some profoundly. One person whose life it changed was Harold Nelson. He was a sociology professor at the University of Texas–Pan American in Edinburg, Texas, and like me, was in his mid-sixties. He had taken many mortal risks during the 1960s civil rights campaign in the South. Now he had flown up to the vigil, stayed awhile, gone home, and found himself drawn back. After it ended, he uprooted his life and moved to Washington to work with Alice and Dianna at the GHRC. "Like my dad," Dianna said, "Harold lived his beliefs. He would give me comfort, solace, and wisdom in the days, months, and years that followed and teach me by his example." For my own part, Harold became one of my closest friends, at the vigil and during the years that followed. We often joked about how close the Doomsday Clock was coming to midnight. Ho-ho.

Week Four of the vigil passed with no official response to Dianna's demand for information. With her permission, her friends at the Assisi Community decided to up the ante yet again by offering themselves and recruiting others to "risk arrest." They found lodgings as needed, arranged for cars to fetch them upon their release from jail, and discussed their plans with the police, all for orderly, peaceful civil disobedience. Starting early Monday morning, April 29, and every morning for the rest of the vigil, a large circle of Dianna's supporters sang and prayed at her encampment. Leaving one person to guard it, they then walked across Pennsylvania Avenue and onto the sidewalk where a fence of black iron bars stood between them and the White House lawn. Notable among them would be Father Joe Nangle or Brother Vianney Justin of Assisi wearing his brown Franciscan robe with its cowl and rope belt and carrying a wooden cross that rose well above everybody's heads. More singing and praying. Dianna would stand on the opposite curb with Marie Dennis or Pat Davis or Mary Fabri on her right and me on her left. Behind us, most pedestrians kept on walking. A few stopped to watch. Paddy wagons waited along the curb to our left.

It was okay to walk on the sidewalk past the White House, but illegal to stop where the group stopped. A policeman in a white shirt would warn them to leave or face arrest. They would not move. He would warn them again. Roughly two thirds of them, including the Franciscan with the cross, would walk back across the street and line the curb on either side of Dianna. The others, who had decided to "risk arrest," would be warned a third time. Rather than move, they would hold their hands behind their backs for the policemen to bind their wrists with plastic cuffs and guide them, one by one, up a step and through the back door of a van. All the while, the group with Dianna would be singing, shouting encouragement, and sometimes cheering. This choreographed civil disobedience let Dianna's supporters make their point and the police make theirs. How civilized, I thought, free expression and the rule of law. At first, Dianna hated to watch the arrests because they reminded her of being held prisoner in the Politécnica. For me, they looked festive.

After the last paddy wagon drove off, the mornings passed quietly until the offenders, whom the police had processed and released, walked up the sidewalk to the cheers and hugs of the rest of us at the briefly non-silent vigil. All told, more than a hundred and twenty people were thus busted, including activist Father Phillip Berrigan, activist Bishop Thomas Gumbleton, and Daniel Ellsberg who had released the Pentagon papers. Catholic nuns, including a good number of Dianna's sisters from Kentucky, made up the largest group. For the most part, the police were not rough and seemed respectful. The officer driving one of the vans told his prisoners that he was doing his best to avoid the potholes that pock Washington's streets because he had been educated by nuns.

Jennifer had fretted at not being able to do more for Dianna. Now she got herself arrested four times and found it liberating. I said I thought she got a terrific kick out of it. "Oh, yeah, that was fun," she laughed. "I got real kick out of seeing forty or fifty elderly nuns and priests standing there being arrested for the first time in their lives out of support for Dianna. I thought that was really moving."

One morning, Jennifer and Margaret Swedish were the last two people to be cuffed and ushered into a van. After all her years of working for human rights and attending acts of civil disobedience, this was Margaret's first arrest. The two women stood alone holding hands. Then the sidewalk was empty.

Adriana Portillo-Bartow came from Chicago during Week Five. "I decided without thinking," she said, "that I wanted to go and be with her."

Dianna: "Having Adriana present at the vigil meant so much to me. The intensity of her desire to know what happened to her daughters gave me strength. If I could help her I would, no matter what that took."

On warm, sunny Thursday, May 2, Jennifer chose not to be arrested so she'd be sure she was free to speak at a midday ceremony on the richly green grass near a corner of the Capitol where several Congressmen were to present Dianna with a copy of the letter that 103 of them had given to President Clinton. Adriana and I decided to walk to the ceremony. It was farther than we thought, and by the time we showed up, Jennifer was speaking at a lectern and several Congressmen were standing behind her. Dianna, wearing a long dark dress and the blue and white Mayan shawl, and looking graceful and much too thin, was sitting in a shiny brown desk chair that looked incongruous on the grass.

Jennifer spotted Adriana in the crowd and called her over. Dianna rose from her chair. There they stood with their arms around each other, the great white dome of the Capitol towering behind them, sisters in the struggle, standing together at the calm, clear eye of the storm.

During Week Five of the vigil, Dianna was gone much of the day. Most of us did not know why and did not ask. In fact, Dianna was in a hotel room with forensic artist Jeanne Boylan and Mary Fabri. She chose Alejandro first. "He represented the US government and what it was capable of doing and denying. For years I'd been told I'd imagined that he was an American. I wanted to reveal his face, to show the world the absolute, undeniable gringoness of his features."

Boylan gently asked Dianna to talk about Alejandro's several features. Dianna took Mary's hand to anchor herself in the present. It didn't work. Terrifying for her but helpful for Boylan, the present vanished, and she was back *with* Alejandro. Boylan said that the first time this happened, Dianna hyperventilated and passed out. Later, she curled up in a ball on the bed and wept. After about an hour, she had to call it a day. But she kept coming back, and the sketch that Boylan drew, Dianna said, looked as accurate as a photograph. So did the sketches of the three Guatemalans that she and Boylan finished, painfully and finally, later on the same day that she, Adriana, and Jennifer had stood together beneath the Capitol.

On Friday, May 3, the Intelligence Oversight Board delivered several thousand pages of declassified documents, many heavily blacked out, to Dianna's lawyers. ("Documents" is a wonderfully weighty word; a Post-it Note on your refrigerator is a document; so is this page.) They, Dianna, and a few friends dove in. The documents bore exactly the sort of peripheral information that one would expect from people who wanted to look honest but hide the truth. Back in Manhattan, we called this "boxcar-ing." You drop a boxcar load of largely worthless papers on the opposing lawyers, outsiders think you've done something, and the lawyers have to examine all the papers. These IOB papers confirmed some information that Jennifer had extracted a year ago, but, Dianna said, "We didn't find anything about me that was new or different." But in spite of everything, she still wanted to trust our government. Thus the government finally broke its silence to Dianna, though with far more show than tell.

Dianna was down from a hundred and ten to eighty-five pounds now, growing weaker, and close to suffering organ damage. There was little or no chance that the government would produce useful documents soon. Those 103 Members of Congress had just signed onto her cause. Most importantly, she had rousted the four torturers out of her head (or so she thought) and onto Jeanne Boylan's big white sketchpad. As we gathered in the circle before the people crossed the street to be arrested on Monday morning, the second day of Week Six, we were told that she was ending her vigil and would hold a press conference in a nearby Marriott at 11:00. A contingent crossed Pennsylvania Avenue anyway, and not long after the police vans drove them off, little groups of us—my wife Nancy had just joined the vigil—walked to that hotel.

As the time for the press conference drew near, its valiant but very human subject hid out for as long as she could with Mary Fabri in a restroom. An imposing array of TV cameras atop tall tripods, cameras with protruding lenses suspended against people's chests, floodlights shining over all, and far too many bodies milling or on chairs jammed much of the hot, windowless room. Dianna made her way through the pack and stood before the lights looking frighteningly slender with her blue and white Mayan shawl around her shoulders and lawyer José Pertierra at her side to introduce her and, I supposed, to catch her if she fell. Four tall easels behind her held four large rectangles of blank white paper.

Her words today improved on the statements she had repeated so painfully during previous years. Thanks to the vigil, she had now seen enough documents to cite specifics of what she called the Embassy's double-dealing and cover-up, and she had the faces of the torturers to unveil. At last, her presentation was going into the video cameras and microphones, onto the reporters' pads, and through them out to America and the world.

The climax came when she lifted the four white cover sheets, one by one. Behind the first three were Boylan's big sketches of the Guatemalan torturers; Dianna told us the role of each man as she lifted his cover and nearly went into a flashback. Her mother Amby, confronted by the faces of the men who had ravaged her little girl, gasped and began to sob. Her sister Barbara was sobbing. Even reporters wept. As Dianna peeled back the final sheet, she said, with emotion overflowing, "This is Alejandro!"

Here is the face of a real man, I thought, yet if he took off his wig, beard, and dark glasses, he could be hard to recognize. "This is Alejandro," she repeated fervently. "He is not a figment of my imagination. He is real."

After the press conference, Dianna felt elated. She led a large group of us back up the Pennsylvania Avenue sidewalk to her encampment, where she made a ceremony of burning a set of the four faces in a clay pot with sacramental sage. "I was free," she wrote later. "The Guateman, the Policeman, José, and Alejandro were out of me." Would that it were so. Pulling forth those faces like long-impacted wisdom teeth with Boylan's gentle coaching was a major step in her recovery, but she would realize soon enough that she was not free.

Though she was still quite weak the next morning and had endured another assault on her credibility by a hostile interviewer on national television the previous evening, she returned to the park and thanked the homeless people who had supported and protected her through the long weeks of the vigil.

The Facts at Last

I was sitting at my desk in Norwalk on a warm spring day in 1998 when Angie Berryman phoned from her office in the AFSC head-quarters in Philadelphia and invited me to be the Quaker on an ecu-menical delegation that was planning to attend the presentation of the REMHI Report in Guatemala City. By then I was fairly out of touch with events in Guatemala and had no idea what REMHI meant. As Angie explained, it was the Spanish acronym for the Project to Re-cover the Historical Memory, that is, the truth commission, of the Archdiocese. Courageous Bishop Juan Gerardi Conedera, head of the Archdiocese's Human Rights Office, and a dedicated team had interviewed thousands of survivors of the terror and written a huge report of their findings. Nancy and I decided that I'd accept Angie's invitation far more readily than we had, the invitation to accompany Adriana and her girls nine years earlier.

Peace had come to Guatemala at the end of 1996, thanks in good part to State Department official Dr. Richard Nuccio, who had met with the guerrilla leaders and convinced them that Communism was not worth continuing to fight for.* With peace came opportunity. Gua-temalans wanted to know the truth about the terror that had killed so many of them. So did the Church and the United Nations. So did a small minority of Americans. To a wondrous extent, we got it.

A dozen or so of us delegates stayed in a secure and cozy inn within walking distance of the Central Square. Guatemala City was full of bustle and felt wonderfully safe compared to my 1989 visit. Once we were walking on a busy sidewalk together with a squad of soldiers and felt no tension or fear. We had arrived a few days before the REM-

---

* Nuccio's success reminded me that a few years earlier, David Astor, Dr. Stefan Szymanski of the London Business School, and my daughter Erin had arranged to show leaders of the African National Congress how market capitalism works better than Communism, as related in "Erin and the ANC."

HI Report was to be presented and were able to visit two men who had coordinated its creation, Edgar Gutiérrez and, I believe, Carlos Martin Beristain. We also talked with a human rights activist named Frank LaRue, two or three US Embassy officials, and most interestingly, the people in the office of the UN Commission for Historical Clarification, called the CEH for its Spanish acronym, who were busily working on their own report about the reality of the terror. They told us that the army was putting enormous pressure on them to allocate responsibility more or less equally between the military and the guerrillas—a falsehood that the Guatemalan and US governments had long asserted and most US media had long suggested.

The REMHI Report drew banner headlines in Guatemala City's newspapers on the morning of April 24. That sunny afternoon, some three thousand people filled the massive Metropolitan Cathedral beside the vast Central Plaza, where Jennifer Harbury had fasted to save her husband and pursued the same truth three and a half years earlier. The crowd was festive, almost jubilant, in spite of the Report's grim subject. Rigoberta Menchú, wearing her brightly colored Mayan *trajé*, sat in the front row. Ours was the only US delegation present, and we were deeply moved as Mayan survivors, wearing equally colorful garb, came forward to receive copies of the Report from mostly taller, whiter bishops. When Bishop Gerardi's turn came to speak, he invoked a familiar teaching of Jesus, the same teaching that adorns the lobby of the CIA's headquarters: "The essential objective that has motivated the REMHI Project during its three years of work [is] to know the truth that will make us all free."

In Guatemala, the truth could also make you dead. Listening to this tall, elderly man with glasses bridging his aquiline nose, we knew he had great courage: to have served in the blood-soaked diocese of Quiché, to close the diocese in an effort, which proved futile, to call the world's attention to the terror, and now to produce this compendium of truth that would surely infuriate the army. Yet as I sat among the warm, triumphant crowd, it did not cross my mind that the man in the pulpit might soon join the host of Guatemalans martyred for telling the truth.

Gerardi's team had trained 600 "animators" who interviewed 6,500

witnesses, some 8% of whom were perpetrators, many of them con-
science-stricken. In all, the REMHI team analyzed human rights violations against a representative 54,000 souls, mainly Mayas in the
countryside, and produced a four volume, 1,400-page report, which
they had prudently had printed abroad.

The Report, *Guatemala: Nunca Mas!* (*Guatemala: Never Again!*), is
precise, historic, and heart-rending. Contradicting years of US official
and media misinformation but vindicating what human rights activists
like Sister Alice and the GHRC had been saying all along, it found
that soldiers and paramilitaries committed 88% of the crimes; the
guerrillas committed 7%; persons unknown committed 5%. Out of
422 massacres studied, the Report blamed the military for 401 (95%)
and the guerrillas for sixteen (4%). Of the 22,500 civilian killings considered, it found that the military murdered 90% and the guerrillas
6%. The bodies of 30% of the murder victims showed marks of torture. One in ten victims were children, often tortured in front of their
parents. Of 4,600 people who were disappeared, 85% were attributed
to the military and 7% to the rebels; only 715 of those 4,600 souls
were ever seen alive again. As to the human rights crimes not studied, there is little doubt that the military and guerrillas were guilty in
similar proportions. In his foreword to the English edition, Thomas
Quigley, of the US Conference of Catholic Bishops, called the Report
"not exhaustive but fully representative." Sophia Canek would start to
read a summary of the Report but find it too painful to continue.

The REMHI team agreed that the incidence of rape was vastly un-
der-reported because Mayan women and girls were extremely reluctant
to talk about it. The Maya, who tend to marry in their teens, consider
it important (as Americans once did) for a bride to be a virgin. "Every
day, government soldiers rape women in the villages," Sophia told me,
"and the soldiers are never punished." According to Beto, rapes were
so common that the resulting children created a social problem for
the Maya in the highlands. Dr. Antonio Martinez on official torture:
"Rape is used almost all the time with women and with some men,
especially if they're younger."

The Report demolished the US major media's decades-long thrust
that most of the civilian dead were caught in "crossfires" or other com-

bat between the military and guerrillas.* In fact, the Report traced only one tenth of one percent (0.1%) of the deaths to combat.

After the presentation in the cathedral, there was a quietly festive reception in an adjoining, cloistered yard. I went up to Rigoberta Menchú and gravely gave her greetings from Sophia and Enrique. A friend translated my English into Spanish. She replied in Spanish, and he told me what she'd said. Later I returned to the refreshments table. Ms. Menchú was standing behind it. Smiling, she asked me in perfect English, "Would you like some wine?"

The CEH stood fast. Its Report, *Guatemala: The Memory of Silence*, which appeared in February 1999, concluded that more than 200,000 people had been killed or disappeared during the terror. It attributed 93% of the 42,000 cases it examined to the military and only 3% to the guerrillas. It recorded 669 massacres, attributing 626 of them (again 93%) to the security forces. 83% of the victims it studied were Maya, and included "the complete extermination of many Mayan communities," while 17% were *ladinos*. It also concluded that the army had deliberately targeted and destroyed Mayan parts of Quiché and Huehuetenango departments to an extent that amounted to "acts of genocide."

Unlike REMHI, which did not discuss foreign intervention, the CEH blasted the United States for its complicity in the crimes of the military. It found that 91% of the human rights violations it studied occurred during 1978–1984, and were most intense from 1981 through 1983. This was during the first years of the Reagan Administration, which had given a green light to the terror, and Adriana's last years in Guatemala. She had testified for both the REMHI and CEH teams and told me she was very pleased especially with the CEH Report.

> I presented my testimony to the [head of the team], and he promised me right then that the case was going to be included. How could they say it wasn't an important case? We're talking about children.

---

* "Cross-fire" sounds good. After law officers shot ten hostages dead at New York's Attica prison, Governor Nelson Rockefeller speculated that hostages may have been caught in a non-existent "cross-fire." See "Attica."

I find it curious that although both the REMHI Report and the CEH Report resulted from separate, reputable investigations, and each largely confirms the other, American writers seldom mention the former and treat the latter as the sole, unconfirmed, source of the truth.

A month after the UN's CEH Report came out, President Bill Clinton told a forum of Guatemalan leaders during a rare presidential visit,

> For the United States, it is important that I state clearly that support for military and intelligence units which engaged in violence and widespread repression was wrong, and the United States must not repeat that mistake.

Did the many revelations that Jennifer sparked about CIA complicity in the terror, the disciplining of CIA officials that resulted, and the attention that Dianna's vigil received from Mrs. Clinton and White House officials help to move the President to say these words? The 1993 UN truth commission report that concluded that government forces in El Salvador had committed roughly 85% of the human rights crimes—in which the US was equally complicit—during its "civil war," failed to move Clinton to make any such admission.

Clinton's admission of US guilt in Guatemala was bold and honorable. The major media reported it, though without a context that would have explained it. Yet for people who knew the facts, his words did not suffice. Sister Dianna: "Are a few words all we owe when we created and maintained an army that slaughtered hundreds of thousands? With that sort of impunity, what will keep us from doing it over and over again?" Adriana: "But here the United States is in Columbia doing the same thing. What is going to be the result? Years ago, it was Communism that they were fighting. Now it's drugs they're fighting. The bogey man."

The Guatemalan army did not invent the lumping of guerrillas indiscriminately with civilians who might or might not be helping them. Rather, it was an integral part of the "national security doctrine" that our Defense Department used itself and taught to Latino military officers at the School of the Americas. The US Army and CIA had similarly killed as many as 26,000 civilian suspects and enemy fighters during their infamous Phoenix Program in Vietnam. The Reagan people tried to distinguish between "authoritarian" regimes that we supported and "totalitarian" regimes that we opposed. But as the *Times's* Harrison Salisbury famously pointed out, "There is little difference to the man to whose testicles the electrodes are applied whether his torturer is 'totalitarian' or 'authoritarian.'"

In 1999, Orbis Books published an abridged version of the REMHI Report in English. Ann Buttwell, of the Assisi Community, who was one of the leaders of our delegation, assisted in editing the translation. It's full title is *Guatemala Never Again! REMHI, Recovery of Historical Memory Project, The Official Report of the Human Rights Office, Archdiocese of Guatemala.* The words of a few survivors, as quoted in the Report, suggest what really happened behind its stats:

> [T]hey killed the men, shot them in the head, and then burned the bodies. They shut the women and children up in a school, threw grenades at them, and burned their bodies. Young women were raped, then tortured and killed. The killing began at 8 a.m. and lasted until 5 p.m. when the army left. It was a battalion of 500 soldiers. [I] saw a river of water, but it wasn't water—it was the melted fat from the bodies that were being burned.
>
> —Petenác, Huehuetenango, 1982

> We were fleeing to Santa Clara, we could not return to the village because there was no life there. Upon arriving at that community, we began to plant corn, malanga, and sugarcane. When the army came, it chopped everything down and burned the houses.
>
> —Santa Clara, Chajul, Quiché, 1985–87

> They had cut out his tongue. His eyes were blindfolded with a wide bandage or wide tape and there were punctures everywhere on his rib cage, and it seemed that one of his arms was broken. And I could tell that it was him only because I had lived with him for many years and I knew about certain scars.

—Cuilapa, Santa Rosa, 1981

And that officer told us [civil patrollers] that if we didn't
kill them, they were going to kill all of us. And that's how
it came about that we had to do it. I don't deny that, yes, we
had to do it because they threatened us.
    —Chiché, Quiché, 1983

The soldiers had begun to kill, without a word. They
weren't asking whether anyone had done something wrong
or not; they were killing that day.
    —Coban, Alta Verapaz, 1981

What we have seen has been terrible: burned corpses,
women impaled and buried as if they were animals ready for
the spit, all doubled up, and children massacred and carved
up with machetes. The women too, murdered like Christ.
    —Cuarto Pueblo, Ixcán, Quiché, 1985

Who could comfort me? I no longer had my mother; my
father was afraid to be with me. Because the only consola-
tion they offered me was that they were going to come and
kill me and my children.
    —Pozo de Agua, Baja Verapaz, 1983

We went five or six months without tasting a single tor-
tilla. They hacked the children to pieces with machetes. If
they found sick people, bloated with the cold, they finished
them off. Sometimes they set them on fire. I have no one
left. My parents are dead, and I feel as if I have a knife in
my heart. When the patrol came, they hacked them apart
with machetes, and some were drawn and quartered. Well,
we waited until they had finished killing them, and then we
went back to look for them. We found them and gave them

a burial of sorts.

—Chama, Alta Verapaz, 1982

We were crowded onto the patio of the house. On the fifth or sixth day, the army ordered us to bury the dead. We found a hole in a ravine, piled them up, and set them on fire. It made us ill to do this. We have lost our appetites. Among them, I saw one whose thorax was opened up; his heart, his lungs, everything was hanging out. Two or three months later they were dug up by their relatives. They were moved to the cemetery, but it wasn't any use by then, it was just water and bone.

—Tierra Caliente, Quiché, 1981

They removed his teeth when they killed him and his nose swelled up a lot. I've never seen a dead person look anything like what they did to my son. I'll never forget it, because they pulled out all of my poor son's teeth.

—Nebaj, Quiché, 1983

When the army returned, they went to tell my uncle, "Look, you, go and bury those people, we finished off a whole family. They are bad folks." When we got there, oh, but it was horrible. I can't forget it. Even though some say you have to put the past behind you, I can't….we went to the kitchen and there was the whole family, my aunt, my daughter-in-law, her sons and daughters; there were two little children hacked to pieces with machetes. They were still alive. The boy, Romualdo, lived for a few more days. The one who couldn't last any longer was Santa, the one with her guts hanging out. She only lasted half a day and then she died.

—San Jose Xix, Chajul, Quiché, 1982

The soldiers said, "Don't worry, we're going to take good

care of your wife." The poor man had to watch everything they did to her, torturing the poor woman [until she] couldn't take anymore. The soldiers raped her one by one. After that they went to ask the husband for money to buy pills because she was in bad shape.

— Santa Maria Tzeja, Ixcán, Quiché, 1982

Two evenings after the celebration in the cathedral, when I was safely back home, assassins smashed Bishop Gerardi's head with a cinder block, leaving him lying in his blood and brains on the floor of his garage. He had to be identified by the ring he was wearing. Three years later, three army men were convicted of the murder and sentenced to thirty years in prison. But justice came at a price: a judge's home firebombed; fourteen witnesses killed; and death threats that forced two judges, three prosecutors, and several witnesses to flee the country. In his 2007 book, *The Art of Political Murder: Who Killed the Bishop?*, Francisco Goldman made the case that the men found guilty were only the tip of a military iceberg that had arranged the murder.

I was horrified and disgusted to read the above and many similar testimonies in the Report that had cost Bishop Gerardi his life. Nancy and I knew when we joined Sanctuary that the US-backed forces in Guatemala were doing horrible things to innocent people, and we learned more as the years passed, but we had not visualized the degree of the barbarity sampled above. Besides being horrified, we felt reassured that we had done right by joining the movement and all the sorrier for the massive barbarity that our nation's leaders had chosen to abet.

Since Bishop Gerardi risked and finally gave his life to report the truth, I thought that the least we Americans might do is ask our public servants to disclose it. Adriana, Jennifer, Dianna, Father Roy Bourgeois, Sister Helen Prejean, Father Joe Nangle, and Prof. Phillip Berryman all told me they wanted a US truth commission to report on our complicity in Guatemala. "We think of Guatemala as being a repressive country," said Father Dan Jensen, pointing out that Guatemala had two truth commissions "whereas I doubt very much one would ever happen here. So who is being repressed?" And I'm afraid

Tom Wicker was right when he told me:

> Where you've got a real culpability on something like
> Guatemala, I would be amazed if you ever had [a truth com-
> mission]. The best you're going to get is your book, or maybe
> somebody'll write a better book. Who's going to appoint
> such a commission, the President? Congress? They're all cul-
> pable. You don't appoint commissions to investigate yourself,
> particularly when you know you're guilty.

The truth is that it may have been only a little holocaust in Guatemala, but it was in good part ours. The greater truth is that Guatemala
was not an isolated case. Rather, it was a paradigm for US interventions and complicity in mass murders around the world—some lesser,
some worse. The ship of state moves on, and in its wake, melted fat
churns like water from the pyres of people who do not matter except to
God and their loved ones. What have we come to, and why?

After the Vigil

Washington has seen many vigils but, Alice told me some years later,
people were still talking about "the vigil," and everyone knew they
meant Dianna's long vigil in 1996. I might almost say it rose above
other vigils the way Denali rises above the other mountains in Alaska.

On June 30, 2001, Scott Simon asked Dianna on NPR's *Weekend
Edition* what she wanted then. "To get the US government to renew
its commitment to ending torture in the world," she replied, "and one
way to have that happen is, we're calling on the US government to
discontinue any aid to governments that are engaged in torture." A
noble but futile request.

Simon wrote to me later, "God bless her for her courage.... I have
never had the impression that Dianna Ortiz is merely out for her own
interests (although that would be understandable, too) .... I am moved
by her determination not just to survive, but also to turn her fury
towards the crime that blighted her life into a movement to help others...."

Scott Simon's recognition that Dianna wanted to help others was a
shining exception. No matter how strongly or often Dianna stressed

the fact that she was acting for the people of Guatemala, our main-stream media, when they mentioned her at all, commonly portrayed her as seeking information and justice solely for herself. By omitting her main motive, they portrayed this most selfless person as being simply self-seeking. All the better to reduce her impact, since the US was not about to stop aiding governments that use torture. It still isn't.

When the vigil ended, Dianna went back to working at Alice's commission and living with her friends at the Assisi Community. From early February until mid-March of 1997, she took a break and visited Nancy and me in our home and then the brothers at the Weston Priory; Mary Fabri visited her for a few days while she was staying in one of their guesthouses. She had never experienced the likes of a Vermont winter, but she seemed to enjoy it as much as many (but not all) Vermonters do. Nancy, the monks, and I had no agenda except to let her relax as she chose.

It warmed my heart to watch her and Nancy hit it off, though it wasn't a surprise since they shared the same outlook on many subjects. Our coffee mug that has a picture of Edward Hopper's "Night People" on it (which I still use) reminded her of the late nights that she and other survivors living in Chicago's Su Casa would hang out in a coffee shop in order to put off going to bed and risking nightmares. Often she would sit on a dark green cushion of our window seats and type on her laptop remarkably fast using only one hand. She wrote very well, as you may have noticed in previous stories, and was now in the early stages of the book that Pat Davis would help her with and Orbis Books would publish in 2002 called *The Blindfold's Eyes: My Journey from Torture to Truth*. It is a powerful, eye-opening memoir. And timeless, especially since torture remains an issue in America. On a final page, "The damage torture does can never be undone. If I survived for any reason, it is to say that."

From Margaret Swedish's review in that November's *Central America/Mexico Report:*

Dianna has written an unsparingly intimate account of her torture and betrayal, of her journey out of this hell back to some semblance of truth and even trust, and a fierce sense of her own dignity—because her dignity is one of the things her torturers tried to destroy.

But the story does not end the way one would hope—there is … no closure of this case, no one brought to justice, no US official who has yet come forward to even admit that a North American was present in the secret detention center. In that sense, the stonewalling worked. Once again, the US government has managed to skirt one of its darkest secrets—that torture, support for torture, or at the very least silence about it … have been used as tools of US foreign policy.… And that even when the targets are US citizens, the response will be not the defense of its citizens, but co-operation in the cover-up.

In 2004, the Abu Ghraib prisoner torture (a.k.a. "abuse") scandal would shed a bit of light on that secret, and President George W. Bush would publicly apologize to the Iraqi victims and their families as though this were a one-off aberration and the CIA's black sites, the School of the Americas, and Guantánamo did not exist.

One day I made the mistake of asking Dianna whether the scars from the cigarette burns on her back were still visible. (I didn't want to look, only to know.) She got upset and angry with me. I was mortified and phoned Alice. She, who had been seeing Dianna nearly daily for several years, told me that she was always making these mistakes, and Dianna would get over it. It surprised and reassured me that a person who knew Dianna so well would still step on the landmines that the torturers had sown in Dianna's mind. The next morning to my great relief, she forgave me.

I was sorry that she still believed she had murdered the other woman in the torture chamber (described in "Confession"). As she watched me, I wrapped my purple bandanna around the handle of the iron shovel we kept on the hearth and poked the fire in the woodstove. You didn't participate with the machete any more than the bandana participated when I poked the fire, I said. She understood but didn't believe me.

As it happened, Dianna was born on my birthday and abducted on

Nancy's birthday. She and Nancy have the same middle name, Mae. Sometimes a coincidence is just a coincidence. Being of the Order of St. Ursula, she was formally "Sister Dianna Ortiz OSU," and quite amused when someone would call her Sister Osu.

She joined a project that led to her interview torture survivors from around the world in order to write about the treatment of survivors from the survivors' perspective.

> I realized torture survivors needed a group like Coalition Missing that would provide mutual support and come together for lobbying and public education efforts. So, with a few other survivors, I formed the Torture Abolition and Survivors Support Coalition International (TASSC). Alice allowed TASSC to be a project of the GHRC, lending us her staff, machines, and advice, and she allowed me to run the organization out of her office.

In 2002, Dianna would lead TASSC onto its own as a separate 503(c) non-profit organization with ample quarters at the edge of The Catholic University of America a brisk walk uphill from the GHRC.

Every year starting in 1998, the year that TASSC was formed, it held a Survivors Week attended by perhaps fifty to a hundred survivors from around the world. They would meet privately to talk things over among themselves—survivors share a special bond and understand each other in ways that the rest of us don't—and with two therapists, Dr. Mary Fabri, who came from Chicago each year, and Dr. Judy Okawa, who treated survivors in the Washington area. The other main activity during the week was to lobby members of Congress, or more often their staffers, in the House and Senate Office Buildings. The week ended in a vigil opposite the White House, with many North Americans joining in, on June 26, which is the date that the United Nations designated as the annual International Day in Support of Victims of Torture.

Five Junes between 2001 and 2009, I took the train from Vermont to Washington and helped out in whatever way I was asked to, from sweeping TASSC's front walk to shepherding groups of survivors through the DC subway system to driving them from or to one of

Metro Washington's three airports. The vigils themselves meant setting up and later taking down a platform, a little wall on which various
papers would be posted, and a PA system in Lafayette Park—or in the
nearby DuPont Circle park for a time after the 9/11 attack—lining up
a nearly continuous series of speakers, having a grand march around
the area by the survivors and their supporters, and catching whatever
sleep we could on the ground. I recall, probably because I was cold,
having a long talk one night with Judy Okawa on a DuPont Circle
park bench while Alice, who was in her seventies, tried to sleep on
another bench under a blanket that was too thin to keep her warm.

I forget what we did about food at the vigils but would remember if
it weren't adequate. On non-vigil nights I usually slept in Alice's guestroom or in a Catholic University dormitory that was given over to the
survivors. As the years passed, the vigils shortened from twenty-four
hour to twelve hours or fewer. Dianna was too busy for me to see
much of her during these weeks. I saw more of Alice and much more
of Harold Nelson. Since women ran the show, he and I naturally hung
out together, a pleasure for me and I believe for him. While I was in
Vermont, we would discuss the world on the phone.

In June of 2014, Nancy accompanied me to Survivors Week, and
it was our privilege to stay at the Assisi Community, where Father
Joe Nangle, Marie Dennis, Dianna, Harold, and a number of other
activists lived and Jennifer stayed when she was in town—to pray with
them in the morning and dine with them in the evening. Though
Harold was nearly blind by then, he managed to navigate through the
subways by himself and, to everyone's happy surprise, show up at that
year's vigil. I can still see Dianna gently guiding him past the trees
and occasional people as Nancy and I walked with them one afternoon on the long sidewalk to Assisi's front stoop.

During my early decades, I had accepted the privilege I was born to,
as I think most people do unless they learn better. Apart from a few
downers, my life was more than pleasant. But starting with the Attica
aftermath and accelerating during Sanctuary and other solidarity endeavors, the privilege I cared about was being able to befriend dedicated people like the ones Nancy and I stayed with at the Assisi Community and join them as I could in their efforts to help strangers in need.

In 2008, Dianna stepped down as Director of TASSC for a well-earned change of pace, yet she continued to speak out at times, and she was soon doing peace and social justice work that did not constantly involve her with torture and the tortured. She died of cancer in 2021 at the age of sixty-two. She was tempered in a terrible fire that smoldered on. Though Alejandro, his superiors, and their lackeys destroyed much of her inner self and poisoned her against much of the self that remained, she became a stronger, deeper person and far more effective than she had been. She expanded her ministry from teaching Mayan children, to pressing for the human rights of Guatemalans, to doing all she could to end torture, nurture survivors, and promote peace everywhere. She had long feared that if she touched people, she would contaminate them with the evil of the torturers that she imagined was within her. In fact, she touched millions of people in America, Guatemala, and across the world with her courage, compassion, gentleness, and perseverance. For Nancy, me, and many, many others, she was a saint.

On Good Friday back in 1997, a late winter snow covered the meadows and wooded mountains outside the weathered barn of the Weston Priory as perhaps two hundred people crowded quietly into the warm interior. The passages that the brothers had chosen for the service included the call for truth and justice that Dianna had given at the start of her 1996 vigil. Listening to a gray-robed monk read her words, I realized that she has passed into the history of faith, even as she continued to serve her fellow human beings and a Church that was founded upon a person who endured torture unto death of the sake of humankind.

Epilogue

Inner Journey

Starting in 1973 with my stint as an Attica riot prosecutor, my idea of privilege began to change. Up until then I had been surrounded by mostly decent people, but then and thereafter I met and often worked with many people who were not only decent but also were doing their best to better the world and the lot of the people across it. Quite a few of them populate these stories, and I assure you there were many more. It was and is a privilege to know them.

It seems fair to say that the spiritual journey that my parents launched me on had much to do with my slow transition from conventional privilege to a privilege that matters. In any event, the journey has played a major role in my life. Its formal venues were the Church of the Holy Trinity in Brooklyn, a large brownstone structure bedecked with glorious stained-glass windows; the First Congregational Church of Darien, Connecticut, a white wooden building with clear windows; the simple meetinghouse of the Wilton (Connecticut) Friends; a library's upstairs room with the Wilderness Friends Meeting of Shrewsbury, Vermont; the stone chapel and large gray barn-chapel of the monks of the Weston (Vermont) Priory; and the living rooms and Zoom gatherings of members of the Priory's informal congregation.

But it was also in the work-a-day world, the great outdoors, and the inside of my head that I went my spiritual way, reading books, talking with people, listening, and thinking things over. Paradoxically perhaps, the account that follows may look like a narrow memoir of physical events, but these events nudged my spiritual steps forward and sometimes back.

The quiet adventure of becoming a Quaker, which began when I was forty-seven, centered around my perceptions of the mysterious God, whom I came to see as the source of all reality. God was the focus, too, during my youth as an Episcopalian and my young adulthood in the United Church of Christ that was housed in the aforementioned Congregational Church. While switching Protestant denominations did not change me, joining the Quakers did, gradually guiding me to become more circumspect, patient, and detached from material values even as I pursued social activism and gave more thought to my quest for spiritual truth. I would probably have come to the Quaker Way sooner if I had pondered more, but I didn't ponder much until I became a Quaker. That was my Catch-22.

In the beginning, God was not at all mysterious, and my first brush with the Ultimate Being was only mildly interesting. The second encounter terrified me, but a few years later, God would see me safely through the terrors of the night. The first came when I was three years old and saw God in a dream. He, definitely *He*, was reclining on a sort of couch with his large head to the right and his body trailing off at the left. He had a deep brown face—today He would be called a Black—and wore white clothes and a hat that rose in its middle and tapered fore and aft like the hats that British admirals used to wear. He did not move or speak, I was not scared, and bland as the scene was, it is the earliest dream I remember.

Before falling asleep on another night, I happened to look at the window across the room and saw a face I thought was God's looking in at me. Terror seized me. I turned to the wall, curled up, and stayed there. It took several nights and maybe weeks before I ventured to straighten out one leg before going to sleep, and more time before I straightened them both. I know I was still three because I could see the window from the bed; in my new bedroom after turning four, I couldn't. The face in the window was too far above the ground to belong to a person. It was probably city lights shaped by wrinkles in the glass.

In the house my family moved to, I slept directly above my parents' bedroom. Nightmares did not grip me often, but those that did were fierce. I'd lean out of the bedclothes and pound on the floor. Mommy would trundle up the stairs, place her warm body next to mine and lie there until my terror faded. As time passed, she taught me to memorize the Twenty-third Psalm, and I found that by repeating those words and calling up those images in darkness, I would calm down and find peace by myself, that is, with God's help. "The Lord is my

shepherd; I shall not want...." The terrifying face in the window became a friend who banished terror. I heard later that we are supposed
to fear God, but except for the brief time between the face and the
psalm, I never did.

It must have been my parents who taught me to say my prayers
before going to sleep. I would repeat the Lord's Prayer to myself as I
lay on the side of the bed that I kept holy. Then I'd sleep, or lie awake,
on the other side. Refusing to lie on the holy space except for praying
deprived me of a cool spot to move to on hot nights, but I stuck with
it. After a while, I put meaning into the rote repetitions of the prayer
by making myself recall eating bread, needing to forgive someone and
be forgiven, yielding to a temptation, and resisting another. My days
never seemed to lack these elements.

For grades one through six, my parents sent me to Brooklyn Friends
School in a venerable, red brick building a healthy nine blocks' walk
from home—it was safe for a kid to walk alone through that part of
Brooklyn back then. The school day began with assembly in the large
adjoining Quaker meetinghouse. There was no Quaker silence. Our
principal, Douglas Grafflin, a good-looking man with a black mustache who I thought resembled movie actor Errol Flynn, would often
read us one or another of the psalms. The Twenty-third was my favorite there too, especially after he explained that in those days, having
your head anointed with oil was not as bad as it sounded.

Our teachers at Friends School never tried to turn us into Quakers, though they did encourage us to think for ourselves and stand
our ground against the group if we were pretty sure we were right—a
lesson that would serve me well during the Attica adventure. During
sixth grade, I developed a mild crush on our teacher, Janice Bush.
Gazing up from my desk, I'd compare the profile of her lovely neck
and chin to the prow of a graceful ship. That Christmas, she gave water guns to all of us boys. This was a Quaker no-no, she explained after
we returned from vacation, and I learned with dismay that well-meaning Mrs. Bush had been admonished for her generous deed. I enjoyed
squirting my younger brothers, David and Tigger, with the water gun,
and it never crossed my mind that I'd one day be a Quaker.

Our father always said grace before Sunday dinner, which usually centered around a chicken that he would carve and mashed potatoes that we'd hollow out and fill with the gravy our mother made. "Oh, Lord, for what we are about to receive, make us truly thankful." I still say those words of gratitude for whatever is coming and often add to them, rather than sit before a meal in the silence of a Quaker grace.

Our mother read children's versions of Bible stories to my brothers and me, and later our father gathered us together on Sundays and read from a narrative version of the Bible. Apart from those readings, our parents kept largely silent about faith—part of the middle-class aversion to discussing what matters, I suppose. My brothers and I sort of knew that they believed in God, wanted to be good people, and expected the same of us. When we were sick in bed, Mom and Dad read us many books, sometimes up to three hours a day—*Alice in Wonderland, Wind in the Willows, The Jungle Books, Treasure Island, The Hobbit...*. That was wonderful of them and launched my lifelong love of reading. I sometimes wonder, though, whether it contributed to my reading to myself at a slow, read-aloud speed.

The Sunday school at the Church of the Holy Trinity led me to several lessons about Christianity that made this church different from most I've been to since. The first arose from not attending. I was so shy that, rather than mix with classmates I barely knew, I often accompanied my parents to the adult service. Happily for me, they accepted my evasions, so of course it took a while to know my classmates well enough to end my fear. What I learned in church came, not from the senior minister's sometimes impassioned sermons, of which I retained little or nothing, but simply from looking at the mix of Black and white parishioners sitting in the pews around us. This mingling of races seemed so normal that I gave it no thought. That's how things are, like the white marble sculpture of the Last Supper up front and the richly colored stained-glass windows.

I would learn later that a white and Black congregation was far from normal; that it had taken the courage and compassion of the man who thundered from the pulpit above me, the Reverend John Howard Melish, to lead Holy Trinity to be the first integrated church on Brooklyn Heights. Two decades later, the Reverend Martin Luther King, Jr., could still call eleven o'clock on Sunday morning "the most segregated hour of Christian America"; but in this church in the 1930s and 1940s, my parents and I were sitting in the future as it ought to be.

My earliest memories of the assistant minister, Reverend William Howard Melish, the son of the senior minister, are of him leading worship for all the Sunday school classes in the front pews under one of the church's side balconies before we adjourned to the adjoining parish house and climbed the stairs to our separate classrooms. On Easter, he would stand on a little stepladder and hand a potted red geranium off the shelves built into a big, dark brown, wooden cross to each of us Sunday school kids.

When I was thirteen, the teacher of my Sunday school's confirmation class told us to memorize, among other things, the Apostles' Creed in our *Book of Common Prayer.* The last paragraph says:

I believe in the Holy Ghost; The holy Catholic Church,
The Communion of Saints; The Forgiveness of sins: The
Resurrection of the body: And the Life everlasting. Amen.

No problem, I thought, with the Holy Ghost, as the Holy Spirit was called back then; but why did we Episcopalians say we believed in the Catholic Church? No problem about the forgiveness of sins because forgiveness is in the Lord's Prayer and sounded like a good idea, but what was The Communion of Saints and what did it have to do with me? The resurrection of people's bodies struck me as bizarre and still does. Will the corpses arise as real people or simply zombies or what? Will they eat, pee, bicker, copulate, live forever, die again in auto accidents? How do you resurrect a body that's been cremated or shattered in war? The proactive part of my spiritual journey began, not with what I memorized, but with what I began to question.

One winter morning that same year, when our Sunday school teacher was out sick, my class trooped up the wooden stairs to join the senior class, which Howard Melish was teaching. That hour has stayed with me much like the book my mother read to me about the violence at Dunkirk in "Security." Mr. Melish told us about white people lynching Black people in the South, which had happened often and was still happening; and he showed us photographs of those barbaric murders. I felt horror and am glad I did, especially since the people who were doing the lynchings looked untroubled. In fact, the photos depicted festive parties and the smiles on almost everyone except the humbly clothed person hanging from a limb with his or her head bent to one side. That morning Mr. Melish parted the curtains of the sheltered Brooklyn I was growing up in and showed me human beings acting like beasts, not Nazis but Americans. He also showed us, as I later understood, that confronting such realities is a proper job for a church, however many churches choose to keep the curtains drawn and the parishioners oblivious.

On a warm Sunday afternoon, when Brooklyn's forsythias wore their yellow glory, came confirmation, the ceremony that sealed our membership in the Episcopal Church. My classmates and I knelt on the long red cushions before the gold-colored railing that separated the ministers from the congregation in the church sanctuary while our parents lined the pews behind us. An elderly man wearing an air and vestments of authority placed his hands on each of our heads and said whatever words it took to confirm us as Episcopalians. I had never seen the man before, would never see him again, and understood that he was the Suffragan Bishop of Long Island, whatever "suffragan" meant. (It's a weighty word for *assistant*.) Then came communion, the first wine I'd ever tasted. That's pretty good, I thought. I wanted another sip but didn't think I should ask for it. For the occasion, my parents gave me a copy of the magnificent King James Bible in a black leather cover. Though the leather has long since cracked and flaked, the pages remain as sound and the words as majestic as ever. It is still the version I prefer—*Fear not* is so preferable to *Do not be afraid*—when I think its English is accurate and understandable.

Early on, I was led to believe that one's beliefs matter the most and correct actions will flow from them. Later I noticed that the Apostles' and Nicene Creeds sketched a story we were expected to believe, but otherwise mattered little to my life or the lives of anyone I knew. In fact, I saw later, the story often served as a diversion, while statesmen and clergy enlisted Scriptures to justify heinous deeds like wars, slavery, and all manner of cruelties. The Scriptures, it seems, serve evil as well as good.

I decided during high school that since God has given us a pretty wonderful life and world to live it in, I trusted that God does right about whether or not to give us an afterlife. I shared this thought with my friend Jim Keller, probably in 1948 while I was sixteen and we were illegally drinking rum cokes in Armando's Bar on Montague Street, where poet Bob Dylan would later sing of revolution in the air. Jim became a Presbyterian minister who served mainly disadvantaged people in The Bronx, Cuernavaca, Mexico, and Lawrence, MA. In his 80s, he continued his ministry by remaining a political activist and sometimes preaching. It helped in a crowd of demonstrators, he told me, to be wearing his clerical collar. My conclusion about an afterlife remains unchanged. I am very grateful to God for this life, and if God has arranged for us to continue into another one, so much the better.

The Cold War was in full swing by the time I finished high school, and my father was snarling at the dinner table that the younger Reverend Melish, *Howard* as I came to call him, "should stop preaching politics from the pulpit." I did not know what terrible preachments Dad meant except that they concerned the Cold War. Adding to Howard's offenses, he was a founding member of the National Council of American-Soviet Friendship. That was fine during the war when the US was helping the Soviets, which inflicted around 80% of all the battle casualties the German military sustained; but after the Iron Curtain clanged down, Howard found himself on official lists of alleged subversives. Dad, who was on the vestry, the church's governing body of laypeople, was doing his best to oust Howard—a long, bitter process that involved the police, Episcopal church law, and New York courts, about which more later.

I have never sorted out how the conflict between Dad and Howard—the two men who had taught me the most about God—affected me except I suppose it was deeply. Some years later, I read a book of Howard's controversial sermons. They struck me as being mild, scholarly, and sensible.[9] His main point was that since the US and USSR both existed, they needed to get along with each other. As it turned out of course, the US and Soviet Union, after much bluster and a few brushes with nuclear oblivion, did get along throughout the Cold War. There had been no way to foretell that we would be so lucky (or blessed) during the years that Howard was urging coexistence from the pulpit and President Eisenhower's sanctimonious Secretary of State John Foster Dulles was playing an insane game of brinkmanship (a.k.a. "chicken") with life on Earth. "Blessed are the peacemakers; for they shall be called the children of God." (Matthew 5:9) But Dad, who cared deeply about being right, went along with Dulles's bellicose lunacy. As did Eisenhower and much of the US Establishment.[10]

"You were a privileged little kid," my refreshingly blunt cousin Josephine told me some years ago. My father, and the station in life that my family had reached through him, had indeed brought me up with privilege. For me that changed. Since men of my age were nearly certain to be drafted into the army after college, I took the course for the Reserve Officers Training Corps (ROTC) in my freshman year, in order to go in as a second lieutenant; but by spring, I decided to stop squandering a course a year of my precious Harvard education on the military—a decision that brought me some hardship but more benefits than I'd expected. I dropped ROTC and went through the army as an enlisted man, mostly as a private first class, from August 1953 until June 1955, the last part quartered in the former Nazi SS barracks outside of Wiesbaden, Germany. I had stepped out of one social class and into another. There I had no privilege, received flak from my platoon lieutenant and sergeant, both of whom resented my Harvard degree, and had the satisfaction of finding that without my unearned advantages, I could do okay among my unprivileged comrades (See "Men."). "Love thy neighbor as thyself." As I did not realize, at the time, getting along in the army bolstered my fragile regard for myself.

Beyond teaching me about law, my three years at Harvard Law School showed me how essential it is to question things, especially what we take for granted. Studying law, reading novels, and much conversation have helped me to see the points of view of other people, especially those I disagree with or dislike. While I do not love most neighbors as myself, I try to recognize that they are all as human as I am. During our disagreements, I try to appreciate whatever it is they may be facing and feeling, though I'm sure my effort often falls short. In my youth, I tried to listen closely when a girl was telling me off and respect what she got right.

When my dear Aunt Livy died in 1960, I flew from New York for her funeral in Cincinnati at the Episcopal church that had been her spiritual home during her ninety-eight years. The service came straight from the venerable *Book of Common Prayer*. Not once did the minister tell us anything about Olivia Bell or mention her name or even that she had been a woman. All that this kind and generous woman had ever been was simply and repeatedly *Thy servant*. The coldness of that one-text-fits-all service gave me the final push out the door of the Episcopal Church, though I have met several admirable Episcopal priests since then and probably admire Howard Melish more now than I did then. A service *for* Aunt Livy? If Episcopalian preachers won't express compassion for one of their own, I thought, how much compassion may they feel for strangers? The Quaker memorial services I've attended since then have been the opposite, all about the person who died, as one attendee then another has stood up in the silence and reminisced, sometimes bringing tears or laughs and always flashes of the person's humanity.

Kay and I moved from Brooklyn to Norwalk, Connecticut, in 1962 shortly after our daughter Erin was born; and we joined the First Congregational Church (a United Church of Christ) in nearby Darien, mainly because of the churches we tried out, its minister's sermons meant the most to us. Its worship services were refreshingly simple. I found its Statement of Faith direct and practical and still believe much of it. I served on several church committees and as a deacon, often drove Erin and Brian to the Sunday school, and was soon teaching Sunday school myself. Weekdays I commuted to work in lower Manhattan, still one of the younger men on the station platform as the train rushed in. Those were good years apart from deepening difficulties that led Kay and me to divorce. She was and is a very decent person, but our marriage became impossible and was, we saw, hurting our children. Erin at age four watched our verbal fights and unerringly took the side of the one who was losing.

The divorced came in 1967 as described in "Sunrise, Sunset." Painful as it was for me and may well have been for Erin and Brian that we were no longer living together, I still believe that the divorce made the best of a destructive situation. A zillion conversations with other divorced people during my years single persuaded me that while many marriages should not have occurred, most divorces should have. Yet Kay and I would not trade our children for anything. Nancy feels the same about the three that she had by her first husband—as most divorced parents I've talked with feel about the children they had while married.

While Jews had always been part of my life and four fifths of my current progeny are Jews, 1968 saw the start of what I think of as my Jewish period. That winter I went to work for Mermelstein, Burns & Lesser, a midtown firm of fourteen lawyers, of whom I was the only gentile. It felt good to learn more than I'd known about Jewish history and current customs. Since several of the lawyers had sons the right age, I started going to bar mitzvahs and drinking in the middle of the day. Later that year, I fell in love with Iris. Though she struck me at first as looking Irish, she was a Jew of Russian heritage. The next year, we married in a simple service in her living room. Around then, everyone was singing, "Those were the days my friend. We thought they'd never end," but thirteen months later, I left her. She was a good woman and had three fine children. I fondly recall our good times and do not blame her or myself or anyone else for our problems, but when I asked the psychiatrist I'd consulted about Kay whether I'd left Iris too soon, he said that he didn't know what took me so long.

She had a nice circle of friends, all Jews as best I recall, and I enjoyed attending synagogue and their parties and being part of their community. Bar and bat mitzvahs then too. At one party, a woman said, "Isn't it nice that we're all members of the tribe." About half the people knew I wasn't, but none of them contradicted her. Iris never considered becoming a Christian, nor did it occur to me to become a Jew, but our different faiths were more a bond than a problem. For several Septembers after we parted, I missed the High Holy Days. Two failed marriages made me very cautious, and I would remain single until Nancy chanced into my life nine years later.

Shortly after I joined the First Congregational Church, the associate minister's wife had invited me to teach Sunday school. What a surprise! How could I? Once she assured me that the church provided a lesson book, I said yes and followed the book during the first shaky Sundays. Soon though, I was dividing the hour between the lesson in the book and the pertinent stuff in the week's newspapers.

Ten years of teaching junior high, which was hard but fun, and senior high, which was all fun, were among my richest learning experiences. Occasionally a student created a simple version of what some great philosopher had said, like Kant's categorical imperative or Pascal's wager—showing me, years before Quakers told me, that truth lies within many people. There was no lesson book at all for the high school class, which gave me a freedom to roam that I and, I think, those lively youngsters, appreciated. They changed me from supporting the war in Vietnam to opposing it. One evening, I joined one of their peace vigils, my first ever. To tease my most challenging student, James Lumsden, who couldn't stand President Nixon, I occasionally reminded him that Nixon was his brother in Christ. James became a UCC minister and lifelong friend. I hope that his doctoral dissertation on the spirituality of rock music will sooner or later inspire many congregations. His daughter Jesse is my beloved goddaughter.

At some point I thought it could be helpful for these attractive teenagers to discuss sex, but I didn't feel competent to lead the discussion. Two of the students' mothers readily agreed to do it, which made me happy until the morning they led the class. On and on they went with high-minded platitudes, while I kept thinking, yeh, but what do you do (or not) in the backseat at two a.m.? So, regarding the mothers' earnest session as largely irrelevant, I took the plunge. Two students were evidently in love and told us they read Walt Whitman to each other, though not that they were physically intimate until the girl misspoke. They were a sweet couple, and no one embarrassed or criticized them. Another girl, who was less selective with her intimacies, told me ruefully that she was a bitch. I assured her that she wasn't, and hoped she believed me. One of the boys told me several years later that the discussions had kept him celibate for two years. I wasn't sure how, but don't think it did him any harm.

Except for a contact high at a Springsteen concert and incidental smoke at other concerts, I have never ingested weed, and I made a point of mentioning this to show my classes and my children that it is fine to enjoy rock music without it.

During the time I "taught" these high schoolers, I believed, and advocated the belief, that the purpose of life is to live. Period. Now I see that belief as only a starting point for what we may do while living fully.

Back in law school, my ambition had been *to work on interesting cases with able and congenial men.* (There were scarcely any women lawyers then.) Before graduating I received an offer that, unfortunately, I never thought of refusing, from the prestigious Wall Street law firm, Dewey, Ballantine, Bushby, Palmer & Wood, as described in "Sluggish Compass." Thus shackled to an American dream that I didn't care all that much about—looking back now, I suppose that, without giving it enough thought, I had absorbed my father's and many other lawyers' vision of success—I worked long and hard to achieve it.

For what? Practicing law is a service business, and the questions are, service to whom and what? I found the cases fascinating, the men were mostly congenial, and it did not occur to me that I was devoting my life's work to helping large corporations make their contributions to their stockholders' and our nation's prosperity by either obeying the law or sliding around it, and thus obtaining the justice of the privileged, often at the expense of the rest.

In the end, it was not my discernment but the firm's that spared me from continuing to serve that sort of justice, when they passed me over for partnership. That hurt. I saw it as a failure that stopped me, at least for a while, from doing the work I enjoyed. Only later did I realize that my failure was in not recognizing how badly I had fit with the firm and how sharply its purposes diverged from what were and would become mine. Not making partner marked an involuntary turning point that spared me from years of pressure-driven, well-paid mediocrity and freed me for all that followed.

By the 1970s, my goal was *putting together an interesting life.* Still not very spiritual.

Almost without my noticing it, my direction was shifting, and my goal was broadening: *Putting together an interesting life* became *leading a helpful and interesting life.* My endeavors that I believe were the most helpful to other people—that is, Attica, Sanctuary, and all the solidarity work that followed—made my life more interesting than ever, as I would not know until I was in their midst. And I believe that helping others *is* spiritual, *is* what God wants us to do, rather than banging on about whether Jesus walked on water.

As the years rolled by, I do not recall ever articulating my core beliefs to myself or anyone else, even though they seemed to guide much of what I said and did. Neither being passed over (let go, fired) by Dewey Ballantine nor two significant later events affected these beliefs except maybe to clarify and strengthen them.

The first event was an actual adventure arose from the notorious 1971 riot at New York's maximum-security prison called Attica, which is what I've called the story that describes it.

My occasional boyhood dream was to grow up and have an adventure like one of the Lone Ranger's or maybe like Jim Hawkins's in Robert Louis Stevenson's *Treasure Island*. One day I realized that, in a white-collar way, Attica was it. More recently, I had admired the honesty and courage of Frank Serpico, a New York City cop who blew the whistle on the corruption of many other cops and was shot in the face (non-fatally) for his pains. Fortunately, I wasn't.

Outwardly the decision to resign from the prosecutor's office and go public about its cover-up changed my life. Not to have made it —to have returned to the charade that the prosecution honestly could not convict any police of their crimes—would likely have continued my career in whatever direction it was going, but it would have changed the inner me. I did not consider doing that.

Before Attica happened into my life, the rebel side of me had been present but not dominant. After Attica, this would change, as the stories in "Beyond the Law" suggest.

A sound reason for appearing radical (if I now do) dawned on me several years ago as I listened to a tape of Brown University's Professor Arnold Weinstein giving a lecture on Nathaniel Hawthorne's classic *The Scarlet Letter*. The story's heroine, Hester Prynne, is partly ostracized from her 17th Century Puritan community in Massachusetts for the sin of adultery. While this psychic exile makes her daily life hard, it gives her a new ability to see her society from the outside, free from the fears, taboos, and no-no's that bind and blind its members. I, too, was ostracized from a goodly part of our society for the sin of kicking the official anthill and rocking the ship of state—as I was keenly aware at the time. The experience left me, I believe, with a new measure of the outsider's perspective, and it helped me to look afresh at the world and question much that I had previously accepted with little or no thought.[11] As I wrote in chapter 1 of *Turkey Shoot*, Attica freed me in ways in which I had not known I was not free.

A highlight, perhaps *the* highlight, of going public about the Attica cover-up was the talk I gave at Hampshire College, the smallest and reputedly most progressive college in the Pioneer Valley of Massachusetts. I could feel that the audience was with me, I ended with a quote from the Jackson Browne album, *Late for the Sky*, and the audience gave me a standing O, the first my host told me he'd seen the students give a speaker. During the question period, a young woman asked me, before Attica, hadn't I been part of the System? I paused, reflected, and said yes.

Another great student audience for my Attica talk came at the John Jay College of Criminal Justice in Manhattan in 2018, the year after my Attica book was republished. I had long thought that this would be an ideal venue for the talk, and it was gratifying that it was. It's really nice to feel that scores of young minds are with you and care about what you care about and may go on to do something about it.

I have often thought since answering the young woman at Hampshire College that I should have considered her question years sooner. I came to see, too, that much as many large corporations keep the nation reasonably healthy and wealthy if not wise, my work on Wall Street had, in its modest way, helped to preserve and protect big businesses' privilege to do much as they pleased. As Marxists are wrong to claim that people are so good that the state can wither away, capitalists are wrong to claim that corporations are too good to need much regulating—an obvious fact that would have been heresy to mention at Dewey Ballantine. They may make more money without proper regulations, but they often screw more people.

One overcast day in the 1970s, my father stood in his pajamas and bathrobe looking feeble and small beside his bed in a Manhattan hospital. He was in his eighties and had had a small stroke—if a stroke is ever small—that sapped his remaining vigor. I put my hand on his shoulder and silently tried to transfuse some of my strength into him.

He was soon able to go home, but during the few years he had left, he walked haltingly and was never again his old self. Long afterwards, I concluded that while physical strength is not transferable, love is. I hoped that Dad had taken my gesture as a mark of my love for him. What I tried to do, I suppose, followed instinctively what we are told that Jesus did repeatedly, imparting life and God's love that, we are told, overcame many ailments and cured many people.

Since Dad and Howard Melish were the two people who taught me the most about God during my early years, it finally came to me in the 1970s that I would like to talk things over with Howard. Not wanting to be disloyal to my father, I asked him if it would bother him if I did. No, not at all. I had several warm visits with Howard and his wife Mary Jane in their basement apartment, which was a refreshing walk across Brooklyn from my parents' basement apartment. The more I learned about Howard's life, the more I admired him. For instance, that he and his father had integrated Holy Trinity as related above, that Red-baiting Senator Joseph McCarthy had attacked him in the 1950s, and that he was the only white American called on to speak at the memorial for W. E. B. Dubois in Ghana in 1963.

Memorably, Howard told me about a fraught Easter that happened while I was away at college. On Holy Saturday, he happened to be up in the church balcony when several of the men who wanted to oust him came in below. He lay down between the pews. They changed the locks on the doors to the church and checked the locks on the beautiful stained-glass windows on the main floor. After they left, he unlocked one of the windows and climbed into the courtyard outside. The next morning when the hostile congregation arrived with a supply priest to celebrate Jesus's resurrection, they found that Howard and his father were already conducting a service with their supporters. For a while, rival services went forward from opposite sides of the chancel while a police car circled the block.

Mary Jane told me about comforting my mother after her baby, her only daughter and my only sister, Mary Elizabeth, died in December 1941 at the age of five days due to the RH factor, which could not be cured back then. That was the only time I ever saw my father weep. It hurt Mary Jane that my mother had sided with my father against her husband. There was nothing I could say.

I probably told Howard and Mary Jane about trying to prosecute the police who perpetrated the Attica massacre. That's not something I usually talk about, but I probably thought he'd be interested and approve of what I'd done.

A picture over the Melishes' mantelpiece of a young Black woman with a huge Afro looked familiar. Howard and Mary Jane had taken Black high school students from the South into their home (as part of an AFSC program) so they could experience decent education in an integrated school. I suspect that the Melishes' passion for justice and against racism nourished this girl's similar passion, which had begun as she grew up in 1950s Birmingham, Alabama. Howard told me that she had been accepted at Mount Holyoke College, but he persuaded her to go to Brandeis, where she encountered Herbert Marcuse, went on to study philosophy in Frankfort, Germany, and became the radical Angela Davis.

From talking with Howard, I felt that whether or not the rift between him and Dad had closed, a wound that I was barely conscious of inside my own mind had healed.

During my last visit, Mary Jane served lunch, and Howard couldn't eat much. As I was leaving, he walked me up the steps to the sidewalk and said he was going to see a doctor about his stomach; did I think it would be all right if he waited until his regular doctor returned from a trip? Not sure what to say and sensing that he wanted me to agree, I said yes. Did my answer matter? The next I heard, he had stomach cancer, which soon killed him. He was seventy-six. His memorial service at Holy Trinity, from which my father had helped to expel him three decades earlier, closed a circle for him, or for his mortal remains, and for me. I decided—I don't know why—that this service was the last time I would take communion, a decision I have honored many times and rarely departed from.

While First Congregational was filled with good people, the goodness of many of them extended only to the Darien town line, and it dismayed me that their idea of social responsibility mostly meant writing checks. Time and again, I would offer them a more active choice, usually to no effect. It embarrassed me one Saturday, for instance, that after two Maryknoll nuns and I arranged that they would make the long drive from their motherhouse in Ossining, NY, and present a peacemaking program, very few parishioners showed up. I think it was four of them, plus four from the Wilton Quaker Meeting, and our friend Evelyn Harris. The sisters led a fine program and tried to ease my embarrassment at the shabby turnout.

Around then I noticed that more and more as I sat in one white pew or another in church on Sunday mornings, I was tuning out the words of the service and thinking my own thoughts.

Nancy grew up in a Methodist Church but had been a Quaker for some years when we met. Almost right away, we started going to her service one Sunday, mine the next, and chatting with people during the coffee hours afterwards. I soon realized that I was more at home with her people than mine. Imagine my delight, too, at finally finding faithful people who have no creed; most of whom value compassionate deeds over correct beliefs and simple living over the status, wealth, and the junk that so many Americans seek; who question convention and authority; who honor the leadings of each person's Inward Light; take social responsibility seriously; and respect dissent while encouraging each other to seek truth. What a combination! If the winter of '74-'75 had been my darkest, '79 was a very good year. Even so, it took me until 1983 to become formally a Quaker.

At first I considered it presumptuous to accept the Quaker belief that a bit of God resides in each person. Now I dare to believe it's true, though I still think it may be more accurate to call it an echo of God. Whatever it is, I am certain it is my best self and I had best heed its still, small voice. What I appreciate perhaps more than Quakers' few beliefs are its principles (*testimonies* in Quakerese): simplicity and simple living, the equality of everyone, peace, integrity, community, stewardship of the Earth, and service to others.

I'd have joined the Quakers sooner if Rev. Sam Fogal had not been in trouble at First Congregational. Sam was a profoundly good person who did his best to do God's work as he saw it and actually lived his values, which were close to mine. That made him too liberal a pastor for most of the congregation. When his second wife left him, they took her departure as a reason (excuse) to push him out. (I asked myself whether he would have kept his job if he'd chained her in the basement.) After supporting Sam as best as I could at the Congo, I joined the Wilton (Connecticut) Friends Meeting and thus the Religious Society of Friends.

Sitting in silence at the Quaker meetings, as a large fire in the stone fireplace at the front of the meeting room blazed and crackled and gradually burned down to red embers, was both more peaceful and more challenging than the structured services I had always attended, where stuff to listen to or read or sing or mutter filled every moment and I did not need to think about anything. In the silence, once I put aside current concerns as best I could, I had to confront the world and myself. There was no escape from what matters. There still isn't.

One summer while Nancy and I were camping on Cape Breton Island, an Episcopal priest on the adjoining tent site chided me for the difficulty of Quakers' "entrance requirement." He meant the ability to sit through an hour of silence. Most people who I've watched try it out grew terminally antsy. In fact, the US has fewer silent Meetings than "programmed" Meetings, which have a minister and services of hymns, prayers, and sermons much like other Protestant churches. I treasure the hour of group silence, though during the early years it sometimes made me impatient. Sitting in silence with fellow Friends means much more to me than sitting silently alone, which I seldom do for very long.

Among my fondest memories of childhood are the simple, beautiful nativity pageants that our music teacher, Louella Vail, staged every year on the morning that our Christmas vacation at Brooklyn Friends began—fourth graders Mary sitting and Joseph standing in colored robes beside the cradle at the front of the dimly lit Meeting House, the shepherds and the wise men with their gifts coming forward to behold the imaginary infant, candle bearers entering in white robes holding electrically lit candles before them and singing "Gloria in excelsis Deo." I try to balance this warm memory against the absence of Quaker ritual in silent meetings. I was lucky enough to have had it both ways, but most kids don't.

The summer before I started at Harvard, my mother had me read *This Side of Paradise*, F. Scott Fitzgerald's 1920 novel that introduced

America, and in 1949 me, to Princeton during the dawn of the Jazz Age, when Mom had been in college at Radcliffe. Pointing me to this book suggested a side of her youth that she never mentioned and I wish I'd asked her about. Towards the end of her life, I saw that she was reading books about religion. Again, she didn't mention them, and I wish I'd asked.

In 1981, early in absorbing the Quaker Way, I wrote, "I want to love and be loved and live consistently with God's will and further His"—I was still saying His—"will if I can."

Nancy was teaching fourth grade when we married, I was still practicing law, and we lived in Norwalk. In 1983, we had enough money to have a two-bedroom house built in the silence and beauty of the forest on a mountainside in Weston, Vermont. We drove to it as often as we could and moved for good in June 1990. Only then did we discover the nearby Weston Priory and the dozen or so Benedictine monks (their number has varied some) who lived there and held services open to everyone. We loved to listen to them sing the songs they had written, accompanied by the guitars that two of them played. Like Quakers, the brothers* made their decisions by consensus and occasionally sang "Simple Gifts." More importantly, their outlook on life was much like ours; I have often thought they'd make good Quakers—further proof, I hope, that different faiths grow similar as they converge on truth.

When I first saw the brothers, some in their prime, some older, they struck me as looking like a non-threatening law firm, if there can be such a thing. They were gentle yet willing to say what needed saying, welcoming of everyone who came their way, and committed to finding and doing God's work in the world here and now, fine examples for everyone who encountered them. Their songs are recorded and widely sold and sung. Nancy worked one day a week in the Priory gift shop for eleven years and often told me about the fascinating visitors from all over the world she'd have talked with. I came to see the Priory as a lighthouse whose rays shone far beyond the mountains of Vermont.

Unwittingly I suppose, the brothers changed our lives in several ways. First came the Sanctuary Movement. While Nancy and I were

---

* People tend to capitalize the b in "brothers" until they learn that the brothers don't.

still living in Connecticut, we would sometimes attend Saturday afternoon vespers at the Priory, sometimes arriving early to listen to an undocumented Mayan refugee (illegal alien) named Enrique Canek relate in Spanish, with brother Richard translating, the terror, torture, rape, and murder that, he, his family, and many thousands of other survivors had fled and his people were still experiencing, especially in the western highlands of Guatemala. How horrible! Since most US media were either shamefully silent or blandly (more shamefully) misleading about US support for this barbarity, we were shocked.

The brothers had taken Enrique, his wife Sophia, and their five children into Sanctuary in 1984—in violation of federal criminal law. As Nancy and I listened to Enrique, we felt moved to become involved. It was mainly his reports, which we passed on to the Wilton Friends, together with several books and the input of Quakers from the Hartford (Connecticut) Friends Meeting, which had already joined the movement, that convinced our Meeting to declare Sanctuary.

Another way that the brothers affected us was through their Eucharist liturgies. They would read from Scripture, then sit in a silence out of which one and another and another would reflect on the readings in a conversational tone yet often deeply—as if in a speeded-up Quaker meeting. Nancy and I did not partake of the bread and wine, and these reflections were at the heart of why we attended these Eucharists.

For me at least, the brothers illuminate the illogic of many people who claim that various words or deeds must be either religious or political. The two categories obviously overlap; many words and deeds are both religious and political. Some of the brothers' writings, for instance, sound like planks from a Senator Bernie Sanders' liberal platform, and their participation in Sanctuary can fairly be called political, yet I am certain that they based their positions on their Christian faith and understanding of the Scriptures. I'm equally certain that Rev. Howard Melish was acting on his faith when he "preached politics from the pulpit" that alienated my father. For me, the main point is not the religious or political label, but whether the words and deeds aim to help people, especially those in need.

Yet another way the brothers changed Nancy and me arose from the committed Catholics plus a few Protestants and Jews who had come together in a lay community around them—not a formal congregation but close to it—which eventually called itself the Motley Group. Starting in 1991 and continuing for many years, Nancy and I would regularly join a dozen or more of these people on Wednesday evenings to share in a pot luck supper and a time of reflections on the Scriptures and often on the ways in which these ancient writings meshed (or not) with the news of the day—somewhat like the Sunday school classes I'd taught. Listening to what these people said opened my mind to ideas and points of view that would never have occurred to me on my own. Time and again, I discovered what I thought by listening to what I said during the gatherings, and I was grateful that the group tolerated my heterodoxies. Nancy's and my involvement with the brothers and the Motley Group did not weaken our commitment to the Quaker Way. It deepened it.

One of my most satisfying days as a Quaker came on March 23, 1986, when the Wilton Meeting reached unity on declaring Sanctuary and joining this movement of civil disobedience (non-violent criminality) that would come to include roughly five hundred churches, synagogues, and Quaker meetings that offered shelter to, and stood in solidarity with, undocumented refugees (illegal aliens), as described in "Sanctuary."

Doing Sanctuary was solidly within the Quaker tradition of non-violent witness and action. I saw it as implementing the Quaker testimonies of *peace* (which would come faster if our government stopped pouring gasoline on the fires), *integrity* (we were countering the official falsehoods that denied the violence and US complicity and the human toll they were taking), *justice* (our government was flouting the Refugee Act of 1980 by denying asylum to many thousands who desperately deserved it under the law and common humanity), *equality* (deserving refugees from Communist countries readily received asylum) and *social responsibility*. Woody Schempp of our Meeting summed it up more simply, "We heard a knock on the door, and someone on the other side was suffering."

The movement sometimes called itself "the new underground railroad"— not that it equaled the old one in risk or effectiveness; but it was in that tradition, and many people's suffering would have been worse without it. Doing Sanctuary was most enriching for Nancy and me. We felt good about doing it. We met wonderful refugees and North Americans, and a number of both remain our friends today. It led us to other witness and action—for instance, to demonstrating at Fort Benning, Georgia, against the School of the Americas, as also as described in "Sanctuary."

I did not and do not minimize the fact that doing Sanctuary meant committing acts of serious civil disobedience. Each act of harboring or transporting an illegal alien is a crime that can cost a perpetrator up to five years in a federal prison; yet several thousand people in those five hundred Sanctuary congregations, including Nancy and me, felt strongly enough about it to do it often—like having refugees spend the night in our house or driving them to take a shower or speak in a church.

A strapping young Salvadoran guerrilla in green fatigues who was attending the same Sanctuary conference as Nancy and I near Phila- delphia brought me, unbeknownst to him, face to face with a dilemma that I might have confronted sooner had I been more reflective. I fully supported his cause of ending the oppression of his people, but I con- sidered the guerrilla war morally wrong and probably counterproduc- tive. By joining his cause, was I abetting the killings that he was part of? After several days and sometimes nights of pondering, I decided, no, the fact that he was pursuing our cause in a harmful way should not deter me from pursuing it non-violently. I wonder now why it took me that long to figure that out. A nun I knew sometimes sent money to guerrillas to buy arms. I did not consider doing that.

It may look paradoxical that during the Attica adventure I strove to uphold the law while officials around me were breaking it, where- as during Sanctuary I was constantly breaking the law while officials were also breaking it by the manner in which they enforced it. Nancy and I broke the law to save innocent lives, but the government's law- less denials of asylum resulted in uncounted thousands of tortures and killings. On both occasions I was following my conscience and sense of justice and humanity. I was and am at peace with those decisions.

One day I remarked to Tom Wicker, who had retired from the *New*

York Times and was living in Vermont, that Jennifer Harbury had done a great deal to open up what the US had been doing in Guatemala.

> She sure did. There was a good deal of coverage and a lot of outrage over her case; but even then, you haven't had any kind of a national movement developing. I'm just perhaps overly cynical, but my own view is that it's not a very large group who are capable of moral outrage. I think the vast majority of Americans couldn't give a damn about these things one way or the other as long as they're left alone. It's only when the body bags start arriving and the draft begins to hit home, or maybe when you can't buy something that you want because there's a shortage, or you lose your job, then you can begin to get morally outraged.

Margaret Swedish agreed with Tom Wicker in general, but told me that she found hope in the people who committed themselves:

> One of the hardest things is to try to show people in the United States the world. They don't want to see it—because people do have consciences, and they don't want them bothered. Let somebody else worry about that because I don't want to change. But the more I am out talking with [Central America solidarity] groups and asking them, "What keeps you going, why are you still doing this?" it kept coming back to the way people connected with that world and began to feel empowered, working alongside Central Americans to the point of taking enormous risks. If we can stop thinking we have to change the world in our lifetime and get past that disillusionment that a lot of people are in, we begin to realize we actually have an impact. It's very empowering.

Reflecting on Margaret's words, I saw that it was the very steps that Jennifer, Adriana, and Dianna took in pursuit of their quests that helped to empower them, refreshing their strength to carry on.

I'm afraid that there's much history that supports Tom's and Margaret's conclusions about so many citizens' disinclination to respond to the information that Jennifer offered them—Jennifer and Dianna and Adriana and Sister Alice and the whole Sanctuary Movement and SOA Watch, Americas Watch, Amnesty International, *Sojourners*, *National Catholic Reporter*, Global Exchange, the American Friends Service Committee, and others. Thank goodness for the thousands upon thousands of citizens who did respond. While it's hard to measure their effect, if any, it seems obvious, especially today, that it's essential to strive for justice, human rights, and the equality of everyone, no matter what the odds against success may be. We would have been remiss to have given up, and speaking for Nancy and myself, it felt good to persist.

Many or most of the efforts by the above people and groups would not have been necessary if our government had done the right thing in the first place and left Guatemala alone. But back in the early 1950s, the United Fruit Company of Boston, which didn't want to pay a price for cheating on its property taxes in that country, tasked the ace P.R. man Edward Bernays, well-connected lawyer Thomas "Tommy the Cork" Corcoran, and a number of others with persuading the Eisenhower Administration of the lie that the duly elected government of Jacobo Arbenz needed to be overthrown in order to prevent a Communist takeover. According to Harvard professor of Latin American history John Coatsworth, in his Introduction to the 2005 Harvard Edition of the highly regarded *Bitter Fruit: The Story of the American Coup in Guatemala* by Stephen Schlesinger and Stephen Kinzer, "every serious work on Guatemala in the 1950s … conclude[s] that while the Arbenz government was reformist or progressive the probability of a communist regime coming into power was virtually nil."

The 1954 CIA coup, which Eisenhower had authorized after the folks with various interests in peddling the lie had convinced him and much of Washington that the lie was true, launched the Guatemalan tragedy. Promptly after the coup succeeded, the CIA's chosen dictator, using CIA-provided lists, executed several thousand Arbenz supporters. During the period I've written about in this memoir, the toll reached around 200,000 civilians.

In 1992, Erin converted to Judaism and married her business school classmate Michael Cohen, who is an Israeli; they raised their daughters Noa, Maia, and Edie in the Hebrew faith and at London's Liberal Jewish Synagogue. When people ask me how I feel about Erin's conversion, I say, accurately if glibly, "Better a good Jew than an indifferent Christian." I want Erin to be happy with her chosen faith and husband, and I believe she is.

One sunset on the French coast, Nancy and I drank wine on a peaceful strip of sand called Omaha Beach and considered the reinforced concrete German gun emplacements, still largely intact, and the huge cemetery behind them that the Germans in the emplacements had filled with the bodies of Americans half a century before. War is hell, but Hitler had to be stopped.

After I had gazed upon the lofty magnificence of the cathedral at Chartres and Paris's Notre Dame, it felt good to return to our simple, white-painted Meeting House in its clearing in the Connecticut woods. Splendid as those cathedrals are and much as they may have been built as tributes to God, I wondered what got preached inside. Does their magnificence inspire more godly conduct than the words shared in humble houses of worship?

In the same vein, I used to think that Christianity somehow centered on the land where Jesus walked and taught, lived and died. Only after a tour of the Holy Land in 1993 did I realize that the Biblical sites of two thousand years ago are forever gone. Our journey around Jerusalem and Galilee showed me how little a particular venue matters, at least to me, and that we in Vermont are not in the boondocks of our faith after all. For me that fascinating visit to the Holy Land—if one tract of earth can be holier than another—was just that, a visit not a pilgrimage.

During my first sixty-seven years, I enjoyed the blessing of a body that usually did what I asked it to, until the spring of 1999 when my immune system attacked me, stripping the sheathing off many nerves, like insulation off an electric cord, so that signals from my brain to my hands, arms, legs, and feet vanished along the way.* What a gift

---

* The name for this is vasculitis. I'm told it is a serious disease and my case could have been much worse.

it was to learn that a number of people in the Priory community were praying for me! I had counted on Nancy and my children for support, but the news of these others, which reached me in the hospital, was a humbling surprise. I wept warm tears. Their prayers were answered at least to the extent that they buoyed my spirits and, I believe, hastened my recovery. Later, all the nerves revived except for a few in my feet and shins.

During the '80s, thanks mainly to my becoming a Quaker and Nancy's and my doing all that went with joining the Sanctuary Movement, my goal finally became to put together a *helpful life* and if interesting, so much the better. The original goal of working on interesting litigations (so self-centered!) had faded away, and by 1986 I had left the law almost entirely. It was not until I reached my fifties—later in life than, until recently, most people lived—that I realized that I wanted to do what I could for peace, justice and people in need, by activism like doing Sanctuary, helping other people who shared these goals, participating in demonstrations, and mainly by writing about stuff that furthers these goals. In almost the words of the prophet Micah (6:8), I have tried to act justly, love compassion, and walk humbly with my God.

If I have an overriding regret, it's that I didn't pause sooner, back when most of my life lay ahead, to consider—widely, carefully, and every so often—the course my life was taking and how I might best spend the rest of it. Surely it would have helped to know myself better earlier and set aside time to think those subjects through. Despite a few bumps in the road, I've been remarkably fortunate in the life I have led.

Nancy's activism and mine took us onto many streets and sidewalks and parks, usually to hold up placards protesting US wars and torture. These were good experiences. Whether they did any good in the grand scheme, I do not know; but they did *us* good and helped to relieve the frustration that comes from passively reading, listening to, or watching the news about one US resort to violence after another. Faced with these outrages, we'd have felt remiss if we had remained stuck on our duffs and not taken to the streets from time to time. The protest groups we joined usually received many honks, smiles, and friendly hand waves from the passing motorists who paid us any heed, and only occasionally a shouted epithet or raised middle finger. This held true for the *war* against Panama (the invasion, conquest, and military occupation that the craven media falsely called merely an "invasion") or Iraq or Afghanistan or again Iraq. Our placards read "US Out of Central America" and "War Is Not the Answer" and "Troops Yes, War No." The placard of our friend Art Brinton said with Quaker simplicity, "No War."

The most intense part for me came in the spring of 1996 when I joined the people accompanying Sister Dianna Ortiz for the last eleven days of her thirty-six-day vigil and helped Sister Alice Zachmann to manage the logistics, as described in "The Vigil." Nancy left her work in Vermont to be there for the last two days. I have related this inspiring event in "The Vigil" and more fully in a chapter of *Sisters in the Storm*. Was this activism political? Sure, but so what? Many of the best and worst things that people do are both political and spiritual. Mainly it meant acting on my deepest spiritual convictions, and it meant the same for Nancy.

Opposing the US-started and abetted reign of terror in Guatemala, doing Sanctuary, and later by my writing and doing what I could for the four women who were opposing it seemed like useful things to do.

Not until I was well into writing these pages did I begin to see how intimately my spiritual and secular journeys blended into one another.

Shortly after Nancy reached her sixties, she ran a New York City marathon with her daughter Katrina and son Curt, starting at the toll plaza of the Verrazano Bridge in Staten Island, across the bridge into Brooklyn, then into Queens, across the 59th Street Bridge into Manhattan, up into The Bronx, back into Manhattan, and into its into Central Park, to finish at 26.2 miles. They weren't speedy, but they ran all the way—no walking, didn't "hit the wall" (suddenly lose energy) which many runners do—and crossed the finish line holding hands and feeling a great sense of accomplishment, three out of thirty-three thousand wholly heterogeneous runners. Katrina's husband Jim, Curt's fiancée Annie, and I cheered them on as they passed us on Brooklyn's Fourth Avenue, again on First Avenue in Manhattan, and again shortly after they entered the park.

All along the route, spectators two, three, or more deep lined the sidewalks, shouting "Good Job!" and other encouragements. This was a November 1st, and many runners still wore their colorful Halloween costumes. The whole event was upbeat, outgoing, friendly, so different from the impersonal quotidian rush. The people of New York City do have hearts, and today they opened them.

One sunny Sunday morning when Kate Brinton and I were the only people at our Quaker Meeting, we decided to carry our chairs to the lawn downstairs from the meeting room and sit in silence in the sunshine. Kate and her husband Art were Quaker role models for Nancy and me in Vermont, as a couple named Fred and Mary Green and an Englishman named John Perry had been in Connecticut. (Except for Howard Melish, and much as I admired Sam Fogal, I had had no role models in my previous churches.) I found it a luxury for that hour to sit still like a cat and watch the world as the white moon dropped down the blue sky behind the branches of a spruce tree across the road and a rocky little river from where we sat. Three years earlier, Kate had been demonstrating on a City of Rutland sidewalk against the impending US attack on Iraq. A year or so after that bright Sunday morning, she died at the age of eighty-nine.

One day as I contemplated a spruce tree standing straight, tall, proud, and dead in a forest, it passed through my mind that it's not always easy to accept the reality that death, especially one's own, is an essential part of life. Yet if we look around, it's hard not to see it is.

Late in 2014, I joined group of a dozen and more mostly elderly men who met every two weeks in the Priory visitors' center and lately on Zoom. It's called a faith-sharing group; we spend most of the hour sharing our thoughts about spirituality and life but not politics. Most of the men are Catholics, some are oblates of the Priory, and I am the only Quaker. (The women of the Priory community have a similar group.) We spent the first two years focused on the writings of Thomas Merton; and the discussions have ranged widely around our lives and world, growing more personal as our trust in each other grew until the group became a brotherhood. Happily, everyone listens to everyone else and no one tries to dominate the conversation. My main contribution is listening, since these guys have read and thought about much that I have not. When someone asks me for the Quaker view on some religious subject, I usually report that we don't have one.

Some people have mystical experiences that they attribute to God. Not me. Unlike many sincere and reverent people, I do not strive to feel God's presence or experience God or be with God while I am in this life. Why, I wonder, would it please God for me to do that? Seeking to hear and heed the still, small voice, probably of God, within me is the best I seem capable of. I hope it's enough.

Suppose I experienced moments of spiritual ecstasy, then what? Such exalted ecstasy is not my goal. Is my approach to faith too cerebral? I don't know. I do seek to know more about God. And I can think of no greater adventure in an afterlife than talking things over with God or some manifestation of God, or an angel if there is one, and souls who have gone before me.

Scholar of religions Karen Armstrong wrote in her Charter for Compassion, with input from more than a hundred nations, "The principle of compassion lies at the heart of all religious, ethical and spiritual traditions, calling us always to treat all others as we wish to be treated ourselves." I agree.

Ms. Armstrong also wrote that "religious belief becomes a reality to us only when accompanied by the bodily gestures, intense mental concentration and evocative ceremonial of ritual." Speak for yourself, Ms. Armstrong! As a Quaker who worships in a silence with like-minded people, without gestures or ritual, I disagree and am disappointed that so broad-minded a person is here so exclusionary. My faith brings me peace. I do not seek ecstasy.

Jesus said we are commanded to love God, but do I? While *love* has many meanings, what can it mean to love an incomprehensible Mystery? It's certainly not the love I feel for Nancy or Erin or Brian or my other family or friends. I feel enormous admiration, respect, and gratitude for God and trust in God. "How Great Thou Art" is my favorite hymn because I feel so strongly the greatness of God. It's Nancy's favorite hymn, too. Hearing it moves me to tears. Is this enough? Again, I don't know.

Some time during her seventies, Nancy said, "We should never lose the little kid within us." The truth and beauty of her words struck me immediately. Thinking on them later, they reminded me of Jesus: "Suffer little children, and forbid them not, to come unto me: for of such is the kingdom of heaven." (Mathew 19:14) I expect he didn't mean when the kids were being bratty or acting out. I know she didn't.

Nancy, who sees things mostly the way I do and often more clearly, says that God is out-of-doors. She sees God in the way a humming bird hovers seemingly motionless in a fitful breeze. Quite like a German woman who spirited a Jewish stranger and many others I suppose beyond the Nazis' grasp,[12] Nancy says, "When we meet our Maker and are asked, 'What did you do to change the world?' I'd hate to say, 'Nothing.'" Amen.

In May of 2017, Nancy and I attended an Episcopal memorial service in which—so differently from my Aunt Livy's service—the congregation remembered the person who had died by his name, his nature, and much that he had said and done. It was a memorial Eucharist for my friend Don Conover. When my turn came to speak, I quoted two of his thoughts that he had shared with me. The crowd that filled the church responded warmly, and Don's words later appeared in the church bulletin. Towards the end of the service, I partook of the bread and wine, one of the few times since the memorial for Howard Melish three decades earlier. I did it for Don and for Patti Kohlmayer Conover, the love of his life, who sat bravely in the first pew. During his final days, Don told me on the phone that he had been torn between wanting to escape the pain from his cancer and to remain with Patti as long as he could. Towards the end, morphine eased the pain, and he died peacefully in her arms.

Since the spiritual journey I've been relating has led me to considerable peace and a zillion thoughts and questions about Christian doctrine, it wouldn't be fair to record the events that shaped the journey without also saying where they took me. I have recorded my conclusions at length in a book of mostly very short essays that I wrote along the way and self-published with the expert guidance of Kitty Werner of Waitsfield, Vermont, *Overdue Heresies and the Search for Truth* (Fresh Look Press, 2024).* It seeks, not to persuade anyone of anything, but to prompt readers to reach, affirm, or rethink their own conclusions

---

* Originally titled *Overdue Heresies and Other Reflections of a Quaker Seeker.*

about faith and Christian orthodoxy, whether theirs resemble mine or not. Here is a summary of some of the main thoughts:

God is largely a mystery who has always existed and created the Cosmos and all that's in it. We may infer from the size and intricacy of creation that God has vast power and intelligence, but there is no basis for attributing gender to the one God, and it's a mistake, no matter how well-intended, to try to confine God within lofty human adjectives like omnipotent, omniscient, and benevolent. Does God love us? I expect so, or God would not have created us (through evolution) to probably be the highest form of life on this exceptionally benign planet. We all are invested with souls, though not at or near conception. Why would God put a soul into tiny particles of human flesh, at least 10% to 20% of which will quickly die by miscarriages? A holy trinity? One God is good enough for Jews, Muslims, and me.

Jesus was conceived in the usual way, and became filled with God's spirit. Don Conover said that God's "ultimate intervention was to send Jesus to earth to make plain what the good life should be." The extent, if any, to which Jesus performed miracles has no bearing on the godliness of his teachings and example. Why would God, who chooses to remain mysterious, care what people believe about God or Jesus or Mohammad or Buddha or Mary's virginity, so long as they treat each other decently? What we do matters far more than holding any approved set of beliefs, though some of what we believe informs what we do.

Sin is overrated. If a deed or thought does not, or is not likely to, harm oneself or another person, why is it a sin? It is a harmful sin for clergy, butters in, and moralists to burden people with unearned guilt. What we feel cannot be a sin; what we do about it can.

The Bible, Science, Atheism. While I am neither a philosopher nor a scientist, I have learned many realities about the Cosmos that neither the men who wrote the Bible nor theologians before the Twentieth Century could have known, but that modern astronomers, physicists, biologists, and other scientists have since discovered and that students in a decent high school science course are now taught. Popular books by atheists like Christopher Hitchens and Richard Dawkins use recent scientific discoveries, often soundly, to expose factual errors in ancient Scriptures. I use them to illustrate the magnificence of God's creation. How can we properly appreciate what God had done, or thank God for our existence, if we have little or no idea of what the sciences have revealed about the wonders of God's Creation? For this reason, basic sciences should be taught in Sunday schools.

Afterlife. Is there one? I hope so. If there is, I suspect it isn't Heaven and Hell, but we simply continue as the person we became on Earth, though free from infirmities of mind and flesh like Alzheimer's disease. I suppose that the God who gave us one life could easily give us a second; but if that is not God's way, it does not lessen my gratitude to God for this life.

Has my spiritual journey brought me closer to God? I don't know. Was it supposed to? I'm not sure. I'm happy to say that it has brought me closer to people, and I suspect that also means closer to God.

Does God intervene in the quotidian world? I'm pretty sure I would not have survived my youth if God did not. Critics of President Ronald Reagan said he was dumb but lucky. Whether that was true of him, it was certainly true of me when I jumped backwards onto the unknown slab of wood ("Curiosity"), and dove over my girlfriend's head into shallow water ("Chivalry") and drove the family car without checking the tire treads ("Wonderful"), and put out the fire on the smoke generator ("The Right Thing), and decided not to sit out a snowstorm in a remote diner on Route 20 ("Luck?"). That last decision was the dumbest of my life and nearly cost it. I thank God I survived. Did God's interventions save me, or was I just damn lucky five times?

Fortune or God also saved Nancy during her youth. After her family moved from Middletown, Ohio, to Ithaca, New York, she and her sister June shared an upstairs porch that had windows to the outdoors, a door into the house, and no heat. When June went off to college, Nancy had the porch to herself. Then their sister Shirley went off to college. One frigid autumn morning that happened to be on a weekend, Nancy snuggled under her covers, which included an electric blanket, pulling them over her head against the cold. Shirley happened to have come home that weekend and happened to open the porch door in time to see that the electric blanket was on fire. She called their father, who threw the burning blanket out a window, saving Nancy's life. Three happenstances converging at the critical few minutes, or were they the hand of God?

Considering the nuclear accidents and misunderstandings to date, the Cuban Missile Crisis and other confrontations, and the thousands of missiles that US and Russia have long been insanely pointing at each other, my survival seems far less miraculous than that of humankind. I've stopped taking chances. Leaders of the nuclear powers have not.

What matters to me in my faith today? To keep on seeking. To act on what I believe, and to work for peace and social justice as I can, mainly now by writing. I am a Quaker in good part because the Quaker Way encourages these efforts and it feels so comfortable to be one. The chance to sit in silence with like-minded Friends and get in touch with the best part of me, which may be divine—to listen with the ear of my heart and maybe sometimes hear the voice of God, as St. Benedict asked us to do—is what I treasure most about the Quaker Way. How blest I was to find Nancy, and it through her.

I wrote this spiritual memoir, in good part, to see what it would say. Three take-aways surprised me: First, how little attention I paid to the direction of my life and contents of my faith until my late forties when, not coincidentally, I met Nancy and became a Quaker. Second, how many secular events struck me as having affected my spiritual course. Third, how little I care whether the mysterious Almighty is a trinity or Mary was a virgin or Jesus walked on water or I "experience" God, compared to the fulfillment I finally felt from trying to live the Scripture-based testimonies and do my bit to help strangers in need. I know myself better for having written and then read this memoir, even the first tales. It has given me fresh insight into my many mistakes and my inner peace. God gave me wonderful life, and it would have been ungrateful to piss it away. At this point, I don't think I did.

I'm told that as we age, our thoughts revert increasingly to our early years. The past long gone draws near. Autumn, which came on earlier back then than it does today, sometimes prompted my mother to sing a song to my brothers and me that she must have learned while she was a girl growing up in Lexington, MA, early in the last century:

"Come, little leaves," said the wind one day.
"Come o'er the meadow with me and play.
Put on your dresses of red and gold,
For days grow short and nights grow cold."[13]

Nearly every year until recently, Nancy and I would drive into Canada, which has excellent campgrounds, pitch our tent, and sleep on mats inside it. We always felt that being close to God's earth brought us closer to God. As we were driving to camp in Canada a few years ago, I said something that, uncharacteristically, I had been holding back from her: I sometimes grieve our passing, which can't be very far away. She promptly replied that she had been grieving it too. We pitched the tent by the edge of a woodland lake on a flat patch of gravel near the car and turned our blue canvas chairs to face the water, then stood together by the tent and pondered the lake and the sunlit green forest on the far side, beyond our empty chairs.

Ramallah Friends

During a family trip to Israel in April of 2011, Nancy and I visited the Ramallah Friends School. Our Friends Meeting had been making modest donations to the RFS for several years, and we had become increasingly interested in the School. Its director, Joyce Ajlouny, spent a night as our guest while she was touring in New England the previous October and had invited us to visit it and her if we passed that way.

Ramallah is about ten miles (forty minutes by bus) north of Jerusalem in what I was taught to call the West Bank, meaning the land between the west side of the Jordan River and the land that is now Israel. In Israel we heard it (and Gaza) referred to as the Palestinian territories. In Ramallah, people simply called it Palestine, as do most nations of the UN. The population of Ramallah had grown enormously in recent decades, in good part, Joyce told us, because it was the de facto capital of the yet-to-be-declared Palestinian state.

Nancy and I made our way to the Damascus Gate on the north side of the old walled city of Jerusalem and quickly found a small green and white No. 18 bus a few blocks away. For 6.50 shekels (about $2) each, we rode through hilly urban streets northwards and were soon passing beside the Israeli security barrier. Some called it a "fence" though it was a smooth concrete wall that looked to be around fifteen feet high, was topped with barbed wire, and had a sort of barbed wire balcony that projected out from the concrete near the top. On reaching the Qaland-iya checkpoint, which resembles an overgrown US toll plaza, the bus stopped momentarily and continued on. We saw Israeli soldiers there, but, seeming unconcerned about who left Israel, they paid us no heed.

As the bus approached the terminal at the end of the line, we spotted "Ramallah Friends School" emblazoned high on a building to our left, marking the "Boys' School," which is actually the co-ed upper school (grades 7 to 12). With green lawns, hedges, and trees that separate stately stone buildings, it looked more like a college campus than a typical US high school. A tennis court on which youngsters were playing sat to the left of the large front gate. Below it were the administrative offices in a low building that included Joyce's family home, much as a parsonage may adjoin an American church. The "Girls' School," which is the co-ed lower school, was some blocks across the city. Total enrollment was about 1,200 students, a third of them Christians and the rest Muslims. When Joyce was a student, she said, she was not conscious of who was of which faith. Though the school, which began about 140 years ago, had no endowment, it was able to provide financial aid to nearly 20% of the students.

There were only six or so Quakers living in Ramallah—Joyce herself is a birthright (born) Quaker—yet the School gives a value-driven education which emphasizes, as its website put it, "the traditional Quaker testimonies of truth, equality, justice, discipline, peace, tolerance, service, creativity, and simplicity," values that help particularly in enduring the oppression of the Israeli military occupation. Many RFS graduates have become prominent in the Palestinian community, so that the School has become a force for enlightenment and reconciliation—to the extent that such may be possible.

Joyce had arranged for us to visit the Amari Play Center in the capable hands of a woman I'll call Amina, who was a refugee and worked for the Center. She drove us through city streets and into the Amari Refugee Camp, parking at the curb outside the building that housed the Center. There wasn't any gate or fence to tell us we were in a refugee camp, just a sign at the head of the street that sloped down into it.

The Play Center consisted of two large rooms filled with maybe thirty or forty preschoolers, some shy and some friendly as kids are, and several teachers who controlled them gently and well. What impressed Nancy and me the most was the fun the kids were having and how happy they looked. Watching their smiles, hearing their laughter, and sharing a few words that neither of us understood, I thought sadly on the future awaiting them as they grow up under the humiliating, tedious, and sometimes brutal Israeli occupation. How many occupations are benign?

The Amari Refugee Camp is essentially an urban slum comprised of mostly tall buildings separated by a few wide streets and mostly narrow alleys with not quite adequate sewage and some garbage in the gutters. The camp was established to house a portion of the 750,000 Palestinians whom Israeli Jews ejected by force and terror from their homes in 1948 when Jewish militias destroyed upwards of 400 venerable Palestinian villages, an event that Palestinians know as the Nakba (Catastrophe). Some refugees from that time are still living in the camp; during the first eighteen or so years, Amina told us, they had lived in tents. Currently the camp was home to over 10,000 souls, about half living in poverty, in a little over half a square mile. The unemployment rate was about 27%. Many additional refugees lived outside the camp.

Amina asked us if we'd like some lunch in the camp. Absolutely! We entered a simple, spacious restaurant that served up good sandwiches of falafel, salad stuffed inside of pita pockets, and delicious tea that was poured into cups paved with sugar and loosely filled with crushed mint leaves.

Then it was back to the RFS for Joyce's tour. She led us across the busy avenue outside the main gate and up into the shaded pathways of the school's large, widely varied organic garden, where both the students and people from the community learn ecologically sound ways to grow food. Then it was on to an eighth-grade class that she told us would be in English and included one of her sons. I expected the subject to be English, but, no, it was a science class. The School aims to make all students fluent in both Arabic, which is the first language of most of them, and English. These eighth graders were already discussing scientific questions with their teacher *in English*. Wow!

As we walked across the campus again, Joyce spotted a group of eleventh graders lounging about the stone steps of another building. Would we like to meet them? They were friendly, relaxed, direct, and of course chatted with us in English. One talked enthusiastically about the college she is applying to in Lebanon. Almost 95% of the RFS students went on to college, about 30% in the US and Canada with another 20% in Europe and the largest number in Ramallah. Palestinians, Joyce said, have more college graduates per capita than any other Arab country. About half the RFS graduates who matriculated abroad returned to live in Ramallah, and most of the rest stayed in touch.

I asked these students how they felt about the current US intervention on behalf of the rebels in Libya. They smiled. Two said they favored it. One was strongly opposed and explained why. It was refreshing to see them so politically aware and civil to each other when they disagreed.

All RFS students are required to do at least 150 hours of community service. The School's stresses tolerance and listening to opposing views. For example, over the objections of some parents, Joyce had the students read *The Diary of Anne Frank*, to help them see that Jews have their own legacy of horror and there is another side to the present conflict.

However happy and well-adjusted the students seemed, as this group did, they all carried the experience of the Israeli occupation inside them. The School had counselors to help them to unpack their anxieties, live with their nightmares, and deal with their fear and anger at being shouted at by Israeli soldiers who shot Palestinians with impunity even back then.

After we wished this group well, there were other people to meet, buildings to visit, classes to watch, and a girl practicing on a cello to encourage. Driving over the hilly streets afterwards, we stopped to go inside the Ramallah Friends Meeting House, which has a vaulted stone ceiling and a garden outside, an enclave of quiet in the bustling city.

We tried to take Joyce to dinner, but she wouldn't hear of it, saying it would violate Palestinian hospitality. So she treated us to a delicious meal featuring salmon in a restaurant downtown. Back in the car, she pointed to a gleaming white obelisk we were passing and said it had been erected for the late Palestinian leader, Yasser Arafat. Accustomed as we were to hearing the US media demean Arafat, this tribute to him surprised us. Palestinians honor him for refusing to give up the substantial rights that a deal with Israel that he was offered would have required.

It was dusk now, and Joyce pointed out an extensive spread of buildings that covered the hilltop across the valley that holds the Am-ari Refugee Camp. Floodlights shone outwards in all directions as though the hilltop wore a golden crown. That's an Israeli settlement, Joyce said, one of the many that surround Palestinian cities. Those floodlights told us that for all their power, those settlers worried about keeping safe.

When our No. 18 bus stopped at the Qalandiya checkpoint during our return to Jerusalem, nearly everyone (Palestinians, we assumed) got off and entered a chain-link fence enclosure to be let through (or not) one by one and resume their ride into Israel. Two Israeli soldiers board-ed the now nearly empty bus, one standing with his weapon at the front while the other walked back and glanced at our passports. The bus drove through, stopped in an adjoining parking lot, and we were asked to board another bus that was standing nearby and was soon filled with the passengers who had been allowed through the enclosure.

Switching buses, we supposed, kept everyone from having to wait while the first bus was searched for explosives, a procedure that struck us as a sensible way of dealing with a real threat. The bus then rolled along the wall towards Jerusalem. The wall was problematic, not be-cause the Israelis felt, with good reason, that their safety required it, but because they situated it so as to slice off pieces of Palestinian land for themselves.

Before visiting Ramallah, I had told a Jewish friend that the Is-raelis' displacement of Palestinians reminded me of the displace-ment of Native Americans by the European immigrants who were her forebears and mine. She replied that the cases differed because Jews had lived on this land two thousand years ago. That's a familiar rationale not only for the creation of Israel on 78% of old British Mandate Palestine, but also for Israel's ongoing fragmentation and annexation of the Palestinian remainder by settlements, connecting roads, and the wall. I couldn't help musing that if this rationale gained currency in Vermont, Nancy and I might see members of the Abenaki Nation roll up our driveway to put us out of our home and maybe bulldoze it.

More poignantly perhaps, I mentioned to another Jewish friend that many Palestinians still have the keys to the homes they had to flee. He replied that many descendants of Jews who fled their homes in Spain and Portugal during the 1490's still have the keys to those houses. I wondered how long it takes for hope to die and a key to become merely a keepsake.

It was clear to Nancy and me that Israelis desperately needed to live in safety; and that Palestinians desperately needed to live not only in safety but also with their land restored, no more military occupation, and the same freedoms that Israelis now enjoy. Graduates of this Quaker School, we thought, might actually contribute to reaching a fair resolution of the conflict, if such a resolution was possible, and in the meantime help their fellow Palestinians to abide under the Israeli occupation.

Six years after our visit, Joyce became the General Secretary (head) of the American Friends Service Committee. She and her husband now live in Bethesda, Maryland.

On October 7, 2023, came the horrific attack by Palestinians of Hamas on Israelis near Gaza. This prompted the Israelis to fight back in self-defense and also to inflict vastly disproportionate carnage plus starvation and property damage on Palestinian civilians, all with US help reminiscent of our help in the mass killing of civilians in Guatemala and El Salvador a few decades earlier, related in previous stories.

I believe that all people are created equal. While many people don't, surely the agony that an Israeli mother feels is much the same as the agony that a Palestinian mother feels on seeing her child shot dead or blown apart. Or an American mother would feel.

Some years ago, my daughter Erin, her newborn daughter Noa, her husband Michael, and his parents nearly celebrated Noa's birth in a coffee shop in Rishon LeZion, near Tel Aviv, on the afternoon that a Palestinian blew it up, killing a number of people. But attacks like that, though horrific and counterproductive, are not unprovoked. The same is true for the October 7 attack. How are a people supposed to react when another people, who believe they are superior human beings, expel them from their ancestral land or occupy it, demean them, restrict them, and harm and kill them with impunity? Certainly, many Native American nations reacted violently when my forebears from Europe did this to them. Why would one expect Palestinians who have been treated similarly to react differently?

Israel clearly has the right to defend itself and the further right to determine for itself, without interference by other nations, the ways to exercise that right. But, with equal clarity, exercising these rights provides zero justification for far exceeding the legitimate needs of self-defense by indiscriminately killing tens of thousands of children, women, and civilian men; burying more thousands alive under rubble; starving two million people, many of them to brain damage and death; depriving them of life-saving medical care; and destroying homes, schools, mosques, hospitals, universities, and other elements of Palestinian culture that were doing fairly well in spite of long-imposed restrictions by Israel. I had thought better of Israel than that it would inflict such cruel, lawless, and needless devastation on fellow human beings. It has encouraged me to see many Israelis protest against it.

Similarly, Israel's legitimate defense against Hamas has not justified Israeli settlers and soldiers in destroying Palestinian life and property with impunity in the West Bank and annexing (taking without the owners' permission) Palestinian land, which is wrong when Russians do it to Ukrainians, but many say is okay when Israelis do it to Palestinians.

US complicity in all this, and its efforts to stifle knowledge about it and criticism of it, make me sad for my country. Where are free speech, truthful news, the vigorous interchange of ideas, the right to dissent and protest, due process of law, and compassion for the lives of others?

Do I hold Israel to a higher standard than other nations? Yes. The US massive and nearly *carte blanche* support for Israel's deeds makes the US complicit when Israel does wrong. If Americans convince

Israel to lessen its guilt, our guilt *ipso facto* lessens.

The conduct of Israelis and Americans in Gaza and of Israeli settlers and soldiers in the West Bank has, illogically but predictably, inflamed antisemitism across the world. My first memory of feeling the sting of this curse came in high school when my friend John Hermann took antisemitic remarks in silence (as related in "Old Sport"). I detest it all the more now that four-fifths of my progeny are Jews. It should be obvious that Jews in general have had zero to do with Israel's destruction of civilian lives and property in Gaza and the West Bank.

It is equally illogical to claim that criticizing the excesses of the Jews who run a small nation in the Middle East is necessarily "antisemitic," which means hating or being hostile towards all Jews everywhere. People who plead this dodge remind me of the school boy who is very obnoxious but says it's because he's Jewish that the other kids don't like him. Many Jews, non-Jews who are not antisemitic, and especially those of us who admire Jews for the vastly disproportionate number of Nobel prizes they have won, have all criticized these excesses.

If thirty or so years ago, the much discussed two-state solution had resulted in the Israelis and Palestinians living side by side, each on their own land, it seems most likely that the tragedy that broke out on October 7, 2023, and continues as I write this nearly two years later, would not have occurred. Rather, these two peoples, who worship the same God, would now be living in peace and security, if not in total harmony; a few thousand dead Israelis and scores of thousands of dead Palestinians would still be alive; anti-Semites would be denied their current jollies; Israel would not be a pariah nation in the eyes of many; and Palestinians and Israeli Jews would be able to celebrate the births of their children and grandchildren and mine without fearing for their lives.

Is a peaceful resolution of the conflict along these lines still possible? Would reaching it help to restore Israel's standing in the eyes of many people and nations? Wouldn't it finally enable both peoples to live in peace?

Reading and Writing

Reading has been one of the joys of my life.

Mom and Dad read to my brothers and me a lot until we could

read for ourselves, as we all did thereafter. In recent decades, I have finished only about twelve books a year, partly because I read slowly and partly because I read magazines. The books that have drawn me to reread them include *The Hobbit, Heart of Darkness, The Great Gatsby,* and *A Farewell to Arms.* It's long been hard to decide whether to pick up a book or a magazine, usually *The New York Times Book Review, The New Yorker, National Catholic Reporter,* and more recently *The New York Review of Books.* Ever since Dr. Kastendieck's high school English classes ("Teacher"), I have underlined all the non-fiction I read, except in borrowed books of course. This helps me to focus, whether or not I'll ever look at the underlined words again. Some people admire war heroes, statesmen, exceptional athletes, and so on; I admire staff writers at *The New Yorker.*

Writing has been another joy.

I've always enjoyed it and might have chosen to make it my career but for three strikes against it: I didn't think my work would earn enough to support me and a family. Much as I enjoyed the books of Fitzgerald, Hemingway, and John O'Hara in college, I didn't want to live as they had. Finally, I wanted to experience enough life to find stuff worth writing about. Perhaps I should have become a reporter, as Hemingway, O'Hara, and many other writers did. But then I'd have missed Attica and doing Sanctuary and so much more.

Writing the humor column for the high school weekly paper was fun and often surprised me by what I came out with. During college, I took two short-story-writing courses—John Updike was in one of them and drew sketches of people during class—and a seminar on writing non-fiction with the noted poet Archibald MacLeish. Fitzgerald's notes in *The Crack-up* intrigued me. Then and ever since, I've jotted down my ideas and observations.

Between graduating from college in June 1953 and entering the army that August, I began to write a novel about a college student who isn't sure what to do with his life; I never got back to it. The short stories I wrote in the army, mainly in the palatial enlisted men's club in Wiesbaden, Germany, are somewhere in my uncollected papers, a.k.a. the mess. I originally called the stories that comprise the first part of this book *Embers.* The first three letters are for my children, Erin and

Malcolm Brian. I got a license plate for my car that said EMBERS. The word reappears in this book's epigraph.

My mother used to read the *New York Herald Tribune*. My father read the *Times*. When I went to work on Wall Street, I chose the *Trib* because, moderate Republican that I was back then, I found it livelier. Starting in the spring of 1962, I was sending it letters to the editor, and it was printing a fair number of them. Studying which were printed and which weren't helped me to sharpen my style. Ever since then, I've been sending letters to nearly every publication I read. My record wasn't too bad with the *Times Book Review*, and not so good with the daily *Times,* though it did publish two of my Op-Eds about Attica. I look back with chagrin on several naively portentous letters that the *Trib* and *Times* published during the mid-sixties supporting the US war in Vietnam. It took the passion of my senior high Sunday school class in 1970–1971 to persuade me to oppose it. I, then Nancy and I, have opposed every US war since. Even today it's helpful to consider which of my letters get published versus which don't.

During or shortly after my stint with Legal Aid in the City's Criminal Court, ("Prohibition"), I wrote a file memorandum of my experiences to show other young lawyers at the firm who might consider doing the same thing how things worked and what to expect. It took more time and grew larger than I'd expected, 178 pages (noted in "Sluggish Compass"). I put it between brown covers and titled it *Rough Justice: Five Weeks in Criminal Court*—rough justice being quite an understatement of what I found there. I asked the court's Administrative Judge (chief judge) John Murtagh if he would read it with an eye to my possibly getting it published. He kindly replied:

> I commend you for an excellent analysis, particularly considering that this was your introduction to the court.... Even though you were most perceptive, greater experience would be required to properly interpret what takes place in the court.

I truly appreciated his taking the time to read it and of course the comments he made, but couldn't help wondering whether his last line meant that if the judges fail to believe the cops who they know are likely lying, the system would probably break down.

My first serious shot at writing a book came in the '70s when I was entering my forties and attending Charlotte Hoffman's writers' workshop in Stamford, Connecticut. It resulted in *The Flying Dutchman*, which I describe in "Work in Progress." The next book, which I believe served the public interest as well my need to relate an adventure, was *The Turkey Shoot: Tracking the Attica Cover-up*, which brave and innovative Barney Rosset, bless his heart, published in his Grove Press in 1985 after I'd received more than forty rejections from more than thirty publisher—probably fewer if I'd known to try Barney sooner. Charlotte's group were a great help during the nearly ten years it took me to write it. Tom Wicker of the *Times* encouraged me to finish it, and he wrote a succinct and generous Foreword. My greatest help and encouragement came from Nancy after we met and married in 1979.

Of the difficulties in getting the book published, Tom Wicker said in his Foreword:

> [O]ver a period of years, I tried with no success to help him to get this book before the public. I became convinced that New York's establishment publishers either thought the public had lost interest in Attica, or that Bell's book was too hot to handle, or both.

Skyhorse Publishing republished the book in 2017 as *The Attica Turkey Shoot: Carnage, Cover-up, and the Pursuit of Justice*, which is a half-line summary of the story the book tells; it doesn't claim that anybody caught up with justice. So much happened in the Attica saga after the original *TS* came out that the new edition contains a 57-page epilogue, which took me nearly a year to write. In 2022, Skyhorse brought it out as a paperback that is the definitive version.

Banish the Bull. During the 1980s I put together a satiric dictionary that tried to give words their real meanings, and an attractive young agent named Laura Gross, who had moved here from London, tried to sell it but couldn't. A few examples: *travel*: expander of mind and bladder. *war of choice*: war of aggression. *advertising*: thou shalt covet. *gravity*: universal tidier up. *true love*: infatuation that outlives consummation. *free world*: our side. Looking it over now, I see that it needs work.

Sophie Harrison. Somewhere during the '70s, I believe, I began collecting information to write about a woman named Sophie Ridgely Dashiell Lytle Harrison, who was the grandmother of my Aunt Sophie. The first Sophie (actually Sophia) was born in Baltimore in 1826, and her family soon moved to Tennessee. At age twenty, she married William Lytle, who was twice her age and had six children living at home; she bore him five more. The fierce Civil War Battle of Stones River (called Second Murfreesboro by the Union) was fought in part on the Lytle plantation during three days starting on December 31, 1862. A small, solid cannonball (which Aunt Sophie inherited and I have hefted) crashed through the front door of the mansion and buried itself in the wooden floor near Sophie as she was carrying across the hall the baby who became Aunt Sophie's mother. After the battle, Union Army soldiers occupied the area for a time in part at least to protect Sophie, who was in her mid-thirties and a widow by then, and was flying the Union flag. A twenty-two-year-old Union Army lieutenant named Carter Bassett Harrison, who was a grandson of the first President Harrison and younger brother of the second, was quite taken with Sophie. They married, scandalizing the town, which hated him at first but loved him by the time he died. When Sophie was old and again a widow, a mob came onto her property to lynch a Black man. She picked up a shotgun and started for the door to stop it, but her family restrained her. The next morning, she had the tree on which the poor man died cut down. Sanctuary happened, and I never wrote the book.

Blood Sport. My father's Irish first cousins, Tommy and Wilfred Haughton, served in the Ulster Division of the British Army during World War I. Wilfred was in transportation, where he contended with a lot of trucks and mud, and survived the war. Tommy was a lieutenant in an infantry outfit called the 12th Royal Irish Rifles. Two German machine gun bullets took him on July 1, 1916, the first day of the Battle of the Somme, one of the 19,240 British soldiers killed during that bloodiest day of any British war, a needless death in a needless battle in a needless conflict. His grave is in a British military cemetery in Beaumont-Hamel. His parents believed that his death served a useful purpose, and they never got over their grief. In 1958, Kay, and I had a refreshing visit with Wilfred and his family at their home in Cullybackey, County Antrim, north of Belfast in Ireland and learned a bit about Finn mac Cool and other mythic Irish figures.

Among my father's papers were a trove of letters from Tommy and Wilfred's mother, Katy, to her sisters-in-law, my grandmother Agnes Elizabeth "Lily" Haughton Bell and my great aunt Sara Haughton in Cincinnati. The letters told the news that the boys wrote from France, the reports of Tommy's death, and the details that emerged about how it happened. I planned to write a book, first called *How Tommy Died* (a British soldier is a Tommy), that would alternate the letters with my reflections on war, rather like my reflections on religion in *Overdue Heresies*, but I never got around to it.

After finishing *Turkey Shoot*, I began another novel, this time a fraught love story that I can't remember the point of. The members of Charlotte's workshop to whom I read chapters were tolerant and polite but didn't seem impressed. In 1986 or '87 I dropped it to write a play that I hoped would recruit people to the Sanctuary Movement. It is:

Cry Uncle!, which I originally titled *A Conspiracy of Love*, presents a complete jury trial in an hour and a half. A good-hearted minister and an outspoken nun are in the dock for taking into his church an undocumented Guatemalan refugee whose husband was murdered by a death squad. The audience is the second jury. The play was stage-read at a number of churches and other venues and usually led the audiences to lively discussions afterwards. In one church, a member of the congregation who was a federal judge donned his black robe and played the federal judge. Anyone who wishes to consider producing the play should contact me or my successors—no charge for non-commercial productions.

Ghost Train from the Border. Some time after finishing the play, I began to write an oral history of Sanctuary, in the manner of Studs Terkel's oral histories, which I have enjoyed and still admire. The research gave me a wonderful chance to dig into the life-changing experiences of many mostly wonderful people. The first pages of "Sanctuary," above, come from the first pages of *Ghost Train*. Ninety or so interviews explored in particular their decisions to join the movement, oppose our government, take the risks, and accept the inconveniences. But after tediously transcribing forty or so interviews on fairly primitive equipment, I put the project aside, briefly I expected, to write a quick book about three valiant women, Sister Dianna, Adriana, and Jennifer, which I called....

Sisters in the Storm: Life and Death on the Receiving End of US Power, which tells the stories of the Sister Alice and the other three women whom you have met in "Beyond the Law." There went the next six years, plus quite a bit of time afterwards. The manuscript was long. Cutting it and cutting it again, I worked it down to 670 pages, 205,000 words.

After selling the new edition of *Turkey Shoot* to Skyhorse back in 2016, my agent was not able to sell *Sister* or my books called *Roses in the Night* and *Overdue Heresies.* So, in the spring of 2023, I had lunch with my old friend Kitty Werner, who knows the publishing business, to see if she could help me in the hugely hard task of finding a new agent. Instead, she persuaded me to self-publish, as she had helped several dozen other writers. She formed my LLC, which I call Fresh Look Press. With her patient and expert help, I published *Roses* in 2023 and *Heresies* in 2024.

Roses in the Night: Mayan Sisters Confront CIA-Backed Terror, is a fact-based novel about two remarkable women. Maria, mindful that the US-backed army has wiped out hundreds of Mayan villages, struggles to save her own village from soldiers' rapes, bullets, and flames. Her sister Brenda tries to lead a normal life in Texas, Manhattan, and Vermont after being raped and tortured by CIA-advised secret police in El Salvador. Both women strive to defeat the denial that grips them at first, to face an abyss, and make the hard choices they must make if they are to persevere. The character of Brenda, who is one of the roses of the title, is modeled on a trilingual Mayan friend; she is named for the brave Salvadoran participant in the Sanctuary Movement whom I interviewed in "Border Witness." Other friends survived torture by several US-backed regimes in Latin America. I wrote the book for them, for the voiceless millions on the receiving end of ill-considered US power, and for my beloved country, which can do better. Pat Davis, who is now the President of the Board of the GHRC, wrote a particularly preceptive blurb for *Roses*. I had made a cold call to Professor Karen Fondacaro of the University of Vermont, who is a clinical psychologist and has worked with survivors of torture from more than thirty countries, and asked her whether the advice I have a therapist give in *Roses* is plausible. She said yes and ended up writing a blurb that amounts to a highly astute and favorable review of the book.

Overdue Heresies and the Search for Truth collects my religious reflections of the previous forty years. Its short and very short essays aim to prompt readers to reach, reaffirm, or rethink their own conclusions about God, Atheism, Jesus, Miracles, Sin, Salvation, and many other elements of the Christian tradition. The book asks many questions and questions many traditional answers. I do not seek to persuade anyone of anything; rather, I encourage readers to enjoy disagreeing with me. The book is especially for people who are spiritually inquisitive or question major parts of their church's doctrines; atheists and other "Nones"; students seeking fodder for late-night bull sessions; and seekers of truth. It is not for people who seek certainty or believe they have found it.

If it were not for Kitty Werner and her skill and patience, *Roses*, *Heresies*, and this book would probably not be in print. Instead, they'd still languishing in my MacBook and backup thumb drives while I continued the search for an effective agent who sees merit and sales potential, such as they are, in my writings.

I still hope to finish *Sisters*, which won't take much work besides the drudgery of endnoting, and *Ghost Train*, which will. But given the chances that I shan't—I'm 94—I wrote the stories in "Beyond the Law" about my roles in Sanctuary and the four women's stories. Though those roles were brief and small, they meant a lot to me. If by any chance I do finish those books, I hope to return to *Flying Dutchman* ("Work in Progress"), which is a fun book and, I think, offers some useful insights. What's there now isn't too bad but needs shortening and sharpening.

Delore

Delores Barbeau—Delore to all who knew her—and Carol Olstad were a devoted couple, devoted to each other, to their faith, and to helping people in need. At the time they settled in Weston, Delore was stocky, imaginative, and pleasantly assertive. Carol was a year older than Delore, larger, quieter, funnier, and very artistic. Where Delore sought the foreground, Carol preferred to stand quietly back; and being an illegal alien—a Canadian who, I believe, had overstayed her visa—required her to lie low.

Delore became a Maryknoll nun after finishing high school. They sent her to Bolivia, and put her through medical school there. The US-backed government of Hugo Banzer, which came to power in the 1970s, was a brutal dictatorship; and Banzer himself was an army officer trained by the US School of the Americas. It bothered Delore to see her friends being tortured and sometimes murdered by Banzer's thugs, while being a Maryknoll sister kept her safe. So she resigned from the sisterhood and subjected herself to those risks.

Carol grew up in Alberta, became a registered nurse, went to Bolivia, and teamed up with Doctor Delore. As they aided the sick and injured, each of them became the love of the other's life. After Delore was "thrown out of Bolivia," as she put it, she and Carol went to Nicaragua during the 1980s when it had discomfited our government to see the Sandinista rebels oust the longtime-US-backed Somoza regime. F.D.R. had famously said of the then-current Somoza, "He may be a son of a bitch, but he's our son-of a bitch." Now the Reagan Administration was sending its so-called Contra fighters from their CIA bases in Honduras into Nicaragua at night to try to overthrow the Sandinista government by shooting people. During the day, Delore and Carol would go forward to patch up the surviving wounded, who were mostly campesinos who happened to live in the wrong place. Eventually the Sandinistas were indeed overthrown, not by the CIA's mercenaries, but by a democratic election whose results the Sandinistas neither denied nor contested.

After twenty-five years of all this, Delore and Carol were ready to settle down. Like a number of other people, they moved to Weston in good part to be near the monks of the Weston Priory. During the early years there, Delore would drive to Boston—which took me more than three hours, but she had a heavy foot—several times a week to serve as an emergency room physician at Massachusetts General Hospital. She must be a pretty good doc, I thought, given the reputation of Mass General. Around Weston, Delore made house calls day or night as needed. In 2014, the Vermont Chapter of the American Academy of Family Physicians chose her their Physician of the Year.

Carol helped people in other ways, but kept the low profile. If she were deported to Canada, Delore would have followed, thus ending the life they richly deserved. Though it became possible for gay couples to marry in Vermont, they declined to do so, so as not to create a public record that might reach the immigration authorities.

During the Priory's Eucharist services, a brother read from a Gospel, there was silence, then several brothers, sitting in their robes, related in a conversational tone the reflections that the passage had prompted within them. Nancy and I never heard a congregant share a reflection, and it never occurred to us to share except at dinner with friends afterwards. Until Delore started sharing hers from wherever she was sitting in the congregation. Her reflections fit in, and it was nice to hear a woman's point of view, which occasionally differed from the men's.

When our friends Dick and Agnes Dougherty had had enough years of hosting the Wednesday evening potlucks and Scripture discussions, Carol and Delore, who had a big living room then, took over for a time. Since what was said at these discussions did not leave the room, Carol would share her thoughts and amusing stories.

Delore shared her thoughts all the time, and I paid particular attention when she did. She was one of the most creative and prolific thinkers—ordained or not—about matters spiritual that I've ever known. She said her spirituality consisted of being sufficiently awake to catch the God that was happening around her and within her. "They killed Jesus," she said, "because he had a big mouth."

She cared about the local community, and in 2009 she and her friend Gloria Dawson co-founded a non-profit called Neighborhood Connections which provided advocacy, education, and social services for people who need them in Londonderry, Weston, and eight more nearby towns. Nancy and I were fortunate not to need those services but enjoyed many of their annual bang-up, fundraising dinner parties.

One day I noticed that my pulse was bouncing all over. I had had a silent heart attack an unknown time previously, and my mother's heartbeats had galloped erratically during the weeks before the strokes that took her. But I felt fine, had my usual energy, and was scheduled to see my doctor in a couple of days. I figured I'd ask him about this then. But when my pulse bounced just as erratically the next morning, I worried enough to phone Delore.

"Get down to the clinic right away," she said—eight-miles that I felt up to driving, no need to bother Nancy. As soon as I walked in, Delore slapped me onto a gurney, popped an aspirin under my tongue, mentioned atrial fibrillation, and said something about getting out the paddles to shock me back to normal. To my relief, she decided not to. My body had a complex history, and I didn't want jolts of electricity from someone who didn't know what it was. I was relieved, too, not to have to say no, no, no to Doctor Delore.

Instead, she phoned Nancy and the Londonderry Rescue Squad, whose ambulance drove me the twenty or so miles to the Spring-field Hospital, where Nancy met me and I did not want to stay. We persuaded Dr. Roger Fox, Delore's boss who happened to be there then, to let Nancy drive me to Blair Brooks, my regular doc, at Dart-mouth-Hitchcock, my regular hospital. By then Nancy and I were beginning to feel as apprehensive as my symptoms warranted. The thirty-mile drive provided plenty of time for our worries to mount. By the time we parked near the ER, I admit to being quite con-cerned.

But Delore had made a third phone call. As we entered the ER lobby, Carol was standing there to greet us with reassuring hugs and smiles. She had made fifty-mile drive simply to be with us, and it was wonderful to see her. She stayed the forever it took for the staff to check me over and wheel me off to the cardiac ward. Dr. Brooks did not use paddles. He waited. Around five the next morning, I wan-dered into the room where a man was monitoring the wavy green lines that traveled across a separate screen for each patient in the ward. I asked him about my green lines. They showed that my heartbeats had returned to normal.

Over the years, Nancy and I called on Delore for medical help a good many time, and she never let us pay her. Then it happened that she and the directors of the clinic fell out over the complaints she kept making that a physician they had recently hired was incompetent. She was right, but he had buddied up to the directors and played golf with some of them, They dearly wanted him to stay and her to go. I can only guess whether her outspokenness and sexual orientation figured in their feelings. She did not contest being fired, but wanted a number of benefits. I got on the phone with their lawyer and became the Manhattan mouthpiece that most people never see—loud, rapid, harsh. I enjoyed doing that but didn't like the me that did it. During the next half-hour, their lawyer agreed to everything I asked for. How much due to my stridence, how much to their eagerness to be rid of her, I can't know; but I felt that at last I'd done something that repaid a part of all that Delore had done for Nancy and me.

As I mentioned, she had given up the protection of Maryknoll in Bolivia so as to share the same risks as her friends. She had obviously not been killed, and I think most of us assumed she had not been tortured. That was not true. A few of years ago, I asked her to help me describe, in a novel I was writing, the meltdown of a fictitious woman twenty years after being tortured. I thought Delore had watched enough PTSD explosions in her friends to get it right, but she shocked me by saying that she herself had been tortured many times, that it was part of the life they had led there.

While talking about her traumas, she was her usual affable, matter-of-fact self. I knew she had cancer, but not, as she must have known, that it would soon take her; and she never let on. Carol had died several years earlier, and I'm sure that Delore hoped they would rejoin each other in whatever Hereafter awaits us.

As the years had passed, an incurable disease within Carol's lungs had worsened, her brother died of it, and we all knew that her time was running out. But love sometimes lengthens life. The love and support in which the monks of the Priory immersed their brother Philip while he was dying of Amyotrophic Lateral Sclerosis (ALS) may well be why he lived months, if not years, longer than expected. An outpouring of love for Reverend William Sloane Coffin may have kept him alive for three years after the media reported that his heart was about to quit. The same for Carol Olstad, who live far longer than expected. She and Delore took a final trip together, then another final trip, then another.

On a warm September day when it was clear that Carol's time was finally up, Nancy received a phone call: Could she and I come to the little cottage on the grounds of the Priory where Carol and Delore were living then? We drove right over. In their small, cozy living room beside a green meadow, Nancy, who was a justice of the peace, joined them at last in holy matrimony. I was the witness, and the four of us talked for a while after the simple ceremony, old friends knowing we would not talk like this again. With no time left for deportation proceedings against Carol, the marriage was duly recorded in the town office. Less than a month later, she left us; and a decade later Delore would be buried beside her in the Priory's cemetery. Heading Carol's obituary in the *Rutland Herald* was a line from one of the brothers' songs, "All I ask of you is forever to remember me as loving you."

David Bell

In my earliest recollection of my brother David, I was three-and-a-half, he was two, and the family lives in Brooklyn at 111 Columbia Heights, on the side of the street whose houses do not have the magnificent view of New York harbor and the towers of lower Manhattan. We were playing together in the back yard, probably in the sandbox, and I did something naughty enough so our parents put me in the house for a time. A walk-way with a low stone border framed the grassy center of the yard. A few steps descend from the rear door of the house to the walkway, and I was so eager to get back to playing with David that I tripped on the steps and hit my forehead on the stone border. The scar took decades to disappear.

Often in the morning, David and I would climb into one or another of our parents' twin beds and ask them to tell us a story. A favorite was "The Fire in Brooklyn," about a two-day blaze in 1935 that destroyed a warehouse that faced the waterfront down on the Furman Street below our block. The fire sent thirty-three firemen to various hospitals, and all of us had to sleep in the back of our house because smoke from burning rubber was seeping into the front rooms.

Either in that house or at 38 Grace Court, which we moved into later that year right after Tigger was born, David became afflicted with asthma. Many a night, Mom had to prop him up in a sitting position in his bed and stay up with him to make sure he could breathe. She burned a powder called Asthmador that was supposed to relieve his distress, and two or three times, she took him off to the Pine Barrens of New Jersey for a few days, on the advice of Dr. Charles Weymuller, the family physician, so that the pitch-scented air could lessen his distress. He eventually got over the asthma, though years later the draft board wouldn't take him into the army because he'd had it. He not only overcame the asthma, he became very athletic.

Mom and Dad often read to us. The A. A. Milne series was among the earliest. It struck me that my family would be the characters. I grabbed Christopher Robin for myself and named David Winnie-the-Pooh. Our brother Richard became Tigger because he was a bouncy baby, Dad Rabbit, and Mom Eeyore. For some reason, I have always associated *Wind in the Willows* with David.

Growing up, David, Tigger, and I sometimes fought but mostly had fun together. In Brooklyn we invented several lively games, and we built out of used crates and large wooden blocks two airplanes that we could get into. We dug a "hobbit hole" in the back yard and crawled briefly inside it, then tracked more mud into the house than I'm sure Mom appreciated. David had two pieces of bad luck in the backyard. Once he fell out of the magnolia tree, which we liked to climb in, and broke his collar bone. Another time, when he was holding onto the top of one of the spiked fences that separated our yard from those on either side, his hands slipped, and a black iron spike went up through his chin.

We had two lives in Brooklyn, the sheltered one of Brooklyn Friends School and then Poly Prep, and the street life of stick ball, stoop ball, roller skating, and occasional fights with kids who invaded our quiet, dead-end block. Traveling to and from Poly, though, wasn't so sheltered. We'd take an elevator down into the BMT subway from the entrance on Montague Street beside the Church of the Holy Trinity, which was then the family's church, and take a Fourth Avenue local to the end of the line, maybe talking with fellow students, doing homework, or reading discarded copies of the *New York Daily News*, which cost two cents and often ran sex stories on page four. Then it was ride on a Poly bus or walk through the Bay Ridge section of Brooklyn to the school's park-like campus. When it came to the street fights with other kids near home, it didn't matter how much David, Tigger, and I might have been squabbling among ourselves; we always stuck together against the outsiders.

Good as our life was in Brooklyn, we treasured our time in Easton, Connecticut, which our parents called "Redding" because the property was close to the Easton-Redding line and most of their friends had homes in Redding. After a few years of phoning them long-distance from our Easton party line, our parents switched to a Redding party line. Dad helped us to learn tennis and baseball. He had a tennis court built in a meadow behind the barn, relying on the natural clay that lay beneath the sod, and he charged each of us with removing one thousand stones each spring that had worked up through the surface during the frosts and thaws of winter. After the war ended and gasoline became plentiful, we usually drove to courts with truer surfaces.

Indoors, Dad and we three boys engaged in lively games of Double Canfield, the four of us playing our own hands and racing to beat each other in adding cards to the piles in the center of the table. Mom helped us with our tennis too, and often drove us to a Westport, Southport, or Fairfield beach—we sometimes sat on the station wagon tailgate with our feet dangling over the road—for a day of swimming, lying in the sun, and telling her what sandwiches we wanted her to make us from a basket of ingredients she called her Bellateria. After lunch we had to wait an hour before going back in the water. Her brother Russell had drowned and she didn't want us to.

We often rode our bikes a mile down the valley to play with John Niles and his visiting cousins Joe and Tom Arnold, or two-and-a half miles up the valley to visit Jimmy and Sylvia Farmer. David and I followed our parents in playing lots of tennis, Tigger not so much, and David and I became a strong men's doubles team by local standards, winning the town tournament in 1955. He and I also played baseball on Sunday afternoons at the Boys' Club field on Redding Ridge or visited another town's field, wearing hot, scratchy, gray, wool uniforms with the red lettering of the Redding town team.

Among the various summer jobs we had, the most interesting for me and later for David was the day camp that we ran for younger boys, taking them off their mothers' hands for a few hours a day to nearby Putnam Park, the Boys' Club field, and other venues to play games, explore, and otherwise have fun. ("Trees" describes an accident in my camp.) An older friend named Timmy Treadwell had started the camp, I did it for two summers with Sherman Briscoe then Bob Sanford. (Bob's father Jesse coached the town baseball team.) Then David did it with Jimmy Farmer. David, Tigger, Jimmy, and Sylvia waited table or bussed at the landmark Spinning Wheel Inn restaurant on Redding Ridge. Somehow I didn't.

David's first two years at Bowdoin College in Brunswick, Maine, overlapped my last two at Harvard in Cambridge. I visited him at least twice, and I'm quite sure he visited me at least once, though I don't recall the specifics. He was majoring in English and would tell me about the authors he was studying, Aldous Huxley among others. He belonged to the Zeta Psi fraternity, which had great Dixieland jazz bands playing at their frat house on both Saturday evenings I was there. It was good to see him happier than I believe he had been at Poly.

After college, he worked in Manhattan as a claims adjuster for Liberty Mutual Insurance Company, then for the BBDO advertising agency. On weekends, he was playing a lot of tennis at Nancy Paine's court in Easton (She was the editor-in-chief of *Harper's Bazaar*.), and I often joined their group. Nancy's daughter Gillette "Jill" Dauphinot was very attractive, intelligent, and gentle; and for quite a while several of us in the group (though maybe not David or Jill) assumed that they would eventually marry. Mary Shute's arrival on the scene ended the talk about Jill. If the Shutes had not started spending summers in Redding and David and Jill had married, he might well have missed the love of his life, Betsy.

While David and Mary lived in Stuyvesant Town in Manhattan and Kay and I were on Brooklyn Heights, we would visit each other for dinners, pleasant evenings that continued after they moved to Wilton to the house that David would live in for the rest of his life, and we moved to Norwalk a short drive away.

I was pleased and relieved to spend some time at David and Mary's right after Kay and I split in June of 1967. Three years later their home became my refuge during my trial separation from Iris in April 1970 and our final split that Memorial Day weekend. During breakfasts over the years, David introduced me to "Imus in the Morning" and later to "Morning Joe," whose show Nancy and I came to watch almost daily. He also introduced me to my first post-Iris romance, with a truly nice woman who had just joined AA.

David and I continued to be a good part of each other's lives during my single-parent years (most of the 1970s) and after I married Nancy and he married Betsy. After Dad died in 1981 and Mom moved from Brooklyn and Easton to a condo in New Canaan, he and I saw her often and did what we could to take care of her until she died in 1985. We grew closer to her, geographically and personally, than we had ever been in our adult lives, and discovered that she harbored politically liberal views similar to ours. We never knew this while our rock-ribbed Republican father held sway. Though he and Mom were a close and loving couple, I suspect that he didn't know it either.

It relieved me greatly that David accepted a golden handshake (early retirement) from the Lipton Tea Company and ended his years of the long, hazardous, daily drives between Wilton and Englewood Cliffs, New Jersey, across Westchester County, New York, and the Hudson River.

After Nancy and I moved to Vermont in 1990, our visits with David and Betsy became fewer, though he and I kept in pretty close touch by phone. (Their visits included detours into New Hampshire for essential beverages.) It gave me warm feelings that David would keep track of Nancy's and my airline flights during our travels to visit our far-flung children, and would remind me to make my quarterly tax payments. I don't follow football, but I'd be happy for him when his beloved Giants won and sad for him when they lost. During Nancy's and my thirty years in Weston, Vermont, we enjoyed many afternoons on his and Betsy's deck when it was warm enough and cozy evenings in front of their wood-stove, with Betsy's array of appetizers and delicious dinners. So often that we came to think of their guestroom as *our room*.

David died peacefully and painlessly at home with loved ones on

April 4, 2024, a week after he turned ninety-one. I still miss picking up the phone to talk things over with him. Our talks always felt good, and he would tell me he appreciated them too. If there is a Hereafter, I hope we can continue them.

I admire David enormously, and am so glad I told him (albeit in the muted Bell manner), for his generous, loyal, and persevering commitment to doing volunteer work at the Stamford (Connecticut) Hospital, mostly in its emergency department, and driving to and from it in all kinds of weather. A picture of him in his red hospital jacket hangs proudly on our living room wall of family photos. I have long believed that throughout history the very best people, of whatever faith or none, are the ones who have given freely of themselves to help strangers in need. The Good Samaritan teaches this, Jesus practiced it, and the life I've seen affirms it. During the twenty-three years after David left Lipton, he helped strangers in need during each of the twenty-three thousand hours that he volunteered at the hospital. Well done, David! May you rest in peace.

Dear Companion

Many couples will tell you the casual choices and odd chances that brought them together. For Nancy and me, they began with my decision to spend an evening at a tennis party for single adults that the Unitarian Church of Westport, Connecticut, arranged at the indoor courts in nearby Darien on the same evening of March 1979 that Nancy and her date made the same decision. I asked the most attractive woman in sight, who was Nancy, to be my partner. Tennis was not her forte, but I wasn't there to win at tennis, and we remained partners for most of the evening. (I assumed that her date, whom I knew slightly, was busy prospecting.) After my shower, Nancy was still sitting in the lobby, so I was still able to ask her for her phone number, which I had neglected to do before. "It's in the book," she said. Phone books still existed in those days, and I knew the one she meant.

On our first date, I took her to a classical music concert in Norwalk; she has often thanked me since for introducing her to classical music. Picking her up at her home in Danbury, I was struck by the vitality of her three teenage children, and more impressed when she told me that she and they had just re-shingled the roof of her Cape Cod house. They brought the shingles up the ladder, and she sat on the roof and nailed them on. During the long drive back that evening, we stopped to dance at a roadhouse that no longer exists. On parting, we kissed goodnight.

By the end of May we were inseparable. She would spend the night at my house in Norwalk or I would spend it an hour's drive north in hers. Her bed was a single, and we slept surprisingly well for being in such close quarters. Later I built us a double bed, not a queen or king size which would have put us too far apart.

That August we took a three-week drive tent-camping in Vermont, Maine, Nova Scotia, and Newfoundland. The adventure began with a bluegrass concert at the Stratton Mountain ski resort, the first of many such concerts we would attend. This was the first tent-camping I'd done since sleeping beside another soldier in a two-man pup tent on maneuvers in Germany twenty-five years before, and the experience with Nancy was considerably preferable. Our tent was the large, heavy canvas one that she and her children had used when the four of them tent-camped across the country several years earlier in her tiny Ford Pinto. Her husband had concluded that raising children was not for him, so he left Nancy to raise them herself, another feat that impressed me with her caring, resourcefulness, abilities, and energy.

Having two failed marriages behind me, I was very cautious about trying again. Having been married only once, Nancy was less so. Her father had died of Alzheimer's disease earlier that year, and most of his nine siblings had it or had died of it, telling me from the outset that the chances were better than even that she would develop it. So what? By the end of the August camping trip, we had decided to marry. Three months later, on the cold clear afternoon of December 8, we stood facing each other in the Wilton Friends Meetinghouse, she in a lovely purple dress, and "in the presence of God and these our friends" we married each other in the manner of Quakers, with no one officiating, "for as long as we both shall live."

Her daughter Katrina, sixteen, was her maid of honor. My son Brian, fourteen, was my best man and gave the main toast at the reception. The next morning her son Curt and my daughter Erin picked us up at the Silvermine Tavern in Norwalk, where we'd spent the night, and drove us to the airport to fly to our honeymoon on a small island in the Bahamas.

Our families merged quite well considering that each of us had invaded the monopoly that the other's children had on their parent's affections. All five children were glad that their parent had found happiness, though for four of them it was more complicated than that. It's natural and common for children of divorce to resent invaders; these kids are not to blame though sometimes to be avoided. I've always been grateful that Nancy's Chris accepted me at once. It took a while for Erin and Brian to accept Nancy. (What was not to accept about my sweetheart?) Curt and Katrina took longer to accept me. But their reservations vanished many years ago, and all five children have been warmly loving and supportive for both of us as the years have passed.

Nancy, who was forty-two when we married, and I, who was forty-eight, tried to have a child, but it didn't work. We did, though, sort of adopt two virtual daughters, Suzanne Greene McLone, whose father was Nancy's brother Roy, and Curt's wife, Cindi Nagy Detzer.

Though my father's mother came from a long line of Irish Quakers and I had gone to Brooklyn Friends School for grades one through six, it had never crossed my mind to consider joining the Religious Society of Friends. Until meeting Nancy, who had been a Quaker for quite a few years, opened the door to my spiritual home. She and I shared the values of Friends —simplicity, integrity, peace, equality, community (I was a bit slow on this one), and care of the Earth.

By the time I met her, I had been single for nine years and grown very fond of several women, though none whom I wanted to spend the rest of my life with. Imagine my delight, then, at finding the ideal partner, who often said what I was thinking and vice versa, whose ideas about how to live and treat other people were much the same as mine, who shared my anger at injustice and my love of reading, whom I could truly love and be loved by in return. I suspect that the two summers Nancy had spent while still in high school, looking after the children of migrant farmworkers—then and still, perhaps the most unfairly treated, essential laborers in the nation—may have "radicalized" her the way that Attica did the same for me, enabling us to mesh on that level too. I cannot imagine most women putting up with some of the activities that we have joined in—like risking prison in the Sanctuary Movement. She has enabled me to live the life that suited me best, and, I believe, I have done the same for her. Ever since that blessed evening of tennis, I've been happier than I'd imagined I could be.

Nancy's family lived in Middletown, Ohio, until her father became the basketball and baseball coach at Cornell and they moved to Ithaca, New York, where she did most of her growing up. She and I attended several of her high school class reunions there, and it warmed my heart to see how much her classmates liked her.

During our early years together, most of our evenings were quiet. She was an excellent third and fourth grade teacher, conscientious and creative, and required her students in both grades to read a book and write an essay each week. In order to do their handwritten essays justice, she read each one three times, usually in the evenings while I read or worked on my Attica book. We were together during the last seven of the ten years it took me to write it, and she was my number one editor.

Since she was a particularly patient teacher, most of the school's ADHD students were assigned to her. Her fellow teacher and longtime friend Karla Franke told me that her students loved her, and she dearly loved them. One year, one of her girls seemed particularly lonely and troubled. Nancy started having lunch with her and befriended her in ways that showed she loved and approved of her. Years later the girl, now a woman, told Nancy that she had saved her life.

Nancy was my number one editor, too, in designing our dream house. We sold her Cape in Danbury in 1981 and with the proceeds bought ten acres of woods far back on the side of Terrible Mountain in Weston, Vermont. The town looked tidy, but we had no idea what an excellent place it was or that the Weston Priory of Benedictine monks was up the road. We chose it because it lay between our two favorite downhill ski mountains, Okemo and Magic. I had been designing my dream house since my teens, each one simpler than the last. Now I designed one we could actually have someone build. I kept bringing my drawings to Nancy, and she kept telling me where to change them. We finally took them to a local designer-builder, and because the house was tall, we asked him whether it would fall over. He said it wouldn't, so we asked him to build it. The result was a small, two-bedroom house with a large, high-ceilinged living room and a wall of windows facing several mountains across a broad valley.

Once there, we did a lot of cross-country skiing and snowshoeing in the woods, but nearly no more downhill skiing at the crowded, increasingly expensive, nearby ski mountains. It occurred to me later that the former outings were more in tune with the contemplative Quaker Way, and the latter, with loud, commercial America. All the same I have sometimes missed swooping in wide arcs down a well-groomed white slope. One winter's afternoon as the sky was tinting pink, Nancy and I skied out of a forest trail onto a white meadow and heard the Priory's distant bell announcing vespers. We could have been in England eight hundred years ago.

Most of our friends in Weston were the people on our road and the lay community of the Priory. Nancy was well known, too, in the town, being at various times a docent at the local museum, the assistant town clerk, and the president of the Women's Club. For eleven years she worked a day a week in the Priory's gift shop. She was elected to four terms as a justice of the peace, and officiated at a number of straight and gay couple weddings. Thanks to the governor of New Hampshire's office, she was able to officiate at Curt and Cindi's wedding in that state; and Chris enabled her to legally marry him to Celine Sakaguchi in California. She sat with the couples first, if they wished, and helped them compose the vows they would say to each other. I was not nearly as well-known as she was in Weston and sometimes referred to myself as Mr. Margaret Thatcher, an allusion to the anonymous husband of a recent UK prime minister.

For as long as I can remember, Nancy and I would hold hands everywhere we walked. People coming towards us often smiled, and some said how nice this was to see. In recent years, holding her hand has helped me to not tip over.

Much of the town shared my pride in Nancy when a local newspaper reported that she had completed the New York City Marathon. She had long been a runner and a biker, jogging or pedaling with apparent ease up the long, steep hills around Weston. Katrina got her into competitive running in her fifties, and she came in first in her age-group in a number of half-marathons. At age sixty-one, she ran the New York City marathon with Katrina and Curt, crossing the finish line holding hands, as described in "Inner Journey." Her children's partners and I were able to watch them run past on Brooklyn's Fourth Avenue and, thanks to the subway, again on Manhattan's First Avenue and again in Central Park towards the end of the race. It was such an uplifting experience that we did it again a few years later.

It was fun, too, supporting Nancy and Katrina while they trained. I would sit in the car at various points on their route with water for them and the *New York Time* for me, and take them to lunch afterwards on a pier in Newport, Rhode Island, or wherever we happened to be. One day while I was following Nancy on my bike in Weston, she tripped and fell on her face. I urged her to get herself checked by Doctor Delore and/or Nurse Carol whose house was just down the road. She wouldn't, and insisted that she had to keep walking so as not to break her training schedule. To my consternation, she soon resumed jogging. X-rays later showed that she'd broken two ribs, but she kept to her schedule. She, Curt, and Katrina ran the second marathon faster than the first, again holding hands as they finished.

An added pleasure of getting together with Nancy was joining her large and mostly lovely family. Her mother Ethel was a wonderful person whom we drove to visit in Crystal Lake, Illinois, every summer as long as she lived. Her brother Roy, sisters Shirley and June, June's husband Ben, and a number of their children became close friends. We visited Shirley in Ithaca and June and Ben in Denver, or they visited us, nearly every year; we had pizza and beer with Roy every two weeks after he moved to Vermont. With June and Ben, we enjoyed Aspen often, and also Santa Fe, Monument Valley, Mesa Verde, and other Native American sites in the Southwest, Prince William Sound and Denali Park in Alaska, prehistoric mound-builder sites in Ohio, and a sailing adventure with a third couple off Guadeloupe in the Caribbean. Ben, who was a psychiatrist and had sailed across the Atlantic with some other guys in a small boat, was our captain. He's the only person I ever took orders from for a week without getting pissed off.

Family always meant so much to Nancy. Every two weeks for many years, she typed out a newsletter for our children, her siblings, close friends, and a few other relatives, about a dozen people in all. First she typed them on our electric typewriter, then on an improved one, then on a small, barrel-shaped Apple computer, and finally on a flat Apple, through 2014. I would proofread them and maybe add a bit—she proofed my stuff, too, and made suggestions I usually took—make the copies, and post them snail mail. Our pile of them is huge, and they're great fun to read, which I don't do often enough. There is so much of her in them. They are a good part of what made her the family's matriarch.

London, where Erin was raising her family, was obviously not a convenient venue—nor were Oakland and San Francisco where Chris and Brian settled—but we usually saw them every year or so; and London made a good base for visiting Scotland, Ireland, Wales, and countries on the Continent. Norway, where Nancy's mother's father came from, was our favorite, Ireland was a treasure, and the city of Prague was very dear.

Nearly every summer for thirty years or so, Nancy and I took tent-camping trips to Nova Scotia or Quebec, most often ending up at Broad Cove on northern Cape Breton Island or Forillon National Park at the east end of the Gaspé Peninsula, where we looked out at a line of cliffs lined up like the prows of ships side by side towards the Atlantic and, with luck, at minke whales rising out of the bay below the cliffs. As the years passed, our tents grew larger, so that eventually we could sit inside on rainy days and look out through the mosquito netting; and our drives grew shorter, so that we often found a lakeside tent site in Mont-Orford National Park in Quebec about thirty miles past the Vermont border.

While camping, we would read, bike, hike, explore the areas and their restaurants, and take in the nature lectures that the Canadian parks offered. Sometimes we drank with the folks in nearby tent sites. One year we camped across the USA, and I vividly recall the struggle to set up the tent during a wind that was whipping across the Badlands of South Dakota. I am forever grateful that Nancy got me into tent-camping—close to the Earth, mildly demanding, inexpensive, and fun.

348 Tales From America's Golden Age

During our first thirty or so years of visiting then living in our house in Vermont, we heated it entirely by a woodstove in the living room and an electric blower in the basement. For the first seven years we drove up to it nearly every chance we got—every other weekend during the winters—moving in for good in 1990, and living there until 2020, the heart of our life together, until our children, health care providers, and common sense convinced us that it was too remote—nearly a mile and a half up a dirt road, which mooshed into deep ruts during mud season, then a steep, L-shaped driveway—and its three flights of stairs were too many for us to live there safely anymore.

In one of my dearest memories, Nancy is sitting on the floor of our little guestroom with lines of color photos spread on the carpet before her. She always cherished the album of black-and-white pictures of her childhood that her father had made for her, and she began making albums for her children as well as for her and me back in 1988, sending off cans of film from both our cameras to a lab with notes saying how many copies to make of each print. Then she'd create a large album with photos selected for each of her children and a larger album for her and me with all the year's photos in it. Most scenes that she took were of her children and grandchildren; mine were of a mix of people and scenery. Year after year through 2011, she created these treasures of her love. When one of Curt's marriages was breaking up, his wife savagely destroyed his albums, and Nancy was able to replace many of the photos for him.

She and I did not look through these albums as often as I now wish we had. There were always books we were reading or projects in progress or phone calls or our two Netflix movies a month. We'd spend more time in our old age enjoying the memories that the pictures recalled. But by then, Nancy's ability to enjoy pictures, or even remember what they were about, had faded, and I was left to turn the pages alone.

During her seventies, her memory began to fail faster than most people's. Our primary care doc at Dartmouth-Hitchcock referred her to a neurologist named Aleksandra Stark, who ordered a PET scan and diagnosed her in April 2017 as having mild cognitive impairment, which was the first stage of Alzheimer's Disease. Some people never grow worse, and I prayed for a while that this would be true for Nancy. It wasn't. Dr. Stark referred her, as she had to, to the Vermont Department of Motor Vehicles. They tested her. She failed. They canceled her driver's license, a blow that hurt deeply and angered her whenever she remembered it, which gradually stopped happening. She kept insisting she was an excellent driver, which was true. We had taken turns driving on our many long trips, and I slept easily while she was at the wheel. But it had become likely that she would be too disoriented to react safely to a sudden challenge on the road. I am so grateful that knowing up front the chances that she'd get Alzheimer's did not deprive me of the best years of my life.

In 2019, once we decided to leave our dream house, we visited seven or eight retirement homes around Vermont and adjacent New Hampshire where there's a good meal served at least once a day, prompt medical attention is available as needed, and we'd have no upkeep on the property. Though several were enticing, we easily chose Morgan Orchards high on a hillside in the town of Randolph Center in the geographic center of Vermont, sixty miles north of Weston, with trains running once a day to and from New York City. We met nice people at several residences, but the ones here seemed particularly nice and interesting. Our apartment looks out on the Green Mountains and ever-changing sunsets. As far as I can tell, the residents loved Nancy, especially when she spoke up during our monthly wine-tastings.

In 2019 too, I had open-heart surgery: a valve replaced and three bypasses. It perked me up and, as it turned out, enabled me to be her main caregiver up until October 2024. During most of our years together, she read books continuously and sometimes paused to tell me stuff she thought I'd like to know about, but that slowed and stopped. She still enjoyed listening to music, though, and watching the news as long as we were together. Some evenings we'd sit on the couch playing one YouTube piece of music after another on the computer. When she was lying in bed and I was sitting on the edge of it, she'd often reach up and rub my back. We usually kissed goodnight. I expected all this to fade. Her diagnosis became "severe Alzheimer's," and her two older sisters died of it. Much of the time, her intelligence and humor shone through.

During our first year or two at the Strode Independent Living apartment house—one building of Morgan Orchards; the Menig Nursing Home is the other—we would walk up through the north end of lovely Vermont Technical College (before it became a campus of Vermont State U.) and around its large athletic field, a total of about a mile. She was always very considerate about going at my pokey speed, and sometimes I'd get her to go ahead at her speed and wait for me or return to me.

Then it was a shorter walk, across the meadow from Strode to the flagpole by the woods, and we'd sit on the bench there for maybe twenty minutes or half an hour watching our tiny part of the world where usually nothing was happening. After Nancy fell and broke her hip in 2023, it became an even shorter walk, she pushing a walker, out the dining room door, around the south end of Strode, and around the parking lot in front of it, again sitting on a bench along the way to watch the world. All this may not sound like much, but I treasured it and wish we could do it, all or any of it, again.

The subject of a support group that I attended on Zoom was "grieving for the living." I have long been grieving for Nancy—so many times at or past the verge of tears—at the sight of the purple dress she wore at our wedding and many times since and will never wear again. Or the music box that she cherished because it was her mothers. Or simply at the thought of what's happening to her and none of it is her fault and how unfair it is. It helps to remember how lucky I am that she has been with me so long, that many diseases could have taken her years ago.

I had long felt that if Alzheimer's became her fate, I would do all I could to keep her as contented, comfortable, and cherished, and as free from fear, confusion, and anxiety, as I could. I also wanted to keep her with me in our apartment as long as possible, hopefully all the way. People have told me that I kept her at home longer than most people would have. Moving her away from me was terribly hard for me, and I put off doing it as long as I could. But when she fell three times in two weeks and cracked a vertebra, I started looking at nursing homes and memory care providers in earnest.

On October 15, 2024, Curt, Katrina, and I placed her in memory care in Kendal at Hanover (NH), where the staff treated her very well. She soon seemed to be adjusting to her new quarters, though she said several times that she wanted to go home. I replied that I wished she could but she was getting better care now than I could give her and I would visit her as often as I could—which I did. She seemed to accept this. It was the hardest decision I have ever made, and I grieved more during the year we lived apart than I ever had before. I'd have been disappointed in myself if I had not grieved for what was befalling my sweetheart.

She believed that we should never lose the little child in ourselves. She never did.

One day at Kendal, when Katrina was massaging her shoulders, her happy toothless smile blossomed, and she said, "I have a lot of clothes, so you could stay here for a long time." On March 20, 2025, she was able to be moved into the Menig Nursing Home diagonally across the street from our apartment, and I became able to spend time with her nearly every day.

While she was living her entire life between lying in bed and sitting in her wheelchair, and the nursing home staff was lifting her from one to the other with a hoist and feeding her pureed food and thickened liquids with a spoon, she still expressed her love and affection with her hands and a few intelligible words. Her grip on my hand was firm as I sat beside her. She'd return my squeezes and I hers. Or she'd stroke the back of mine with her other hand or bring it to her lips. As I was leaving for the day on June 12, she pierced my heart by saying, "Can't I stay with you?"

The times when she kissed my hand made me particularly happy. The last time was on October 5th. She made me very happy, too, when she'd stroke my forearm or the back of the hand that was holding hers, or simply when she'd smile at me. Ravaged as she was by Alzheimer's, she still found these ways to show her love.

The last time with my arm was on the 13th. That evening, a severe seizure started her on a rapid decline, and the last I saw of her precious smile was when I stood to leave her at sunset two days later. I was with her all the next day, and she had a visit from her friend Karla at noontime. I held her hand till the setting sun stopped shining on the autumn leaves beyond her window. She died peacefully the next morning shortly after sunrise.

Our children, their partners, and our friends and relatives were wonderfully supportive of her during her illness and of me then and afterwards. They were thoughtful and kind, paid us many visits, made her happy while she could still be happy, and helped me often and well. In this, she and I were blest.

A favorite CD of ours has Dolly Parton, Emmylou Harris, and Linda Ronstadt singing "My Dear Companion." After the disease had begun to seriously change her, my own version of the words lodged in my head: Where have you gone, my dear companion? We have been so fortunate to be so close for so long. It is my fondest hope that you will be you again and we shall remain together hereafter.

Endnotes

1 *Time Magazine*, Sept. 14, 2020; Heather Cox Richardson, "Letters from an American", Feb. 15, 2025.

2 This question is the final sentence of Ernest Hemingway's 1926 breakthrough novel *The Sun Also Rises*.

3 Scott Fitzgerald tried characterizing people as canine or feline. For me this worked with Ronson and Raycroft but not with everyone.

4 I relate the former in *The Attica Turkey Shoot* and summarize the latter in *Overdue Heresies and the Search for Truth* (Fresh Look Press, 2024).

5 "Letters from an American", January 15, 2023.

6 *New York Times*, January 3, 1995, page 1.

7 Much of this paragraph and all its quotes are based on my interviews with Eileen on December 3, 1993 and May 31, 1994, and with Gus on November 26, 1991.

8 As the brothers described the retreats on their website.

9 *Strength for Struggle: Christian Social Witness in the Crucible of These Times* (Bromwell Press, 1953).

10 An excellent book on Dulles and his brother Allen, who headed the CIA from 1953 until President Kennedy fired him in 1961 for the Bay of Pigs debacle, is Stephen Kinzer's *The Brothers: John Foster Dulles, Allen Dulles, and Their Secret War* (Times Books, 2013).

11 Most of this paragraph also appears at pp. 383-384 of *The Attica Turkey Shoot*.

12 The German woman is quoted by Bernt Engelmann in his book, *In Hitler's Germany* (Pantheon, 1976, paper), p. 85.

13 A slightly different version of these words was written by the American poet George Cooper. He ended, "Summer is gone, And the days grow cold." I prefer my mother's version.

Acknowledgments

As always, I am deeply grateful to my wife Nancy Greene Bell, my main inspiration and supporter, for remaining my first editor in writing and so much else as long as she was able.

I am also deeply grateful to my daughter Erin Elizabeth Bell and to Nancy's and my niece and virtual daughter Suzanne Greene McLone, who brought the perspective of a younger generation to her detailed editing of all the stories. And to Dee Quinn Miller, my brother Richard, and my cousin Laura for their encouragement and constructive suggestions.

And to Kitty Werner for her artistry, expertise, patience, and advice in designing the book and in shepherding me through this, my third self-publishing venture with her. Were it not for her, this memoir would still be only a file on my MacBook.